ADAM SMITH

IV

Lectures on Rhetoric and Belles Lettres

THE GLASGOW EDITION OF THE WORKS AND CORRESPONDENCE OF ADAM SMITH

Commissioned by the University of Glasgow to celebrate the bicentenary of the Wealth of Nations

I

THE THEORY OF MORAL SENTIMENTS

Edited by A. L. MACFIE *and* D. D. RAPHAEL

II

AN INQUIRY INTO THE NATURE AND CAUSES OF THE WEALTH OF NATIONS

Edited by R. H. CAMPBELL *and* A. S. SKINNER; *textual editor* W. B. TODD

III

ESSAYS ON PHILOSOPHICAL SUBJECTS
(and Miscellaneous Pieces)

Edited by W. P. D. WIGHTMAN

IV

LECTURES ON RHETORIC AND BELLES LETTRES

Edited by J. C. BRYCE

This volume includes the *Considerations concerning the First Formation of Languages*

V

LECTURES ON JURISPRUDENCE

Edited by R. L. MEEK, D. D. RAPHAEL, *and* P. G. STEIN

This volume includes two reports of Smith's course together with the 'Early Draft' of the *Wealth of Nations*

VI

CORRESPONDENCE OF ADAM SMITH

Edited by E. C. MOSSNER *and* I. S. ROSS

Associated volumes:

ESSAYS ON ADAM SMITH

Edited by A. S. SKINNER *and* T. WILSON

LIFE OF ADAM SMITH

By I. S. ROSS

The Glasgow Edition of the Works and Correspondence of Adam Smith and the associated volumes are published in hardcover by Oxford University Press. The six titles of the Glasgow Edition, but not the associated volumes, are being published in softcover by LibertyClassics.

ADAM SMITH
Lectures on Rhetoric and Belles Lettres

EDITED BY

J.C. BRYCE

GENERAL EDITOR

A.S. SKINNER

LibertyClassics

INDIANAPOLIS

This Liberty*Classics* edition of 1985 is an exact photographic reproduction of the edition published by Oxford University Press in 1983.

Liberty*Press*/Liberty*Classics*
7440 N. Shadeland
Indianapolis, Indiana 46250

This reprint has been authorized by the Oxford University Press.

©Oxford University Press 1983

Library of Congress Cataloging in Publication Data

Smith, Adam, 1723-1790.
  Lectures on rhetoric and belles lettres.

  Reprint. Oxford [Oxfordshire]: Clarendon Press; New York: Oxford University Press, 1983.—(The Glasgow edition of the works and correspondence of Adam Smith; 4)
  Includes index.
  1. English language—Rhetoric. 2. English language—Style.
I. Bryce, J.C. II. Title.
[PE1407.S47 1985]   808   85-6884
ISBN 0-86597-052-1 (pbk.)

  10 9 8 7 6 5 4 3 2 1

Cover design by JMH Corporation, Indianapolis.
Printed & bound by
Rose Printing Company, Inc., Tallahassee, Florida.

Preface

This volume, consisting of a version of Adam Smith's first work, may in a double sense claim as its 'onlie begetter' John Maule Lothian (1896–1970), himself a son of the University of Glasgow, M.A. 1920; he discovered the manuscript, and the careful scholarship with which he edited it has enormously eased the labours of anyone who now studies it. Both publicly and privately he acknowledged the help he had received over the classical references from Professor W. S. Watt of the Chair of Humanity in the University of Aberdeen, and as Professor Watt's beneficiary at one remove I wish to add my own thanks. My longest-standing debt in this field is to that great scholar who taught so many to take seriously the literary criticism of the eighteenth century, David Nichol Smith; and he delighted to recall his own beginnings as an academic teacher in Adam Smith's University. Gaps and errors are of course my own. 'What is obvious is not always known, and what is known is not always to hand'. Johnson's wry comment must haunt the mind of anyone who tries to annotate a text as densely allusive as the present one.

The contribution of Professor Andrew Skinner to this book far exceeds what even the most generous General Editor might be expected to make. That the materials ever reached printable shape, or after arduous and complex proof-reading became presentable, is due entirely to his determined energy and wisdom. My personal as distinct from my editorial debt to him is for all he has taught me in conversation and by his writings about the central role of the *Rhetoric* in Adam Smith's work as a whole. To the secretaries of the Glasgow Political Economy Department, especially Miss Chrissie MacSwan and Mrs Jo Finlayson, I am very grateful for the skill and patience with which they typed extremely awkward copy. I have enjoyed the counsels of Mr Jack Baldwin of Glasgow University Library's Special Collections; of Professors D. D. Raphael and M. L. Samuels; and of Mr J. K. Cordy of the Oxford University Press, who in addition has shown apparently inexhaustible patience. I am also grateful to Mary Robertson for her invaluable assistance in compiling the index.

1982   J.C.B.

Contents

Key to Abbreviations and References

WORKS OF ADAM SMITH

Corr.	*Correspondence*
EPS	*Essays on Philosophical Subjects* included among which are:
Ancient Logics	'The History of the Ancient Logics and Metaphysics'
Ancient Physics	'The History of the Ancient Physics'
Astronomy	'The History of Astronomy'
English and Italian Verses	'Of the Affinity between certain English and Italian Verses'
External Senses	'Of the External Senses'
Imitative Arts	'Of the Nature of that Imitation which takes place in what are called the Imitative Arts'
Stewart	Dugald Stewart, 'Account of the Life and Writings of Adam Smith, LL.D'.
Languages	*Considerations Concerning the First Formation of Languages*
TMS	*The Theory of Moral Sentiments*
WN	*The Wealth of Nations*
LJ(A)	*Lectures on Jurisprudence, Report of 1762–3*
LJ(B)	*Lectures on Jurisprudence, Report dated 1766*
LRBL	*Lectures on Rhetoric and Belles Lettres*

OTHER WORKS

JML	*Lectures on Rhetoric and Belles Lettres*, ed. John M. Lothian (Nelson, 1963)
LCL	Loeb Classical Library
OED	Oxford English Dictionary

Note: symbols used in the textual apparatus are explained on pp. 7 and 27.

Introduction

1. *The Manuscript*

In *The Scotsman* newspaper of 1 and 2 November 1961 John M. Lothian, Reader (later titular Professor) in English in the University of Aberdeen announced his discovery and purchase, at the sale of an Aberdeenshire manor-house library in the late summer of 1958, of two volumes of manuscript 'Notes of Dr. Smith's Rhetorick Lectures'. They had been part of the remainder of a once extensive collection begun in the sixteenth century by William Forbes of Tolquhoun Castle, and in the late eighteenth century the property of the Forbes–Leith family of Whitehaugh, an estate brought to the Forbeses by the marriage of Anne Leith. In September 1963 Lothian published an edition of the notes as *Lectures on Rhetoric and Belles Lettres Delivered in the University of Glasgow by Adam Smith, Reported by a Student in 1762–63* (Nelson).

Identification of the lecturer was easy. It had always been known that Smith gave lectures on rhetoric; his manuscript of these (Stewart, I. 17) was among those destroyed in the week before his death in obedience to the strict instructions he had given, first to Hume in 1773, then in 1787 to his literary executors Joseph Black and James Hutton. Lecture 3 of the discovered report is a shortened version of the essay on the First Formation of Languages published by Smith in 1761. Further, Lothian found later in the 1958 sale volumes 2–6 of manuscript notes of lectures on Jurisprudence, and though they bore no name they turned out to be a more elaborate version of the lectures by Smith reported in notes discovered in 1876 and published by Edwin Cannan in 1896. A search in Aberdeen junk-shops was rewarded, thanks to the extraordinary serendipity which Lothian's friends always envied him, by the finding of the missing volume 1. These volumes have the same format and paper as the *Rhetoric* and the same hand as its main text.

When the Whitehaugh family acquired these manuscripts is not known. Absence of mention of them in three successive catalogues of the collection now in Aberdeen University Library has probably no significance; these are lists of printed books. No link between the Forbes–Leiths and the University of Glasgow has come to light. The most probable one is that at some point they engaged as a private tutor a youth who had been one of Adam Smith's students and who knew that he would endear himself to his notably bookish employers by bringing them this otherwise unavailable work by a philosopher already enjoying an international reputation as the author of the *Moral Sentiments*. Such private tutorships were among the most usual first employments of products of the Scottish universities in the eighteenth century; and of Smith himself we learn from the obituary notice in the *Gentleman's Magazine* of August 1790 (lx. 761) that 'his friends wished to send him abroad as a travelling tutor' when he came down from Oxford in 1746 after six years as Snell Exhibitioner at Balliol—though WN V. f. i 45 suggests that even after his happy travels with the young Duke of Buccleuch in 1764–66 he had doubts about the value of such posts. Still, both his successors in the Chair of Logic at Glasgow had held them. Of course the discovery of a Whitehaugh tutor among the graduates of, say, 1763–64 would not necessarily bring us nearer to identifying the note-taker, who may have been another student. Such notes circulated very widely at the time. Indeed, given the celebrity of this lecturer it is surprising that the *Rhetoric* should have turned up so far in only one version. The attempt to match the handwriting of the manuscript with a signature in the Matriculation Album of the relevant period has been thwarted by the depressing uniformity of these signatures; entrants were calligraphically on their best behaviour.

In the matter of provenance an interesting possibility is opened up by a letter from John Forbes-Leith to James Beattie, Professor of Moral Philosophy at Marischal College, Aberdeen in 1779 about his family's library (JML xi, quoting *Proceedings of the Society of Antiquaries of Scotland* LXXII, 1938, 252). The *Rhetoric* is not mentioned, but its subject-matter lay so much in Beattie's field of interest that one is tempted to wonder whether he was in some way instrumental in acquiring the manuscript. A similar possibility is that Smith's successor as Professor of Moral Philosophy in 1764, Thomas Reid, who maintained his contacts with friends in Aberdeen long after his move to Glasgow, may have obtained the notes and handed them on to Whitehaugh. Reid is known to have been anxious to see notes of his predecessor's lectures: 'I shall be much obliged to any of you Gentlemen or to any other, who can furnish me with Notes of his Prelections whether in Morals, Jurisprudence, Police, or in Rhetorick'—so he said in his Inaugural Lecture on 10 October 1764 as preserved in Birkwood MS 2131/4/II in Aberdeen University Library.

The manuscript of the *Rhetoric*, now Glasgow University Library MS Gen. 95. 1 and 2, is bound in half-calf (i.e. with leather tips) and marbled boards. In the top three of the six panels of the spine is incised blind in cursive: 'Notes of Dr. Smith's Rhetorick Lectures: Vol. 1st.' and '. . . Vol. 2nd'. The pages are not numbered; the present edition supplies numbering in the margin. The gatherings, normally of four leaves each, have been numbered on the top left corner of each first page, apparently in the same (varying) ink as the text at that point. Volume 1 has 51 gatherings, of which the 14th is a bifolium, here given the page-numbers 52a, v.52a, 53b, v.53b, to indicate that it is an insertion. Volume 2 consists of gatherings 52–114; 94 has six leaves; and 74 has a bifolium of different paper stuck in loosely between the first and second leaves with no break in the continuity of the text, and a partially erased 'My Dear Dory' written vertically on the inner left page, i.e. ii. v. 90 under the note about Sancho Panca. The pages measure 195 × 118 mm, but gatherings 1–4 only 168 × 106 mm (of stouter paper than the rest), and 5–15 185 × 115 mm. The watermark is LVG accompanied by a crown of varying size and a loop below it, and in some of the gatherings GR under the crown. This is the L. V. Gerrevink paper commonly used throughout much of the eighteenth century. The chain lines are vertical in all gatherings. The first page of each of the earlier gatherings is much faded, as though having lain exposed for a time before the binding was done.

Three hands, here designated A, B, and C, can be distinguished. Hand C, using a dark ink, appears in only a few places in the earlier pages, and may be that of a later owner of the manuscript: sometimes merely touching up faded letters. An appreciation of the nature and authority of the notes depends on an understanding of the activities of scribes A and B, who (especially A) were responsible for transcribing them from the jottings made in class. The scribal habits, of which the textual apparatus will furnish the evidence, rule out the possibility that the pages we have were written while the students listened.

There is an apparent contradiction between two reports of Adam Smith's attitude to note-taking. According to his student John Millar, later Professor of Law: 'From the permission given to students of taking notes, many observations and opinions contained in these lectures (on rhetoric) have either been detailed in separate dissertations, or engrossed in general collections, which have since been given to the public' (Stewart I. 17). The *Gentleman's Magazine* obituary (lx. 762) records that 'the Doctor was in general extremely jealous of the property of his lectures . . . and, fearful lest they should be transcribed and published, used often to repeat, when he saw any one taking notes, that "he hated scribblers".' The paradox is resolved if we remember the advice given by Thomas Reid, and by many a university teacher before and since, that those who write most in class understand least, 'but those who write at home after carefull recollection, understand most, and write to the best Purpose', and that this reflective reconstruction of what has been heard is precisely what a philosophical discourse requires (Birkwood MS 2131/8/III). The general success with which our scribes grasped the structure and tenor of Smith's course, as well as much of the detail, exemplifies what Reid had in mind. Even the exasperated admissions of failure—'I could almost say damn it', 'Not a word more can I remember' (ii. 38, 44)— confirm the method by which they are working. In some cases the scribe begins his transcription with a heading which will recall the occasion as well as the matter, as when he notes that Smith delivered Lectures 21 and 24 'without Book' or 'sine Libro'; and he is careful to give Lecture 12, the hinge between the two halves of the course, the title 'Of Composition' because it begins the discussion of the various species of writing.

Our manuscript is the result of a continuous collaboration between two students intent on making the notes as full and accurate a record of Smith's words as their combined resources can produce. The many slips and gaps which remain should not blind us to the great pains taken. Working from fairly full jottings, Scribe A writes the basic text on the recto pages (except, oddly, i. 18–68 when he uses the verso pages), and thereafter two kinds of revision take place. He corrects and expands the text, writing the revision above the line when only a word or two are involved. Unfortunately the additions of this kind are far too numerous to be specially signalized without overburdening the textual apparatus, and they have been silently incorporated in the text. In any case it is impossible to distinguish those added *currente calamo* from those added later, except of course where the interlined words replace a deletion (and these are always noted here). When the addition is too lengthy to be inserted between lines, Scribe A writes them on the facing page (i.e. a verso page, except at i. 18–68) at the appropriate point, and often keys them in with x or some other symbol. All such additions on the facing page are, in this edition, enclosed in brace brackets { }. Scribe A's sources for his additional materials no doubt varied; some of it was certainly 'recollected in tranquillity' as Reid would have recommended; some of it such a tirelessly conscientious student would acquire by consultation with a fellow-student, or perhaps one of the sets of notes in circulation from a previous year. There is reason to think that some of the material had simply been inadvertently omitted at the first transcription.

The second revision, much less extensive but very useful, is Scribe B's. Apart from a few corrections of A's words, B makes two sorts of contribution. He fills in a good many of the blanks clearly left by A with this in view—alas, not enough, though he is obviously in many ways better informed than A. This comes out also in the sometimes substantial notes he writes on the verso page facing A's text, with supplementary illustration and explanation of the points there treated. These are enclosed in { }, with a footnote assigning them to Hand B. They raise the same question of source as A's notes. From the fact that B never himself deletes or alters what he has written and generally arranges his lines so as to end exactly within a certain space, e.g. opposite the end of a lecture (i. v. 116; ii. v. 18), we may deduce that he is working from a tidy original or fair copy: another set of notes? The order in which A and B wrote their inserted matter varied: at i. 46 A's note is squeezed into space left by B's, and similarly at ii. v. 30 and elsewhere: but normally B's notes are clearly later than A's, as at i. v. 146, and at ii. v. 101 B's note is squeezed between two of A's although the second of these was written (in different ink) later than the first.

There is a noticeable falling-off in verso-page notes from about Lecture 16 onwards: inexplicable, unless Scribe A was becoming more adept in transcription. Certainly the report of the last lecture is much the longest of them all, but Smith probably, like most lecturers, used more than the hour this time in order to finish his course. Scribe A relieved the tedium of transcription by occasional lightheartedness. There is the doodled caricature of a face (meant to resemble Smith's?) 'This is a picture of uncertainty', at ii. 67: at ii. 166 'WFL', i.e. 'wait for laugh', is inserted then deleted; at ii. 224 the habitual spelling 'tho' is for once expanded by the addition of 'ugh' below the line. Of special interest is the added note at i. 196 recording the witticism of 'Mr Herbert' about Adam Smith's notorious absent-mindedness. The joke about Smith must have been made just after the lecture and the note added shortly after the transcription in this case.

Henry Herbert (1741–1811), later Baron Porchester and Earl of Carnarvon, was a gentleman-boarder in Smith's house throughout the session 1762–3. On 22 February 1763 Smith wrote to Hume introducing him as 'very well acquainted with your works' and anxious to meet Hume in Edinburgh (Letter 70). Hume (71) found him 'a very promising young man', but refers to him on 13 September 1763 (75) as 'that severe Critic, Mr Herbert'. There is a letter from Herbert to Smith (74) dated 11 September 1763.

To suggest that Herbert may have been the source of at least some of the additional notes would be an unwarranted use of Occam's razor. No one enjoying this degree of familiarity with the lecturer and consulting him on the content of the lectures would have left so many blanks unfilled; and Smith would certainly not knowingly have helped to compile notes of his talks. It is also worth noting that the Rhetoric lectures, unlike those on Jurisprudence etc. (see LJ *14–15*), were not followed by an 'examination' hour in which additional points might be picked up.

The well-marked scribal habits of Scribe A point to his having suffered from a defect of eyesight, some sort of stenopia or tunnel-vision. He is prone to various forms of haplography, omission of a word or syllable which resembled its predecessor: 'if I may so' (*say* omitted), 'coing' (*coining*), 'possed' (*possessed*). He writes 'on the hand', adds r to the, and imagines he has written 'other'. Angle brackets ⟨ ⟩ have been used for omissions here supplied. There are frequent repetitions of word or phrase; these have been enclosed in square brackets [ ]. There are innumerable instances of anticipation of words or phrases lying ahead: most of these have been corrected by the scribe when his eye returns to his original jottings. In one case he anticipates a phrase from the beginning of the following lecture (i. 116, 117), showing that on this occasion he had allowed a weekend to pass before transcribing Lectures 8 and 9—Friday and Monday, 3 and 6 December. He often tries to hold in his mind too long a passage, writing words that convey the sense and having to change them, when on going back to his jottings he finds the proper words. He starts to write 'object' and has to change it to 'design'. Most of the many overwritten words in the manuscript are examples of this, and unfortunately it is seldom possible to decipher the original word; where it is, it has been noted. The scribe's memory of the drift of Smith's meaning no doubt played a part; but here as elsewhere he is eager to record the master's *ipsissima verba*. He frequently reverses the order of words and phrases and restores the proper order by writing numbers above them.

The aim of the present edition has been to allow the reader to judge for himself the nature of the manuscript by presenting it as fully as print will allow; but in the interests of legibility several compromises have been made. Where the punctuation is erratic or accidental it has been normalized: e.g. commas separating subject from verb, 'is' from its complement, a conjunction from its clause, and the like. The original paragraphing has been retained where it clearly exists and is intended. Not all initial capitals have been retained. The scribe usually employs them for emphasis or to convey an impression of a technical or special use of a word; but in 'Some', 'Same', 'Such', 'with Regard to', 'in Respect to', 'for my Part', 'for this Reason', etc., the capital has been ignored. Frequently used abbreviations have been silently expanded: such are y^s (*this*), y^m (*them*), y^r (*their*), y^n (*than*), y^{se} (*those*), nëyr (*neither*), oy^r (*other*), Bröy^r (*Brother*), p̈t (*part*), aġst (*against*), figs (*figures*), dïs (*divisions*), nom̈ve (*nominative*), and others of similar type. It has not been possible to record the many changes of ink, pen, and style of writing (from copperplate to hurried), though these are no doubt indicative of the circumstances in which Scribe A was working. The misnumbering of Lecture 5 onwards has been corrected, and noted.

To sum up the textual notation used:

{ }	notes on page facing main text—'Hand B' if relevant
⟨ ⟩	omissions supplied conjecturally
[ ]	erroneous repetitions
deleted	deleted words not replaced above line
replaces:	words corrected in line above a deletion
changed from:	original word decipherable beneath *over-writing*
superscript indicators:	normally refer to the *preceding* word or words, to which reference is made.

2. *The Lectures*

The notes we have date from what was apparently the fifteenth winter in which Adam Smith lectured on rhetoric. Disappointed of a travelling tutorship on coming down from Balliol, and after two years at home in Kirkcaldy in 1746–8, he 'opened a class for teaching rhetorick at Edinburgh', as the obituary in the *Gentleman's Magazine* (Aug. 1790, lx. 762) puts it; and it goes on to remark on an advantage enjoyed by Smith and frequently to be noticed in later years: 'His pronunciation and his style were much superior to what could, at that time, be acquired in Scotland only'. The superiority was often (as by Sir James Mackintosh in introducing the second edition of the 1755–6 *Edinburgh Review* in 1818) ascribed to the influence of the speech of his Glasgow Professor Francis Hutcheson, as well as to his six Oxford years. His awareness of language as an activity had certainly been sharpened by both experiences of different modes—differences so often embarrassing to his fellow-countrymen, speakers and writers alike, in the mid-century. *The Edinburgh Review* no. 1 named as one of the obstacles to the progress of science in Scotland 'the difficulty of a proper expression in a country where there is no standard of language, or at least one very remote' (EPS 229); and two years later, on 2 July 1757, Hume observes in a letter to Gilbert Elliott of Minto (Letter 135, ed. J. Y. T. Greig, 1932) that we 'are unhappy, in our Accent and Pronunciation, speak a very corrupt Dialect of the Tongue which we make use of'. The background of desire for 'self-improvement' and the part played by the many societies in Edinburgh and elsewhere are described in JML xxiii–xxxix, and D. D. McElroy, *Scotland's Age of Improvement* (1969). Smith 'teaching rhetorick' in 1748 was the right man at the right moment.

In the absence of advertisement or notice of the lectures in the *Scots Magazine* (these would have been unusual at this time: not so ten years later) we do not know exact dates; but A. F. Tytler in his *Memoirs of the Life and Writings of the Honourable Henry Home of Kames, containing sketches of the Progress of Literature and General Improvement in Scotland during the greater part of the eighteenth century* (1807: i. 190) gives this account:

It was by his [sc. Kames's] persuasion and encouragement, that Mr Adam Smith, soon after his return from Oxford, and when he had abandoned all views towards the Church, for which he had been originally destined, was induced to turn his early studies to the benefit of the public, by reading a course of Lectures on Rhetoric and the *Belles Lettres.* He delivered those lectures at Edinburgh in 1748, and the two following years, to a respectable auditory, chiefly composed of students in law and theology; till called to Glasgow. . . .

The 'auditory' included Alexander Wedderburn (who edited *The Edinburgh Review* 1755–6), William Johnston (who became Sir William Pulteney), James Oswald of Dunnikeir (a boyhood friend of Smith's from Kirkcaldy), John Millar, Hugh Blair, 'and others, who made a distinguished figure both in the department of literature and in public life'. When on 10 January 1751 Smith wrote (Letter 8) to the Clerk of Senate at Glasgow accepting appointment to the Chair of Logic there and explaining that he could not immediately take up his duties because of his commitments to his 'friends here', i.e. in Edinburgh, the plural shows that he had sponsors for his lectures besides Kames, and it has been supposed that these were James Oswald and Robert Craigie of Glendoick. There is independent evidence that at least in his last year at Edinburgh if not earlier he also lectured on jurisprudence; but Tytler is quite clear on the duration of the rhetoric course; and after Smith's departure for Glasgow a rhetoric course continued to be given by Robert Watson till *his* departure for the Chair of Logic at St Andrews in 1756. This was only the beginning: one of Smith's first 'auditory', Hugh Blair, on 11 December 1759, began a course on the same subject in the University of Edinburgh, which conferred the title of Professor on him in August 1760 and appointed him to a new Chair of Rhetoric and Belles Lettres (destined to become in effect the first Chair of English Literature in the world) on 7 April 1762. Smith's original lectures were presumably delivered in one of the Societies, the Philosophical being the most likely because since the '45 its ordinary activities had been suspended, and Kames would have seen the courses as a way of keeping it alive. In 1737 Colin Maclaurin, Professor of Mathematics (see Astronomy IV. 58), was instrumental in broadening the Society's scope to include literature and science.

*   *   *

When Adam Smith arrived in Glasgow in October 1751 to begin teaching as Professor of Logic and Rhetoric he found his duties augmented owing to the illness of Thomas Craigie, the Professor of Moral Philosophy, the work of whose classes was to be shared by Smith and three other professors. We hardly need evidence to prove that, hard-pressed as he was, he would fall back on his Edinburgh materials, including the Rhetoric, which it was his statutory duty to teach. Craigie died in November and his Chair was filled by the translation to it of Smith in April 1752. Throughout the eighteenth century the ordinary or 'public' class of Moral Philosophy met at 7.30 a.m. for lectures on ethics, politics, jurisprudence, natural theology, and then at 11 a.m. for an 'examination' hour to ensure that the lecture had been understood. A 'private' class, sometimes called a 'college', attended by those who had already in the previous year taken the public class and were now attending that for the second time—or even third—but not the examination class, met at noon, normally three days a week. Each professor used the private class for a course on a subject of special interest to himself. Hutcheson had lectured on Arrian, Antoninus (Marcus Aurelius), and other Greek philosophers; Thomas Reid on the powers of the mind.

Adam Smith chose for his private class the first subject he had ever taught, Rhetoric and Belles Lettres. Here a question arises. Rhetoric was now in the domain of his successor in the Chair of Logic, James Clow. There is no record of a protest from Clow, as there was in Edinburgh from John Stevenson, who had been teaching logic and rhetoric for thirty-two years when Blair's Chair was founded. Several explanations suggest themselves, apart from personal good-will. The phrase 'Belles Lettres', though it did not mollify Stevenson, differentiated in a decisive way the two Glasgow courses. Clow's emphasis seems to have rested on rhetorical analysis of passages, in keeping with the discipline of logic (see JML xxx quoting Edinburgh Univ. Lib. MS DC 8,13). More important, at Glasgow a public class was not the offender. In any case Smith's rhetoric students had attended Clow's class two years before, and the opportunity (which Smith knew they enjoyed) of making correlations can only have been philosophically beneficial. Similar opportunities were opened by their hearing at the same time—and having already heard—Smith's discourses on ethics and jurisprudence. The lectures on history and on judicial eloquence would be illustrated by those on public and private law. And we must not forget that these students were simultaneously studying natural philosophy, theoretical and practical, the fifth year subjects of the Glasgow Arts curriculum. Such juxtapositions were then as now among the great benefits of the Scottish University system, and without them Scotland would not have made the mark she did in philosophy in Adam Smith's century. In particular, Smith's students must have noted the multi-faceted relationship between the ethics and rhetoric, in three broad areas. First, Smith employed many of the general principles stated in TMS in *illustrating* the different forms of communication; for example, our admiration for the great (ii. 107 and below, section 4), or for hardships undergone with firmness and constancy (ii. 100). Smith also drew attention to the influence of environment on forms and modes of expression (ii. 113–16, 142 ff., 152 ff.) in a manner which would be familiar to those who had already heard his treatment of the rules of conduct. Secondly, Smith's students would note the points at which the rhetoric *elaborated* on the discussion of the role of sympathy and the nature of moral judgement and persuasion (cf. TMS I. i. 3–4; cf. *18–19* below). The character of the man of sensibility is strikingly developed in Lecture XXX (ii. 234 ff.) while the argument as a whole implies that the spoken discourse could on some occasions affect moral judgement. Thirdly, Smith's students would perceive that the arguments developed in the lectures on rhetoric *complement* the analysis of TMS, where it is remarked that:

We may judge of the propriety or impropriety of the sentiments of another person by their correspondence or disagreement with our own, upon two different occasions; either, first, when the objects which excite them are considered without any peculiar relation, either to ourselves or to the person whose sentiments we judge of; or, secondly, when they are considered as peculiarly affecting one or other of us' (TMS, I.i.4.1).

Objects which lack a *peculiar* relation include 'the expression of a picture, the composition of a discourse . . . all the general subjects of science and taste'.

Smith's lecturing timetable is set out in LJ *13–22*, with references to the sources of our information. On the Rhetoric lectures, two accounts by men who had heard them show with what clarity they were remembered more than thirty years later. The first was given by John Millar, Professor of Law, who had heard them both in Edinburgh and Glasgow, to Dugald Stewart for a memoir of Smith to be delivered at the Royal Society of Edinburgh in 1793 (Stewart I. 16):

In the Professorship of Logic, to which Mr. Smith was appointed on his first introduction into this University, he soon saw the necessity of departing widely from the plan that had been followed by his predecessors, and of directing the attention of his pupils to studies of a more interesting and useful nature than the logic and metaphysics of the schools. Accordingly, after exhibiting a general view of the powers of the mind, and explaining so much of the ancient logic as was requisite to gratify curiosity with respect to an artificial method of reasoning, which had once occupied the universal attention of the learned, he dedicated all the rest of his time to the delivery of a system of rhetoric and belles-lettres. The best method of explaining and illustrating the various powers of the human mind, the most useful part of metaphysics, arises from an examination of the several ways of communicating our thoughts by speech, and from an attention to the principles of those literary compositions which contribute to persuasion or entertainment. By these arts, every thing that we perceive or feel, every operation of our minds, is expressed and delineated in such a manner, that it may be clearly distinguished and remembered. There is, at the same time, no branch of literature more suited to youth at their first entrance upon philosophy than this, which lays hold of their taste and their feelings.

The second report, written after 1776 in a letter from James Wodrow, Library Keeper at the University of Glasgow from 1750 to 1755, to the Earl of Buchan and preserved in Glasgow Univ. Lib. Murray Collection (Buchan Correspondence, ii. 171), reads:

Adam Smith delivered a set of admirable lectures on language (not as a grammarian but as a rhetorician) on the different kinds or characteristics of style suited to different subjects, simple, nervous, etc., the structure, the natural order, the proper arrangement of the different members of the sentence etc. He characterised the style and the genius of some of the best of the ancient writers and poets, but especially historians, Thucydides, Polybius etc. translating long passages of them, also the style of the best English classics, Lord Clarendon, Addison, Swift, Pope, etc; and, though his own didactic style in his last famous book (however suited to the subject)—the style of the former book was much superior—was certainly not a model for good writing, yet his remarks and rules given in the lectures I speak of, were the result of a fine taste and sound judgement, well calculated to be exceedingly useful to young composers, so that I have often regretted that some part of them has never been published.

With this stricture on the style of WN, incidentally, may be compared the remark made by Lord Monboddo to Boswell that though Smith came down from Oxford a good Greek and Latin scholar, from the style of WN 'one would think that he had never read any of the Writers of Greece or Rome' (Boswell, *Private Papers*, ed. Scott and Pottle, xiii. 92); and even his friends Hume, Millar and Blair took this view. On the other hand John Ramsay of Ochtertyre (*Scotland and Scotsmen in the eighteenth Century*, published 1888, i. 462) thought that in view of the purity and elegance with which he ordinarily wrote it was 'no wonder, then, that his lectures should be regarded as models of composition'. A kindred activity of Smith's in his Glasgow days is recorded in the Foulis Press Papers, extracted by W. J. Duncan in *Notes and Documents illustrative of the Literary History of Glasgow* (Maitland Club 1831, 16): in January 1752 he had helped to found a Literary Society in the University, and 'he read papers to this society on Taste, Composition and the History of Philosophy which he had previously delivered while a lecturer on rhetoric in Edinburgh'. Of these, two were parts I and II of the essay on the Imitative Arts—this on the evidence of John Millar who was a member of the Society (EPS 172)—an essay which Smith told Reynolds he intended publishing 'this winter', i.e. 1782–3 (Reynolds, letter of 12 September 1782, in *Correspondence of James Boswell*, ed. C. N. Fifer, Yale UP 1976, 126).

What modifications the lectures on rhetoric underwent between 1748 and the session in which our notes were taken it is almost impossible to determine. There are few datable post-1748 references. Macpherson's Ossian imitations, 'lately published' (ii. 113), appeared in 1760, 1762, 1763. Gray's two Pindaric odes, if the reference at ii. 96 includes them, belong to 1757; the *Elegy in a Country Churchyard*, of which Smith became so fond, to 1751; Shenstone's *Pastoral Ballad* to 1755. Rousseau's *Discours* (i. 19) appeared in 1755 and was discussed by Smith in the *Edinburgh Review* no. 2 (EPS 250–4). All of these references, except perhaps the last, could easily have been inserted without radical revision of the text. The unmistakable reference to Hume's *History of England* at ii. 73, whether we read 'so' or ('10' in the added marginal note, raises a complex question. The *History* appeared in instalments, working backwards chronologically, in 1754, 1757, 1759, and was completed in 1762, after which date the reference becomes relevant. On 12 January 1763 Smith must have read out what had stood in his manuscript for some years, and then in the last moments of the lecture made an impromptu correction when recollecting a friend's very recent publication. Why this afterthought is also recorded by Scribe A in an afterthought is perhaps not in the circumstances all that mysterious.

The general continuity of the lecture-course from 1748 to 1763, details apart, is established by its structure and by the set of central principles which inform all twentynine reported lectures and which could not have been added or superimposed on the argument at some intermediate stage of its development. Basic to the whole is the division into 'an examination of the several ways of communicating our thoughts by speech' and 'an attention to the principles of those literary compositions which contribute to persuasion or entertainment'.

To set this out in summary: first section, linguistic: (*a*) Language, communication, expression (Lectures 2–7, i. 85); (*b*) Style and character (Lectures 7–11).—Second section, the species of composition: (*a*) Descriptive (Lectures 12–16); (*b*) Narrative or historical (Lectures 17–20); (*c*) Poetry (Lecture 21); (*d*) Demonstrative oratory, i.e. panegyric (Lectures 22–23); (*e*) Didactic or scientific (Lecture 24); (*f*) Deliberative oratory (Lectures 25–27); (*g*) Judicial or forensic oratory (Lectures 28–30).

Two features of the course enable us to make a plausible guess at the contents of the introductory lecture—whose absence, by the way, tends to prove that this set of notes was not prepared with a view to sale. At the heart of Smith's thinking, his doctrine, and his method of presentation (the three are always related) is the notion of the chain (see ii. 133 and cf. Astronomy II. 8–9)—articulated continuity, sequence of relations leading to illumination. Leave no chasm or gap in the thread: 'the very notion of a gap makes us uneasy' (ii. 36). The orator 'puts the whole story into a connected narration'; the great art of an orator is to throw his argument 'into a sort of a narration, filling up in the manner most suitable . . .' (ii. 206, 197). The art of transition is a vital matter (i. 146). Smith is concerned with this on the strategic level just as contemporary writers on Milton and Thomson were on the imaginative. As a lecturer, giving an exhibition of the very craft he is discussing, he insists that his listeners know where they have been and where they are going. Dugald Stewart notes in his *Life of Thomas Reid* that 'neither he nor his immediate predecessor ever published any general *prospectus* of their respective plans; nor any *heads* or *outlines* to assist their students in tracing the trains of thought which suggested their various transitions' (1802: 38–9). In Smith's case the frequent signposts would have made such a prospectus superfluous, and readers of the lectures are more likely to complain of being led by the hand than of bafflement. What all this amounts to is that the opening theme-phrase 'Perspicuity of stile' must have been clearly led up to.

The other habit of Smith's gives a clue to how this may have been done. He often shows his impatience with intricate subdivisions and classifications of his subject, such as had long made rhetoric a notoriously scholastic game. La Bruyère speaks of 'un beau sermon' made according to all the rules of the rhetoricians, with the *cognoscenti* in the preacher's audience following with admiration 'toutes les énumérations où il se promène'. But though Smith thinks it all very silly and refers anyone so inclined to read about it in Quintilian, his teacherly conscience compels him to ensure that his students have heard of the old terms. Lecture 1 no doubt defined the scope of this course by saying what it was not going to include. At least since the anonymous *Rhetorica ad Herennium* early in the first century B.C. the orator's art had been divided into invention, arrangement, expression, memory, and delivery; Quintilian's words (*Institutio Oratoria* III. iii. 1;

and passim) are *inventio, dispositio, elocutio, memoria,* and *pronuntiatio* or *actio.* Smith in effect sees only the second and third as important, the third (style) occupying Lectures 2–11, the second underlying virtually all that Lectures 12–30 discuss.

It is to be hoped that for the sake of clarity one other traditional division was at least mentioned. As early as i. 12 'the didactick stile' is compared with that of historians and orators, and the phrase and the comparison occur repeatedly throughout the lectures as if their meaning was already known. The central place occupied in Smith's whole conception of discourse by the 'didactick stile' becomes clear in the lecture (24) devoted to it, where it emerges as not only a mode of expression but as a procedure of thought: the scientific (ii. 132–5), that concerned with the exposition of a system, the clarification of a multitude of phenomena by one known or proved principle. Perhaps this was too early in the course; but the analogy with music set out in Imitative Arts II. 29 (see below, section 5) by which many notes are related both to a leading or key-note and a succession of notes or 'song', and the observation that this is like 'what order and method are to discourse', would have proved helpful to the many who, then as later, find it harder to apprehend pattern in language than in sound or colour. Smith makes things harder by equating, at i. 152, the ancient (indeed Aristotelian) division of speeches into Demonstrative, Deliberative, Judicial, with his own philosophical division into narrative, didactic, rhetorical (i. 149). This, it must be admitted, involves some straining. 'It is rather reverence for antiquity than any great regard for the Beauty or usefullness of the thing itself which makes me mention the Antient divisions of Rhetorick' (i. 152); but in this case he could have been less scrupulous, since Quintilian (III. iv) asks 'why three?' rather than a score of others. He is echoing Cicero; and Jean-François Marmontel, author of the literary articles in the *Encyclopédie* vols 3–7 and *Supplément* (collected in *Eléments de Littérature,* 1787) pours scorn on the terms themselves: *Deliberative* speech, where the orator exerts all his energy to proving to the meeting that there is nothing at all to deliberate; *Demonstrative,* which demonstrates nothing but flattery or hatred (and, he should have added, the orator's virtuosity—not showing but showing off); *Judicial,* aiming at demonstrating, and leaving it all to the judges' deliberation. In any case Smith in the end does not scrap the ancient divison but simply adds the *Didactic* to it: Lectures 22–30.

By chance our notes begin at what Smith thought of first importance: style, language. 'Nobis prima sit virtus perspicuitas' said

Quintilian (VIII. ii. 22, echoing Aristotle's σαφὴς λέξις, *Rhetoric* III. ii. 1), and defined the main ingredient in perspicuity as *proprietas*, each thing called by its *own*, its properly belonging name. The root meaning of *perspicuity* is the quality of being seen through, and the subject of Smith's lectures may be said to be what it is that language allows to show through it, and how. For Smith there is much more to this transparence than the handing over of facts or feelings, and the first paragraph introduces some of this. Words are no mere convenience; they are natives of a community, as citizens are—and as i. 5–6 shows, of a particular part of the community. The Abbé du Bos devoted I. xxxvii of *Réflexions critiques sur la poésie et sur la peinture* (1719) to showing the kind of force the words of our own language have on our minds. When an English-reading Frenchman meets the word *God* it is to the word *Dieu* and all its associations that his emotions respond.

A more immediate motive for this paragraph can best be indicated by a well-known story about the poet of the *Seasons*. After completing his Arts course at Edinburgh, James Thomson's first exercise in the Faculty of Divinity was the preparation of a sermon on the Jod section of Psalm cxix. When he read it to his class on 27 October 1724 it was severely criticised by his professor, William Hamilton, for its grandiloquence of style, quite unsuitable for any congregation. Thomson, discouraged, gave up his studies, went off to London, and spent his life writing poems whose highly Latinate diction has often been remarked on: as was that of his fellow-countrymen in his own century. The Scoticisms against which Scottish writers were put on their guard, as by Hume and Beattie, were partly of this kind, and have been attributed to the Latin base of Scots Law as well as of Scottish education. Hutcheson was the first professor at Glasgow to lecture in English, and this, quite apart from his teaching, was seen as a help to the students in unlearning their linguistic tendencies. A. F. Tytler (*Kames*, i. 163) emphasises the influence of another Scottish professor in the same direction, that of the Edinburgh mathematician Colin Maclaurin, his 'pure, correct and simple style inducing a taste for chasteness of expression . . . a disrelish of affected ornaments'. Scots youths were encouraged towards 'an ease and elegance of composition as a more engaging vehicle for subjects of taste, in the room of the dry scholastic style in which they had hitherto been treated'. They were 'attracted to the more pleasing topics of criticism and the belles lettres. The cultivation of style became an object of study', replacing the ancient school dialectics. This, if only Tytler had provided evidence and illustration, would parallel the linguistic programme of the Royal Society as outlined by Sprat in its *History* in 1667: 'this trick of *Metaphors*', 'those specious *Tropes* and *Figures*', to be replaced by positive expressions 'bringing all things as near the Mathematical plainness as they can'.

A much wider context for Smith's lectures is thus created, though we must not forget the immediate one suggested by i. 103: 'We in this country are most of us very sensible that the perfection of language is very different from that we commonly speak in'. Periodically throughout the history of style there occur combats between the respective upholders of the plain and the elaborate: Plato versus the sophist Gorgias; Calvus charging Cicero with 'Asianic' writing as opposed to Attic purity. Smith's teaching comes at such a moment. While he was a student John Constable's *Reflections upon accuracy of style* enjoyed something of a vogue. Not published till 1734 (reprinted 1738), this attack on the highly figurative language of Jeremy Collier's *Essays* (1697) had been written in 1701; and in the meantime Collier's 'huddle of metaphors' and conceits had been sharply criticized in John Oldmixon's adaptation of the influential *La manière de bien penser dans les ouvrages d'esprit* (1687) by Dominique Bouhours— *The arts of Logick and Rhetorick* (1728). Behind all of them lies another combat: the Chevalier de Méré's strictures on the verbal extravagances of Voiture in *De la Justesse* (1671), which gave Constable his title. These oppositions are of many kinds, and all differ from the one Smith sets up between the lucidity of Swift and the 'pompousness' of Shaftesbury—the shaping motive of much of Lectures 7–11. This is perhaps the earliest appreciation of Swift as writer; political and quasi-moral objections prevented his critical recognition till late in the century. Smith's admiration rests on something central in the *Rhetoric*: 'All his works show a complete knowledge of his Subject . . . One who has such a complete knowledge of what he treats will naturally arange it in the most proper order' (i. 105–6). Shaftesbury is a dilettante and does not know enough. Above all he has not kept up with modern scientific advances; he makes up for superficiality and ignorance by ornament (i. 140–1, 144). That his letters 'have no marks of the circumstances the writer was in at the time he wrote. Nor any reflections peculiarly suited to the times and circumstances' is the most telling fault. The writing does not *belong* anywhere or to any one.

It is his criticism of the reverence paid to the figures of speech (whether departures from normal use of word, *figurae verborum*; or unusual modes of presentation, *figurae sententiarum*—Cicero, *Orator* xxxix–xl; Quintilian IX. i–iii; *Rhetorica ad Herennium* Book IV) that leads Smith to his decisive formulations of beauty of language. 'When the sentiment of the speaker is expressed in a neat, clear, plain and clever manner, and the passion or affection he is possessed of and intends, *by sympathy*, to communicate to his hearer, is plainly and cleverly hit off, then and then only the expression has all the force and beauty that language can give it'. Figures of speech may or may not do the job. See i. 56, 73, 79. 'The expression ought to be suited to the mind of the author, for this is chiefly governed by the circumstances he is placed in'. Language is organically related not merely to thought in the abstract (see section 3 below); it bears 'the same stamp' as the speaker's nature. Ben Jonson, writing about 1622 (*Timber or Discoveries*), observed: 'Language most shewes a man: speake, that I may see thee. It springs out of the most retired and inmost parts of us, and is the Image of the Parent of it, the mind. No glasse renders a mans forme or likenesse so true as his speech'.

The discussion of this relationship is introduced by a nice piece of Smithian economy. The character-sketches of the plain and the simple man not only illustrate two styles and lead on to Swift and Temple (i. 85–95); they offer the student models of *ethologia*, the form prescribed (according to Quintilian I. ix. 3) to pupils in rhetoric as an exercise, and they prepare for the instruction in character-drawing in Lecture 15 and the discussion of the Character as a genre—invented by Theophrastus, edited by Isaac Casaubon in 1592, introduced in England by Joseph Hall in 1608, and practised by La Bruyère, who is Smith's favourite because his collection is a microcosm of society and of mankind. When Hugh Blair, as he tells us, was lent the manuscript of Smith's lectures (he no doubt remembered hearing this passage) when preparing his own, it was from these *ethologiae* that he drew hints: 'On this head, of the General Characters of Style, particularly, the Plain and the Simple, and the characters of those English authors who are classed under them, in this, and the following Lecture, several ideas have been taken from a manuscript treatise on rhetoric, part of which was shown to me, many years ago, by the learned and ingenious author, Dr Adam Smith; and which, it is hoped, will be given by him to the Public' (*Lectures on Rhetoric and Belles Lettres*, 1783, i. 381). The Theophrastan form influenced the historians; see the collection *Characters of the Seventeenth Century*, ed. D. Nichol Smith (1920). It is significant that the first critic to publish a series of studies of Shakespeare's characters, William Richardson, the Glasgow Professor of Humanity from 1773, was a student of Adam Smith's; his *A philosophical analysis and illustration of some of Shakespeare's remarkable characters* appeared in 1774, and two more volumes in 1784 and 1788.

Boswell, another student who heard the Rhetoric lectures (in 1759), was struck by Smith's emphasis on the personal aspects of writers, and he twice recalled the remark about Milton's shoes (absent from our report; it should have come at ii. 107): 'I remember Dr. Adam Smith, in his rhetorical lectures at Glasgow, told us he was glad to know that Milton wore latchets in his shoes, instead of buckles' (*Journal of a tour to the Hebrides* §9). 'I have a pleasure in hearing every story, tho' never so little, of so distinguished a Man. I remember Smith took notice of this pleasure in his lectures upon Rhetoric, and said that he felt it when he read that Milton never wore buckles but strings in his shoes' (*Boswell Papers* i. 107). Such was the training of the future author of the greatest of all biographies of a man of letters. In no. 1 of the *Spectator* (1 March 1711) Addison 'observed, that a Reader seldom peruses a Book with Pleasure 'till he knows whether the Writer of it be a black or a fair Man, of a mild or cholerick Disposition, Married or a Batchelor, with other Particulars of a like nature, that conduce very much to the right Understanding of an Author'. John Harvey included in his *Collection of Miscellany Poems and Letters* (1726: 84–88) a parody of this *Spectator*, with a fictitious life of himself.

Beauty of style, then, is *propriety* in the exact sense of the word: language which embodies and exhibits to the reader that distinctive turn and quality of spirit in the author 'qui lui est *propre*', as Marivaux insisted in the *Spectateur français*, 8e feuille (8 September 1722). Our pleasure is, as Hutcheson noted in his *Inquiry into the original of our ideas of Beauty and Virtue* (1725: I. sec. IV. vii), in recognizing a perfect correspondence or aptness in a curious mechanism for the execution of a design. It is characteristic of Smith that his aesthetics should thus centre on correspondence, relation, affinity. What he finds wrong with Shaftesbury's style is that he arbitrarily made it up; it has nothing to do with his own character (i. 137–8). When the principle is extended from persons to societies—'all languages . . . are equally ductile and equally accommodated to all different tempers'—very wide and illuminating prospects open up. Good examples are Trajan's Rome as formative background for Tacitus (Lecture 20), the comparison of Athens and Rome as contexts for Demosthenes and Cicero (Lecture 26), and the association of the rise of prose with the growth of commerce and wealth (ii. 144 ff.). Indeed the accounts of historical writing and of the three types of oratory are made the occasions for elaborate excursus on different kinds of social and political organization, ancient and modern.

'*By sympathy*' (i. v. 56): this phrase in the formulation of the highest beauty language can attain is one of the very few which Scribe A underlines, and pains had clearly been taken by Smith to bring out the parallel between his ethical and rhetorical principles. Just as we act under the eye of an impartial spectator within ourselves, the creation of an imaginative self-projection into an outsider whose standards and responses we reconstruct by sympathy or ability to feel as he does, so our language is enabled to communicate our thoughts and 'affections' (i.e. inclinations) by our ability to predict its effect on our hearer. This is what is meant by seeing the Rhetoric and TMS as two halves of one system, and not merely at occasional points of contact. The connection of 'sympathy' as a rhetorical instrument with the vision of speech and personality as an organic unity need not be laboured. Again, it should be obvious how often Smith's concern is with the sharing of sentiments and attitudes rather than mere ideas or facts. The arts of persuasion are close to his heart for this reason. The opening of Lecture 11 is a key passage. The conveying to a hearer of 'the sentiment, passion or affection with which [his thought] affects him'—'the perfection of stile'—is regulated by a 'Rule, which is equally applicable to conversation and behaviour as writing'; 'all the Rules of Criticism and morality when traced to their foundation, turn out to be some Principles of Common Sence which every one assents to'. One of the most frequent terms of critical praise in the Rhetoric is 'interesting', bearing its original and normal eighteenth century sense of *involving, engaging*, as at ii. 27 where, thanks to Livy's skill, 'we enter into all the concerns of the parties' and are as affected as if we had been there. The reason why history is enjoyed is that events which befall mankind 'interest us greatly by the Sympatheticall affections they raise in us' (ii. 16). The good historian shows the effects wrought on those who were actors or spectators of the events (ii. 5; cf. ii. 62–3). Knowledge of the plot of a tragedy is an advantage since it leaves us 'free to attend to the Sentiments' (ii. 30). A variation on this is acutely described in dealing with the picture of Agamemnon's sacrifice of Iphigenia, by Timanthes (ii. 8); cf. i. 180, Addison on St Peter's. Indeed the entire treatment of the art of description in Lectures 12–16 is profoundly instructive of Smith's main interests. Even minutiae such as the arrangement of words in a sentence (i. v. 42–v. 52b) repay an attention beyond the merely grammatical.

The species of writing are so intimately bound up with each other that Smith finds it difficult in Lectures 12–30 to demarcate them sharply. By instinct, as already noted, he is a historian in the sense that he sees narrative as the very type of human thought-procedure; but his interest in it is also that suggested by Hume's description of history's records as 'so many collections of experiments by which the moral philosopher fixes the principles of his science'. (William Richardson used similar terms about his studies of Shakespeare's characters in 1784). The first paper read to the Literary Society in the University, on 6 February 1752, was 'An essay on historical composition' by James Moor, the Professor of Greek (*Essays*, 1759). Moor's elaboration of the kinship of history and poetry, the unified pattern which both exhibit in events, throws interesting light on the position occupied by Lecture 21 in Smith's progression. Bolingbroke compared history and drama; and Voltaire wrote to the Marquis d'Argenson on 26 January 1740 (*Correspondence* ed. T. Besterman, xxxv. 373): 'Il faut, dans une histoire, comme dans une pièce de théâtre, exposition, noeud, et dénouement'. There may be an echo of the ancient assimilation of history and poetry in 'the Poeticall method' of keeping up the connection between events, other than the causal (ii. 36); and history, like poetry, is said to 'amuse' (ii. 62), and to have originated with the poets. Leonard Welsted expounded this view fully in his *Dissertation concerning the perfection of the English Language* (1724). For Quintilian (X. i. 31) a history *is* a poem: 'Est enim proxima poetis et quodammodo carmen solutum'. There was indeed much collocation by the ancient rhetoricians of all these genres—history, poetry, rhetoric, philosophical exposition—as in Cicero's *Orator* XX. 66–7. The Muses are said to have spoken in Xenophon's voice (*Orator* XIX. 62). They are all combined by Fénelon in the educational project he outlined to the French Academy, first in 1716. That panegyrical eloquence 'tient un peu de la poésie' as Voltaire maintained in the *Encyclopédie* article on Eloquence is also Smith's view (ii. 111–2).

The lecture on poetry (21), delivered extemporaneously, is both instructive and disappointing. The post-Coleridge student looks for more analysis of short poems; these are of little interest, naturally, to the philosopher. More important, why does not Smith of all critics tackle the problem of the pleasure afforded us by tragedy? This is specially strange since Hume, who had offered a highly ingenious answer in his essay on tragedy in 1757, expressed dissatisfaction with the treatment of sympathy in this context in TMS I. iii. 1. 9 (Corr. Letter 36, 28 July 1759), and the second edition of TMS contained a footnote on the question. The insistence in the lecture (ii. 82) on the tragic writer's heightening of the painful nature of his story in order to lead to a satisfying 'catastrophe' is an oblique solution of the problem and one frequently given: the difference between suffering on the stage and in real life resides in the artifice of the former. 'The delight of tragedy proceeds from our consciousness of fiction', said Johnson in the Preface to Shakespeare (1765)—though Burke in 1757 took the opposite view, because 'we enter into the concerns of others'. Kames in *The Elements of Criticism* (1762: I. ii. 1 sec. 7) discusses 'the emotions caused by Fiction'. The function of Lecture 21 is to prepare for the arts of persuasion used by the orator, playing down or exaggerating as the need demands, by describing the similar arts of the good story-teller. Tragedy and Comedy both *arrange* events so as to culminate in true conclusiveness. Note that Smith's imagination is as tuned to good *cadence* as is his ear.

That is why he delights in rhyme. Boswell reports that when Johnson was extolling rhyme over blank verse, 'I mentioned to him that Dr. Adam Smith, in his lectures upon composition, when I studied under him in the College of Glasgow, had maintained the same opinion strenuously, and I repeated some of his arguments'. Johnson had no love for Smith, but—'had I known that he loved rhyme as much as you tell me he does, I should have HUGGED him' (*Life of Johnson*, ed. Hill-Powell, i. 427–8). Dugald Stewart associates this bias with Smith's ascription of our pleasure in the Imitative Arts (e.g. I. 16, III. 2) to admiration of *difficulté surmontée* (Stewart III. 14–15). The phrase is by Antoine Houdar de La Motte in his controversy with Voltaire over *Œdipe* (1730). La Motte opposed both the Unities and Rhyme in drama: 'toutes ces puérilités n'ont d'autre mérite que celui de la difficulté surmontée'. Both Voltaire and Smith counter this argument by pointing to the observed triumph over observed obstacles, as a source of our surprised delight in all the arts, both plastic and literary. Stewart (III. 15) wonders whether Smith's 'love of system, added to his partiality for the French drama', may have led him to generalize too much in this. Rhyme is not in fact explicitly mentioned in our manuscript at ii. 74 ff., but it is implicit in *couplet* and reference to Pope. Cf. TMS V. i. 7.

'The principles of dramatic composition had more particularly attracted his attention' (Stewart III. 15); and though the dogmas about unity of Time and Place had often been attacked since Corneille's *Discours* in 1660—in Farquhar's *Discourse upon Comedy* (1702) and Kames's *Elements of Criticism* (1762: chap. xxiii)—it is pleasant to find Smith transferring the question to 'Unity of Interest' (ii. 81). This time he is on La Motte's side. In the first of his *Discours sur la Tragédie* (1730) this is made the supreme law of dramatic art: but, as Smith remarks, the phrase is susceptible of many interpretations, and it is a little surprising to find him not following La Motte's thesis that concentration of the audience's *sympathy* on a group of characters— always present, always acting, animating and vivifying the action of the piece—is what constitutes 'unité d'intérêt', as they are 'tous dignes que j'entre dans leurs passions'. 'That every part of the Story should tend to some one end, whatever that be' is of course also a typically Smithian formulation.

Beside the remark on Comedy (ii. 82) we must place the full account of the comic at i. 107–v. 116. Smith's interest in the laughter-provoking (we must remember that that is simply what the eighteenth century words ridicule and ridiculous mean) was no doubt kindled early by Hutcheson, whose criticism of Hobbes's view—'the passion of laughter is nothing but sudden glory arising from some sudden conception of some eminency in ourselves' (*Leviathan* vi)—first appeared in the *Dublin Journal* 10–12 (June 1725), collected as *Reflections on Laughter* (1750). Smith's approach is proper to someone preoccupied with comparison: unexpected incongruities arising from the aggrandisement of the little (as in mock-heroic) or diminution of the grand. At i. 112 he seems to allude to Leibnitz: 'All raillery includes a little contempt, and it is not just to try to make contemptible what does not deserve it' (Remarks on Shaftesbury's *Characteristicks*, 1711; printed in Masson's *Histoire critique de la République des Lettres*, 1715). He does not accept therefore Shaftesbury's notion of laughter as a 'test of truth'. For Smith on wit and humour cf. the review of Johnson's *Dictionary* (EPS 240–1).

Johnson would not have *'hugged'* Smith for his words on tragi-comedy (ii. 83–4). This 'mixed' kind, described in *Spectator* 40 as monstrous, was several times vigorously defended by Johnson for its truth to life: e.g. *Rambler* 156 (14 Sept. 1751), as well as the Preface to Shakespeare in 1765.

To one tradition of rhetorical instruction Smith is faithful, in the readiness with which he quotes poetic examples side by side with prose. At i. 9 he refers to Samuel Clarke's preface to his edition of the *Iliad* (1729) in praise of Homer's perspicuity—such, says Clarke, that no prose writer has ever equalled him in this his 'perpetua et singularis virtus'. Clarke also makes an interesting distinction between the poet's *ars* and his *oratio*; so in our day Ezra Pound has insisted that poetry must have the qualities of good prose.

Like that later polymath Coleridge, Adam Smith nursed till his last days the hope of producing a *magnum opus* of immense scope. 'I have likewise two other great works upon the anvil; the one is a sort of Philosophical History of all the different branches of Literature, of Philosophy, Poetry and Eloquence' (the other being his Jurisprudence); 'The materials of both are in a great measure collected, and some Part of both is put into tollerable good order'. So he wrote to the Duc de La Rochefoucauld on 1 Nov. 1785 (Corr., Letter 248). This was no doubt why in 1755, in a paper read to Cochrane's Political Economy Club, he gave 'a pretty long enumeration . . . of certain leading principles, both political and literary, to which he was anxious to establish his exclusive right; in order to prevent the possibility of some rival claims . . .' (Stewart IV. 25). Unfortunately Stewart does not tell us which 'literary' principles were listed. Smith describes the opinions as having formed the subjects of his lectures since he first taught Mr Craigie's class 'down to this day, without any considerable variation'.

One envies the eighteenth century the freedom and width of vision made possible to them by their not circumscribing the word *literature* and narrowing the scope of its study as we have since done. Our two scribes enable us to glimpse that first work which would have become the foundation of the tantalizing 'Philosophical History' of all literature.

3. *Considerations concerning the First Formation of Languages*

It may be worth remembering that the dissertation Adam Smith delivered, as by statute required, on 16 January 1751 to justify his induction into the Chair of Logic and Rhetoric at the University of Glasgow was entitled *De origine idearum*. In the absence of the text of this we cannot know in what sense *idea* was used. His first published essay was on a semantic subject. For the first number of the *Edinburgh Review* which he had helped to found in 1755 he chose to review Johnson's newly issued *Dictionary*, and he made his review an exercise in the systematic distinction and arrangement of the meanings of words: *but* and *humour* as examples. He found Johnson's treatment insufficiently 'grammatical', i.e. philosophically analytic (EPS 232–41) and offers an alternative plan. There is evidence to support the statement of A. F. Tytler in his *Memoirs of the Life and Writings of the Honourable Henry Home of Kames . . . containing sketches of the Progress and General Improvement in Scotland during the greater part of the eighteenth century* (1807: i. 168) that of all the articles in the two numbers of the magazine this was the one which attracted most attention—and the implications of Tytler's long sub-title help us to understand why. Tytler admits that though Smith's article 'displays the same philosophic views of universal grammar, which distinguish his *Essay on the formation of Languages*' his metaphysical discrimination and ingenuity were less suitable than Johnson's method 'for conveying a critical knowledge of the English language' (170).

Light is thrown on the beginnings of Smith's interest in language in a letter which he wrote on 7 February 1763 to George Baird who had sent him an Abstract of *An Essay on Grammar as it may be applied to the English Language* (1765) by his friend William Ward. The letter (69), which was printed by Nichols in *Illustrations of the Literary History of the Eighteenth Century* (iii, 1818, 515–16), expresses surprise that Ward, mentioning various definitions of nouns, 'takes no notice of that of the Abbé Girard, the author of a book, called, 'Les vrais Principes de la

Langue Françoise'. . . . It is the book which first set me a thinking upon these subjects, and I have received more instruction from it than from any other I have yet seen upon them. . . . The grammatical articles, too, in the French Encyclopedie have given me a good deal of entertainment.' The comments on Ward's design offer a useful introduction to Smith's own thinking.

I approve greatly of his plan for a Rational Grammar, and I am convinced that a work of this kind, executed with his abilities and industry, may prove not only the best system of grammar, but the best system of logic in any language, as well as the best history of the natural progress of the human mind in forming the most important abstractions upon which all reasoning depends. . . . If I was to treat the same subject, I should endeavour to begin with the consideration of verbs; these being, in my apprehension, the original parts of speech, first invented to express in one word a complete event: I should then have endeavoured to shew how the subject was divided from the attribute; and afterwards, how the object was distinguished from both; and in this manner I should have tried to investigate the origin and use of all the different parts of speech, and of all their different modifications, considered as necessary to express all the different qualifications and relations of any single event.

Smith is too modest to say that all this—'taken in a general view, which is the only view that I can pretend to have taken of them'—he did in fact set out in an essay published two years earlier, but, as Stewart tells us (II. 44), he was proud of the 'considerations concerning the First Formation of Languages': 'It is an essay of great ingenuity, and on which the author himself set a high value' and justly—it is a masterpiece of lucid exposition which any summary can only blur. Stewart's comments (II. 44–56) are the most perceptive ever made on it. He saw that its value lies, not in the possible accuracy of the opinions, but in its being a specimen of an entirely modern kind of inquiry 'which seems, in a peculiar degree, to have interested Mr Smith's curiosity.' To this Stewart applied the now famous phrase '*Theoretical* or *Conjectural History*', and he finds examples of it in all Smith's writings. In the absence of direct evidence, 'when we are unable to ascertain how men have actually conducted themselves upon particular occasions' we must consider 'in what manner they are likely to have proceeded, from the principles of their nature, and the circumstances of their external situation.' 'The known principles of human nature'; 'the natural succession of inventions and discoveries'; 'the circumstances of society'—these are the foundations on which rests Smith's thinking 'whatever be the nature of his subject'; astronomy, politics, economics, literature, language. 'In most cases, it is of more importance to ascertain the progress that is most simple, than the progress that is most agreeable to fact; for . . . the real progress is not always the most natural' (56). Stewart is stressing the timelessness of Smith's argument, which still makes sense even after the birth of comparative philology in 1786 with Sir William Jones's demonstration before the Royal Asiatic Society of the kinship between Sanskrit, Greek, Latin, and the Germanic and Celtic languages. Smith instinctively uses the historical *mode* for his exposition of principles in this context while exhibiting the powers of the mind operating in their most fully human and characteristic activity: comparing, classifying, abstracting. The primacy he gives to language, which entails that something like Lecture 3 must have come early in his Rhetoric course right from its first delivery, rests on his vision of language as the embodiment of the mind's striving towards the 'metaphysical', towards conceptualization.

'Essay', 'Dissertation', 'Considerations': the last is the appropriate title, since three (of quite different kinds) are offered. The first, 'theoretical history' proper, has two sections: (a) on nouns, adjectives and prepositions (1–25); (b) on verbs and pronouns (26–32). That mere chronology is not Smith's real concern is shown by his beginning with nouns, although he believes verbs are the most ancient part of speech, which starts with the presentation of a single undifferentiated event as in the impersonal verb. He does so because the inflectional systems of the noun are well adapted to exhibiting his analysis of the process of abstraction: from classes of things, to modification by quality, gender, number, and relationship—and even within relationships, a hierarchy or range of degrees of the metaphysical, there Smith's vision of the organic connection between thinking and speaking becomes clear. No one will attribute to him the naive notion that early man first conceived the relations *by*, *with*, or *from*, and then invented the device of adding -o or -e to the root of the noun to express them. Language and thought are generated together, as d'Alembert maintained in the 'Discours préliminaire' to the Encyclopédie in 1751. He too had learned from the Abbé Gabriel Girard's *Les vrais principes de la langue françoise, ou la parole réduite en méthode conformément aux lois de l'usage* (1747) to see 'parts of speech', not as dead terms in school grammar, but as operations of the human intellect, and 'grammar' itself as the image of logic. Girard's book is a perfect example of the beautiful unity and harmony he finds in the linguistic works of the spirit.

The second Consideration (33–40) moves from conjectural to actual history: the breakdown of the inflectional system which results from peoples of different tongue living together and being defeated by the intricacies (as they see them) of each other's speech-structures: the Germanic Lombards confronted with Latin, or (Smith might have added) the invading Norse-speakers meeting the English. The simplification in question can be observed by anyone listening to a foreigner wrestling with his elementary English. 'Elementary' is the right word, speech reduced to its elements, all verb-forms reduced to the infinitive. Something comparable produces the various kinds of pidgin and creole throughout the world.

The third Consideration (41–45) is an assessment of the damage wrought by this breakdown: modern analytic languages are, as compared with earlier synthetic ones, more prolix (since a multiplicity of words must replace the old inflections), less agreeable to the ear (lacking the pleasing symmetries and variety of the inflections), and more rigid in their possibilities of word-ordering (differences of case-endings make for flexibility in arrangement without ambiguity).

Most of the many mid-eighteenth century investigators of the beginnings of language are interested in more superficial senses of the word 'origin': fruitless searches for a reason why a particular sound was ever chosen to denote a particular thing or idea, as in the *Traité de la formation méchanique des langues et des principes physiques de l'étymologie* (1765) by Charles de Brosses, parts of which were in circulation from 1751 and found their way into articles in the *Encyclopédie*; or speculations on 'universal grammar' and the causes of differences among languages, like the *Hermes* of James Harris (1751). How simple-mindedly Smith's highly original essay could be read is illustrated by the widely known *Elements of general knowledge* (1802), lectures which Henry Kett had been delivering since 1790: how did Adam Smith's two incredible savages ever get into the situation in which he imagines them inventing speech? (i. 88–9). Kett is put down by the percipient L. Davison in 'Some account of a recent work entitled *Elements of General Knowledge*' (1804: ii. 87–88), who sees that Smith *assumes* language and is interested simply in how it proceeds.

Smith's connection with *The Philological Miscellany* (1761) in which his essay first appeared is obscure. An anonymous contributor to *The European Magazine, and London Review* for April 1802 (xli. 249), writing from Oxford on 10 April 1802, after a reference to an article on Smith in the previous issue and high praise for the review of Johnson's *Dictionary*, goes on: 'in 1761 was published, I believe by Dr. Smith, "The Philological Miscellany"', and in it Dr. Smith's 'Considerations concerning the first Formation of Languages' first appeared. No authority for attributing the volume to Smith is given; and what in any case is meant—the compiling, or the translating of the French articles? Smith's essay is the only one to be first published here. The others are almost all from the *Mémoires* of the Académie des Inscriptions et Belles Lettres, apparently specially translated for this collection of papers on historical, classical and miscellaneous learned questions, such as Smith showed an interest in, in his letter to the *Edinburgh Review* no. 2, 1756 (EPS 242–54). The editor of the *Miscellany* 'proposes to enrich his Work with a variety of Articles from the French *Encyclopedie*, and with curious Dissertations on Philological Subjects by foreign writers.' But no further volumes appeared.

Note on the Text

In Adam Smith's lifetime five authorized editions of this essay were published, for which the sigla *PM, 3, 4, 5, 6* are here used:

[*PM*] THE | Philological Miscellany; | CONSISTING OF | SELECT ESSAYS | FROM THE | MEMOIRS of the Academy of | BELLES LETTRES at PARIS, and | other foreign ACADEMIES. | TRANSLATED into ENGLISH. | WITH | ORIGINAL PIECES by the most Eminent | WRITERS of our own Country. | VOL. I. | [double rule] | Printed for the EDITOR; | And Sold by T. BECKETT and P. A. DEHONDT, | in the Strand. 1761. | (8vo: pp. viii + 510).

Pp. 440–79 contains: *Considerations concerning the first formation of Languages, and the different genius of original and compounded Languages.* By Adam Smith, Professor of Moral Philosophy in the University of Glasgow. *Now first published.*—The Table of Contents lists the essay in the same words. This volume, the only one of a projected twice-yearly series to appear, was published in May 1761. The British Library copy has on its fly-leaf the note: 'Presented by M.ʳˢ Becket Oct.ʳ 9. 1761.'

[*3*] THE | THEORY | OF | MORAL SENTIMENTS. | To which is added | A Dissertation on the ORIGIN OF LANGUAGES. | By ADAM SMITH, L.L.D. | THE THIRD EDITION. | . . MDCCLXVII.—The essay is on pp. 437–78, headed and listed in Table of Contents as in *PM*, but omitting 'By . . . *published*'.

While this edition of TMS was going through the press in winter 1766–67 Smith wrote to his publisher William Strahan:

The *Dissertation upon the Origin of Languages* is to be printed at the end of *Theory*. There are some literal errors in the printed copy of it which I should have been glad to have corrected, but have not the opportunity, as I have no copy by me. They are of no great consequenc⟨e⟩ (Letter 100).

Seven verbal changes were nevertheless made in the text. Smith, it may be noted, here gives the essay the same title as do the title-pages of the early editions of TMS, and as Dugald Stewart in his *Account of the Life and Writings of Adam Smith*, I. 26, II. 44 (see EPS).

[*4*] THE | THEORY | OF | MORAL SENTIMENTS. | [as *3*] THE FOURTH EDITION . . . MDCCLXXIV. The essay is on pp. 437–76, headed as in *3*.

[*5*] THE | THEORY | OF | MORAL SENTIMENTS. | [as *3*] THE FIFTH EDITION . . . MDCCLXXXI. The essay is on pp. 437–78, headed as in *3*.

[*6*] THE | THEORY | OF | MORAL SENTIMENTS. | [as *3*] THE SIXTH EDITION . . . MDCCXC. The essay is on pp. 403–62 of vol. ii.

The present text is that of 1790, the last for which Smith was responsible. He had worked long on the 'considerable additions and corrections' now included in the *Theory*. An account of the early editions, and of Smith's carefulness over proof correction in general, is given in the introduction to TMS in the present edition: especially *47–9*. The 'Considerations' remained entirely unchanged in substance throughout their five editions, and only a selection of variants from before 1790 need be recorded.

4–6 replace in lower case the initial capitals which *PM* and *3* consistently give the following words: Philosopher, Grammarians, Adjective, Schoolmen, *Green* (§4), Nouns, Metaphysics, Masculine, Feminine, Neutral, Genders, Substantive, Termination, Prepositions, Superiority, Inferiority, Genitive, Dative, *Arbor* (§§13 ff.), Grammar, Languages, Nominative, Accusative, Vocative, Cases, Variations, Declensions, Numbers, Conjugations, Verb, Logicians, Citizen, Optative, Mood, Future, Aorist, Preterit, Tenses, Passive, Participle, Infinitives, Law, Court, Verse, Prose (in the order of first occurrence).

4–6 replace with what we should regard as 'modern' forms the following spellings in *PM* and *3*: concret, antient, accompanyment, surprized, forestal, compleat, indispensible, acquireable.

In the matter of punctuation, only students of eighteenth century typographical usage (or whim) will be interested in omissions and insertions of commas in intermediate editions, and they will consult the original texts. In no case is the meaning affected by these variations, though the delivery of an elocutionist declaiming the text might be. No logical or grammatical principle can be seen to be uniformly dictating the many changes from edition to edition. On the whole *4–6* agree as against *PM* and *3*; but six of *3*'s changes of *PM* are reversed by *6* and/or *4*, *5*. Only variants involving points heavier than comma are here recorded. We cannot know how many are authorial.

The seventh edition (1792) follows 6 in capitals, spelling, italics, and generally in punctuation. The other early editions have not been collated. They include: 1777 (Dublin: title-page 'the sixth edition'), 1793 (Basel), 1797 (8th), 1801 (9th), 1804 (10th), 1808 (Edinburgh: title-page 'the eleventh edition'), 1809 (Glasgow: title-page 'the twelfth edition'), 1812 (11th), 1813 (Edinburgh). In *The Works of Adam Smith* vol. v (1811) the 'Considerations' are on pp. 3–48, printed as in 6. They are included in Smith's *Essays* (1869, 1880). A French translation by A.M.H.B[oulard], *Considérations sur la première formation des langues, et le différent génie des langues originales et composées*, was published in Paris in 1796; also one appended to the third French translation of the TMS: *Théorie des sentimens moraux*, trans. from ed. 7 by Sophie de Grouchy, Marquise de Condorcet (1798, revd. 1830): 'Considérations sur l'origine et la formation des langues', ii. 264–310.

4. *Rhetoric and literary criticism*

A student of the traditional rhetoric who reads the present work as he runs (or—as Smith would put it—'one partly asleep'), may possibly as he encounters familiar topics, concepts and terminology, conclude that this is the well-worn old story: a story so often in the past a dreary one. Smith in speaking of the many systems of rhetoric both ancient and modern observed that they were generally 'a very silly set of books and not at all instructive' (i. v. 59). Such a reader will have missed the motive which gives unity and direction to the lectures and the framework of thought which transforms the old discipline; above all he will be ignoring the delight which informs the whole and its details.

Steele remarked early in the century that 'it is a very good service one man renders another when he tells him the manner of his being pleased'. Smith began lecturing at a time when the study of rhetoric was turning increasingly, especially in Scotland, to the study of taste. Hugh Blair opens the *Lectures on Rhetoric and Belles Lettres* which he first delivered in 1759 by summing up their twofold aim: 'Whatever enables genius to execute well, will enable taste to criticise justly'. Smith was a natural teacher of literature. One of his students, William Richardson, in a life of Archibald Arthur who later occupied the Glasgow Chair of Moral Philosophy (and who had himself studied under Smith), records: 'Those who received instruction from Dr. Smith, will recollect, with much satisfaction, many of these incidental and digressive illustrations, and even discussions, not only in morality, but in criticism, which were delivered by him with animated and extemporaneous eloquence, as they were suggested in the course of question and answer' (Arthur, *Discourses on Theological and Literary*

Subjects, 1803: 507–8). Richardson's words, though in the first instance about Smith's 'examination' hour, are known to be true of his lecturing in general; and it is significant that in the account of the lectures on rhetoric which follows (515), 'taste' is the first topic to be mentioned, before 'composition'. Arthur himself followed Smith's method 'and treated of fine-writing, the principles of criticism, and the pleasures of the imagination . . . intended by him to unfold and elucidate those processes of invention, that structure of language, and system of arrangement, which are the objects of genuine taste'. Double evidence, in effect, of Smith's attitude to the first subject he had chosen to teach. George Jardine, another student of Smith's who, as Professor of Logic and Rhetoric at Glasgow from 1787, continued to teach along the lines his master had laid down, likewise concentrated on 'the principles of taste and criticism'. Thomas Reid, writing about 1791 in the *Statistical Account of Scotland* (vol. 21, 1799 735), describe Jardine's current practice thus: after dealing briefly with the art of reasoning and its history, he

dedicates the greater part of his time to an illustration of the various mental operations, as they are expressed by the several modifications of speech and writing; which leads him to deliver a system of lectures on general grammar, rhetoric, and belles lettres. This course, accompanied with suitable exercises and specimens, on the part of the students, is properly placed at the entrance to philosophy: no subjects are likely to be more interesting to young minds, at a time when their taste and feelings are beginning to open, and have naturally disposed them to the reading of such authors as are necessary to supply them with facts and materials for beginning and carrying on the important habits of reflection and investigation.

It is significant that accounts of the tradition in rhetorical teaching acknowledged as stemming from Adam Smith so often dwell on the 'taste and feelings' of the students.

The title 'Rhetoric and Belles Lettres', which presumably (though we do not know) was Smith's own choice to describe his course, seems to go back to Charles Rollin's appointment to the Chair of Rhetoric at the Collège Royal in Paris in 1688. Rollin's lectures were published in 1726–8 as *De la manière d'enseigner et d'étudier les Belles-lettres, par raport à l'esprit et au coeur*—later changed to *Traité des études*. Apart from the suggestions of the subtitle the book cannot be shown to have taught Smith anything in the field of criticism. He needed no one else's instruction on *l'esprit et le coeur*.

His pleasure as a critic is in several ways that of a philosopher. He is stimulated by prose and poetry which clearly reveal the author, and his eye (and ear) are made attentive by the conception he has worked out of the relation between the writer and the man. Theories, as Pater saw, are useful as 'points of view, instruments of criticism which may help us to gather up what might otherwise pass unregarded by us'. Rhetoric had, at least since the first century BC, always been taught with copious illustrations from writers, and students had been trained by exercises in the close analysis of texts. The opening paragraphs of *Biographia Literaria* show how lively, and fruitful, this tradition still was in Coleridge's schooldays. For Smith there is no separation between the two instructions, in handling language and in the enjoyment of that handling by the masters of the crafts. As we might have predicted, his most characteristic method is the comparative, the pin-pointing of an author's essential quality by putting his work alongside that of a practitioner in the same field or a kindred one: Demosthenes and Cicero, Clarendon and Burnet. This method, used systematically over a great range of examples, is his most distinctive contribution to the literary criticism of his age—especially when we remember that the values he invokes in his judgements are, not narrowly technical, but comprehensively human and humane—common-sense, to use his own word. In English criticism only Dryden, e.g. in the *Essay of Dramatic Poesy* and the Preface to the *Fables*, had so far used comparison in an extensive and self-conscious way. Smith certainly knew the examples in the rhetorical treatises of Dionysius of Halicarnassus (Demosthenes with Thucydides, Plato with Demosthenes, Isaeus with Lysias, etc.) and in Quintilian's *Institutio Oratoria* Book X; but perhaps his immediate model was the series of comparisons of ancient writers published by René Rapin in 1664–81.

This was the age of collections of *The Beauties of . . . Shakespeare, Milton, Pope, Poetry,* and so on. Many of Smith's lectures must have delighted their audience by sounding like some such judiciously selected anthologies. He read extensively from the texts in class, often in his own translation (an art he took great pleasure in and found instructive in its own right: Stewart I. 9): hence the variation in length in the reported lectures. The immense popularity of these lectures was the result of their offering the spectacle of Smith's suppleness in moving easily over the whole field of ancient and modern writing and of his inventiveness in making illuminating connections.

If we cannot number Adam Smith among the greatest critics, we need not fall into the ill-temper expressed by Wordsworth in a footnote to his Essay Supplementary to the Preface (1815); on the notion 'that there are no fixed principles in human nature for this art [the admiration of poetry] to rest upon', he adds: 'This opinion seems actually to have been entertained by Adam Smith, the worst critic,

David Hume not excepted, that Scotland, a soil to which this sort of weed seems natural, has produced'. The premise of this remark is so mistaken, and the quantity of Smith's literary criticism in the printed works, especially TMS and EPS, so fragmentary and scanty, that the violence of Wordsworth's language is difficult to explain. A clue occurs in a letter he wrote to John Wilson in June 1802, commenting on the offence given to 'many fine ladies' by supposedly indelicate or gross expressions in certain of the *Lyrical Ballads* (*The Mad Mother* and *The Thorn*), 'and as in the instance of Adam Smith, who, we are told, could not endure the ballad of *Clym of the Clough*, because the author had not written like a gentleman' (*Early Letters*, 1935, 296). This is a clear reference to the interview by Amicus with Smith printed in Appendix 1. The article was reprinted in *The European Magazine* for August 1791 (xx. 133–6), in *The Whitehall Evening Post*, and thence (with misprints and omissions) in a miscellany of essays dating from the sixteenth to the late eighteenth centuries entitled *Occasional Essays on Various Subjects, chiefly Political and Historical* (1809). The editorship of this last is ascribed by the B.L. Catalogue to the lawyer and mathematician Francis Maseres, the 'Baron Maseres' of Lamb's essay on the Inner Temple, i.e. Cursitor Baron of Exchequer. The identity of Amicus is unknown. He has been wrongly said to be Adam Smith's old student David Steuart Erskine, later 11th Earl of Buchan (1742–1829), who in fact, under his pen-name Ascanius, criticised the article of Amicus in *The Bee* of 8 June 1791 (iii. 166 f.): 'I knew him too well to think he would have liked to have had a pisgah view of such frivolous matters obtruded on the learned world after his death'—yet he goes on: 'He had no ear for music, nor any perception of the sublime or beautiful in composition, either in poetry or language of any kind. He was too much of a geometrician to have much taste.' Only if we think the notorious and flamboyant eccentricity of Lord Buchan extended to writing an article under one pseudonym in order to condemn it under another can we accept him as Smith's 'friendly' interviewer. In any case he collected all his *Bee* articles for 4 May 1791 to 25 December 1793 in *The anonymous and fugitive essays of The Earl of Buchan*, vol. 1 (1812) so that, as the preface explains, 'no person may hereafter ascribe to him any others than are by him, in this manner, avowed, described, or enumerated'. So all we know of 'Amicus' is that, as the 'we' of his defence of Allan Ramsay shows, he was a Scot. As to Lord Buchan, though he had his own odd ways of showing his regard for 'the reputation of my excellent preceptor and amiable friend' and recalled 'having had the happiness to live long and much with him', the regard was genuine, and in some remarks on literary immortality he groups together Homer, Thucydides, Shakespeare, Adam Smith (*Essays* as above, 213, 246–7, from *The Bee*, 29 May 1793 and 27 June 1792 respectively). Incidentally, his denial to Smith of a 'perception of the sublime' would have been rebutted by Edmund Burke (who had just written a book on *The Sublime and the Beautiful*): on 10 Sept. 1759 he wrote to Smith praising the 'lively and elegant' style of TMS and adding 'it is often sublime too, particularly in that fine Picture of the Stoic Philosophy towards the end of your first part which is dressed out in all the grandeur and pomp that becomes that magnificent delusion' (Corr. Letter 38).

Despite the introductory assurance of authenticity by the editor of *The Bee*, Dr. James Anderson, who had himself known Smith, the moral propriety of reprinting yet again the gossip of Amicus may rightly be questioned. John Ramsay of Ochtertyre, writing at the beginning of the nineteenth century in *Scotland and Scotsmen in the Eighteenth Century* (1888: i. 468) remarks that Smith's table-talk would be precious, 'but the scraps of it published in the *Bee* do no honour either to his memory or the discretion of his friends'. Dugald Stewart (V. 15) contrasts the opinions which 'in the thoughtlessness and confidence of his social hours, he was accustomed to hazard on books, and on questions of speculation', though having much truth and ingenuity in them, with 'those qualified conclusions that we admire in his writings'; and what he said as the fancy or the humour took him, 'when retailed by those who only saw him occasionally, suggested false and contradictory ideas of his real sentiments'. But the Amicus piece has often been quoted (see Rae, *Life*, 365–71). Smith himself seems to approve of curiosity about the great—'The smallest circumstances, the most minute transactions of a great man are sought after with eagerness. Everything that is created with Grandeur seems to be important. We watch the sayings and catch the apothegms of the great ones with which we are infinitely pleased and are fond of every opportunity of using them . . .' (LRBL ii. 107). We are after all publishing lectures which Smith died believing he had saved from publication as not in a worthy state. Of course (there is a difference) these *had* in one sense been 'published'. In 1896 Edwin Cannan sought to justify the publication of the Lectures on Jurisprudence by quoting Smith's own words about the limits on testamentary provisions. In LJ (A) i. 165–6 they run: '. . . we should permit the dying person to dispose of his goods as far as he sees, that is, to settle how it shall be divided amongst those who are alive at the same time with him. For these it may be conjectured he may have contracted some affection. . . . But persons who are not born he can have no affection for. The utmost stretch of our piety can not reasonably extend to them.' *Mutatis mutandis* Smith's suppressions need not inhibit us.

Johnson's remark in *Rambler* 60 is not inopportune: 'If we owe regard to the memory of the dead, there is yet more respect to be paid to knowledge, to virtue, and to truth'.

5. *System and aesthetics*

On 9 July 1764 Boswell wrote from Berlin to Isabella de Zuylen (Zélide): 'Mr. Smith whose moral sentiments you admire so much, wrote to me sometime ago, "your great fault is acting upon system", what a curious reproof to a young man from a grave philosopher'. The letter opens: '. . . You know I am a man of form, a man who says to himself, Thus will I act, and acts accordingly' (*Letters*, ed. C. B. Tinker, 1924, 46). In the absence of Adam Smith's letter (strange, considering what mountains of paper Boswell preserved) we cannot tell with what irony he wrote to his former student; but the incident draws attention to the two uses in the eighteenth century of the word and the concept 'system'. While Smith was giving these lectures two of the most powerful critiques of the idea appeared: in the wittiest and subtlest of all such attacks, *Tristram Shandy* (1759–67), Sterne presents a hapless philosopher-father's attempts to make his son's upbringing conform to theory, the Shandean system—the form of the novel itself criticises the notion of rigid form; and in 1759 Voltaire produced, in *Candide*, a demolition of the optimistic scheme of the universe, a series of disastrous frustrations of the illusion that all is for the best in the best of all possible worlds. Marivaux is fond of pillorying 'les faiseurs de systèmes' (e.g. in *Lettres au Mercure*, May 1718 etc.), who are what 'le vulgaire' call 'philosophers'; and Shaftesbury had already in 1711 (*Characteristics:* Misc. III. ii) defined a formal philosopher as a 'system-writer'. 'System-monger' comes in about the same time. On 27 Sept. 1748 we find Lord Chesterfield advising his son to 'read and hear, for your amusement, ingenious systems, nice questions, subtilely agitated with all the refinements that warm imaginations suggest', and less sardonically he complains: 'The preposterous notions of a systematical man who does not know the world tire the patience of a man who does'. Cf. Stewart's (V. 15) 'too systematical' of Smith; and the 'man of system' apt 'to be very wise in his own conceit', in TMS, VI. ii. 2. 17.

'System' in the good sense is exemplified by Johnson's defence of *The Wealth of Nations* against Sir John Pringle's charge that Smith was not equipped to write such a work since he had never taken part in trade: '. . . there is nothing which requires more to be illustrated by philosophy than trade does' (Boswell, *Life of Johnson*, ed. Hill-Powell, ii. 430). Another example, used by James Wodrow in a letter to the

Earl of Buchan (Glasgow Univ. Lib., Murray MS 506, 169) is the comparison of Smith's accounting for the principal phenomena in the moral world from the one general principle of sympathy, with 'that of gravity in the natural world'. Still another is set out by Smith in a letter (30, dated 4 April 1759) to Lord Shelburne on the course of study his son Lord Fitzmaurice should pursue in his future years at Glasgow, after completing his Philosophical studies. He should, says Smith, attend the lectures of the Professor of Civil Law, as the best preparation for the study of English Law even though Civil Law has no authority in the English Courts:

The civil law is digested into a more regular system than the English Law has yet been, and tho' the Principles of the former are in many respects different from those of the latter, yet there are many principles common to both, and one who has studied the civil law at least knows what a system of law is, what parts it consist of, and how these ought to be arranged: so that when he afterwards comes to study the law of any other country which is not so well digested, he carries at least the Idea of a System in his head and knows to what part of it he ought to refer everything that he reads.

Compare this with the motive underlying the system of meanings laid out in the review of Johnson's *Dictionary* (EPS 232–41).

That something more than mere tidiness and intellectual coherence is involved for Smith is illustrated by a passage in Imitative Arts (II. 30, cf. section 2, above):

A well-composed concerto of instrumental Music, by the number and variety of the instruments, by the variety of the parts which are performed by them, and the perfect concord or correspondence of all these different parts; by the exact harmony or coincidence of all the different sounds which are heard at the same time, and by that happy variety of measure which regulates the succession of those which are heard at different times, presents an object so agreeable, so great, so various, and so interesting, that alone, and without suggesting any other object, either by imitation or otherwise, it can occupy, and as it were fill up, completely the whole capacity of the mind, so as to leave no part of its attention vacant for thinking of any thing else. In the contemplation of that immense variety of agreeable and melodious sounds, arranged and digested, both in their coincidence and in their succession, into so complete and regular a system, the mind in reality enjoys not only a very great sensual, but a very high intellectual, pleasure, not unlike that which it derives from the contemplation of a great system in any other science.

In other words, to watch the explanation of a great diversity and multiplicity of phenomena from a single general principle is to be confronted with beauty: 'the beauty of a systematical arrangement of different observations connected by a few common principles' (WN V.

i. f. 25; cf. EPS, *13* ff). We remember that Smith's dominant interests while a student at Glasgow under Professor Robert Simson (Stewart, I. 7) were mathematics and natural philosophy; this is where he learned 'the idea of a system'—as set out in Astronomy IV. 19.

The issue is most clearly stated in LRBL (ii. 132–4), in the lecture (24) on scientific and philosophical exposition, the 'didacticall' method. One may either explain phenomena piecemeal, using a new principle for each as it is encountered, e.g. the 'System of Husbandry' presented in Virgil's *Georgics* following Aristotle's procedure; 'or in the manner of Sir Isaac Newton we may lay down certain principles known or proved in the beginning, from whence we account for the severall Phenomena, connecting all together by the same chain'. This *enchaînement* (the favourite term among French thinkers of the time) is in every branch of study—ethics, physics, criticism—'vastly more ingenious and for that reason more engaging than the other. It gives us a pleasure to see the phaenomena which we reckoned the most unaccountable all deduced from some principle (commonly a wellknown one) and all united in one chain, far superior to what we feel from the unconnected method. . . .' (Cf. TMS, VII. ii. 2. 14).

The task Smith set himself in the *Rhetoric* was to substitute a 'Newtonian' (or Cartesian, cf. ii. 134), a philosophical and 'engaging' explanation of beauty in writing, for the old rigmarole about figures of speech and of thought, 'topics' of argument, subdivisions of discourse, characters of style and the rest. In this sense his lectures constitute an anti-rhetoric; and though they could not by themselves rescue the word *rhetoric*, or for that matter the phrases *belles lettres* and *polite literature*, from the bad press they suffered from, they exerted a profound and revolutionary influence which has still not been properly investigated, on Hugh Blair, Kames, William Richardson, George Campbell, and those they in turn taught.

'There is no art whatever that hath so close a connection with all the faculties and powers of the mind as eloquence, or the art of speaking.' So George Campbell introduces *The Philosophy of Rhetoric* in 1776. To come closer to describing Smith's central informing principle, the formulations of two French writers whose work he knew well may help. 'Le style est l'homme même'. This famous and generally misunderstood remark was made by the naturalist Buffon on his admission to the French Academy in 1753, in what came to be called his *Discours sur le style*. He is contrasting the inert facts of unanimated knowledge with what language does to them. 'Ces choses sont hors de l'homme' they are non-human. But utter them, and *how* you utter them, is 'very man', 'man himself'. From a different angle Marivaux, in *Le Spectateur français* of 8 September 1722 (Huitième feuille), attacks the notion that you must write in the manner of this or that ancient or modern author, and aims 'prouver qu'écrire naturellement, qu'être naturel n'est pas écrire dans le goût de tel Ancien ni de tel Moderne, n'est pas se mouler sur personne quant à la forme de ses idées, mais au contraire, se ressembler fidèlement à soi-même ... rester dans la singularité d'esprit qui nous est échué. ....' Be like yourself: it was a lesson, Smith believed, the much admired Shaftesbury had never learned.

Bibliographical Note

Adam Smith's life and thought:

John Rae: *Life of Adam Smith* (1895). Reprinted with 'Guide to John Rae's *Life of Adam Smith*' by J. Viner (1965).

William R. Scott: *Adam Smith as Student and Professor* (1937; reprinted 1965).

R. H. Campbell and A. S. Skinner: *Adam Smith* (1982).

A. S. Skinner: *A System of Social Science, Papers relating to Adam Smith* (1979).

T. D. Campbell: *Adam Smith's Science of Morals* (1971).

The *Rhetoric*:

W. S. Howell: *Eighteenth-Century British Logic and Rhetoric* (1971). The section on Smith, first published in 1969, was reprinted in *Essays on Adam Smith*, ed. Andrew S. Skinner and Thomas Wilson (1975).

V. M. Bevilacqua: 'Adam Smith's *Lectures on Rhetoric and Belles Lettres*' (*Studies in Scottish Literature*, 3 (1965), 41–60). See also *Modern Language Review*, 63 (1968).

For J. M. Lothian's edition, see Abbreviations.

R. Salvucci: 'La retorica come teoria della comunicazione' [on A.S.] *Sociologia della comunicazione*, 1 (1982). See also R. Salvucci, *Sviluppi della problematica del linguaggio nel XVIII secolo: Condillac, Rousseau, Smith* (1982).

A. S. Skinner: 'Adam Smith: Rhetoric and the Communication of Ideas' in *Methodological Controversy in Economics: Historical Essays*, A. W. Coats ed. (1983).

Languages:

Articles on 'Considerations' by C. J. Berry and S. K. Land in *Journal of the History of Ideas*—respectively 35 (1974), 130–8; and 38 (1977), 677–90.

LECTURES ON RHETORIC
AND BELLES LETTRES

Delivered in the University of Glasgow by
ADAM SMITH

Reported by a Student in 1762–3

Lecture 2$^{\text{d.}}$

Friday. Novr 19

Perspicuity of stile requires not only that the expressions^a we use should be free from all ambiguity proceeding from synonimous words but that the^b words should be natives if I may ⟨say⟩ so of the language we speak in. Foreigners though they may signify the same thing never convey the idea with such strength as those we are acquainted with and whose origin we can trace.—We may see an instance of this in the word Unfold; a good old English word derived from an English Root; and consequently its meaning must be easily perceived^c. This word however has within these few years been most unaccountably thrust out of common use by a French word of not half the strength or

2 significance, to wit Develope.^{1} This word tho of the same signification | with unfold can never convey the idea so strongly to an English reader. {In the same manner unravell is thrown out to make room for Explicate^d.} The words of another Language may however be naturalized by time and be as familiar to us as those which are originally our own, and may then be used with as great freedom; but here liquewise we may see the effect of the words being well known to us or not; for instance, the words unsufferable and intollerable which are both borrowed of the Latin language and compounded of words of the same meaning are of very unequall strength. The reason is that the word Untollerable has not been so long introduced amongst us and therefore does not carry the same power along with it. We say that the

3 cruelty and oppress⟨ion⟩ | of a tyrant is unsufferable, but the heat of a summers day is untollerable. Insufferable^e expresses our emotion and indignation at the behaviour of the Tyrant, whereas intollerable^f means only that their is some difficulty and uneasiness in supporting the heat of the Sun.

The English language perhaps needs our care in this respect more than any other. New words are continually pushing out our own originall ones; so that the stock of our own is now become but very

---

^{a} *replaces* word ^{b} *MS* they, y *deleted and* words *written above* ^{c} *MS* perceeived ^{d} *after* for *Hand B(?) supplied* Develope, *which Hand C deleted and replaced with perhaps* Explicate *in dark ink* ^{e} *replaces* The one ^{f} *replaces* the other

^{1} *OED* gives these dates of first use in the relevant senses: *develop*, 1742; *explicate*, 1628; *insufferable*, 1533, but *unsufferable*, 1340; *intolerable*, 1435, and as an intensive (like *awful* or *terrible*), 1544. Smith is a sensitive witness to a contemporary trend or fashion; but his distinction between *insufferable* and *intolerable* is not clearly confirmed by *OED*; it is a deduction from *suffer* and *support*.

small and is still diminishing. This perhaps is owing to a^g defect which our language labours much under, of being compounded of a great

4 number of others. | {No author has been more attentive to this point than Swift; we may say his language is more English than any other writer that we have.} Most terms of art and most compounded words are borrowed from other languages, so that the lower sort of People, and those who are not acquainted with those languages from whence they are taken^h can hardly understand many of the words of their own tongue. Hence it is that we see this sort of people are continually using these words in meanings altogether foreign to their proper ones^i. The Greeks used compounded words but then they were formed from words of their own language; by this means their language was so plain that the meanest person would perfectly understand the terms of art and

5 expressions of any | artist or philosopher. The word Triangle would not be understood by an Englisman who had not learned Latin, but an Italian would at the first understand their triangulo or a Dutchman their thrienuik.^{2}

Our words must not only be English and agreable to the custom of the country but likewise to the custom of some particular part^j of the nation. This part undoubtedly is formed of the men of rank and breeding. The easiness of those persons behaviour is so agreable and taking that^k whatever is connected with it pleases us. {It is commonly said also that in France and England the conversation of the Ladies is the best standar⟨d⟩ of Language, as there is a certain delicacy and agreableness^l in their behaviour and adress, and in generall we find that whatever is agreable makes what accompanies it have the deeper impression and convey the notion of agreableness along with.} For this reason we love both their dress and their manner of language. On the

6 other hand many words as well as | gestures or peculiarities of dress give us an idea of some thing mean and Low in those in whom we find them. Hence it is that words equally expressive and more commonly used would appear very absurd if used in common conversation by one in the character of a gentleman. Thus perhaps 9/10 of the people of England say, Is'e dot, instead of I will do it, but no gentleman would use^m that expression without the imputation of vulgarity. We may indeed naturally expect that the better sort will often exceed the vulgar in the propriety of their language but where there is no such excellence we are apt to prefer those in use amongst them, by the association we

---

g *replaces* one   *h* must be at a great loss *deleted*   *i* proper ones *replaces* own
j part *added by Hand C in margin*   *k* it carries alon *deleted*   *l* ness *added by Hand C*
m replaces say

---

^{2} No doubt a Scot's mishearing (for 'three-corner') of *driehoek*.

7 form betwixt their words and the behaviour | we admire in them. It is the custom[n] of the people that forms what we call propri⟨e⟩ty, and the custom of the better sort from whence the rules of purity of stile are to be drawn. {As those of the higher rank generally frequent the court, the standard of our language is therefore chiefly to be met with there[o]. In countries therefore which are divided into a number of sovereignties we cannot expe⟨c⟩t to meet with any generall standard, as the better sort are scattered into different places[p]. Accordingly we find that in Greece and Modern Italy each State sticks by its own dialect without yielding the preference to any other, even though superior in other respects as the Athenians were.}

Our words must[q] also be put in such order that the meaning of the sentence shall[r] be quite plain and not depend on the accuracy of the printer in placing the points, or of the readers[s] in laying the emphasis on any certain word[t]. Mr. Pope often errs in both these respects; as 1st In that line, Born but to die, and reasoning but to err.[3] The sense of this line is very different in these two cases, when we put the accent in both

v.7 members on but, or in the one on born and in the other on Reasoning. | {The former I imagine was Mr Pope's own meaning tho Mr Warburton gives it a different turn. But if that had been Mr Popes meaning[u] Mr Pope had more properly have used though for but and then there had been no ambiguity, though the line would not have been so strong as in the way it stands at present if taken in the common

8 and apparent meaning} | [v]We have an example of the latter sort, when it is not easy to know what member of the sentence a word belongs to in this line

great master death and god adore[4].

Here we will find the meaning[w] altogether different if we place the pause before or after the word death.

{We may here observe that it is almost always improper to[x] place *and* in the beginning of a member of a[y] sentence, tho it may be some times tho rarely proper to begin a sentence in that manner, and then there is no danger of ambiguity.}[v]

---

[n] *replaces* common use   [o] *original order* to be . . . chiefly *changed by numbers written above*   [p] *last four words replace* divided and do not live better   [q] only be free *deleted*   [r] shall *added by Hand C above line*   [s] *original order* reader or of the printer *changed by numbers written above*   [t] *MS* words, s *deleted*   [u] *last eight words replace* in which case   [v]–[v] *line across page, and catch-phrase* We have an *to lead in p. 8; rest of v.7 consists of the interpolation* We may . . . ambiguity, *keyed in on p. 8 by marginal* We may *after* death   [w] the meaning *added above line by Hand C* (?)   [x] begin a sentence with *deleted*   [y] *changed from* the *by Hand C*

[3] *Essay on Man*, ii.10. Cf. Smith's discussion of *but* in his review of Johnson's *Dictionary*, §3 (EPS 236–8).

[4] *Essay on Man*, i.92; Pope wrote 'teacher Death'.

Another ambiguity also to be avoided is that where it is difficult to know what verb the nominative case belongs to, or what noun an adjective agrees with. The Antient languages were much more liable to this ambiguity than the modern ones, as they admitted of a greater
9 freedom in the arrangement of the words. As an example | of this we take that line of Juvenal, Nobilitas sola atque unica Virtus,[5] where the ambiguity is owing to the not distinguishing whether *sola* agrees with *virtus* or *Nobilitas*.

This line*z* may serve as an instance of the ambiguity proceeding from the Verb not being ascertain'd to belong to one substant⟨ive⟩ more than*a* another:

In this alone beasts do the men excel[6],

where one would be apt to think the author meant that the beasts excelled men ⟨in⟩ this alone, whereas the conterary is certainly the meaning. — — —

{The best authors very seldom fall into this error, as Thucidides, Xenophon and severall others; nay Dr Clerk[7] says he has found but one instance in all Homer. This indeed may be turned in very different ways; but as the rest is so exact this one probably proceeds from the error of some transcriber*b*; It is*c* wonderfull no more errors of this sort have crept in during so long a tract of time, and may serve to shew the surprising*d* accuracy of that writer.

Mr Waller again is a remarkable instance of the defect of this quality, and as he pays very little regard to grammaticall rules his sense is sometimes hardly to be come at, tho this method will often serve to discover the meaning of other obscure writers. The characterists[8] are extremely free from this, and would be the book most easily construd.}

A naturall order of expression free of parentheses and superfluous
10 words is likewise a great help | towards perspicuity; In this consists what we call easy writing which makes the sense of the author flow naturally upon our mind without our being obliged to hunt backwards and forwards in order to find it. {When there are no words that are superfluous but all tend to express something by themselves which was not said before and in a plain manner*e*, we may call it precision; tho

---

z of *inserted above line: sc. Juvenal* *a* more than *replaces* or *b* and *deleted*
c more *deleted* *d* is *before* surprising, instances of the *after it, both deleted*
e last five words written upwards in margin replace *and no part any decorant* (?deliberate) trope

---

[5] viii.20; Juvenal wrote 'sola est atque . . . .
[6] Not traced.
[7] The philosopher Samuel Clarke (1675–1729) edited the *Iliad* in 1729.
[8] This might refer to writers of 'Characters' (see Introduction, p. *17*), but is probably an error for *Characteristicks of Men, Manners, Opinions, Times* (1711), the collection of treatises by Anthony Ashley Cooper, 3rd Earl of Shaftesbury (1671–1713), so often discussed by Smith.

this word is often taken to mean a stiff and affected stile such as that [as that] of Prim[9] and others of the puritan writers.}

Bolingbroke especially[j] and Swift have excelled most in this respect[g]; accordingly we find that their writings are so plain that one half asleep may carry the sense along with him, {even tho the sentence be very long[h], as in that in the end of his essay on virtue.[10]} Nay if we happen to lose a word or two, the rest of the senten⟨c⟩e is so naturally connected with it as that it comes into our mind of its own accord.

10 | On the other hand Writers who do not observe this rule often become so obscure that their meaning is not to be discovered without great attention and being altogether awake. Shaftesbury sometimes runs into this error by endeavouring to throw a great deal together before us[i].

Writings of this sort have a great deal of the air of translations from an other language, where a certain stiffness of expression and repetition of synonymous words is very apt to be gone into.

Short sentences are generally more perspicuous than long ones as
11 they are more easily comprehended | in one view; but when we intend to study conciseness we should avoid the unconnected way of writing which we are then very apt to run into, and at the same time is of all[j] the most obscure. The reason of this is that when we study short sentences we are apt also to throw out the connecting words and render our expressions concise as well as our sentences. But precision and a close adherence to a just expression are very consistent with a long sentence, and a short sentence may very possibly· want both. Sallust,
12 Tacitus and Thucydides are the most remarkable in this | way; and it is proper to observe that concise expressions and short turned periods are proper only for historians who narrate facts barely as they are, or those who write in the didactick stile. The 3 historians we mention'd are accordingly the chief[k] who have followed this manner of writing. It is [l]very improper for Orators or publick speakers, as there design is to rouse the passions, which are not affected by a plain simple stile, but require the attacks[m] of strong and perhaps exaggerated expressions. No
13 didactick writer has invariably adhered to this stile tho it be proper | to them, unless Aristotle, who never once deviates from it in his whole works, whereas others often run out into oratoricall declamation.

j lines above and below especially *perhaps intend its placing after* and   *g* and *deleted*
h tho the sentence be very long *written above line, deleted, and written on opposite page*   *i* Short
sentences are for the most *deleted*   *j* others *deleted*   *k* in that way *deleted (or? this)*   *l* very
im *replaces* not   *m replaces* aid

[9] William Prynne (1600–69), Puritan author of *Histrio-Mastix* (1633) and some twenty politico-legal works; cf. ii.253 below.

[10] Not Bolingbroke but Shaftesbury: *An Inquiry Concerning Virtue or Merit* (1699; Treatise iv in *Characteristicks*, 1711).

What are generally called ornaments or flowers in language, as allegoricall, metaphoricall and such like expressions are very apt to make ones stile dark and perplex'd. Studying much to vary the expression leads one also frequently into a dungeon of metaphorical*ⁿ* obscurity. The Lord·Shaftesbury is of all authors I know the most liable to this error. In the third volume of his works,¹¹ talking of
14   meditating and reflecting within one-self he contrives an innu|merable number of names for it each more dark than another as, Self conversation, forming a plurality in the same person etc. In an other place he says that his head was the dupe of his heart, where another would have said that he was so intent on obtaining a certain   ⁰
that he could not help thinking he would obtain it. But it is plain this author had it greatly in view to go out of the common road in his writings and to dignify his stile by never using common phrases or even
15   names for things, and we see hardly any expression in his works | but what would appear absurd in common conversation. To such a length does he carry this that he wont even call *men* by their own names. Moses is the Jewish lawgiver, Xenophon the young warrior, Plato the Philo⟨sopher⟩ of noble birt⟨h⟩; and in his treatise¹² written expressly to prove the being of God he never almost uses that word but the supreme being or mind, or he that knows all things etc.

{The frequent use of Pronouns is also not agreable to perspicuity, as it makes ⟨us⟩ look to what they refer to: They are however proper where the noun whose place they supply is not the chief or emphaticall one in the sentence. But in that case the repetition of the word itself gives greater strength and energy to the sentence.}

We might here insist on this as well as proper variation of the form of
16   a sentence and how far our language could admit of it; but this as | well as many other grammaticall parts we must altogether pass over as taedious and unentertaining, and proceed to give an estimate of our own language compared with others. In order to this it will be proper to premise somewhat with regard to the origin and design of language in the gen⟨erall⟩.

ⁿ *written above, with a long line under it*   ⁰ *blank of five letters in MS*

---

¹¹ *Soliloquy or Advice to an Author*, parts I and III (1710; Treatise iii in *Characteristicks*, 1711; cf. Miscellany iv, chap. 1, in Miscellaneous Reflections, i.e. Treatise vi).

¹² *A Letter Concerning Enthusiasm*, sections iv–v (1708; Treatise i in *Characteristicks*, 1711); cf. *Inquiry Concerning Virtue*, Bk I. pt iii).

Lecture 3^d.

Monday Nov. 22

Mr. Smith

Of the origin and progress of language[1]

It seems probable that those words which denote certain substances which exist, and which we call substantives, would be *amongst* the first contrived by persons who were inventing a language. Two Savages who met together and took up their dwelling in the same place would very soon endeavour to get signs to denote those objects which most frequently occurred and with which they were most concerned. The cave they lodged in, the tree from whence they got their food, or the fountain from whence they drank, would all soon be distinguished by
18 particular names, | as they would have frequent occasion to make their thoughts about these known to[a] one another, and would by mutual consent agree on certain signs whereby this might be accomplished.

Afterwards when they met with other trees, caves, and fountains concerning which they would have occasion to converse, they would[b] naturally give the same name to them as they had before given to other objects of the same kind. The association of ideas betwixt the caves, trees, etc. and the words they had denoted them by would naturally suggest that those things which were of the same sort might be denoted
v.18 | [by the same words. Thus it might perhaps be that those words which origin[in]ally signifyed singular[d] objects came to be Special names to certain classes of things. [As our Savages made farther advances they would have occasion not only for names to the severall substances near them but also for words to express the relations betwixt those severall objects.][e]

These names however as the objects multiplied would not be sufficient to distinguish them accurately from one another: they would therefore be necessitated to have recourse to their peculiar relations or qualities. These are commonly expressed by prepositions or adjectives.
19 | This is what chiefly difficults Mr Rousseay[2] to wit, to explain how generall names were 1st formed, as they require abstract thought and what is called generallization, before they can be formd according to

---

[a] their *deleted*	[b] *replaces* might be	[c] *From v.18 to v.60 the main text is generally on the*
verso page	[d] *replaces* particular	*verso page*
		[e] As . . . . . objects *cancelled by oblique strokes*

---

[1] A more elaborate version of this lecture was published in *The Philological Miscellany* (1761) as 'Considerations concerning the first formation of Languages, and the different genius of original and compounded Languages'. See p. 201.

[2] See note on Rousseau, p. 205.

his way of thinking: Which he thinks me[a]n at first hardly capable

v.19   of.^{j} | Thus they might express a certain tree by saying the tree above
the cave. But those expressed by prepositions would not go any great
length: they would then call in that [the] of the adjectives, and thus
they might say, the Green tree, to denote one that was Green from one
that was not. The invention of adjectives would have required a much
greater degree of exertion than that of substantives, for these following
reasons. The quality denoted by an adjective is never seen in the
abstract, but is always concreted with some substance or other, and the

20   word signifying such a quality must be formed | from it by a good deal
of abstract^g reflection; besides this quality^h is not seen in any generall
set of things, tho it is a generall quality, but must be at first formed
from some singular object. For this reason we may imagine those
adjectives would be formed before any of the substantives denoting the
abstract[i] qualities of those bodies to which the adjectives are applied.
Thus Green would be formed before Greeness, as the quality tho
abstract in itself is seldom^i considered but when concreted with some
substances realy existing and perceived in some singular one before us,

21   whereas the quality abstracted from any body is never seen | but is only
formed by abstraction and generalization from those bodies where
they are found. It is also necessary before such adjectives be formed
that those who form them have seen other things of the same kind
which have them not. Thus the word Green if it was originally formed
from the colour of a tree would not have been formed if there were no
trees of a different colour. But when there were other trees found of
another colour, they might call such a tree, a green tree; and from
thence other trees, and afterwards other things of that colour might get

v.21 | appellation. From thence too, the quality of greeness would at length
be formed by farther abstraction. When there is so much abstraction
required to form those adjectives that denote colours, which are the
most simple of all, it is plain there would be^j much greater in forming
more complex and general ones.

   But whatever difficulty there might be in the formation of adjectives,
there must be still more in forming prepositions. For that which is
signified by them is not found in any one particular set of things but is
common to all those in a certain relation. Thus above denotes the

v.22   relation | of superiority, below that of inferiority, with regard to
anything in that relation. It is not concreted with any other thing but is
of itself originally abstract. We may say a green tree, or any thing else
is green, but *above* is connected with the relation that two things bear to
one another. It happens too that those prepositions which necessarily

^{f} *rest of page blank* ^{g} *MS* abstraction, ion *deleted* ^{h} must be *deleted*
^{i} *replaces* never ^{j} a *deleted*

most frequently occur are those that are most abstracted and metaphysicall. There is none of which such frequent use is made as of the preposition Of; which at the same time is the most abstract of the whole number of | them all. It denotes^k no particular relation betwixt the things it connects but barely signifies that there is a relation. And if we were to ask an ordinary man what he meant by the word Of he might be allowed at least a weak to consider of it. We may see the generall signification of it from the various and conterary relations it is used to express as betwixt the whole and its^l parts. Thus we may say the son of the father ⟨or the father⟩ of the son; the fir tree of the forest or the forest of the fir trees: Other prepositions can not be used so generally, when we say the tree above the cave and the cave above the tree, | but this cannot be said with regard to the same thing.

When such is the difficulty of forming these prepositions, which are so very requisite, it was naturall for the contrivers of language, whom we are not to suppose very abstract philosophers, would contrive some method to^m answer these purposes by a more easy method. That which was most naturall and obvious and that which we find was the case in all the primitive and simple languages, is to express^n by various modifications of the same word what would otherwise require a preposition. This they | have done by varying the termination of the substantive; the different prepositions whose place was thus supplied gave occasion to the differen⟨t⟩ cases and according as fewer or more of them were thus supplied the cases would be more or less in number in different languages, in some 5, 6 or in others ten.

The agreableness of the same sound repeated or love of Rythme^n made them suit their adjectives to the terminations of the suitable substantives and hence it came to pass that all the adjectives were declined in the same manner as the substantives, tho the signification is noway altered; as, Malus^p, Mali, Malorum, Malis | etc., all signify *evil* and are varied only to make them suit the substantiv⟨e⟩s, as Equus, Equi, Equorum, Equis etc.

As all animalls are of some sex and other things of none and it was requisite to have a distinction in this respect, and the quality in the abstract being not easily comprehended, they rectified this by making another sort of a change in the noun of one sex: hence Equus, Equa: and as those of another quality had no sex they formed here another sort which denoted those of neither of the other two qualities. For the same reason as they suited the adjectives to the declension of cases so also | they would to that of gender, and hence *Equus bonus, Equa bona, pratum bonum.*

^{k} nor *written above, then deleted* ^{l} *MS* it is ^{m} *replaces* do this *(or?* these)
^{n} what *deleted* ^{o} the t *wrongly inserted later* ^{p} mala, malum *deleted*

i.v.23 (margin)
i.v.24 (margin)
i.v.25 (margin)
i.v.26 (margin)
i.v.27 (margin)

As more objects than one of the same sort occurred it was necessary to distinguish betwixt the singular person and those cases where there were more than ⟨one⟩ together; and as abstract numbers are also of difficult comprehension they here likewise invented another variation to denote number, hence the singular, duall and plural number. {The original languages have all the duall as the Hebrew and Sclavonic.} To this de⟨c⟩lension or variety also they accomodated their adjectives for

v.28 the same reason that we before menti|oned. Hence came Equus, Equi, and ἀνηρ, ἀνερε, ἀνερες, and to these the adjectives, bonus, boni, and ἀγαθος, ἀγαθω ἀγαθοι.

Hence we may see how complext their declensions must have become. The substantive nouns declined thro 5 cases in 3 numbers will have 15 varieties, and the adjectives having besides 3 genders will have 45.

Besides these various parts they would have occasion for some words to describe or express certain actions. Every thing we say is either

v.29 affirming or denying something and to do this some other | master sort of word was necessary and this was the reason of the invention of verbs, for without no one thing could be expressed. Hence probably verbs of the impersonall form would be the first invented of any, as they would express a whole sentiment or assertion in this way. So Pluit, Ningit are compleat assertions. The savages we supposed together might for instance use the word venit to express the coming of some terrible animall as a Lion, which they expressed compleatly in one word.

v.30 Afterwards other beasts coming they would naturally use the same | word to give the alarm. So this word would come to signify some terrible beast, then any frightfull object and last⟨l⟩y any approach in the abstract. For the same reasons as they invented number and person in nouns they would in the verbs as[q] a greater or less number might be coming. According to the time different variations would also be made. {They might indeed have used the same word for different tenses had they known the pronouns, but these were not invented in the early times we are talking of, as too abstract. The different words made for different things of the same origin is like the forming of the letters. The first writer would probably use a different[r] character for each[s] word but this would soon be troublesome and occasion some other contrivance; so different flexions of words would be also invented.}

In this complex state languages would probably have continued had it not been for the mixture of different nations. The only thing that

v.31 could have had any effect | was this so great complexity which would make them at a loss and might run them into improprieties of grammar; and so we see the Greeks and Romans were forced to

[q] perso *deleted*   [r] a different *replaces* but an   [s] *replaces* one

instruct their children in the[t] grammar of their own tongue. But the chief cause of the declension from this custom was the intermixture of different nations.[u] When two nations thus met, when ⟨one⟩ was at a loss to express himself in the other language he would be led to supply this
33 defect in[v] | some easy manner. The most obvious is that of the substantive and possessive verbs. The substantive verbs sum with the passive participle would supply all the passive voice, and the auxiliary or rather possessive habeo would by a stranger with the help of the supine be made to supply the whole of the active. The prepositions would be put also in the place of the declensions of nouns.—A Lombard[w] when he had forgot amor for I am loved, would say ego sum amatus, A citizen of Rom⟨e⟩, civis de Roma. For I have loved, Ego
.33 hab⟨e⟩o amatum, | instead of[x] amavi.

These mixtures the more they are multiplied the more the language would lose of its complexness and be supplied in this manner. The simpler the language the more complex. The Greek seems to be very originall as all the primitives are only about 300. The Latin formed of it and the Tuscan is complex but much less so. The French, of the Latin and the native of the country, still less; and the English less still,
.34 being formed from the French and the Saxon. The languages | in this have made advances a good deal similar to those in the constructions of machines. They at first are vastly complex but gradually the different parts are more connected and supplied by one another. But the advantage does not equally correspond. The simpler the machine the better, but the simpler the language[y] the less it will have variety and harmony of sound and the less it will be capable of various arrangement: and lastly it will be more prolix.[z]

---

[t] elements of *deleted*   [u] These who are most simple are all most complex. Thus *deleted*
[v] *32 and v.32 blank*   [w] would *deleted*   [x] ego *deleted*   [y] *replaces* machine
[z] *35 and 36 blank*

1762

Lecture 4^{th a}

Wedinsday Nov. 24

As such great defects have been unavoidably introduced into the English Language by the very manner of its formation, it will be proper to consider how far and by what means they have been remedied.

The first of those defects which comes to be considered is the prolixity necessarily attending a Language which has so few flexions in its Nouns and Verbs. To remedy this, many contractions have been made^b in the words themselves. The *e* which formerly made the finall syllable of the 3^d person[1] of all our verbs has been universally throw⟨n⟩ out where it possibly could, and in many cases where it had been better retain'd, as in Judged; but the generall rule is followd.^c Most of our own native words consist [consist] of but one or two or at most three

v.37 syllables. There are fewer of one | than in any other language whatever. {The Italian and French are compounded of Simple Languages but into the composition of the English there enters a language already compounded viz. the French.}^d When we borrow from other language⟨s⟩ words of more syllables, they are^e shortend by the manner of pronunciation. This is very remarkable in the words refractory, concupiscence: and   ^f of other words too where this cannot be done, we fairly strike off one half, as in Plenipotentiary, Incognito, which in the mouths of some would sound plenipo, Incog.

The pronunciation of^g sentences is likewise shortend in the same manner, by throwing the accent as near the beginning as possible, which makes it much sooner pronounced. This method lies exactly conterary to that in use in the French Language, where the accent

v.38 both in words and periods is thrown on to the last sylable | or the concluding word. The former is what seems most likely to produce a melodious sound as it is a known rule in Musick that the first note of a bar, or the first pitch of any note that is to be repeated with a uniform accent should be sharpest. Whereas the manner of the French pronounciation makes the sentence continually more and more

---

^a *Hand* B(.?), *replacing* 2^d   ^b *both deleted*   ^c *last six words inserted by Hand B in blank left*   ^d *Hand B*   ^e *soon deleted*   ^f *blank of six letters in MS*   ^g *last two words replace* words in which; fronounciation *changed to* fronnunciation; sentences is likewise *is repeated*

---

[1] 'Past tense' and 'past participle' clearly need to be added here; and of course the archaic third person singular *-eth* has not lost its *e* but been superseded by *-s*.

39 precipitate till at last it breaks of short. | {From this contrariety we may
see the reason why a French man will never be able to speak English
with the proper accent, nor an English man French if the habit be
confirmed by time. To shew that the English manner of pronouncing a
sentence, high at first and lower in the end, we need only observe that
it is the manner in which all those speak who have a cant or whine
whether in reading, preaching or crying oysters or broken bellows, the
first is allways the high note and the last part dies away and is hardly
felt.}

The Melody of sound has likewise been attended to in many
respects. The harsh and uncouth gutturalls which so much prevailed
have been allmost entirely laid aside: thought, wrought, taught, are
now pronounced as if there was no gutturall in them.—Ch, which was
*.39 sometime ago pronounced[h] as the greek *X*, is | now pronounced either
as when it ends a word[s] as in charming, change, etc. or as *K* in
character, chimera. The finall syllable ed which has a sound nearly as
harsh as eth is now laid aside as often as possible, and even sometimes
when ⟨it⟩ had better been continued; but when common use which has
the supreme determination in these matters has determined otherwise,
'tis vain to stand out.

Eth as we just now mentioned is softened into *s*; loveth to loves,
willeth to wills. This change however is still faulty as it encreases the
hissing of the language[i], already very remarkable as most of the
pronouns and plurall nouns end in the letter S. But tho the sound may
not be altogether harmonious, yet it is much better than the other,
.40 which as well as *ed* ap|proaches nearly to a whisper and dies away to
nothing.

40 | {The frequent use of the letter S and the hissing thereby occasion'd
is commonly ascribed to the defect of a musicall ear in the English
nation. But this does not seem to be the case[j]. The introduction of it
here is of reall advantage; and besides their is no reason to think there
is any defect in the point of a musicall ear. For there is as generall a
good taste for musick in England as in any other nation unless the
Italians, and what is still of more weight no nation attends more to a
musicall pronounciation, as is hereafter to be observed.

Some authors[k] indeed have wrote constantly eth and ed, as Swift and
Bolinbroke[l], but if they were now to read their own works[m] they would
41 undoubtedly read flows, brings, avowd, | which are certainly smarter
words than floweth, bringeth, avowed, the pronounciation of our more
deliberate and sober ancestors.

[h] e *of* pronounced *deleted*   [i] (which all foreigners observe often) *deleted*   [j] for *deleted*
[k] Some authors *replaces* The sound   [l] *inserted by Hand B in blank left*   [m] changed from
words

"In order also to curtail the Phrases we omitt prefixing the Particles to every word, as in translating the Tittle of the Abbee du Bos's Book,[2] yet this sure is the accurate method and that without which we are exposed to ambiguity. It is thus that we write in Publick Monuments etc. Here again the Generall rule betrays us into an Error.}

v.40 | Besides these alterations on the pronunciation of the consonants, there are severall attempts to remedy the harshness of the language in the pronunciation of the vowels and dipthongs, which are indeed but very few. The first vowel a is softened into the same sound as in other[s] nations is given to the greek η, unless in a few words where it would be dissagreable as in Walk, Talk. The 2^d vowel E is sounded as other nations do the 3^d i, which in the english has a different sound when it is long and when it is short; in the first case it is sound⟨ed⟩ as a Diphthong, as in idol, and in the latter has the same as they give E, as in *intelligible*. The 5th vowel u has also 2 sounds, in one case it is pronounced as the diphthong iu, as in muse, pronounced as eu in Eugen, and in | other cases it has the same sound as in other languages,

v.41   as in undone.[3] The diphthongs also have their full strength, and are sound⟨ed⟩ stronger than in any other languages, as in Faith, mourn etc."

But what has a greater effect on the sound of the Language than all the rest is the harmonious and sonorous pronunciation peculiar to the English nation. There is a certain ringing in their manner of speaking which foreigners can never attain. Hence it is that this language which when spoke by the natives is allowed to be very melodious and agreable, in the mouths of strangers is strangely harsh and grating. {The English have been led into all these practices without thinking of them to remedy the Naturall harshness of their Language, which they have effected}[p].

v.42 | I proceed next to make some observations on the arrangement of words, which will naturally lead[q] to the consideration of what I call stile.

---

n This paragraph in Hand B   *o mourn etc in Hand B*   *p Hand B*
q lead in Hand B at end of a line

---

[2] *Réflexions critiques sur la poésie et sur la peinture* (1719) by the Abbé (Jean Baptiste) Du Bos (1670–1742), one of the most influential works in eighteenth-century aesthetics, appeared in an English translation by Thomas Nugent as *Critical Reflections on Poetry, Painting, and Music* (1748).

[3] Lack of an adequate phonetic notation defeats Smith's attempt to describe the vowel system of English, especially the short (non-diphthongal) i and u; and the scribe has probably failed to understand. In the case of u it is not clear which 'other language' could possibly be intended—or alternatively which variety of English and which words are the basis. For i it looks as if an approximate equivalent is desperately being sought in the 'obscure' vowel e as in French *je*, *ne*, etc. 'Intelligible' was an unlucky example to use, since at least its first e is irrelevant to the statement: unless it simply exemplifies i.

A Period is a set of words expressing a compleat sense without the help of any other.

The members of a period are those phrases which make up that sense, and may frequently have^r a sense of their own, compleat enough without the other and only referring to it by some word or two.

In every^s member there are generally three principall parts or terms

43 | {because every Judgement of the humane mind must comprehend two Ideas between which we declare that relation subsists or does not subsist}^{t}; concer⟨ning⟩^{u} Two of these we affirm some thing or other, and the third connects them together and expresses the affirmation.

·43 One of these is that which is the chief part or subject of the member | and is therefore called the subjective term; the middle one which connects the extremes is called the Attributive^v, and the other of whom the assertion is made is called the objective^w, as of inferiour rank to the former one. These three must generally be placed in the order we have mentioned as otherwise the meaning of the sentence would become ambiguous. It is also to be observed that in sentences expressed by neuter [neuter] verbs their is no adjective^x, it is when the verb is active that the term can be used. In Imperative^y and Interogative expressions the order of the terms is also different.—Besides these terms there ⟨are⟩ other two which frequently occur {tho not necessary to constitute a perfect Member of a Period or Phrase}^{z} and denote the ⟨one⟩ how far,

44 and the other in what circumstances, | the proposition expressed by the ^{a} three forementiond terms is to be understood. The former is called the terminative and the latter the circumstantiall. Tho the other three are a good deal limited in their order, yet these are hardly at all confined, but may be placed in all most any way that one inclines.

The only remaining terms are the conjunctive and the adjunctive. The conjunctive is that which connects the different terms of a sentence or period together. The adjunctive again points out what particular opinion the speaker has of it, the person to whom it is adressed, and such like. {The adjunctive is that which expresses the Habit of the Speakers mind with regard to what he speaks off or the sentiment it excites, as, tis strange, alas, etc. Sir is an adjunctive which denotes your adressing yourself to a particular person; all Interjections are adjunctives.}^{b}

These being the constituent parts of any sentence, it comes next to be

45 considered in what order these | parts are to be placed in the composition of a sentence. Now^c it is plain that must be the best order

---

^{r} *replaces* may ^{s} *last letters blotted through overwriting:* ? each ^{t} *Hand B*
^{u} *added in margin before* Two ^{v} *added by Hand B in blank left* ^{w} *added by Hand B on opposite page, replacing deleted* adjective ^{x} *should be* objective ^{y} *cancelled in MS, and not replaced*
^{z} *Hand B* ^{a} other *deleted* ^{b} *Hand B* ^{c} *written over* and

which most naturally occurrs to the mind and best expresses the sense of the speaker concerning what he speaks. But this is not the simple order in which they would be placed by one that was noaway affected with what he said, but varies according as any of the different terms is the chief or essentiall one in the sentence, as that must first occur to the mind. The most plain order we could suppose and in which ideots etc. speak, would be this. 1st The subjective, 2^d The attributive, 3^d The objective, 4th The Terminative, 5^{thly} The Circumstantiall. The

v.46 conjunctive and adjunctive^d would | probably [be at the] be either of the beginning or end, and the adjuncti⟨ve⟩ in different places according to its different designs.

But this order would very ill suit many expressions, nothing lively or spirited could be said of this arrangement. The generall rule therefore is that whatever is most interesting in the sentence, on which the rests depends, should be placed first and so on thro' the whole. {That the strong member should preceed those of less consequence is also confirmed by the observation already made of ranters, they raise the 1st and most important part of the sentence always to a high note as they are most in earnest.^{e}

Thus would a man always speak who felt no passions, but when we are affected with any thing some one or other of the Ideas will thrust^f itself forward and we will be most eager to utter what we feel Strongest. Eloisa regrets her vain Endeavours to check her Passion and the treachery of her heart.

> In vain lost Eloisa weeps and prays
> Her heart still dictates and her hand obeys.[4]

Make it

> Lost Eloisa weeps in vain and prays
> Still her heart dictates and her hand obeys,

the line tho still a pretty one has lost much of its force. In the same Manner:

> His Soul proud Science never taught to stray.}

Translations which are literally done from one language to another particularly from the antient to the modern are very defective in this respect. They do not indeed stick by the naturall and grammatical

---

^{d} attributive, objective (*replacing* adjunctive), and adjunctive, *added by Hand B* ^{e} *The sentence* That . . . in earnest *is squeezed by Hand A into space left at top of 47 above Hand B's note* Thus would . . . to stray, *which begins opposite* But this order would . . . ^{f} MS thurst

---

[4] *Eloisa to Abelard*, 15–16.— 'His Soul . . .': *Essay on Man*, i.101.

order, but then they frequently ⟨follow⟩ one worse suited to the subject than it would be. The reason is that as the different parts might be
.47 more disjoined in them, | so when they are put into an other language where such liberty can not be taken they only breed confusion. They need a different arrangement before the same spirit can be given the sentence when in an other language. The most animated and Eloquent works whether ancient or modern, if turned into the grammaticall order would appear to be wrote by ⟨a⟩ dull fellow or an idiot. If therefore we find the first turn we give a sentence does not express our sentiment with suitable Life we may reasonably imagine it is owing to some defect in the arangement of the terms (that is to say if the words be proper English) and when we hit this, it is not only language but stile, not only expresses the thought but also the spirit and mind of the author.

48 | {Hence it is that Literary translations have been from the beginning of the world and to its end will be unsufferably Languid and tedious. Any member of the Phrase may thus on certain occasion intrude into the first place, sometimes even the Conjunctive.

An example may be taken from a fine passage in Bolinbroke: There have been in our little world as well as in the Great one Ages of Gold, of Silver and Brass etc.[5]

If our dissatisfaction be owing to the impropriety of our Words, that we will instantly perceive if we understand Language; but oftimes it arises from somewhat that we cannot explain and in this case we may always be sure that it is from the words not arranging themselves in the order of the Ideas.

.48 | Ammianus Marcellinus[6] observed the great Dignity which Livy had given his Stile by his Inversions; he thought therefore that by inverting still more and more frequently he might give a greater Energy to his; but not knowing that which gave propriety to Livys he has become insufferably obscure; ex⟨ample⟩ the beginning of his third Book.

[5] Henry St John, Viscount Bolingbroke (1678–1751): the Hesiodic cliché ascribed here to him (but untraced) does not sum up his view of history. 'You poets have given beautiful descriptions of a golden age, with which you suppose that the world began. Some venerable fathers of the church have given much the same descriptions of another golden age, with which they suppose that it is to end, and which will make some amends for the short duration of the paradisaical state, since the latter is to continue a thousand years'. ('Fragments or minutes of Essays' x.§4: *Works*, 1754, v.107). What he really sees is: 'a sort of genealogy of law, in which nature begets natural law, natural law sociability, sociability union of societies by consent, and this union by consent the obligation of civil laws' (80).

[6] The model imitated by the Latin-writing Greek historian Ammianus Marcellinus (AD *c*.330–395) was rather Tacitus, whose histories he continued from 96 to 378, his extant books xiv–xxxi covering 353–378. The reference is to his close attention to prose rhythm, especially his habit of ending sentences with metrical *clausulae* and exploiting variations of the cursus.

This Generall axiom it is fit to have in view while, we compose, but it is not to be expected nor is it adviseable that we should adjust every Phrase by a minute examination of the order our Ideas have or ought to have.}*g*

g *48 and v.48, the last two pages of quire 12, are in Hand B*

49   # Lecture 5.^a

It is a great defect in the arangement of a sentence when it has what they call a tail coming after it, that is when the sense appears to be concluded when it is not really so. This is always avoided by placing the terminative and circumstantiall term before the attributive. This by rendering the sense incomplete prevents our thinking it is concluded before the wh⟨ole⟩ is expressed. It likewise keeps the mind in suspense, which is of great advantage on many occasions. If these rules be observed the expression, though not perhaps so pompous and regular as that of Lord Shaftesbury amongst the moderns or Isocrates and the other most antient orators, will probably have more force and life, and be every way more natural and Eloquent, than the laboured periods of those authors.

.49   The chief thing they aimed at in the | arrangement of their words was the agreable cadence of the periods. This was much more easily attained in the ancient than modern languages. The similarity of sound in the different members, one great help in this case, was allways to be come^b at without any great labour: Their verbs and nouns generally having the same or similar terminations in the same parts. By this means the cadence of their sentences were easily rendered smoothe and Uniform. But in modern languages the case is very different as neither the verbs nor nouns have such similarity in their terminations. The chief help in our language to a good cadence is to make the

.50   different members end nearly with the same number of words | and those of the same sort. When other ways are attempted or when even this is carried too ⟨far⟩, it often hurts the propriety and perspicuity of the sentence, which are still more to be regarded.

50 | {The ancient authors of the best character generally avoid this by throwing the verb and sometimes the nominative also into the end of the sentence. Livy and Cicero commonly ⟨end⟩ every third sentence in this manner. And later authors thinking to attain their grandeur and dignity by following them in this, frequently carry it too far, so as to end perhaps 2 out of 3 with the verb or nominative. Cicero was ridiculed¹ for his esse [Posse] videatur.}^c

51 | {There is a passage in the Oratio pro Marcello in which there is an

---

^a *MS* 4; *all subsequent lectures are correspondingly misnumbered*   ^b *MS* become (? *-squeezed at end of line*)   ^c *In Hand B keyed by marginal X to above line 1 of v.49*

---

¹ Quintilian (X.ii.18) says some orators think they have done brilliantly and spoken as Cicero would have done 'si in clausula posuissent *Esse videatur*'.

example of Couplets and of Alternate Rhime. Another passage in Shaftesburys Essay on Virtue gives a specemen of his great care.² The passage is a description of a Judicious traveller.}ᵈ

v.50 | In many cases this uniform and regular cadence is not at all proper. Joy and grief generally burst out into periods, regularly decreasing or increasing both in length and the quickness of their movements according as the passion is growing more violent or beginning to subside. {Theᵉ Bursts of Laughter and of Crying observe this Regularity of increase or diminution.}ᶠ Pompous lofty expressions generally run into sentences of a tollerable length and of a slow movement. Cicero has many passages that shew the proper stile of grief and joy in this respect: he often makes use of those stronger passions.

v.51   But De|mosthenes, a man of a more hardᵍ and stubborn materials, never introduces those passions and accordingly has none of those regular and uniform cadences. Lord Shaftesbury may serve as an example of the pompous and grand stile. {Demosthenes never expresses a weak Passion: Joy, grief, or Compassion never once, he is that hard unfeeling man; nor does he ever express Pomp as Cicero often does, he is altogether familiar tho Severe}ʰ

On the other hand indignation has ⟨no⟩ⁱ sort of regularity in its cadence and anger is of all the most broken and irregular. {Indignation everyone knows is the most irregular of all Passions in its movements. It is so in its Expression also, and this it is which gives the Variety to Demosthenes Periods.}ʲ

A good and harmonious sound is also promoted by avoiding harsh clashings of consonants or the hiatus arising from the meeting ⟨of⟩ many vowels. The latter our language is in no great danger [is danger] of. The more frequently vowels and dipthongs occur it is generally the

v.52   sweeter. Waller | has a vast sweetness in his compositions, from the
53   smooth and melodious words he generally makes use of. | {Waller has a

---

ᵈ *Hand B: sentences set out as three paragraphs*   ᵉ loud *deleted*   ᶠ *Hand B*
ᵍ natu *deleted*   ʰ *Hand B*   ⁱ *supplied conjecturally*   ʲ *Hand B*

---

² *Pro Marco Marcello*: the reference is unclear, unless it is to such patterns as 'imperatorum / gentium / populorum / regum' (ii.5). Couplet rhymes are, as Latin terminations make inevitable, fairly frequent: 'aut nobilitate aut probitate' (i.3); 'interclusam aperuisti . . . aliquod sustulisti' (i.2); '[multi quid sibi expediret,] multi quid deceret, non nulli etiam quid liceret' (x.30). For Shaftesbury JML suggested the passage on travel in *Soliloquy or Advice to an Author* (Treatise iii in *Characteristicks*), III.iii; but metrical effects are not obvious in it. Methods of scanning prose metrically were set out by John Mason in *An Essay on the Power and Harmony of Prosaic Numbers* (1749), especially chapters 4–6. In his survey of English prose writers from this standpoint (ch. 8) he takes a low view of Shaftesbury, who 'hath gained the Character of a fine Author' more from his name than his writings. He stresses the importance the ancient critics attached to 'numerous composition': Aristotle, *Rhetoric*, iii.8; Cicero, *Orator*; Quintilian, ix.4.

whole Copy of verses to Delia[3] in which the only harsh words are *Stretch* and *Gods.*

> Delia let not us enquire
> what has been our past Desire
> for if Joys we now may prove
> take advice of present love.

Swift in his Severe Ironicall manner says[4]

> Our Barren climate hardly bears
> one Sprig of bay in 50 years
> yet every fool his claim alledges
> as if it grew on common hedges.}[k]

Swift again is harsh and unpleasant in many of his compositions. This stile suits well enough with the morose humour of that author but would bee very unpleasant in most sorts of compositions.

Long sentences are generally inconvenient and no one will be apt to use them who has his thoughts in good order. This is not to say that we are to be so restricted as Demetrius Phalereus[5] and other authors would have us, as never to have above 3 or 4 members at most in a period. There are many sentences in Bolingbroke and Shaftesbury ⟨which⟩ 53ᵃ have twice that number and | are nevertheless very perspicuous.[l]

52ᵃ | {In the same manner as when we are taken with any Subject and full of it we are eager and impatient to speak of it and bring it in to every Conversation, so[m] whichsoever it is among the Ideas which constitute a Phrase that most deeply affects us, that we bring forth first.

As we are naturally disposed to begin with the most interesting Idea and end with those which are least so, in like manner those who are

---

[k] *Hand B*   [l] *last four words are at top of v.53; 52ᵃ and 52ᵇ (i.e. quire 14), in Hand B, are inserted between 52 and 53*   [m] *whatever it is deleted*

[3] Waller's *To Phillis* ('Phillis! why should we delay'), in *Witts Recreations* (1645) entitled 'The cunning Curtezan'. Line 15 (the first quoted) reads 'Let not you and I inquire'; line 21 (the third), 'For the joys we now may prove'. No alternative version of the poem, to Delia or another, seems to be known; though it appears in three Bodleian MSS.

[4] *On Poetry: a Rhapsody* (1733); lines 7–10 read:

> Our chilling Climate hardly bears
> A *Sprig* of Bays in Fifty Years;
> While ev'ry Fool his Claim alledges,
> As if it grew in common Hedges.

[5] Demetrius (*On Style*, i.16–17) gives two to four as the best number of *cola* or members to a period; Aristotle's definition of the *colon* is quoted from *Rhetoric*, iii.9 (i.34); its structure is examined (i.1–8). The author of the Περὶ ἑρμηνείας, *De Eloquentia*, was formerly identified with Demetrius of Phalerum (300 BC) who is much too early. W. R. Roberts in his LCL edition (1927, 271–7) argues for Demetrius of Tarsus who lived in the latter decades of the first century AD and who may have served in Britain.

v.52ᵃ little attentive to their manner of speaking begin always in a high key |
and end in a low one. This is the manner of all those who have a
monotony, who whine whether in the Pulpit of the Barr or in
Conversation.

When in obedience to the Arrangement of Ideas the objective comes
first it requires the subjective to be placed immediately after.

> Whom have I hurt? No Poet yet or Peer.[6]
> Him haply Slumbring on the Norway foam etc.

52ᵇ | This then is the Rule.

Let that which affects us most be placed first, that which affects us in
the next degree next, and so on to the end.

I will only give one other Rule with regard to the arrangement
which is Subordinate indeed to this great one, and it is that your
Sentence or Phrase never drag a Tail.

To limit and qualify what you are about to affirm before you give
the affirmation has the appearance of accurate and extensive views,
v.52ᵇ but to qualify it afterwards seems a kind of Retractation and | bears the
appearance of confusion or of disingenuity.

Many other rules for arrangement have been given but they do not
deserve attention.}

---

⁶ Pope, *Epistle to Dr Arbuthnot*, 95 (Pope wrote 'has Poet . . .'); Milton, *Paradise Lost*, i.203.

Lecture 6.th ^a

Mr. Smith.

Monday Novr 29 1762

Of what is called the tropes and figures of speech.^b

These are what are generally conceived to give the chief beauty and elegance to language; whatever is sublime and out of the common way is called a figure of speech.

After language had made some progress it was naturall to imagine that men would form some rules according to which they should regulate their language. These rules are what we call Grammar. The Greeks and Romans accordingly have done so, but as their languages were | very complex in their form, particularly in their conjugations and declensions, it was not easy to accommodate these rules to all possible cases. Neither were they made in the best manner they might have been. They were only accommodated to the most plain and vulgar expressions. But when they came to find that many expressions could not be reduced to these rules, they were not candid enough to confess the grossness of their error and allow that these were exceptions to the generall they had laid down but stuck close to their old scheme. That they might do this with the greater appearance | of justice, they gave this sort of expressions the name of tropes or figures of speech. Thus Imperative and Interrogative expressions, which plainly contradict the generall rule That in every sentence there must be a nominative, a verb,^c and an accusative, and in a certain order, were not consider'd as exceptions but as figures of speech; and accordingly we find that amongs⟨t⟩ the first of the *figuræ sententiarum* of Quinctilian[1] and Cicero. They had accomodated their rules to the narrative stile and whatever varied from this was considered as a figure of speech. In these as we mentiond they | tell us all the beauties of language, all that is noble, grand and sublime, all that is passionate, tender and moving is to be found. But the case is far otherwise.^d When the sentiment of the speaker is expressed in a neat, clear, plain and clever manner, and the passion or affection he is poss⟨ess⟩ed of and intends, *by sympathy*, to communicate to his hearer, is plainly and clevery hit off, then and then only the expression has all the force and beauty that language^e can give it. It matters not the least whether the

---

^a MS 5th, *replacing* 3^d   ^b The origin of this name is *deleted*   ^c numbers written above
change the original order a verb a nominative   ^d The beauty *deleted*   ^e and words *deleted*

¹ Quintilian, IX.i.17.

figures of speech are introduced or not. {When your Language expresses perspicuously*ʲ* and neatly your meaning and what you would express, together with the Sentiment or affection this matter inspires you with, and when this Sentiment is nobler or more beautifull than such as are commonly met with, then your Language has all the Beauty it can have, and the figures of speech contribute or can contribute towards it only so far as they happen to be the just and naturall forms of Expressing that Sentiment.}*ᵍ* They neither add to nor take from the beauty of the expression. When they are more proper than the | common forms of speaking then they are to be used but not otherwise. They have no intrinsick worth*ʰ* of their own. That which they are often supposed to have is entirely derived from the expression they are placed in.—When a man says to another, Go Blow the fire, there is no one that will affirm there is any beauty or elegance in this expression; Yet it is as much*ⁱ* a figure of speech and as far from the common or grammaticall form as when Dido says *I peti Italiam ventis,*[2] which every one allows to be a neat and strong expression. But the beauty of it flows from the [the] sentiment and the method of expressing it being suitable to the passion, and not from the figure in which delivered.

v.57

v.58　　The Grammarians however finding that | the best authors frequently deviated from their generall rules and introduced those figures of speech as they called them; and finding also that they were most frequently met with in the most striking and beautifull passages, wisely concluded that these figures gave the passage*ʲ* all its beauty; not considering that this beauty flowed from the sentiment and the elegance of the expression, and that the use ⟨of⟩ figures was only a secondary mean sometimes proper to accomplish this end, to wit, when they more fittly expressed the sense of the author than the common stile. This being often the case in strong and striking passages, was the reason of these being so found in them and this mistake of grammarians in founding the | beauty of a passage in the figures found in it. — — — —

v.59

'Tis however from the consideration of these figures,*ᵏ* and the divisions and subdivisions of them, that so many systems of retorick both*ˡ* ancient and modern have been formed. They are generally a very silly set of Books and not at all instructive; However as it would be

---

ʲ MS perscipuously　　　*ᵍ Hand B*　　　*ʰ* the common form of speaking they are to be used but not otherwise, they have no intrinsick worth *written at top of 57, and deleted*　　　*ⁱ from deleted*
ʲ replaces sentiment　　*ᵏ* however *deleted*　　*ˡ last three words replace* of

---

[2] *Aeneid*, iv.381: 'I, sequere Italiam ventis, pete regna per undas'; the rhetorical device called *permissio*. See Quintilian, IX.ii.49.

reckoned strange in a system of Rhetorick intirely to pass by these figures that have so much exercised the wits of men, we shall offer a few observations on them though not on the same plan as the ordinary writers proceed on.

Whenever then an expression is used in a different way from the common it must proceed either from the words of the expression or 60 from the manner they are used in. | {The first forms what the antients called Tropes, when a word τρεπεται[m] turned from its original signification. The 2^d produces what is more properly called figures of speech.

[n]Hudibras says justly[3]

> for all the Rhetoricians Rules
> are but the naming of his tools.

It is impossible to assign the distinct limits of the antient figures: thus—when the shreek of the fallen angells is said to have torn hells concave[4] this figure might be asserted with equall reason to be a Hyperbole, a Metonyme or Metaphor.}

v.60 | Again, if it proceeds from any thing in the words, it must be either from the words being new and not in common use or being used in a sense different from the common one. No one will venter to form words altogether new and not related to those already in use. Such could never be understood, being mere creatures of his own brain. They must either be formed from words in common use or be old ones brought again into use or be borrowed from some other language. The language we are most ⟨used⟩[o] to borrow from is the Latin, as we think that as all in the character of gentlemen commonly understand this language, our words will be easily understood.[p] Words of this sort are 61 commonly | reckond to add to the dignity of the writing, as they shew the learning of the author; and besides what is foreign has some priviledges always attending it. But as we shewed before, these foreign intruders should never be re⟨c⟩eived but when they are necessary to answer some purpose which the natives cannot supply. That they are many ways prejudiciall to the language has been already shewn and need not again be insisted on.

[m] for *deleted*   [n] *the remainder of this passage in Hand B*   [o] *conjectural;* ? apt
[p] They common *deleted*

---

[3] Butler, *Hudibras*, I.i.89–90;

> For all a Rhetoricians Rules
> Teach nothing but name his Tools.

These lines, among the most often quoted in the poem, Butler himself echoed in 'A Mathematician' in his *Characters* (1759; ed. C. W. Davcs, 119).
[4] *Paradise Lost*, i.542. Milton wrote 'shout', not 'shreek'.

Old words are often introduced into grave and solemn narrations or descriptions, sometimes because they answer the purpose better, as Mr. Pope says the Din of Battle,[5] instead of the Noise of Battle; and sometimes merely because we are apt to think every thing that is ancient is venerable whether it be | so or not. Our forefathers we allwise think were a much soberer and grave solemn sort of people than we are and by analogy every ⟨thing⟩ that relates to them conveys to us the idea of gravity and Solemnity. Spenser has studied this thro all his works; he is much more obsolete than any of his contemporary writers, than Shakespear or Sydney.

Compound words are thought by some to give a great majesty to a language as well as the others; but we see they are generally used rather by the middling than the upper class of authors. Lucretius, Catullus and Tibullus have many of this sort which we will never meet with in Virgill or Horace. {I have seen a greek ode by the fellow of a Colledge on Ad: Vernon[6] more abounding in such Compounds than either Eschylus or Homer.}[q] Milton has but very few; Thompson again never thinks he has expressed himself well but when he has put two or three. | [r]There does not seem to be any great merit in barely tacking two or three words together, unless it be that they are more concise, as tha⟨t⟩ Violet-enammelled Vale of Milton[7] is shorter than the Valley enammeled with violets.[s] But no one surely would admire Colley Cibbers Uncomattible, or the Seceders,[8] Pull-off-the-crown-of-Christ-heresy.[t]

When the alteration of the word is in its signification, it must either be in giving it one to which it has some resemblance or analogy, or when it gets one to which it has no resemblance but is someway connected. Thus when we say, *the slings and arrows of adverse Fortune.*[9] There

---

[q] *this sentence, in Hand B, should perhaps follow* class of authors   [r] But *deleted*
[s] *MS reads* valley *for last two words*   [t] *Hand B inserts on opposite page* off Christs head crown plucking Heresy

---

[5] *The Dunciad* (1743), iii.269: 'Dire is the conflict, dismal is the din'.

[6] Admiral Edward Vernon took the defenceless Porto Bello in November 1739 while Smith was still a student at Glasgow; but the phrase suggests his Oxford days as Snell Exhibitioner at Balliol, 1740–46. Shenstone (*The School-Mistress*, 1742) praises 'Vernon's patriot soul', example of 'valour's generous heat'.

[7] *Comus*, 232: 'the violet-embroidered vale'.

[8] Colley Cibber's *The Lady's Last Stake, or The Wife's Resentment* (1707), I.i: Lord Wronglove speaks of 'pleasures which were a little more comeatable'. Tom Brown had used the word in a dialogue in 1687.
The Seceders were the members of the Secession Church which under Ebenezer Erskine in 1733 broke away from the Church of Scotland in protest against its relation with the state, as the established church. The phrase reported in two forms recalls the banners of an earlier movement rebelling against the usurpation by the secular power of the regality of Christ, 'the crown rights of the Redeemer': the Scottish Covenanters between 1660 and 1690. It is left doubtful above whether the 'heresy' is the secession or the usurpation.

[9] *Hamlet*, III.i.58; read 'outrageous fortune'.

64 is some connection betwixt the crosses of bad fortune and the slings |
and arrows of an enemy. {Rhetorical and Gramaticall paronomasia}
But when we say that one drinks off a Bowl*[u]* for the liquor that is in it
there is here no sort of resemblance betwixt the Glass and the liquor,
but a close connection. The first of these is what the Rhetoricians
call a *metaphor* or *translatio*[v] and the latter is what they call a
metonymie. Of each of these there are severall distinctions which we
shall pass over as of little consequence. {and when we use these words
it shall be in the sense abovementiond.}

In every metaphor it is evident there must be an allusion betwixt one
object and an other. Now as our objects are of two classes, intellectuall
and corporeal, the one of which we perceive by our mind only and the
65 other by our bodily senses; it follows that metaphors may be | of four
different kinds. 1ˢᵗ when the Idea we borrow'd is taken from one
corporeal object and applyed to another intellectuall*[w]* object; or 2ᵈˡʸ
from one intellectuall object to an other corporeal*[x]*; or 3ᵈ betwixt two
corporeal, or 4ᵗʰ betwixt two intellectual objects. When we say the
bloom of youth, this is a meta⟨phor⟩ of the 3ᵈ*[y]* kind. When we say one
covets applause, this is a⟨n⟩ instance of the 4ᵗʰ*[z]* sort of metaphor. The
lust of Fame is an instance of the 1ˢᵗ kind, betwixt a corporeal ⟨and⟩ an
intelle⟨c⟩tual object. {The lust of fame is a transposition of a word from
denoting a Corporeal Passion to another Mentall equally gross and
indelicate.}*[a]* And when we say in the script⟨ure⟩ language, The fields
rejoiced and were glad, The floods clapt their hands for joy,[10] [an] are
an example of the 2ᵈ kind.*[b]*

Now it is evident that none of these metaphors can [can] have any
beauty unless it be so adapted that it gives the due strength of
66 expression to the object to be described and at the same | time does this
in a more striking and interesting manner. When this is not the case
they must either carry us to bombast on the one hand or into burlesque
on the other. When Lee makes his Alexander say, 'clear room there for
a whirlwind or I blow you up like dust';[11] {Avaunt and give a

[u] o *deleted*   *[v]* MS transtatio   *[w]* replaces corporeall   *[x]* replaces intellectual *(interlined then
deleted)*   *[y]* MS hesitates between 3ᵈ and 4ᵗʰ; 3ᵈ seems the second thought   *[z]* changed from 3ᵈ
[a] Hand B   *[b]* sentence squeezed into blank space left before next paragraph

[10] A conflated adaptation of 1 *Chronicles*, xvi.32, and *Psalm* xcviii.8.
[11] Nathaniel Lee's *The Rival Queens, or The Death of Alexander the Great* (1677), III.i.45–7:
Roxana says:

> Away, be gone, and give a whirlwind room,
> Or I will blow you up like dust; avaunt:
> Madness but meanly represents my toyl.

At V.i.349 the dying Alexander says: 'like a Tempest thus I pour upon him'.

Whirlwind room or I will blow you up like dust,}[c] the objects compared are noways adequate, the Strength of A Whirlwind is a much more terrible object than the fury of even an Alexander tho perhaps as dangerous to some individualls. Homer has some metaphors which border near on the burlesque as when he says, Diomed resembled an Ass[12] driven by Boys[d]. Thomson seems to be very faulty in this respect {of Expressing ever too much and more than he felt}; his
v.66 description of the horse will shew this very well [shew this]. | {Compare Thompsons horse with Virgills from which it was translated}[13] Virgill again is always just and exact in his metaphors. Mil⟨t⟩on too keeps them always within just bounds. When he compares the grating of hell gates to the thunder[14] the metaphor is just, but if he had[e] compared the noise of the gates of a city to thunder the metaphor would not have been so just, and still ⟨less⟩ if to the door of a private house, tho perhaps the noise might have been as great as in the former case. Homer is not always so exact in this point; his comparison of Ajax to a gad-fly that continually pesterd the Milk woman[f] is hard on the borders of Burlesque;[15] as also that other where he compares Diomedes to an ⟨ass⟩
v.67 whom the boys are driving | before them, but ever and anon he plucks up some thistle as he passes.

What has been sa[a]id of the justness or propriety of metaphors is equally applicable to other figures, as Metonymies, Similes, and Allegories, Hyperbolls. Metaphors are nearly allied to Metonymies as we observed before. Allegories are also closely connected with them, insomuch that metaphors are called contracted allegory and an allegory is named by some a diffused Metaphor: had Spencer been to use[g] that comparison of Shakespears before mentioned, of the arrows of an enemy to the uneasiness of bad fortune, he would have described
v.68 fortune in a certain garb, throwing her darts arround her and | would[h] those that were under her power.

One thing farther we may observe is that two Methaphors[i] should never be run and mixed together as in that case they can never be both just. Shakespear is often guilty of this fault, as in the line immediately following that before cited, where he goes on, or bravely arm ourselves

---

[c] *Hand B*　　　[d] *last seven words inserted by Hand B into blank left; so the next two interpolations*
[e] said *deleted*　　　[f] *last three words inserted by Hand B in blank left*　　　[g] *replaces* describe
[h] ? wound *intended*　　　[i] *replaces* hyperbolls

---

[12] *Iliad*, xi.558: Ajax compared to an ass in a cornfield beaten by boys.
[13] *Seasons*, Spring 808–20; adapted from *Georgics*, iii. 250–4. Thomson's whole passage 789–830 is from *Georgics*, iii. 212–54.
[14] *Paradise Lost*, ii. 880–2.
[15] JML thought *Odyssey*, xxii.300 ff. the closest approximation to this confused allusion: the panic-stricken suitors compared to cows pestered by a gadfly in spring— the Milk woman is a Freudian slip. Diomedes is again substituted for Ajax; note 12 above.

and stem a sea of troubles. Here there is a plain absurdity as there is no meaning in ones putting on armour[j] to stem the seas. {Shakespears sea of troubles has been converted in a late Edition into a Siedge,[16] but the former reading is so like Shakespears manner that I dare to say he wrote it so.}[k] Thomson has severall slips of this sort tho much fewer than Shakespear. There ⟨are⟩ I believe 3 or four in the 4 first lines of his Seasons. In the 1st line Spring[17] is addressed as some genial quality in the air, but in the next it is turned into a person and | bade *descend, to the sound of musick*, which I believe is very hard to be understood, as well the next, Veild in a shower of dropping roses. What[l] sort of a veil a shower of roses would make, or connection such a shower has with the Spring, I can not tell. These lines which I believe few[m] understand are generally admired and I believe because few take the pains to consider the authors reall meaning or the significance of the severall expressions, but are astonished at these pompous sounding expressions.

The hyperboll is the coldest of all the figures and indeed has no beauty of itself. When it appears to have any it is owing to some other figure with which it is con|joined. To say that a man was a[n] mile high would not be admired as a lofty expression; but when Virgil compares the two Heros Turnus and Æneas coming to battle, to two huge mountains,[18] the grandeur of the two objects is suitable to each other and the hyperboll appears on the same grounds as we determind when a metaphor appears so.

> {Quantus Athos aut quantus Eryx aut ipse coruscis
> cum tonat[19] Ilicibus quantus gaudetque nivali
> vertice assurgens Pater appeninus in auras}[o]

When he compares the ships before the battle of Actium[20] to the Cyclades loosened from their foundations and floating on the sea, the grandeur of the idea of Islands loosend and floating on the sea makes the hyper⟨boll⟩ appear just and agreable. But if he had said the ships

---

j last three words replace arming himself   *k Hand B on v.69*   *l* a shor *deleted*
m MS reads view   *n MS as, s deleted*   *o Hand B*

---

[16] *Hamlet*, III.i.59–60: 'Or to take arms against a sea of troubles/And by opposing end them' 'Siedge': Pope's emendation (1725).

[17] Spring, 1–4:

> Come, gentle Spring, ethereal mildness, come;
> And from the bosom of yon dropping cloud,
> While music wakes around, veil'd in a shower
> Of shadowing roses, on our plains descend.

[18] *Aeneid*, xii.701–3.

[19] For 'tonat' read 'fremit'. Line 703 reads 'vertice se attollens pater Appenninus ad auras'.

[20] The Battle of Actium passage ('pelago credas innare revulsas / Cycladas . . .') is *Aeneid*, viii. 692, and was imitated in the history of Cassius Dio, xxxiii.8.

were half a mile broad, the beauty would be entirely lost tho the
71 hyperboll would be not so great and the fact | asserted nearer the truth.

Besides these many other species of these figures are mentioned, as
the paranomasia, when we dont name but describe a person, as the
Jewish lawgiver for Moses, the   *p* when we call an Orator a
cicero, a brave warrior an Alexander, etc. When we speak improperly
as when we say a brass inkglass, a silver box, etc. these are all made
figures of speech, and in generall when we speak in a manner different
from the common they call it a fig⟨ure⟩. But these we shall pass over
and proceed to the 2^d class of figures.*q*

p blank of six letters in MS   q a blank page (72) follows

Lecture. 7.ᵃ

Wednesday Dec.ʳ 1ˢᵗ 1762

Besides those tropes and fig⟨ure⟩s as they are called, of which we treated in the last lecture, there are others that consist either in the meaning the word is taken in or in the arangement of the words. The 1ˢᵗ they call *figuræ verborum,*ᵇ the 2ᵈ figuræ sententiarum.[1] When we use a fem⟨inine⟩ for a mascu⟨line⟩ or even give an other gender to a neuter, this is a figura verborum. Figuræ senten⟨tiarum⟩, on the other hand, are such as imperative, interogative or exclamatory phrases. But these as we observed above give no beauty of their own, they only are agreable and beautifull when they suit the sentiment and express in the neatest manner the way in which the speaker is affected. | When the common form of speechᶜ well enoug⟨h⟩ describes the thing we want to make known or sufficiently communicates our sentiments, yet perhaps it does not express clearly and with sufficient life the manner we ourselves regard it. If in this case the fig⟨urative⟩ way of speaking is more suited to our purpose, then it surely ought to be used preferably to the other. But we may observe that the most beautifull passages are generally the most simple. That passage of Demosthenes in which he describes the confusion at Athens after the battle of | Elat⟨eia⟩ is reckond by Longinus the most sublime ⟨of⟩ all his writings; and yet there is not one figure or trope through the whole of it.[2] Very often the figures seem to diminish rather than add to the beauty of an excellent passage. Two of the most beautifull passages in all Popes works are those in which he describes the state of mind of an untaught Indian; and the other in which he considers the various ranks and orders of beings in the universe.

> {Lo the Poor Indian whose untutored mind
> Sees God in clouds and hears him in the Wind etc.[3]

ᵃ *MS* 6   ᵇ *MS underlines only this phrase*   ᶜ is to be chosen *replaced by* most expressive in every *which is then deleted*

---

[1] See v.55 n.1 above, and Introduction.

[2] Demosthenes, *De Corona,* 169. This account of the alarm of the Athenians at the news of Philip's occupation of Elateia in 339 BC was admired by several critics: Hermogenes, and Longinus *On the Sublime,* X.7; cf. ii.225 n.3 below.

[3] *Essay on Man,* i.99–112; line 100 reads 'or hears him . . .'; line 106 is 'Some happier island in the watry waste', to rhyme with 'embrac'd'.

'Behold above around and underneath . . .': the passage on the 'vast chain of being' (i.233 ff.) reads:

> See, thro' this air, this ocean, and this earth,
> All matter quick, and bursting into birth.

The words watery waste had been better exchanged for Ocean but that the Rhime required them.

> Behold above around and underneath
> all nature full and bursting into birth etc.}[d]

In the latter of these there is not any one figurative expression, and the few there are in the other are no advantage to it.— —

76 On the other hand there is nowhere more use made of fi|gures than in the lowest and most vulgar conversation. The Billingsgate language is full of it.[e] Sancho Panca, and people of his stamp who speak in proverbs[f], always abound in figures. For we may observe that a proverb always contains one, at least, and often two metaphors.

Upon the whole then, Figures of speech give no beauty to stile: it is when the expression is agreable to the sense of the speaker and his affection that we admire it.

But the same sentiment may often be naturally and agreably
77 expressed and yet the manner be very different | according to the circumstances of the author. The same story may ⟨be⟩ considered either as plain matter of fact without design to excite our compassion, or [it] in a moving way, or lastly in a jocose manner, according to the point in which it is connected with the author.[g] There are variety of characters which we may equally admire, as equally go⟨o⟩d and amiable, and yet these may be very different. It would then be very absurd to blame that of a good natured man because he wanted the severity of a more[h] rigid one. A man of Superior sense and penetration
78 is not ⟨to⟩ be condemned because he | give his assent to the opinion of the Company with the same ease as one of a more soft temper and of less parts (whose[i] character for this reason very often acceptable) will do. Other charac[ac]ters all very commendable can not be blamed because they want some perfections we are apt to admire, for these perhaps are[j] not at all consistent with them, and can hardly meet in the same person. The[k] consideration of this variety of characters affords us often no small entertainment, it forms one of the chief pleasures of a
79 sociall life, and few are so foolish as to blame it or consider it as | any defect.

In the same manner the various stiles in stead of being condemned for the want of beauties perhaps incompatible with those they possess may be considered[l] as good in their kind and suited to the circumstance of the author.[m] This observation confirms what we before observed that the expression ought to be suited to the mind of the author, for this is

---

[d] *Hand B*   [e] *MS* off   [f] *are deleted*   [g] As *deleted*; The v *written opposite on v.76*
[h] ru *deleted*   [i] *replaces* a   [j] *replaces* will   [k] *replaces* These
[l] *last three words added in blank left*   [m] And *deleted*

chiefly governed by the circumstances he is placed in. {The stile of an author is generally of the same stamp as their character. Thus the ⁿ   of   and the   [of] of the flowery modesty of Addison   ⁿ the pert and flippant insolence^u of Warburton and the ^p   of   ^p appear evident in their works and point the very character of the man.}

A Didactick writer and a historian seldom make use of the bolder
80 figures, which an orator frequently introduces | with advantage. The end^q they have in view is different and so the means by which they hope to accomplish that end must be so too.

It is here to be observed that an Orator or didactick writer has two parts in his work: in the one he lays down his proposition and in the other he brings his proof of that proposition. An historian on the other hand has only one part, to wit the proposition. He barely tells you the facts, and if he has any thing as a proof of it, ⟨it⟩ is only a quotation
81 from some other authore in a note or parenthesis. | From this it is that tho the circumstances of an Orator and a didactick writer are very differen⟨t⟩ yet there is a much greater resemblance betwixt their stiles than even^r betwixt the ⟨stile⟩ of the latter and the historians.

The Orator and historian are indeed in very different circumstances. The business of the one is barely to narrate the facts which^s are often very distant from his time and in which he is, or ought to be and endeavours to appear, noways interested. The Orator again treats of subjects he or his friends are nearly concerned in; it is ⟨his⟩ business therefore to appear, if ⟨he⟩ is not realy, deeply concerned in the matter,
82 and uses all his art to | prove what he is engaged in. Their Stiles are no less different. The orator insists on every particular, exposes it in every point of view, and sets of every argument in every shape it can bear. What the historian would have said barely and in one sentence by this means is brought into a long series of different views of the same argument. The orator frequently will exclaim on the strength of the argument, the justice of the cause, or any thing else that tends to support the thing he has in view; and this two in his own person. The historian again as he is in no pain what side seems the justest, but acts^t
83 as if | he were an impartial narrater of the facts; so he uses none of these means to affect his readers, he never dwells on any circumstance, nor has he any use for insisting on arguments as he does not take part with either side, and for the same reason he never uses any exclamations in his own person. {When he does so we say he departs from the character

of the historian and assumes that of the orator. Amongst the ancient historians I remember but three instances of such exclamations in the first person: one in Velleius Paterculus[4] on the death, and the other in Florus on the Eloquence, of Cicero. The third is in Tacitus life of Agricola in the end, on the character of that Roman[u]. Virgil has but three exclamations in the Eneid, one on[e] the love of Dido, another on the death of Pallas, a third on that of Nisus and Euryalus,

Felices animæ si quid mea carmina possunt.}

The Didactick writer, as his circumstances[v] are nearer[w] to that of the orator[x], so their stiles bear[y] a much greater resemblance to each other. The orator often lays aside the dictatorial stile and barely offers his arguments in a plain modest manner, especially when his discourse is 84 directed to those of greater | judgement and higher rank than himself. The didactick writer sometimes assumes an oratorial stile tho it may be questioned whether this be altogether so proper. Cicero often does so. Not only in those writings which are wrote in the manner of dialogue, but where he speaks in his own person, he often runs out into oratorial exclamations, and dwells on the same argument, and repeats it in different manners. Most other writers of this sort often do so[z] as well as he. Aristotle amongst the ancients, and Matchiavel[a] among the 85 moderns are perhaps the only two who have adhered | closely to this peculiar stile of a didactick writer. They trust solely to the strength of their arguments and the ingenuity and newness of their thoughts and discoveries to gain the assent of their readers.

Such is the variety of stiles that those which appear the most like have still a great difference. No two stiles have a great⟨er⟩ connexion than a plain and a simple one, but they are far from being the same.[5]

A Plain man is one who pays no regard to the common civilities and forms of good breeding. He gives his opinion bluntly and affirms 86 without condescending to give any reason for his doing | so; and if he mentions any sort of a reason it is only to shew how evident and plain a matter it was and expose the stupidity of the others in not perceiving it as well as he. {He is not ⟨at⟩ all ruffled by contradiction or any irritation whatever but is at pains to shew that this proceeds from his confidence in his own superior sense and judgement. He never gives

u last six words in Hand B; also following sentence   *v* bear *deleted*   *w* resemblance *deleted*
x so his stile *deleted*   *y MS* bears, s *deleted*   *z* likewise *deleted*   *a Hand B, replacing Hand A's*
Dr Mandeville *deleted*

---

[4] C. Velleius Paterculus, *Hist. Rom.* ii.66; Annaeus Florus, *Epitome*, ii.16 (Cicero's funeral juxtaposed with his fame as orator); Tacitus, *Agricola*, xlv.3; *Aeneid*, iv.65–7 ('heu! vatum ignarae mentes . . .'), cf. iv.408–10 (Dido apostrophised, 'quis tibi tum . . .'); x.501–2 ('nescia mens hominum . . .'), and Pallas apostrophised 'o dolor atque decus magnum . . .' (507–9); ix.446–9 (for 'Felices animae' read 'Fortunati ambo!').
[5] On the Characters see Introduction, p. *17*.

way either to joy or grief; such affections would be below the dignity
and complacence of mind which he affects. Compassion finds littl⟨e⟩
room in his breast; admiration does not at all suit his wisdom;
contempt is more agreable to his selfsufficient imperious temper.} He is
not at all sedulous to please, on the conterary he affects a sort of
austerity and hardness of behaviour, so that when the common
civilities of behaviour would be the most natural and easy manner, he
industriously avoids them. He is so far from affecting any graces or
civilities that he affects the conterary, and renders himself more severe
than his nature would naturally lead him to be. {He despises the
fashion in every point and neither conforms himself to it in [in] dress,
in language nor manners, but sticks by his own downright ways. Wit
87 would ill-suit his gravity, Antitheses or Such like expressions.*b*} | He is
more apt to think that others have ill motives even when they act well
than that they are only in a mistake and do not err knowingly when
they act amiss. {He affirms without mitigation or apology.}*c* In
ordinary conversation he thinks it enough to support what he says that
it is his opinion, and is at no pains to enquire into those of others. Such
a character is what clergymen generally assume, and those come to
age.
   It does well enough in those of superior abilities, who have had
greater opportunities than common, or longer experience, but young
men generally avoid it. Modesty and diffidence are more suited to their
88 years than the assuming arrogance of this | character; which even tho
accompanied with age and knowledge*d* renders the possessor rather the
object of our respect*e* and esteem than of our love.
   The Simple man again, is not inde⟨e⟩d studious to appear with all the
outward marks of civility and breeding that he sees others of a more
disingenuous temper generally put on; but then, when they naturally
express his real sentiments, and do'nt appear constrained, he readily
uses them. He appears always willing to please, when this desire does
not lead him to act dissingenuously. At other times the modesty and
89 affability of his behaviour, his being always willing to comply | with
customs that do'nt look affected, plainly shew the goodness of his heart.
He is not over ready to give his opinion and when he does it 'tis with
that unaffected modesty which displays itself in all his behaviour, and
in nothing more than in his conversation where his diffidence of his
own judgement leads him to offer all the reasons he has to be of that
mind,*f* to shew that he does not assert any thing merely because it is his
opinion. Contempt never enters into his mind, he is more ready to

b sentence written down inner margin of v.85, with last five words at top of v.86   *c Hand B*
d MS age, knowledge and   *e replaces* esteem regard   *f last eight words replace* arguments he
can think of

think well than meanly both of the parts and the conduct of others. His
90 own goodness of heart | makes him never suspect others of dis-
sengenuity. He is always open to conviction and is not ⟨at⟩ all irritated
by others contradicting him, but the reason of this is not any
stubbornness but the diffidence he entertains of his own capacity. {This
leads him to speak very often in the first person to shew the mean
opinion he has of himself, and sometimes to childish prating.} He is
more given to admiration and pity, joy [pity] g⟨r⟩ief and compassion
than the conterary affections, they suit well with the softness of his
temper. This temper is what we often find in young men and in them is
very agreable. Old men are generally not so apt to be of this character.
It renders one more an object of^g love and affection than regard and
esteem.— — — —
91 | When the characters of a plain and a simple man are so different we
may naturally expect that the stile they express themselves in will be
far from being the same.—Swift may serve as an instance of a plain
stile and Sir Wm Temple of a simple one. Swift never gives any reason
for his opinions but affirms them boldly without the least hesitation;
and when one expect⟨s⟩ a reason he meets with nothing but such
expressions as, I have always been of opinion that, etc. because etc. It
seems to me. This we find he does in the begin of his Considerations on
the present state of affairs.[6] He is so far from studying the ornaments of
92 language that he | affects to leave them out even when naturall; and in
this way he often throws out pronouns etc. that are necessary to make
the sentence full but would at the same time lead him into the
uniformity of cadence which he industriously avoids. This however
make⟨s⟩ his stile very close, no word can be passed over without notice,
every other one must be strongly accented to draw the attention of the
hearer, for a word lost would spoil the whole. This makes us read his
works with more life and emphasis than those ⟨of⟩ most others; in
Shaftesbury and Bolingbroke or others who study this uniformity of
caden⟨c⟩e there are many superfluous words which we huddle together
93 | as being of very small importance to the sense of the period. He never
introduces (in his grave works) any sort of figure, and that for the same
reason as he avoids harmony and smoothness of cadence. He never
expresses any passion but affirms with a dictatorial gravity.^{h}
    Temple on the other hand is not anxious about ornament but when
they are naturall he does not reject them; his stile has neither the
hardness of Swifts nor the labourd regularity of Shaftesbury.^{i} The most

^{g} regard. than of love *deleted* ^{h} *three blank lines follow* ^{i} In *deleted*

^{6} *Some free thoughts upon the Present State of Affairs*– *May 1714*, published 1741.

common and received opinions he never ⟨expresses⟩*ʲ* but the most ⟨?⟩
94 manner possible, as That saying that | wit and solid judgement are
seldom or ever found together; which he brings in his character of the
Dutch nation.—He does not avoid a figurative stile when agreable to
his subject, as in the comparison betwixt the life of a merchant and aᵏ
soldier,—{In which there ⟨are⟩ a great many antitheses. These Swi⟨f⟩t
never uses in his grave works, the⟨y⟩ savour too much of the paradox,
that is of wit, to suit his gravity.}—He uses more obsolete words here
than we would expect in a writer of his age. This we never find in Swift.
The knowledge of the world which ⟨he⟩ affects and which he chiefly
imploys to satyrize it and turn it to ridicule, will not allow him to use
anything that is out of the present taste. But Temple is led to them by
the notion that every thing belonging to our forefathers has more
simplicity than those of our times, as weˡ they were a more simple and
95 honest set of men. | His love of a modest simple stile leads him (but in a
different maner from Swift) to use the first person very often, as well as
to run into prating and Quibble. The description he gives of   *ᵐ*
may se⟨r⟩ve as an instance of both the former. When he says, *The earth
of Holland is better than the air,* the the love of Interest stronger than
the love of honour,[7] it is a mere quibb⟨l⟩e on the words earth and
profit, air and honour. Xenophon and most other writers of this sort as
well as he, abound in Jokes we are surprised to find in such grave
writers.

ʲ conjecturally supplied: blank in MS   *ᵏ the written above*   *ˡ for if*
ᵐ blank of eleven letters in MS

[7] *Observations upon the United Provinces of the Netherlands* (1673), ch.4. See i.200 n.12 below.

Lecture. 8.^a

Friday. Dc.^r 1762

Having in the foregoing lecture made some observations on tropes and figures and endeavoured to shew that it was not in their use, as the ancient Rhetoricians imagined, that the beauties of stile consisted, I pointed out what it was that realy gave beauty to stile: That when the words neatly and properly expressed the thing to be described, and conveyed the sentiment the author entertained of it and desired to communicate [to his hearer] by sympathy to his hearers; then the expression had all the beauty language was capable of bestowing on it. I endeavoured to shew also that the form of the stile was not to be
97 confined to any particular point. The view of the author | and the means he takes to accomplish that end must vary the stile not only in^b describing diferent objects or delivering different opinions,^c but even when these are the same in both; as the sentiment will be different, so will the stile also. Besides this I endeavoured to shew that^d when all other circumstances are alike the character of the author must make^e the stile different. One of grave cast of mind will describe an object in a very different way from one of more levity, a plain man will have^f a stile very different from that of a simple man.—There is however no one particular which we esteem, but many are equally agreable.
98 Extreme moroseness and gravity, such that | no risible objects will in the least affect, would not be admired: neither would one of such levity that the smallest incident would make lose himself. But it is not in the middle point betwixt these two characters that an agreable one is alone to be found, many others that partake more or less of the two extremes are equally the objects of our affection. In the same way it is with regard to a spirited and silly behaviour, and every two other opposite extremes in the Characters of men.

These^g characters tho all good and agreable must nevertheless as they are different be expressed in very different stiles, all of which may
99 be very agreable. | And here likewise the rule may be applied that one should stick to his naturall character: a gay man should not endeavour to be grave nor the grave man to be gay, but each should regulate that character and manner that is naturall to him and hinder it from running into that vicious extreme to which he is most inclined.

This difference of stile arising from the character of the author, I endeavoured to illustrate by comparing the Stiles of two celebrated

---

^a *MS* 7   ^b the *deleted*   ^c *replaces* sentiments   ^d not only the *deleted*   ^e *replaces* vary   ^f he *deleted*   ^g different *deleted*

English writers, Swift and Sir Wm Temple, the one as an example of
the plain Stile and the other of a simple one. Both are very good
100 writers; Swift as I observed is remarkable for his propriety and |
precision, the other is not perhaps so very accurate, but he is perhaps as
entertaining and much more instructive. I shall now proceed to make
some farther observation on the Stile of Dr. Swift.

There is perhaps no writer whose works are more generally read
than his, and yet it has been very late,^h that very few in this country
particularly understand his real worth. He is read with the same view
and the same expectations as we read *Tom Brown*,¹ etc. They are
considerd^i as writers just of ⟨the⟩ same class. Swifts graver work⟨s⟩ are
never almost read, they are looked upon as silly and trifling, and his
other works are read merely for their humour.

We shall therefore endeavour to find out what are the causes of this
generall taste: and first Swifts sentiments in Religious matters are not
101 at all suitable to | those which for some time past have prevail'd in this
country. He is indeed no friend to tyranny either religious or civill; he
expresses his abhorr[r]ence to them on many occasions; but then he
never has such warm exclamations for civill or religious liberty as are
now generally in fashion. This would not suit his character, the plain
man he affects to appear would never be subject to such strong
admiration. The levity of mind^j as well as freedom of thought now in
fashion demands^k warmer and more earnest expressions than he ever
allows himself.

Another circumstance that will tend to confirm this opinion is that
the thoughts of most men of genius in this country have of late
⟨inclined⟩^l to^m abstract and Speculative reasonings which perhaps tend
102 very | little to the bettering of our practise. {Even the Practicall
Sciences of Policticks and Morality or Ethicks have of late been treated
too much in a Speculative manner.}^n These studies Swift seems to have
been rather entirely ignorant of, or what I am rather inclined to
believe, did not hold them to be of great value. His generall character
as a plain man would lead him to be of this way of thinking; he would
be more inclined to prosecute what was immediately beneficial.
Accordingly we find that all his writings are adapted to the present
time,^o either in ridiculing some prevailing vice or folly or exposing
some particular character.^p We can not now enter altogether into the

---

^h *perhaps* late, *or* his fate; very *is added above line, perhaps by anticipation*   ^i them *deleted*
^j *MS* me   ^k more *deleted*   ^l *conjecturally supplied*   ^m the *deleted*   ^n *Hand B*
^o being *deleted*   ^p These *deleted*

---

¹ Tom Brown (1663–1704), a prolific writer of satirical dialogues, tracts, fiction, verse; he
translated, among much else, the works of Scarron (1700).

true spirit of these; and besides as I said such confined thoughts do not suit the present taste which delights only in generall and abstract speculations.

103　| But his language may possibly have brought about the generall disregard for his serious works as much as any other part of his character. We in this country are most of us very sensible that the perfection of language is very different from that we commonly speak in.*q* The idea we form of a good stile is almost conterary to that which we generally hear. Hence it is that we con⟨c⟩eive*r* the farther ones stile is removed from the common manner [the] it is*s* so much the nearer to purity and the perfection we have in view. Shaftesbury who keeps at a vast distance from the language we commonly meet with is for this reason universally admired. Thomson who perhaps was of the same

104　opinion himself, is equalled with {Milton}*t* who amongst | his other beauties has this also, that he does not affect forced expressions even when he is*u* most sublime. Swift on the other hand, who is the plainest as well as the most proper and precise of all the English writers, is despised as nothing out of the common road; each of us thinks he could have wrote as well; And our thoughts of the language give us the same idea of the substance of his writings. But it does not appear that this opinion is*v* well grounded. There are four things[2] that are requisite to make a good writer. 1st—That he have a complete knowledge of his Subjects; 2.dly *w* That he should arrange all the parts of his Subject in

105　their proper order; 3dly That he paint | ⟨or⟩ describe the Ideas he has of these severall in the most proper and expressive manner; this is the art of painting or imitation (or at least we may call it so).

Now we will find that Swift has attained all these perfections. All his works shew a comple⟨te⟩ knowledge of his Subject. He does not indeed ever introduce any thing foreign to his subject, in order to display his knowledge of his subject; but then he never omitts any thing necessary His rules*x* for behaviour[3] and his directions for a Servant shew a knowledge of both those opposite characters that could not have been attained but by the closest attention continued for many years. {It would have been impossible for any one who had not given such attention to alledge so many particulars.}*y* The same is apparent in all his political works, insomuch that one would imagine his thoughts

106　had been altoge|ther turned that way.— —

---

q and *deleted*　　　*r* whatever is most *deleted*　　　*s* the it is *replaces* to be　　　*t* Milton W
supplied by Hand B at top of v.103　　　*u* the *deleted*　　　*v* at a *deleted*　　　*w* That he paint if
we may so, the ideas of *deleted*　　　*x* *replaces* directions　　　*y* Hand B

---

[2] Read 'three'; but the scribe may have omitted one.

[3] *A Treatise on Good Manners and Good Breeding* (in the Earl of Orrery's *Remarks on the Life and Writings of Swift*, 1752); *Directions to Servants* (1745).

One who has such a complete knowledge of what he treats will naturally arange it in the most proper order. This we see Swift always does. There is no part that we can think would have been better disposed of. That he paints but each thought in the best and most proper manner and with the greatest strength of colouring must be visible to any one at first sight.*ᶻ* Now that a writer who has all these qualities in such perfection should not make the best stile for expressing himself in*ᵃ* with propriety and precision can not be imagined. {That he does this when he speaks in his own person we*ᵇ* observed already and that he does so when he takes in the character of another is sufficiently evident from his Gulliver or⁴— —}

107   Notwithstanding of all this, perhaps for the reasons already shewn his graver works are not much regarded. It is his talent for ridi|cule that is most commonly and I believe most justly admired. We shall therefore consider how far [far] this talent is agreable to the generall character we have already given of him, and whether or not he has prosecuted it with the same exactness as the other subjects we mentioned. But before we enter upon this it will be necessary to make a few previous observations on [the] this Talent.*ᶜ* {This Leibnit*ᵈ* and after him Mr Locke⁵ supposed to be excited by the viewing of some mean object; but that this is not the case will appear from what follows.}

  Whatever we see that is great or noble excites our admiration and amazement, and whatever is little or mean on the other hand excites our contempt.*ᵉ* A greatt object never excites our laughter, neither does a mean one, simply as being such. It is the blending and joining of those two ideas which alone causes that Emotion.

108 | {*ʲ*The foundation of Ridicule is either when what is in most respects Grand or pretends to be so or is expected to be so,*ᵍ* has something mean or little*ʰ* in it or when we find something that is realy mean with some pretensions and marks of grandeur.} Now this may happen either when an object which is in most respects a grand one, is represented to us and described as mean,*ⁱ* or e contra when a grand object is found in company as it were with others that are mean; [or] or e contra when*ʲ*

ᶻ and *deleted*; strength . . . sight *replaces* precision, was observed on a former occasion, *then* and *deleted*   *ᵃ* and that *deleted*   *ᵇ* MS whe   *ᶜ replaces* subject *ᵈ written in different ink above a blank beginning* sc   *ᵉ* or disdain *deleted*   *ʲ* Ridicule proceds *deleted*   *ᵍ last six words inserted in margin*   *ʰ last three words replace* noble   *ⁱ last eight words replace* but has some particulars that are/do about it as presented (*last five words interlined then deleted*)   *ʲ* one that *deleted*

---

⁴ Supply 'Drapier', which gave Hand A trouble also at i.120 and for which Hand B supplied 'Dyer'.

⁵ Leibnitz, Locke: see Introduction, p. *21*.

our expectation is dessapointed and what we imagined was either grand or mean turns out to be the reverse. These different combinations of ideas afford each a different form[k] or manner of ridicule.

   If we represent an object which we are apt to conceive as a grand one ⟨or⟩ as of no dignity, and turn its qualities into the conterary, the mixture of the ideas excites our laughter tho neither of them seperately would do so. Hence come the Ridicule conveyed to us by burlesque or mock heroick compositions. The circumstances a thing is in also, if
109 their be any great contradiction betwixt the objects, | for the same reason excites our laughter. A tall man is no object of laughter, neither is a little, but a very tall man amongst a number of dwarfs, like Gulliver amongst the Lillyputians, or a little man amongst a set of very tall men as the same Gulliver in Brobdignag, appear = ly[l] ridiculous. There is no real foundation for laughter here but the odd association of grand and mean or little ideas. {In this and similar cases it is the Groupe of figures and no individuall one which is the object of our Ridicule[m]. The Ridicule in the Rape of the Lock proceeds from the Ridiculousness of the Characters themselves, but that of the Dunciad is owing altogether to the circumstances the persons are placed in. Any two men, Pope and Swift themselves, would look as ridiculous as Curl[6] and Lintot[n] if they were described running the same races.} We laugh against our will at the employment of Socrates when we see him in the Clouds[7] of Aristophanes measuring the length of a Fleas Leap by the length of the same fleas foot; or suspended in a basket making observations. If this philosopher had been ⟨seen⟩[o] so employed he[p] would have appeard ridiculous, and the great contrariety of the ideas makes the very supposition appear so.
110 | {The wit of some of the French Comedians as   [q] is founded in this principle. The Lover in fousque[8] is no ways ridiculous but by the circumstances.} The Italian Comedians, at Paris, as they are called, as soon as any grave or solemn tragedy appears on the theatre give the same play, that is the same Incidents[r] applied to some very opposite

---

[k] or stile *deleted*   [l] utterly (?), equally (?)   [m] In this . . . Ridicule, *Hand B*
[n] *inserted by Hand B in blank left*   [o] been *has been changed to* seen *by haplography*
[p] *MS* the, t *deleted*   [q] *blank of six leters in MS*   [r] tur *deleted*

   [6] Edmund Curll and Bernard Lintot, the booksellers who appear in both 1729 and 1743 versions of Pope's *Dunciad*, especially Book ii.
   [7] Lines 143–52.
   [8] No doubt a first attempt at the title of which 'Fouguer' (i.115 n.16) is the second version. The Italian Comedians: the *Gelosi*, allowed to play *commedia dell'arte* in Paris, later presented parodies of tragedies, etc. Expelled 1697–1716 for exceeding their licence; later still, fused with the Opéra-Comique. Writers for them included Regnard, Dufresny, Marivaux.

character. Generalls and Emperors become Burghers or turn[s] mechan-
icks; the ridicule here is owing to the contrast ⟨betwixt⟩ the high Idea
connected with the incidents we have seen attendant on great
characters, and the same incidents happening to persons of a rank so
much lower. When what we expect to find[t] great and noble turns out
otherwise we are in the same manner moved to laughter, and e contra.
A sow wallowing in the mire is certainly a loathsome object, but no one
would laugh at it, as it is agreable to the nature of the beast. But if he
111 saw the sow afterwards in a drawingroom, the case would | be altered.
On the other hand a lean poor looking rawboned horse excites ones
laughter as {that noble animall seems to lay claim to our admiration},
we expect something great and noble in the appearance of that
animall. One would not laugth at a bad prospect, as there ⟨is⟩ no
contradiction in supposing one, unless we had been made to expect a
fine one, but we laugh at a bad picture because we expect that art is
exeersised in some noble manner.

'Tis from such combinations chiefly that ridicule proceeds; we may
laugh too at things we contemn, but in[u] a different manner. A
Coxcomb walking on the Street and looking around him to see those
about admiring him as he expects is a subject of laughter to the graver
sort; but then this laughter that proceeds from an object we contemn is
evidently mixt with somewhat of anger. But if this same coxcomb
112 should slip a foot | and fall into the kennel the grave gentlemen would
laugh[v] but from a different motive, ⟨at⟩ the ridiculous plight such a
fine fellow was in; which was the very condition they at their hearts
would have wished him. Some philosophers[9] as   [w] observing that
laughter proceeds sometimes from contempt, have made ⟨it⟩ the
originall of all ridiculous perceptions. But we may frequently laugh at
objects that are not at all contemptible. A tall man amongst a number
of little men or e contra makes us laugh but we dont contemn either.
Things that have no sort of connexion, but where the ideas we have are
strangely contradictory, excite our laughter. I remember once a
113 mouse[x] running across the area of a chappel spoilt the effect | of an
excellent discourse. Any such trivial accidents excite our laughter
when they happen at any solemn or important work, as a Funerall. Tis
for this reason that we are diverted with those[y] phrases that we are
accustomd to connect in our imagination with noble objects, when we
meet with them applied to mean and trifling ones. Hence comes the

---

[s] *MS* ton; *see note* r   [t] of a gra *deleted*   [u] *replaces* from   [v] at his *above line, deleted*
[w] *blank of fourteen letters in MS*   [x] *original order* a mouse, once *changed by numbers written above*
[y] *replaces* any

---

[9] 'Some philosophers': perhaps Hobbes, See i.107 n.5, and Introduction, p. *21*.

ridiculousness[ness] of Paradoies (or applying whole passages of an author by a sort of translation to subje⟨c⟩ts of a very different sort, and Centos where single phrases are applid.) The Cento of Apuleius,[10] where the Grave and chaste Virgil is made to speak in his own words on a very different Subject and not very chaste language, no where makes us laugh but in the Story of the Marriage. {All the ridicule of Scarrons Virgil Travesti[11] in the same manner proceeds from the Grave⁵ and solemn adventures of Æneas being told in the most ridiculous language and trivial mean expressions.} The Modern Latin

114   Poets, Vida, Sanazarious,[12] etc. are all Paradies on some of the ǀ ancient Latin Poets. They*a* not being on trivial subjects but such as are equally important, do not excite our laughter but are rather taedious and wearisome. The English poets are more originall, they do not usually borrow from others; such dealings would be counted no better than stealing; and for that reason are not so tiresome. The Splendid shilling[13] diverts us by the ridiculous appearance*b* Mi⟨l⟩tons language makes when used to extoll the Charms of a Shilling. {The incongruity of the language to the Subject has also its effect here*c* as well as in works of the conterary sort as Virgil travesti.} But so far is ⟨it⟩ from being a sign of any passages being a mean one that a parrodie has been made upon it, that 'tis rather a sign of the conterary, as the more sublime and Pompous a passage is the*d* greater the contrast will be when the

115   phraseology is applied to triviall ǀ subjects. Thus we see the soliloquy of Hamlet,[14] the last speech of Cato, have undergone more parodies than any others I know, and indeed make very good ones. For the same reason Parodies on the Scriptures tho very profane are at the same time very ridiculous.

{Puns, which are the Lowest Species of Wit,[15] are never witty or

---

ᶜ Langu *deleted*   *a replaces* but   *b* of m *deleted*   *c* also (*already inserted above line*) *deleted* *after* here   *d* more ridicu *deleted*

---

[10] i.e. Ausonius, *Opuscula*, Lib. xvii: *Cento nuptialis*.

[11] Paul Scarron, *Virgile travesti* (1648–52).

[12] Jacopo Sannazzaro (1456–1530). Latin poems: *Elegiae* and *Epigrammata* are personal lyrics. *Eclogae piscatoriae* substitute fishermen for the shepherds of pastoral. *De partu Virginis* treats Christ's birth in classical epic style; criticised by Du Bos in *Réflexions critiques* (1719), I.xxiv.

[13] *The Splendid Shilling: an Imitation of Milton*, by John Philips (in *A Collection of Poems*, 1701), began a vogue for the application of Miltonic style and verse to trivial subjects: his own *Cerealia* (1706) and *Cyder* (1708), John Gay's *Wine* (1708), the Countess of Winchilsea's *Fanscomb Barn*. In 1709 appeared a protest in Miltonic verse: *Milton's Sublimity Asserted*.

[14] *Hamlet*, III.i.56–88; Addison's *Cato*, V.iv, referring either to Cato's dying speech or to the lines spoken over him by Lucius, 105–17.

[15] This sounds already a proverbial phrase, as it has remained. It goes back to Dryden's 'the lowest and most grovelling kind of wit, which we call clenches' (*Defence of the Epilogue*, 1672, §20). The word *pun*, which gradually replaced *clench* or *clinch* from 1660 onwards, was used perjoratively from the start. Addison devoted *Spectator* 61 (10 May 1711) to an attack on it. His strictures in *Spectator* 279 (19 Jan. 1712) on the devils' puns in *Paradise Lost* vi were rebutted by John

agreable but when there is some contrast betwixt the ideas they excite; a mere quibble is never agreable.}

There are two species of Comic writing derived from two species of ridiculous circumstances. The one is when characters ridiculous in themselves are described and the other when characters that have nothing ridiculous in themselves are described in ridiculous circumstances. The *ᵉ*   in the   of   is an instance   of the former and the Lover of   *ᵉ* in the fouguer[16] of   *ʲ* is an

116 instance of the latter. The whole | of Congreves wit consists in the ridiculousness of his similies,[17] as his comparing two persons bespattering one another to two apples roasting, or the young lady newly come to town, gaping with amazement, he compares her wide opend mouth to the gate of her fathers house*ᵍ*.

It is proper to be observed*ʰ* that of all these species of Ridicule: Burlesque, Doggerel, Mock Heroick, Parodies, Centos, Puns, Quibbles and even that sort of Comedy which ridicules characters not from their real defects*ⁱ* ⟨but⟩ from the circumstances they are brought into, are*ʲ* all of the buffoonish sort and unworthy of a gentleman who has had a

116 regular education; | and whenever such an one exercises his wit in this manner, he lays aside that character to assume that of a buffoon at least for the time he does so. The only species of Ridicule which is true and genuine wit is that where Real foibles and blemishes in the Characters or behaviour of men are exposed to our view in a ridiculous light. This is altogether consistent with the character of a Gentleman*ᵏ* as it tends to the reformation of manners and the benefit of mankind.

{The objects of Ridicule are two: either those which, affecting to be Grand or being expected to be so, are mean, or being Grand in some of their parts are mean in others—or such as pretending etc. etc. to beauty are deformed.}*ˡ*

ᵉ⁻ᵉ five blanks of about ten letters each in MS   ʲ blank of four letters in MS   ᵍ before house *illegible word (pony?) deleted; after* house, Lucian has chosen the one of these 2 sorts of comick Subjects and Swift the other *deleted   ʰ that* I mentioned *inserted above then deleted   ⁱ* and of *deleted   ʲ replaces* use   *ᵏ* it is the *deleted   ˡ Hand B at foot of v.116*

Oldmixon, *The Arts of Logick and Rhetorick* (1728), 18: 'Milton, 'tis plain, thought he cou'd not make worse Devils of them, than by making them *Punsters*', just as serious painters give them horns and a tail. 'Of all meanness', wrote Johnson in the *Rambler* 140 (20 July 1751), 'that has least to plead which is produced by mere verbal conceits, which depending only upon sounds, lose their existence by the change of a syllable'.

[16] Cf. i.110 n.8 above. This comedy cannot be identified.

[17] Witwoud, *The Way of the World*, IV.viii ('. . . fell a-sputt'ring at one another like two roasting Apples'); Belinda, *The Old Batchelor*, IV.viii ('I fansied her like the Front of her Father's Hall; her Eyes were the two Jut-Windows, and her Mouth the great Door, most hospitably kept open . . .'). But the 'wit' is not Congreve's; he is creating two comic characters whose affectation is a pretence to wit. Witwoud at one point gives a recital of similes (II.iv) till Millamant cries 'Truce with your Similitudes'. For the distinction see Congreve's *Concerning Humour in Comedy* (1696).

Lecture. 9th ^a

Decr. 6.th   Monday

Mr Smith.

As there are two Sorts of Objects that excite our admiration, viz when an object is Grand, or when it is beautiful, and two that excite our contempt, viz those that are little and mean, or such as are deformed and disagreable in themselves; So there must be too sorts of Ridicule proceeding from the Combinations of these different objects. 1st When mean objects are exposed by considering them as Grand, or 2dly when Grand ones or such as pretend or are expected to be so, are ridiculed^b by exposing the^c meaness and the littleness which is found in them. Swift has chosen the former and Lucian the latter of these Sorts.

118 | The characters of these different men would naturally lead them to choose these conterary Subjects. Swifts naturall moroseness joined to the constant dissapointments and crosses he met with in life would^d make contempt naturall to his character; and those follies would most provoke him that partake most of gayety and levity.^e This was so prevalent a part of his character that we are told he studiously avoided what are called the common forms of Civility and good breeding. When he saw those that had little else to recommend ⟨them⟩ not only have some tollerable character and pass thro life with some sort of applause, but even be preferred before himself,^f the reverence he had for his own good sense and judgement which he thought far above

119 that^g of the common stamp[t]; he would | surely be^h prompted to expose to the ultmost of his power these and such likeⁱ follies and silliness in men. Accordingly we find all his less serious works are wrote with a design to ridicule some one of the prevailing gay follies of his Time. The⟨y⟩ are chiefly levelled against Coxcombs, Beaus, Belles and other characters where gay follies rather than the graver ones ⟨prevail⟩; these he never attacks in any of his works except the Tale of a tub, which was wrote when he was very young and is a work of a very different sort from all the rest. It is much less Correct than those which he wrote when more advanced in life.— — — —

We may observe he never uses that sort of ridicule which may be thrown on any subject by the choise of words, his Language is always correct and Proper and no ornaments are ever introduced nor does he ever write but in a manner most suitable to the Nature of the Subject.

---

^a MS 8th   ^b replaces exposed   ^c replaces their   ^d induce him to contemn deleted
^e tho deleted   ^f whom deleted   ^g that deleted   ^h MS by   ⁱ last four words replace
such; and deleted before next and

120 As his morose temper directed him to make choise of the gayer follies |
of men*ʲ* to exercise his talent for ridicule, so the character of a plain
man which he affected hindered him from ever making us laugh*ᵏ* to
excess at any subject in however ridiculous a light he may set. This he
does when he speaks in his own person. But when he has a mind to
throw a great degree of Ridicule on any subject he puts it into the
mouth of some other person as in Gullivers travells and the Dyers
Letters.*ˡ* Even in these works he never uses any expressions but what
are suitable to his Subject. The most common manner in which he*ᵐ*
throws ridicule on any subjects when he speaks in an other character is
to make them express their admiration and esteem for those things he
121 would [he] expose. As ridicule | proceeds from a combination*ⁿ* of the
Ideas of admiration and contempt it is very evident he could not take a
more effectual method to ridicule any foible or silly object than by
making someone express the highest admiration for it, as the contrast is
here the strongest. In those works that appear the most silly and
trifling, as his Song of Similies*¹* and that other of Ditton and Whiston,
he shews*ᵒ* the folly that then prevailed in a very strong light*ᵖ*— —

Lucian, if we may judge of the man from his works, has been of a
very opposite turn. He was of a merry gay and jovial temper with no
inconsiderable portion of Levity. {He was a follower of the Epicurean
or rather of the Cyrenaic Sect; his principles are all adapted to*�q* that
scheme of life where the chief thing in view is to pass it easily and
happily, and with as much pleasure as we possibly can. And as Life is*ʳ*
short and transitory he lays it down as a maxim that we ought not to
omit any present happiness in expectation of a greater to come butt lay
hold of the present opportunity. Friendship and the exercise of the
sociall affections are in his opinion the chief fund for enjoyment and
consequently chiefly to be cultivated.} The characters which Swift*²*
22 exposes | were those which best suited his taste. Grave men who had
any thing*ˢ* of levity or folly in their character were those that he most

ʲ for the field *deleted*   *ᵏ* ing *deleted*; making us *added above line*   *ˡ* Dyers Letters *inserted by
Hand B in blank left*   *ᵐ* thre *deleted*   *ⁿ* of *deleted*   *ᵒ* changed from* ridicules   *ᵖ* blank line
follows*   *q* prove *deleted*   *ʳ* of a *deleted*   *ˢ* light *deleted*

¹ These two poems are no longer ascribed to Swift. *A new song of new similies* appeared in the
Pope-Swift *Miscellanies in Verse* (1727), iii.207–12, and is included in John Gay's *Poetical Works*,
ed. G. C. Faber (1926), 645–6, and ed. V. A. Dearing and C. E. Beckwith (1974), 376–8.— The
scatological 16-line *Ode for Musick: On the Longitude*, recitativo and ritornello, on W. Whiston and
H. Ditton's *A New Method for discovering the Longitude both at Sea and Land* (1714) circulated in
London in April 1715 and was published in the so-called *Miscellanies: The Last Volume* (1727). It
has been variously ascribed to Swift, Pope and Gay, and was included in Swift's *Works* (1824),
xiii.336, but its author is unknown. Gay wrote a brilliant prose satire on the eccentric Whiston in
Miscellanies, Vol. 3 (1732), 255–76: 'A True and Faithful narrative'.
² The antithesis requires Lucian, not Swift.

despised, as those who[s] went about their follies with an air of
importance appeared most despicable in the eyes of the morose Swift.
Agreably to these different casts of mind, the⟨y⟩ chose different
characters to expose by their wit. Swift as we said exposes none but
Empty Coxcombs, Fine Gentlemen, Beaus, Belles, and any that
encouraged themselves in*ᶦ* employments of no moment or importance
of life. {Lucian exposes only Grave Characters and the Graver pursuits
of men, as the miser and ambitious man}*ᵘ* Lucian on the other hand
has pitched on, for the subject of his ridicule, persons of the most
sollemn and respectable characters, as Gods, Goddesses, Heroes,
123 Senators, | Generalls, Historians, Poets, and Philosophers [as], as those
wherein the Gra⟨v⟩er sort of follies are most commonly found. Of such
personages all his dialogues are composed and those writings in which
he talks in his own person turn chiefly on such follies. His discourse de
Luctu³ will serve as an example both of the Subject and his manner of
treating it. We may observe he never uses any witticisms derived from
language, nor any ornaments of that sort but what his subject naturally
leads him to. He never makes any digressions from his Subject; his
fruitfull Imagination always affording him matter enough on every
subject without being obliged to call in another to his assisstance,
124 perhaps very little connected with it. | His design of surprising and
diverting his reader sometimes leads him into seeming digressions, that
his return to his Subject after keeping one in suspence may be the more
entertaining. One way he often does this in, is by putting the
Comparison before the subject to which it is compared. Thus he puts
the fatall effects of the fever at Abdera before*ᵛ* his complaint on the
number of historicall writers then in Greece. And the same may be
seen in the Comparison betwixt Diogenes tumbling his Tub and his
own labours. {He often brings in the Illustration before that which it
illustrates because commonly it is the most diverting, ex Gr in the
beginning of his Directions for the writing of history⁴   *ʷ* A Graver
author would have followd the Naturall order.}*ˣ*
    By the different ends that Swift and Lucian have had in view, they
have*ʸ* formed a complete system of ridicule. There is hardly any folly of
the gayer sort that Swift passes over and*ᶻ* scarce any of the graver that
125 is ommitted by Lucian. | Either*ᵃ* of them taken alone might be apt to

---

ᶦ ligh *deleted*   *ᵘ* Hand B   *ᵛ* to the historicall *deleted*   *ʷ* blank *of nine letters in* MS
ˣ Hand B   *ʸ* exhausted all the *deleted*   *ᶻ* as few *deleted*   *ᵃ* replaces Any one

---

³ *On Funerals* (LCL iv.112–31), a satire on superstitious expressions of grief inspired by the
mythographers Homer, Hesiod, *et al.*
⁴ *How to write History* (LCL vi.2–73), an attack on the host of chroniclers of the Parthian War,
AD 162–5).

prejudize one [an] in favour of the follies conterary to those he ridicules; But both together form a System of morality from whence more sound and just rules of life for all the various characters of men may be drawn than from most set systems of Morality.

Nor are Lucians works altogether confined to subjects of a ludicrous nature, he has many discourses of a serious cast, recommending the different virtues. These are all very excellent; his manner in them is no less agreable than in his other works; he always keeps to his Subjects and never is necessitated to betake himself to generall praises of virtue in order to recommend any particular one (as has been the fashion for

126 some time) that the discourse migh⟨t⟩ | have the appearance of a complete system and be drawn out to the length of a pocket Volume. In a word there is no author from whom more reall instruction and good sense can be found than Lucian.[b]

124 | {There are scattered thro his works severall Essays very much in the manner of Mr Addison, wherein he illustrates the Virtue he would re⟨c⟩ommend with all the Graces of Serious Composition and yet never departs from the consideration of its Particular Nature, nor launches out into[c] vague and Generall declamations suited to any Virtue

125 whatever and shewing this chiefly that the author is not particularly | acquainted with his Subject. In this respect he may be an excellent moddell to those whose particular business it is to teach morality, in opposition to a very different manner which prevails at present.}[d]

[b] *in large letters in MS*   [c] those *deleted*   [d] *Hand B, v.124–v.125*

Lecture. 10th ᵃ

Monday Dec.ʳ 13 1762

126 There is perhaps no English writer who has more of this Gaiety*ᵇ* than Mr Addison, neither*ᶜ* has he so much as Lucian. This is the chief character of all his prose works: he frequently in the manner of Lucian begins his discourses with a story which he places before the subject itself, as in his address to the Tory Ladies in the Freeholder;[1] but he*ᵈ* never carries [carries] these so far as Lucian does, nor so minutely. This perhaps may be owing to*ᵉ* a sort of modesty which he is said to have

127 been possessed in a very [a] great degree, in the common affairs | of ⟨life⟩ {and which breaths indeed thro all his works}*ᶠ* and which the other author does not appair to have had in any considerable share, from severall stories he tells of himself, as that of his biting the thumb of the Imposter Alexander. {The Ludicrous incident of biting Alexanders thumb is related in his Life of that imposter,[2] than which few things are more entertaining.}*ᵍ* {His modesty hinders him from those*ʰ* bold and extrava⟨ga⟩nt strokes of humour which Lucian uses (he would not for instance put a Ludicrous speech into the mouths of a dead man or a god)*ⁱ* or from throwing out such biting sarcasms in his own person as Swift often does.} The flowryness of Mr Addison naturally lead him to*ʲ* make frequent use of figures in his discourses, the chief of these are metaphors, similies and Allegories. But in the use of these he always displays the modesty of his character. It may seem strange how the use of Allegories especially should seem consistent with that modesty we have attributed to him {as they are the boldest and strongest kind of figures*ᵏ*}, but the manner in which he introduces them is always such as makes it appear that there was nothing forced or uneasy in the

128 reforming them. He often introduces them in the form | of a dream,[3] and at the same time shews us the train of thought that led him into such conceptions, and by this means makes us imagine that the

---

ᵃ MS 9th   *ᵇ of S deleted*   *ᶜ replaces* tho he   *ᵈ but he replaces* he never howe
ᵉ that deleted   *ᶠ Hand B, v.125 foot*   *ᵍ Hand B, below Hand A's* His modesty . . . does
ʰ strong and *deleted*   *ⁱ* and at the same time *deleted*   *ʲ* use *deleted*   *ᵏ* of *deleted*

---

[1] *The Free-holder: or political essays.* 23 Dec. 1715 to 29 June 1716, 55 numbers, often reprinted in one volume; ed. J. Leheny (1979). 'Future Readers may see, in them, the Complexion of the Times in which they were written (55).

[2] Lucian met the false priest Alexander of Abonuteichos, who as 'prophet' of Asclepius conducted mysteries and had a considerable following from AD 150 to 170, and his satire on him is one of his bitterest (LCL iv; reference to p. 145).

[3] Addison on allegory: *Guardian* 152; *Spectator* 55, 63, 183, 315, 464. For dreams and visions, which as suggested are often the vehicle, see *Guardian* 106, 158; *Tatler* 81, 97, 100, 117, 119, 120, 123, 146, 154, 161; *Spectator* 110, 159 (Vision of Mirzah), 275, 487 (essay on Dreams), 505, 558–9.

circumstances he was in naturally Suggested them without his being at any pains about it. {As that where he compares the different characters of men to different musicall instruments.}[4]

In the same manner his similes are always represented as naturally presenting themselves. This modesty we have ascribed to him[l] causes him likewise deliver his sentiments in the least assuming manner; and this would incline him rather to narrate what he had seen and heard than to deliver his opinions in his own person; and at the same time he will not seem to be at great pains to[m] give nice and curious

129 circumstances; it is more consistent with | the naturall modesty of his temper to give us only a few of the most striking and interesting. He[n] neither presumes as Shaftesbury and Bollingbroke, nor dictates as Swift. {Shaftesbury and Bolinbroke display their[o] superior dignity etc. Swift his superiority of Sense.}[p] For the same reason he neither writes with the precision and nice propriety of the latter, nor have his sentences that Uniform cadence in their severall members as the two former writers always affected:[q] His Sentences are neither long nor short but of a length suited to the character he has of a modest man; who naturally delivers himself in Sentences of a moderate length and with a uniform tone. Accordingly we find those of Mr Addeson are of this sort. They generrally consist of 3, 4 or 5 phrases and are so uniform

130 in their | manner that we read them with a sort of monotony. The modest man will not use long sentences as they are either proper for declamation, which he never uses, or bespeak a confusion of Ideas that is not to be attributed to Mr Addison. He would not either deliver himself in short sentences, as that would appear either like Snip-snap or the language of presumption and a dictating temper. {As he does not pretend that every thing he says is of the utmost importance, and an infallible rule, so he is much more lax in his writings than Dr Swift: every word of his writings is of importance; when on the other hand Mr Addison frequently turns up the same thought in the different phrases of a sentence only placing it in a different light,[r] and is rather inaccurate in the use of words and repetition of Synonymes, which the concluding of the Essay on the Pleasures of the imagination[5] will be an example of if examined with that view.[r]}

He frequently makes quotations from the Poets, which gives his writings an air of gaiety and good humour. This Gaiety joined to the modesty that appears in his works has gained him the character of a

---

[l] prevents his *deleted*   [m] choose out *deleted*   [n] has *deleted*   [o] dignity *deleted*
[p] *Hand B*   [q] the Language *deleted*   [r-r] and is ... view, *Hand B*

---

[4] *Tatler* 153.
[5] The pleasures of the imagination are the subject of *Spectator* 411–21 (21 June–3 July 1712).

most polite and elegant writer. His descriptions are not near so animated as those of Lucian, and this may proceed both from his 131 naturall modesty and | from his imagination not being altogether so lively. This will appear to be the case in any of his descriptions if compared with ⟨that⟩ of Jupiter carrying of Europa in Lucian[6] which is remarkably animated, and gives as compleat a notion of the severall transactions as' words can convey.[t]

' any thing can *deleted*   [t] *the rest of 131, and 132 are blank*

---

[6] *Dialogues of the Sea-Gods* (fifteen, a shorter work than the superior *Dialogues of the Gods*) drew on Homer, the pastoral poets, and paintings: LCL vii. 178–237. Reference to no. 15.

¶33

Lecture. 11ᵃ

Wednesday. Dcr:

Inᵇ some of our former Lectures we have given a character of some of the best English Prose writers, and made comparisons betwixt their different manners. The Result of all which as well as the rules we have laid down is, that the perfection of stile consists in Express⟨ing⟩ in the most concise, proper and precise manner the thought of the author, and that in the manner which best conveys the sentiment, passion or affection with which it affects or he pretends it does affect him and which he designs to communicate to his reader.

This you'll say is no more than common sense, and indeed it is no more. But if you'll attend to it all the Rules of Criticism and morality when traced to their foundation, turn out to be some Principles of Common Sence which every one assents to; all the business of those arts is to apply these Rules to the different subjects and shew what their

¶35 conclusionᶜ is when they are so applyed.ᵈ | Tis for this purpose we have made theseᵉ observations on the authors above mentioned. We have shewn how fare they have acted agreably to that Rule, which is equally applicable to conversation and behaviour as writing. For what is that makes a man agreable company, is it not, when his sentiments appear to be naturally expressed, when the passion or affection is properly conveyed and when their thoughts are so agreable and naturall that we find ourselves inclined to give our assent to them. A wise man too in conversation and behaviour will not affect a character that is unnaturall to him; if he is grave he will not affect to be gay, nor if he be gay will he affect to be grave.ʲ He will only regulate his naturall temper, restrain within just boundsᵍ and lop all exhuberances and bring it to that pitch which will be agreable to those about him. But he will not affect such conduct as is unnaturall to his temper tho perhaps in the abstract they may be more to be wished.

¶36 | In like manner what is thatʰ is agreable in Stile; It is when all the thoughts are justly and properly expressedⁱ in such a manner as shews the passion they affected the author with, and so that all seems naturall and easy. He never seems to act out of character but speaks in a manner not only suitable to the Subject but to the character he naturally inclines to.

The three authors we have alr⟨e⟩ady considered seem all to have

---

ᵃ *MS* 10; *the date must be 15 December*   ᵇ *MS* Ino   ᶜ *replaces* effect   ᵈ *134 is blank*
ᵉ *use of the* wri *deleted*   ʲ *replaces* gay, *in Hand B*   ᵍ *last four words replace* curb in impetuosity   ʰ *last six words replace* But as their are not natur   ⁱ *with deleted*

acted agreably to this Rule. Every one speaks in his own stile and such an one as is agreable to his generall character. Hence we see there is a certain uniformity in their maner, there are no passages that remarkably distinguish themselves,[j] their admirers dont seem particularly fond of any one more than the rest, there are none which they

137 get by heart | and repeat with admiration as they would a piece of Poetry.[k] These authors did not attempt what they thought was the greatest perfection of stile but that perfection which they thought most suitable to their genius and temper.

But there is an other English[l] author who though much inferior to these three yet for the same reason as Thomson and others of that sort, had till very lately in this country a character much Superior to that of the others. The reason as we mentioned before was the ignorance of true propriety of language. I believe I need hardly mention that I mean Lord Shaftesbury.

This author seems not ⟨at⟩ all to have acted agreably to the Rule we have given above but to have formed to himself an idea of beauty of

138 Stile abstracted from his | own character, by which he proposed to regulate his Stile.

If we attend to the Character and circumstances of this nobleman we will easily perceive what it was which lead him to this Conduct. He was connected with a father and educated under a tutor, who have no[m] very strong affection to any particular sect or tenets in Religion, who cried up freedom of thought and [and] Liberty of Concience in all matters religious or philosophicall without being attached to any particular men or opinions. If these friends of his were[n] inclined to any one sect it was rather to the puritans than the established Church, as their tenets best suited with that Liberty of Concience they so strenuously maintained. Shaftesbury himself, by what we can learn from his Letters,[1] seems to have been of a very puny and weakly

139 constitution, always | [o]either under some disorder or in dread of falling into one. Such a habit of ⟨body⟩ is very much connected, nay almost continually attended by, a cast of mind in a good measure similar. Abstract reasoning and deep searches are too fatiguing for persons of this delicate frame.[p] Their feableness of body as well as mind hinders them from engaging in the pursuits which generally engross the common sort of men. Love and Ambition are too violent in their emotions to find ground to work upon in such frames; where the

---

[j] non whi *deleted*   [k] They *deleted*   [l] *Hand B(?) wrote* no *above* English   [m] particular *deleted*   [n] any wise *deleted*   [o] particular character which he always *deleted*   [p] And as *deleted*

---

[1] Shaftesbury's letters were published in 1716 and 1721.

passions are not very strong.*q* The weakness of their appetites and passions hinders them from being carried away in the ordinary manner, they find no great difficulty in conforming their conduct to the Rules they have proposed to themselves.*r*

140 | *'*The fine arts, matters of taste and imagination, are what they are most inclined to cultivate. They require little labour and at the same time afford an entertainment very suitable to their*s* temper and abilities. Accordingly we find that Lord Shaftesbury tho no great reasoner, nor deeply skilled in the abstract sciences, had*t* a very neice and just taste in the fine arts and all matters of that sort. {We are told he made some figure as a speaker in bothe houses of Parliament[2] tho not very extraordinary, but we do not find that he was ever distinguished in debate or Deliberation in Politicall matters} Naturall philosophy he does not seem to have been at all acquainted with,[3] but on the other hand he shews a great ignorance of the advances it had then made and a contempt for its followers. The reason plainly is that it did not afford the amusement his disposition required and the

141   mathematicall part particularly required | more attention and abstract thought than men of his weakly habit are generally capable of. The pleasures of imagination as they are more easily acquired and of a very delicate nature are more agreable to them. {The contempt he expresses for such Studies is such as could proceed from no cause but very great ignorance}

Men of this Sort, when they take a religious turn are generally great enthysiasts, and much disposed to mysticall contemplations, on the being and nature of god, and his perfections, and such like topics. But the delicacy of his temper together with the plan of his education gave him a different turn. The scheme of Revealed religion which he was best acquainted with as we said was that of the puritans. The Grosness

142   of their conduct, the little decency or appearance | of devotion that they used in their manner of worship shocked his delicate and refined temper and*u* in time prejudized him against every scheme of revealed religion. The Selfish and confined systems of Hobbs and   *v* could

---

q ,and *deleted*   *r* *v.139 makes false start:* The fine arts and matters of taste and imagination are w   *s* way *deleted*   *t* yet *deleted*   *u* in *deleted*   *v* *blank of five letters in MS* (*The reference is probably to Locke, Shaftesbury's 'preceptor'*).

[2] He was member for Poole 1695–8. In the House of Lords he ardently supported the Whig cause, and despite illness attended the partition treaty debate, travelling from Somerset in one day at Lord Somers's summons. Alone he urged dissolution in the last year of William's reign. He was the author of the anonymous *Paradoxes of State relative to the present juncture . . . chiefly grounded on His Majesty's princely, pious and most gracious speech* [i.e. on 31 Dec. 1701] (1702).

[3] That Shaftesbury's failure to keep up with recent advances in Natural Philosophy was criticised by Smith will not surprise readers of the latter's Letter to the *Edinburgh Review* of 1756 (EPS 242–54).

not agree with the delicacy of his Sentiments. The School philosophy was still less agreable. The futility, Sophistry, Barbarism and Meaness of their schemes was very visibl⟨e⟩ and very disagreable to his turn of mind. This made him desirous of forming some system to himself more agreable to his own inclinations and temper. The intimate acquaintance which he had with the ancients and the great[u] knowledge he had early acquired in the ancient languages inclined[x] him to apply to them 143 in this research. The system which of all others best suited his | disposition was that of the Platonists. Their refined notions both in Theology and Philosophy were perfectly agreable to him, and accordingly his Philosophy and Theology is the same in effect with theirs but modernized a little and made somewhat more suitable to the taste then prevailing. In these he intermixes somewhat of the Philosophy of Hobbs and his precep⟨t⟩or Lockes. This latter as he was of a very different cast from his pupil so his philosophy did not suit with ⟨him⟩, being too metaphysicall and not capable of affording him entertainment to his mind. But tho he endeavours to run down these philosophers yet he sometimes takes their assistance in forming his own plan.

144 | {Such is Lord shaftesburys Undertaking to overturn the Old Systems of Religion and Philosophy as Hobbs before him had done but still more,[y] which Hobbs never had attempted to do, to erect a new one. Let us see how he has executed it, in what Stile and manner}[z]

Such is the subject of Lord Shaftesbury's writings; Let us next consider how far his Stile[a] is suitable to the same character that lead him to this Scheme of Philosophy.

His weakly state of body as it prevented the violence of his passions, did not incline him greatly to be of any particular[b] temper to any great height. His Stile therefore would not be naturally more of one Sort than another. As therefore he was not lead to have any particular Stile, by the prevalence of any particular inclination, it was natural for him to form some Model or Idea of perfection which he should always have in view. {His Letters where we should expect to meet with some distinguishing marks of the character of the man more than in his other writings, are not near so animated as those of Swift and Pope or Ciceros[c] and the noble Romans who corresponded with him. The⟨y⟩ are indeed full of what we call here sentiments (that is morall observations) but have no marks of the circumstances the writer was in at the time he wrote. Nor any reflections peculiarly suited to the times and circumstances.}

As he was of no great depth in Reasoning he would be glad to set off

---

[u] mastery he *deleted*   [x] *replaces* lead   [y] to *deleted*   [z] Hand B   [a] and *deleted*
[b] Shape *deleted*   [c] Corres *deleted*

45 by the ornament of language what was deficient in matter. | This with
the refinement of his temper directed ⟨him⟩ to make choise of a
pompous, grand and ornate Stile. His acquaintance with the ancients
inclined him to imitate them; and if he had any one particularly in
view it was Plato. As he copied him in his Theology and in a great
measure in his philosophy so he seems to have copyed his Stile and
manner also, tempering it in the same manner so as to make it more
suitable to the times he lived in. Theocles in his Rhapsody[+] is exactly
copied from Socrates. But as Socrates humour is often too coarse and
his sarcasms too biting for this age he has softend him in this respect
46 and made his | Theocles altogether polite and his wit such as suits the
character of a gentleman.

{He has indeed succeeded better in this attempt to form a stile than
we could have expected and much better than any one could do in an
attem⟨pt⟩ to form a plan of behaviour. The writer may review and
correct anything that is not suitable to the character he designs to
maintain. But in Common life many accidents would occurr which
would be apt to cause him loose his assumed character and if they are
not immediately catched there is no remedy.

The character which a writer assumes he is not oblidged on any
occasion to maintain without prymeditation, but many Incidents
happen in common Life to which if the manners are not conformed in a
moment the affectation will be betrayed}[d]

Polite dignity is the character he aimed at, and as this seems to be
best supported by a grand and pompous diction that was the Stile he
made choise of. This he carried so far that when the subject was far
from being grand, his stile is as pompous as in the most sublime
subjects.—The chief ornament of Language he studied was that of a
uniform cadence and this he often does[e] in contradiction to precision
and propriety, which are surely of greater consequence. {He has this so
much in view that he often makes the one member of his sentence an
echo to the other and often[f] brings in a whole string of Synonymes to
make the members end uniformly.}[g]

{Socrates always in his longer discourses points out distinctly his
transitions from one subject to an other. But as this looked too formal,
he chose to do this by the more polite and easy manner of beginning a
new paragraph, and he is at pains to tell us that he had reasons for his
order even ⟨tho⟩ we[h] can perceive no connection.

---

[d] *the last two paragraphs* He has . . . betrayed *begin on v.144 opposite* grand and ornate Stile; *the
second paragraph is in Hand B*   [e] when *deleted*   [f] makes *deleted*   [g] *on v.145 interpolations see
Introduction, p. 5*   [h] *changed from* tho

[+] *The Moralists, a Philosophical Rhapsody* (1709), Treatise v in *Characteristicks* (1711).

This is the manner of making Transitions which has come so much in Vogue in Modern times; whatever advantages it may have in Elegance in perspicuity it falls short.

Socrates in Plato is always made to say: having considered this thing we are next to consider such another thing.}

In the Choise of his subject he*i* was allmost the same as Lucian. The design of both was to overthrow the present fabric of Theology and

147 Philosophy but they differed in this: | Lucian had no design of erecting an other in its place. Whereas Shaftesbury not only*j* designed to ⟨destroy⟩ the *Structure* but to build a new Aedifice of his own in its room. He judged, and indeed he judged rightly that this destruction would be easier accomplished and more to the taste of the times by riducule than by confutation. But even in those works where he designs to banter and laugh at his adversary he does it with the same*k* pompous diction as he uses in other works. By this means he hardly ever makes us laugh, only in two places in the whole characteristicks, one in the introduction to   *l* and the other in his description of a match at football a little after. His Similles and metephors are often very

148 ingenious but are spun out to such a | ⟨length⟩ as is*m* tiresome both to himself and his readers {as that of the Indian.} In his Treatise where he ridicules Mr Hobbs there is not one passage which would make us laugh. Mr Hobbs book would make us laugh but his ridicule of it would never affect us.[5]

{As all Copiators*n* exceed the Original, as a painting may be known to be a copy from being larger than that from which they are copies, so those who affect either in behaviour or in Stile carry their imitation too far. One who affects to be merry always laughs the loudest and longest of any in the company. In the same manner as Shaftesbury affects to be pompous, he often*o* exceeds and applies a grand diction to subjects of a very different kind. A Stranger who did not understand the language would imagine the most trivial subjects to ⟨be⟩ something very sublime from the manner and sound of his periods.}

This Nobleman*p* sometimes allows himself even to run into Burlesque, his Pompous Stile and humourous thoughts joined together make it almost unavoidable. But this species of Ridicule is always buffoonish and he surely falls greatly off from the Polite dignity he

---

i has *deleted*   *j* judged *deleted*   *k* gravity and [blank] as wh *deleted*   *l* *blank of ten letters in* MS   *m* tediou *deleted*   *n* *changed from* Copyators   *o* appli *deleted*   *p* This Nobleman *replaces* He even

---

[5] *Miscellaneous Reflections*, I.i. (*Characteristicks*, Treatise vi, 1711). Ibid. I.ii, philosophical controversy compared to a football match. Ibid. V.iii, the Indian. *The Moralists*, II.iv, ridicule of Hobbes; cf. III.i, and *Sensus Communis: An Essay on the freedom of Wit and Humour* (1709), Treatise ii in *Characteristicks*, II.i.

studies to maintain, when he allows himself a species of wit that is greatly beneath the character of a gentleman.—Nay this strenuous advocate for the re⟨finement⟩ and justness of thought even condescends now and then to make use of a pun and those of the silliest kind as where   *q*.

148 | {When Shaftesbury is disposed to be in a Rapture it is always unbounded, overstretcht and unsupported by the appearance of Reason, as for instance in his address to the Sun in his Rhapsody[6] in which address not one Circumstan⟨c⟩e is mentioned which ought to excite Rationall Admiration. Compare this with the Most Rapturous Passage in all Virgil, his Encomion on Rurall Life in the Georgicks.[7]

> O Fortunati nimium sua si bona norunt
> Agricolae etc. etc.

Here every circumstance, every word, has an energy and force in displaying the felicity of the Country and Deprecating the Tinsel and Tumult of a Town Life. Virgil when he is disposed to be in a transport does not run mad}*r*

q blank of six letters in MS   *r Hand B*

---

[6] *The Moralists*, III.i.
[7] *Georgics*, ii.458–9: read 'O fortunatos . . . norint / Agricolas'.

149   Lecture. 12.[th a]

Friday. Decr. 17. 1762.

Of Composition

Before we[b] enter on the different parts and Species of Composition it will be proper to acquaint you with the method in which we are to proceed.

Every discourse proposes either barely to relate some fact, or to prove some proposition. In the first [is the end][c] the discourse is called a narrative one. The latter is the foundation of two Sorts of Discourse: The Didactick and the Rhetoricall.[1] The former proposes to put before us the arguments on both sides of the question in their true light, giving each its proper degree of influence, and has it in view to perswade no farther than the arguments[d] themselves appear[e] convincing. The Rhetoricall again endeavours by all means to perswade us; and for this
150 purpose it magnifies all the arguments on the one side | and diminishes or conceals those that might be brought on the side conterary to that which it is designed that we should favour. Persuasion[f] which is the primary design in the Rhetoricall is but the secondary design in the Didactick. It endeavours to persuade us only so far as the strength of the arguments is convincing, instruction is the main End. In the other Persuasion is the main design and Instruction is considered only so far as it is subservient to[g] perswasion, and no farther.

{One who was to give an account of any controverted point, as of the disputes about the rights of two princes to a throne, would state the claims of each in the clearest light, and shew their severall foundations in the customs and constitution of the country without being or at least appearing to be any way inclined to the one more than the other. But if one was to plead the Cause of one of the contending parties before some supreme court or another Prince (as Edward was made the Judge betwixt Bruce and Baliol)[2] he would not probably think it his business, nor would it be his duty, to[h] lay the cause open before him, he would give all the strength he could to those arguments that supported his side and soften or pass over with little attention those which made against him.}

---

[a] MS 11th   [b] shall deleted; Before inserted later   [c] added above line   [d] realy (?) deleted   [e] replaces lead us to   [f] replaces That   [g] their deleted   [h] give deleted

---

[1] See i.152 below, and Introduction, p. 14.
[2] Interest in the Great Cause (1292) in early eighteenth-century Scotland is shown by among other things the popularity of John Harvey's epic The Life of Robert Bruce, King of Scots (1729; reprinted several times, in 1769 as The Bruciad: an epic poem). Documents in the Cause: Edward I and the Throne of Scotland, ed. E. L. G. Stones and G. G. Simpson (1978).

[i]There are two different Sorts of facts, one externall, consisting of the transactions that pass without us, and the other internall, towit the thoughts[j] sentiments or designs of men, which pass in their minds. The[k] Design of History, compounded of both of th⟨ese⟩ is to relate the
151 remarkable[l] transactions | that pass in different nations, and the designs, motives and views of[m] the most remarkable men in those times, so far as they are necessary to explain the great changes and revolutions of States which it is intended to relate.

In our observations on this I shall observe the following division. 1[t] I shall consider what facts are proper to be narrated. 2dly In what maner. 3dly How they are to be arranged. 4th In what stile these may be most conveniently expressed. 5^{thly} and lastly What writers have succeeded[n] most happily in all these branches. {As there are two kind⟨s⟩ of objects which may become the subject of description I shall consider first the Description of Simple Objects, first of Simple Visible objects, then of Simple Invisible objects. Then we shall consider the description of compound Visible objects as of an Action; next of compound invisible objects as a character; and last of all of the Historicall Style or description of Actions and Characters.— In treating of which I shall observe 5 things etc.}[o] {We shall then proceed to Didactick and Rhetoricall compositions}[p]

The Distinction made by the ancients [was] came pretty nearly to
152 the same. They divided Eloqu|ence into three Parts, according to the three Species which were most in the use amongst.them. The first they called the Demonstrative, 2^d Deliberative; and 3^d Judicial.[q] {It is rather reverence for antiquity than any great regard for the Beauty or usefullness of the thing itself which makes me mention the Antient divisions of Rhetorick}[r]

The demonstrative is so called not because it was that sort which is used in mathematicall demonstrations but because it was chiefly designed to Demonstrate or Point out the Eloquence of the Orator. This was one of the most early sorts of Eloquence. Discourses of this kind were merely for ostentation delivered in the assemblies of the whole People, and were thence called πανηγυρικοι[s] The Subjects of such discourses were generally[t] the Praises or the discommendation of some particular persons, communities or actions, exhorting the people to or deterring them from some particular conduct. As it was more safe to commend than discommend men or actions, these discourses generally

---

[i] We shall begin with the narative or Historicall *deleted*   [j] or *deleted*   [k] Subjc *deleted*
[l] fact *deleted*   [m] those men who were concerned in bringing about *deleted*   [n] best in
those *deleted*   [o] *Hand B, top of v.150; perhaps belongs after* intended to relate *at end of previous
paragraph*   [p] *Hand B, at top of v.151*   [q] *MS* Jundicall   [r] *Hand B*   [s] As *deleted*
[t] either *deleted*

153 turned^u that way, and hence what we call | Elogiums came to be denominated by the name of Panagerick.

The Deliberative was such as they used in their councils and assemblies on matters of Consequence to the State; and the Judicial was that used in proceedings before a court of Justice.

^{v}In treating of this dis⟨course I shall⟩ proceed in it in the same order as I proposed to follow when I come to treat of historicall discourses. 1st of the Facts, 2^d the manner of treating them, 3^d the arrangement, 4th The Stile, and 5th The Writers.

{We shall begin with the historicall, and the most simple part of it is the narration of one simple fact. These are either externall or internall. After having explained their difference we proceed to shew how they are to be expressed, in what order they are to be arranged and in what expressions the idea of them will be best conveyed. Then we shall treat of the expressing a sentiment, and last of all of describing a character. History comprehends all these and we shall therefore treat of it next.^{w}}

First then we are to treat of the facts that are to be described or
154 related. These as we observed are either externall or internall. | We shall begin with the first as most Simple and easily conceived. Mr Addison observes that^x fact⟨s⟩ may be agreable either from their being grand, new or beautifull.^{3} As those facts^y that are agreable will be apt to make the greatest impression we shall consider them first and then we can easily apply the rules laid down for them to objects of other kinds. The Idea ⟨of⟩ a fact^z that is grand may be conveyed^a in two ways, either by describing it and enumerating various particulars that concern it or by relating the effect that it has on those who behold it. {The first of these viz. describing the thing itself by its Parts I call, for it is necessary to give names to things, direct description, the other indirect.}^{b} Milton^4 makes use of the first method^c in his description of Paradise, and of the 2^d in the account Adam gives the angel of the effect Eves presence had on him. ^{d} He makes use of the first
155 again where he described the view which Satan had of the burning | lake. Shakespear again uses the 2^d Manner in the description of Dover Cliff in King Lear.^{5}

^{u} on *deleted* ^{v} I shall follow this order in *deleted*; this dis *is followed by one and a half blank lines, then* and begin with the demonstrative, as it the most Simple and *deleted* ^{w} ut supra *added at foot* ^{x} a *deleted* ^{y} *replaces* objects ^{z} *replaces* An Object (*not deleted*) ^{a} *replaces* described ^{b} *Hand* B ^{c} *replaces* kind ^{d} *blank of six letters in MS*

^{3} *Spectator*, 412: 'the Sight of what is *Great, Uncommon*, or *Beautiful*'. Ibid. 413: the pleasing imaginative effects of the '*Great, New*, or *Beautiful*'. Cf. the opening sections of Astronomy (EPS 33–47) on wonder, surprise and admiration.

^{4} *Paradise Lost*, iv.205 ff. (but it is Eden 'viewed' by its enemy Satan); viii.596 ff.; i.59 ff.

^{5} *King Lear*, IV.vi.11–24; but the imagined view aims at an effect on Gloucester. The description was much discussed in the eighteenth century, e.g. by Johnson (Boswell's *Life*, ed. Hill-Powell ii.87); Addison, *Tatler* 117.

The manner of Describing an object*e* often makes it agreable when there is nothing in the Object that is so.—There would surely ⟨be⟩ nothing agreable in a picture of a dunghil, neither is the object agreable nor can there be anything extraordinary in painting it. {remember mechanicall part whi} For the same reason it would be altogether unsufferable in prose. It might be tollerable if it was done in good language and flowing verses as it would shew the art of the writer. It might please still more if this was done in Burlesque, but neither here does the pleasure arise from the object itself but from the consideration of the ingenuity*f* of the artist in turning grand and sublime expressions to describe | such an object in an accurate manner. Even when there is no burlesque the applying grand expressions or such as seem not easily applicable to the subject please us from ·the same cause. Thus Mr Greys['s]*g* description of the appearance of Harlequin on the Stage[6] will always be agreable. The art required in adapting the Stile and manner and versification of Spencer to*h* an object so different gives us a great opinion of the capacity and skill of the writer. Had it been in prose there would have been nothing agreable in it as all the art of the author in which alone the beauty of it consists would have been lost.

New objects are never agreable in description merely from being new. There must be something | else*i* in them than mere novelty before they can please us much. New objects may have somewhat agreable when we*j* realy behold them and have them present before us, because then they may strike us with wonder*k*; The whole object is at once*l* conceived; But in Discriptions, the Idea is presented by degrees; The object opens slowly up so that the Surprise cannot be great at the novelty of the object. Mr Addison observes that there is no author who abounds ⟨more⟩ in descriptions of this Sort than Ovid.[7] In his meta⟨mor⟩pho[r]ses*m* every change that happens*n* is described in all its stages; we hear of men with the heads and paws of Bears, women who are beginning to take root in the ground and their*o* hair and hands

156

157

---

e is of *deleted*   *f replaces* art   *g Hand B inserted* Greys *in Hand A's blank ending* s   *h* such a su *deleted*   *i* broibe (?) *deleted*   *j MS* they   *k* ; and *deleted*   *l* the o *deleted*   *m* give *deleted*   *n* to t *deleted*   *o MS* these

[6] Not Grey or Gray. It might be an aural error for Richard Graves (1715–1804), whose friend William Shenstone revived the fashion of Spenserian imitation with *The Schoolmistress* (first version 1737) and wrote on the subject in letters to Graves in the 1740s. But the poems by Graves in Dodsley's *Collection of Poems* iv and v (1755–8) include nothing of this sort.— Harlequin appears in innumerable plays and pantomimes of the time.

[7] *Spectator* 417 defines the art of Ovid in the *Metamorphoses* as the continuous and well-timed exploitation of *novelty*; cf. Addison's notes on his translation of *Metamorphoses* ii–iii in *Works* (Bohn edn), i.139–53.

sprouting into leaves.[8] Mr Addison seems to be pleased with these
158 descriptions, | but to me[p] they don't at all seem pleasing, both for the
reason I already mentiond, and because they are so very much out of
the common course of nature as to shock[q] us by their incredibility. For
my part, when I see Tithonus[9] in a picture with the wings and legs of
grashopper, I feel no pleasure at seeing such an unnaturall and
inconceivable object. Novelty indeed joined to any other quality that
makes an object agreable heightens the pleasure we feel in the
description of it.[r]

p but to me *replaces* for my part   *q* our belief *deleted*   *r v.159* is blank

[8] Examples commented on by Addison: *Met.* ii.477 (Callisto changed to a bear by jealous Juno,
then by Jupiter to a constellation named the Bear); ii.367 ff. (Cycnus to swan); ii.657 ff.
(Ocyrrhoe to mare); ii.346 (Phaeton's sisters the Heliades), i.548 ff. (Daphne), also x.489
(Myrrha), all transformations to trees; ii.542ff. (Coronis to raven); iii.198 ff. (Actaeon to stag).
[9] Tithonus changed by his love Eos (the Dawn) to a grasshopper as the only way of releasing
him from shrunken decrepitude as a man, since she had conferred immortality on him: see J. G.
Fraser's note to Apollodorus, *Bibliotheca*, III.xii.4 ff. on the scholiast to *Iliad*, xi.1 (LCL ii.43).
Pictures such as Smith might have seen have not been identified.

Lecture. 13[a]   Mr Smith.   Monday Dcr 20 1762

That way of expressing any quality of[b] an object which does it by describing the severall parts that constitute the quality we want to express, may be called the direct method. When, again, we do it by describing the effects this quality produces on those who behold it, may be called the indirect method. This latter in most cases is by far the best. We see accordingly Shakespeares descriptions are greatly more animated than those of Spenser. Shakespeare as he wrote in Dialogues had it always in his power to make the persons of the Dialogue relate the effects any object had upon them. Spenser describes every thing directly,[1] and has in adhering to this plan described severall objects direc⟨t⟩ly which no other author attempted in that manner. {Spenser was constrained to take this method because he dealt in Allegoricall Personages without Existence or form but what he conferred on them}[c]

161 Pindar, Homer and Milton[2] never attempt to describe musick | directly, they allways do it by relating the effects it produced on some other creatures, Pindar[3] relates the effects it had not only on the earthly beings but even goes to the Heavens and to Tartarus for objects that might strengthen his description. {Mr Hervey[4] has imitated the passage here mentioned in an extremely beautifull manner[d] but tho the circumstances are as well or perhaps better pointed out than in Pindar yet one chief beauty is lost, by his ommitting the effects of the Musick on Jupiter himself, the thunder bolt falling from his hand and the eagle[s] settling herself at that particular moment on his hand. In the merchant of Venice[5] Musick is described by the effects it produces. The man that hath not musick in himself}[e] But this which none of these Great men ever attempted Spencer has not only attempted but has succeeded in[f]: In the account of the knight of temperance destroying the bower of bliss.[6]

[a] *MS* 12   [b] *last four words replace* describing   [c] *Hand B*   [d] *last five words replace* very excellently   [e] *second sentence is a later addition by Hand A, the third by Hand B*   [f] *it deleted*

[1] This ignores (what would be relevant to Smith's distinction) Spenser's habit of presenting objects as observed by a particular onlooker; hence the prominence of verbs like *sees* and *seems*, and the frequent (dramatic and moral) discrepancy between appearance and reality in *The Faerie Queene*.

[2] On Milton, exceptions might be the conclusion of *L'Allegro*, the canzone *At a Solemn Music*, or celestial music at various points in *Paradise Lost*. See S. Spaeth, *Milton's Knowledge of Music* (Princeton 1913).

[3] *Pythian Ode*, i.1 ff.

[4] John Harvey (see above, i.150 n.2), *A collection of miscellany poems and letters, comical and serious* (1726), 62-4, 'To Sir Richard Steele'.

[5] V.i.71-88.

[6] *The Faerie Queene*, II.xii.70-1. Guyon's destruction of the Bower of Bliss follows, 83 ff.

The describing or expressing internall invisible objects is a matter of far greater difficulty. One would imagine that it would be easy to express an externall one in either of the forementioned ways; But we find it requires no inconsiderable degree of skill to accomplish this into
162 considerable perfection. | But whatever difficulty there is in expressing the externall objects that are the objects of our senses; there must be far greater in describing the internal ones, which pass within the mind itself and are the object of none of our senses. We have here no parts into which we can seperate them nor any by describing which we can convey the notion we desire. {The easiest way of describing an object is by its parts, how then describe those which have no parts}^{g}

The causes of these internall facts, or objects are in like manner either internall or externall. The internall are such dispositions of mind as fit one for that certain passion or affection of mind; and the externall are such objects as produce these effects on a mind so disposed. {There can be but two ways of describing them, by the Effects they produce either on the Body or the mind: both these are indirect}^{h} A mind not ruffled by any violent passions, but calm and tollerably serene; filled with some degree of joy not so great as to withdraw the attention, is
163 that | state of mind in which one is most disposed to admiration. Tis in this state the poets have been when they have burst out into those Raptorous expression⟨s⟩ on the pleasures of a Country life. The Calme tranquill scene it affords would then be most agreable. If any beautifull object is presented to one in these circumstances, he is fixt in the place he was in, his arms fall down loose by his sides, or if the emotion is very violent are laid across his breast, he leans forwards and stretches out his neck, with his eyes fixt on the object and his mouth a little opened. The^i affection he feels is mixt with some degree of desire and hope^j towards^k the object and this inclines to draw nearer towards^k it,
164 imagining | that by coming nearer towards it he will enjoy it in greater perfection. {A Cottage Seen at a Certain distance is an agreable object and we are apt to Suppose the Inhabitants of a Cottage (perhaps contrary to Experience) inno⟨c⟩ent and happy}^{l} This^m affection is most apt to take place in those of an easy pleased temper; but not in one where vanity or selfconceit is predominant; such persons are too much engaged with themselves to be greatly affected with other objects.

Any new object affects one with surprise particularly if it be great and important. This affection does not as the other fix the person to his place but makes him start back, his hands streatched out and his eyes staring. The turn of mind most fitted to this is when ^{n} If the

^{g} *Hand* B ^{h} *Hand* B ^{i} *passion deleted* ^{j} *numbers written above change the original order* hope *and* desire ^{k} *in hopes deleted* ^{l} *Hand* B ^{m} *passion deleted* ^{n} *blank of six letters in MS*

Object is grand he is fixt to his place, but does not as in the first case desire to approach the object, he rather inclines to draw back. This is what we properly call admiration. It does not partake of hope or desire but rather of a reverential awe and respect, that gives one a fear of
165 dis|pleasing. {Surprise is most violent on their first beholding the object, but admiration gradually increases, comes to its greatest height and again decreases.} The turn of mind that inclines one most to this is[o]

Other passions affect the body still more violently and distort it in different ways. We do not mean that all these should be described but only such as are most striking and distinguishing.[p] The different passions all proceed in like manner from different states of mind and outward circumstances. But it would be both endless and useless to go thro' all these different affections and passions in this manner. It would be endless, because tho the simple passions are[q] of no great number, yet these are so compounded in different manners as to make a number of
166 mixt ones almost infinite. It would be useless, for tho we | had gone thro all the different affections yet the difference of character and age and circumstances of the person would so vary the affects that our rules would not be at all applicable. Grief is the passion that affects Mezentius, Evander and the mother of Euryalus,[7] but its effects on them are very different. Mezentiuss[r] at the same time[s] {In Mezentius the Effect it produces on a ferocious Tyrant abandond by his Subjects, pursued by the Venegance of heaven, is a contumacious fury and despair. [t] The Grief of Evander was perfect Weakness such as naturally became an old man who had lived in Innocence and Simplicity}[u] Evander is affected with a plain simple grief, The mother of Euryalus displays a sort of vivacity in her grief[v] common to that sex after they have passed a certain age; their passions[w] seem then (conterary to what happens to men) to have acquired greater strength
167 and accuteness than they had before. | {This diversity of the same affection in different characters is finely instanced in the Sentiments of our first Parents on quitting Paradise[8]—Eve she regrets Leaving the flowers and Walks and chief the Nuptial Bower—Adam in a very sublime passage the Scenes where he had conversed with God}[x]

The addition of certain objects tending to the same point are often of

[o] *blank of two and a half lines in MS* [p] The no *deleted* [q] *replaces* be [r] is that of one *deleted* [s] ra (*for* '*rages*'?), *then almost two lines blank* [t] *blank of six letters in MS* [u] *Hand B* [v] conterary to *deleted* [w] their passions *replaces* they then [x] *Hand B*

[7] Aeneid, x.833–908; on Mezentius' hateful character, viii.481 ff. Evander: xi.148–81. The dead Euryalus apostrophised by his grieving mother: ix.475–502.

[8] *Paradise Lost*, xi.268–85 and 315–29 respectively.

great benefit. The L'allegro of Milton and his Il penseroso are^j set out to great advantage by the various additional personages joined in the Scene.— These additionall objects may be of three kinds, 1st such as are immediately effected by the principall objects and tend to give strength to the design in View. 2dly Such as are not produced by the principall object but are connected with it and are of the same kind and tend to produce the same emotion^z and 3dly Such as neither are affected by the object nor are connected with it, but are^a some way suitable to the main design and tend to produce the same emotion.

168 When Vi⟨rgil⟩^{b} describes the tumbling of a torrent down a Rock | he strengthens the Picture by describing a traveller astonished and surprised on^c hearing it below him.^{9} The Rocks themselv⟨es⟩ broken, steep, and hanging over the ground is an object very agreable in a country scene. Titian often added a goat climbing on these rocks to his pleasant^d landscapes; this added greatly to the agreablenes of the Rocks,^{e} but when he drew the Shepherd lying along on the ground and diverting himself with beholding its motions, he made a great addition to the mirth and pleasure of the piece. The Humming of a swarm of Bees and the cooing of a turtle give us ideas agreable and soothing, but this is greatly hightned when Virgil describes Meliboeus^{10} lulled a sleep

169 by their soothing sound. These are examples | of the first kind where the additionall objects are affected by the principall one.^{f} (We may observe here that a landscape is where the chief object is the innanimate or irrationall part, and a historicall where the human figures are designed chiefly to attract our attention.) The 2^d Method is that which Milton makes use of in his L'allegro. The Mi⟨l⟩kmaid singing along, and the mower sharping his Scythe^{11} etc. do not immediately respect the landscape^g described but are^h connected with it and tend to excite the same^i emotion. {Salvator} Rosa^j has drawn many Landscapes^k in which the Rocks, Cascades, Woods and

170 Mountains make | objects. Here he often places a philosopher meditating under the shade of the^l mountain, a magician at the mouth of a cavern, and a Hermit amidst the desarts and Forests. Here neither the Philosop⟨h⟩er is contemplating the mountain, the magician the cavern, nor the Hermit the Desert. But these objects are connected

---

^{y} all *deleted* 　　 ^{z} and tend to pro *wrongly deleted* 　　 ^{a} of the *deleted* 　　 ^{b} *blank in MS*
^{c} *written over* at 　　 ^{d} objects *deleted* 　　 ^{e} *last nine words replace* of itself is a pleasant object
^{f} For *deleted* 　　 ^{g} bef *deleted* 　　 ^{h} of the *deleted* 　　 ^{i} idea *deleted* 　　 ^{j} *inserted by Hand B in blank left*
^{k} of *deleted* 　　 ^{l} object *deleted*

---

　^{9} Perhaps *Aeneid*, ii.304–8: but 'stupet inscius . . . pastor', not 'viator'. The simile imitates *Iliad* iv.452 ff.
　^{10} *Eclogues*, i.54–6.
　^{11} *L'Allegro*, 65–6.

together and excite the same emotion. {A Philosopher Reading on a Book}[m] The Philosopher adds to the awfull majestick appearance of the mountain, the magician to the Gloomy horror of the Cavern. The Hermit tends to excite in a strong degree the emotions we are apt to conceive at the sight of a desert.—Solitude gives us an idea of
171 something | very awfull, we imagine that some Superior beings are generally present in such places, and when we do not see them we conceive them to ⟨be⟩ present tho invisible. The fairies, Nymphs, Fawns, Satyrs, Dryads and such divinities were all inhabitants of the[n] Forest. {If they are ever brought into the City it is in the Silence of the Night which is a species of Solitude}[o] In such places all communication with superior beings is conceived to be had; Propheticall inspirations and Revelations have all been given in solitude. It was not in the Palaces of Troy but on the Solitary mountain of Ida that the Goddesses are said to have presented themselves to Paris. By this means Hermits and other religious persons are fit additions to such solitary places where we would have an awfull and gloomy emotion[p] excited.

{Poussin in his night piece has added the story of Pyr⟨amus⟩ and Thisbe, as of the same sort with the rest, but here there is no connection and the unsuitableness renders the effect not very agreable. The same he has done in[q] others where he has brought in the history of Phocion. This sort where there is no connection seems proper in historicall paintings because[r]}

172 | {We shall now give some generall rules for the description of Objects and 1st The whole[s]} of the objects described should tend to excite the same emotion otherwise the end will not be answered. Where the chief design is to excite mirth and chearfullness nothing should be brought in that is gloomy or horrible, and on the other hand where we would raise awfull grand sentiments the whole must tend that way. Miltons L alleg and Il p {Penseroso}[t] answer exactly to this rule. Thomson seems frequently to have[u] broke throw it. The Plan he laid down of giving an account of the Seasons often lead him[v] to describe objects of different and conterary natures. By which means his descriptions tho sometimes good enough lose their effect, in raising any strong emotion.[w]

173 | 2d Another thing that is necessary is that the description should be short and not taedious by its length. But here there is a difficulty, to

[m] *Hand B* [n] des *deleted* [o] If . . . is *in Hand A the rest in Hand B* [p] of *deleted* [q] *replaces* with [r] -cause *stands alone at top of v.171 blank of six letters in MS* [s] 1st The whole *repeated at beginning of 172* [t] *Hand B* [u] brought *deleted* [v] in *deleted* [w] They ought all to have been arranged in such an order as not to have contrasted one another but tended to the same end *at top of 173, deleted, with five blank lines before* 2d Another thing that is. . . .

attain this conciseness and at the same time bring in those circumstances which give a description vivaciety and force. This may

174 often be accomplished by picking out some of the most curious and | striking circumstances, which may suggest the others to the reader. This Virgil has done excellently in the description of the death of an Argive commander where he says

Sternitur[x] et Dulces moriens meminiscitur Argos—A Poet of less merit would have made him express all the tender sentiments this naturally suggests to the reader[12]. This Thomson has done in the description of the man dying in the Snow.[13]

v.172 | {3[d] A 3[d] Direction may be, that, We should not only[y] make our circumstances all of a piece, but it is often proper to Choose out some niece and Curious ones. A Painter in Drawing a fruit[z] makes the figure very striking if he not only gives it the form and Colour but also represents the fine down with which it is covered. The Dew on Flowers in the same manner gives the figure a striking resemblance. In the same manner in description we ought to choose out some minute circumstances which concur in the general emotion we would excite and at the same time but little attended to. Such circumstances are always attended with a very con⟨si⟩derable effect.}[a]

Conciseness in the expression may also be attained consistently with the Strength of the imagery if every member of a sentence represent

175 one | at least and if possible two or three different Circumstances. This makes the description still more lively. Thus in Milton Il pen and L'all almost every word tends to convey some idea suited to the Subject, and the same may be seen in Virgils account of the horse dying in the Murrian.[14]

{Another direction is that the Circumstance Pointed out be a Curious one, and if such as is not subject to common observation then it will be sure to strike. Thus we are greatly pleased with those Paintings of flowers or fruits which represent the down or the dew, which is not what is commonly observed altho to it the fruit and flowers owe their Lustre}[b]

---

[x] in humum *deleted*   [y] choose out *deleted*   [z] ine *deleted*   [a] *v.172 note is keyed in after* in the Snow *by a caret*   [b] *Hand B, bottom half of* 175

---

[12] Wounding of Antores; *Aeneid*, x.781–2 reads
            sternitur infelix alieno vulnere, caelumque
            aspicit et dulcis moriens reminiscitur Argos.
[13] *Seasons*, Winter, 276–317 (as in 1730–46 editions).
[14] *Georgics*, iii.498–502. Cf. the ox's death at iii.515 ff.

Wednesday
176 Lecture. 14^a Mr Smith.   Decr. 22^d 1762

Having given some generall rules for the description of objects, I shall now proceed to give some particular rules for the description of different sorts of objects. These are indeed the former applied to particular cases, and are no more than common sense dictates to any man tho' he had never heard there was such a rule.

Objects are either corporeal or incorporeal.—Corporeal objects are, again, either Naturall or Artificial. Natural objects may be considered as of two Sorts. Either 1st Such as exist compleatly at the same time, or 2^d Such as subsist in a succession of incidents.

1st In describing such Natural^b objects as exist altogether at the same moment as Prospects, it is not necessary that we should arrange the 177 objects, but | describe them in any order we find easiest. Milton does this in his Description of Paradise[1] and in his L'allegro and Il penseroso. When authors attempt to arrange the objects in such descriptions, the reader endeavours to arrange them in the^c same manner in the idea he forms of the thing described, and is always at a loss to follow it out, as no words can convey an accurate idea of the arrangement of objects unless they be assisted by a Plan. {Such descriptions Require all the attention and Exertion of Mind which is required by a Mathematicall Demonstration}^{d}. Pliny has given us a Description of his Villa[2] in this manner, with great minuteness. But notwithstanding his great exactness his commentators are not at all agreed with regard to the situation of the severall objects described, each has formed a different plan according to the way in which he 178 arranged them in his mind. And I believe if any unprejudized | person were to read the description he would form an arrangement^e of the severall objects in his mind, different from what either of them has given us. {The later Sophists often make use of such descriptions as these. As Achilles Tatius^f etc. They deal very much in description and tell you that on the Right hand was a wood, on the Left a rock and so on}

Mr Balzac^g has in imitation of Pliny given us an account of his Villa

---

^{a} MS 13 ^{b} replaces Corporeal ^{c} written over like ^{d} Hand B ^{e} different deleted; numbers written above confirm the changed order ^{f} MS Statius; Hand A wrote Hercules, Hand B substituted Achilles but left Statius; the next sentence is in Hand B ^{g} Hand B's correction of Blenac

[1] Paradise Lost, iv.205 ff. Cf. i.154 n.4 above.
[2] Letters, V.6. For Achilles Tatius see i.184 n.10 below.

and the[h] arrangement of the severall objects in it.[3] I believe that if it be Mr Balzacs[i] fate to be an ancient and have commentators, they won't agree a whit better thanPlinys have done. The Earl of Buckingham has given a very accurate description of his house and Gardens in a letter to Mr Pope.[4] Yet tho it be very exact and done in an extremely lively maner, any one who sees Buckingham house will find it very different
179 from the idea he had formed from the de|scription.

When therefore we describe a naturall object which can be comprehended in one view we need not be at great pains with regard to the arangement as the reader will arrange them to himself in the manner which suits his taste best; and will not be perplex'd by the arrangement[j] we have given, which will never be sufficient without the assistance of a Plan to give a just notion of the Thing Described.

2[d] If the[k] Circumstances regarding the object to be described are not existent in the same moment, we should deliver them in the same succession as that[l] they existed in. As Virgill does in his Description of the Murrain.[5] This is evident otherwise the order would impose on the Reader.

180 | 3[d] Artificial objects are either intirely the contrivance of men or they are made in imitation of the works of nature. In describing the former {I mean in Poetical descriptions} it is much better to follow the indirect than the Direct description. We form a much better idea of these works from the effects they have on the beholder than by any description of their severall parts. Mr Addison has described St Peters[6] at Rome in this manner, and we form a more distinct notion of the size and proportions ⟨of⟩ that Building from his account than if he had gone to describe each part and given us the most exact dimensions. {without a plan}[m]

4 On the other hand if the objects are imitations of nature they can
181 not be described too minutely | for it is in the exact Symetry and the stableness[n] of the severall parts that the excellence of such productions

---

[h] sev *deleted*   [i] *MS* Blenacs   [j] *replaces* description   [k] Objects *deleted*   [l] *replaces* what   [m] *Hand B*   [n] *first three letters overwritten and illegible:* nobleness.? But *synonym of* exactness *is needed; see 185 foot*

---

[3] Jean-Louis Guez de Balzac (1597–1654): *Lettres* (1624), I.xxxi, Sept. 1622, to Jacques de La Motte Aigron; I.15 in W. Tirwhyt's English translation (1634).

[4] John Sheffield Duke of Buckingham, *Works* (1723), ii.275–87, letter to the Duke of Shrewsbury of which Buckingham sent Pope a copy. Pope replied half-mockingly with an elaborate description of Stanton Harcourt where he was staying in the summer of 1718, and sent an almost identical fanciful account to Lady Mary Wortley Montagu: printed in Pope's *Works* (1737) and in *The Correspondence of Alexander Pope*, ed. G. Sherburn (1956), i.505–11.

[5] *Georgics*, iii.478–566; cf. i.175 n.14 above.

[6] *Remarks on several parts of Italy* (1705; see Bohn edn of *Works*, i.417–18).

consist. Lucians description of Appelles's[u] Painting[7] of the marriage of
Alexander and Roxana is admirable in this way, he gives us a compleat
notion of the whole piece. But if he had wrote[p] on purpose to describe
that picture, and had not mentioned ⟨it⟩ only to illustrate another
subject he would (as he himself hints) have entered much more
minutely in to the severall parts and not only given us an account of
the generall scheme of the piece, but of the chief Lines and Colouring
of every figure in it.

5 Internall objects as passions and affections can be well described
182 only by their effects; these again either internall | or externall.—The
best Rule that can ⟨be⟩ given in this head seems to be that if the passion
is very violent and agitates the person to any high degree, the best
method is to describe it by the externall effects it produces, and these
ought to be enumerated pretty fully and in the most striking and
expressive manner. {The Sentiments which a Violent Passion excites in
the mind are too tumultuous and rapid for your description to keep
pace with}[q]—On the other hand when the passion is less violent we
must have recourse to the internall effects; the externall ones are not
strong enough nor sufficiently remarkable to point out the state of the
persons mind and[r] characterise the passion he feels.—The enumeration
of circumstances also in this case should neither be very full nor very
particular. One or two well chosen[s] often are more expressive than a
183 greater number less striking.—Virgill has | described the passion of
Dido in the departure of Æneas in a very ⟨different manner⟩[t] from that
of Æneas on the same occasion.[8] Her[u] bitter anguish is admirably
pointed[r] out by a great variety of circumstances all externall and very
nicely chosen. The Grief of Æneas again as he does not seem to have
been so deeply affected is expressed by a few well chosen circumstances, and these all internall. The Cause of the Passion may sometimes
be[u] brought in to advantage but is seldom sufficient to characterise it
without the addition of some of its effects.

Homer and Virgil both describe the Joy of Latona on seeing her

---

[u] Apelles *added by Hand B in space left, ending* 's   [p] *replaces* been writing   [q] *Hand B*
[r] distinguish *deleted*   [s] ones *deleted*   [t] *supplied conjecturally*   [u] violent Grief and *deleted*
[v] *MS* painted   [w] well *deleted*

---

[7] Not Apelles but Aëtion, whose most famous painting, the marriage of Alexander and Roxana,
is discussed by Lucian in *Herdotus or Aëtion*, i.e. the virtues of historian versus the painter's (LCL
vi.141–52). Daniel Webb in *An Inquiry into the Beauties of Painting; and into the Merits of the most
celebrated Painters, ancient and modern* (1760), 193–5, draws on Lucian in contrasting the boldness
and novelty of ancient painters' effects as contrasted with the clutter of minutiae in the work of
the moderns.

[8] *Aeneid*, iv.362–87 and 333–61 respectively.

daughter preferred to other Oreads,[x] by a single expression, and this[y]
184 readily suggests the state of mind she was in.— | We may here observe
that[z] Virgils description is somewhat more exact than[a] Homers.[9] That
author barely says she[b] γεγηθεν φρηνα an expression he uses to denote
any kind of joy, and often applies in a very different sense as when he
says γεγηθεν δε ποιμην. Virgil again points out in a very delicate
manner the kind of joy she fel⟨t⟩. Those nice and delicate emotions
were either not greatly felt or not much attended to in[c] the age of the
Greek Poet.

6. In Describing naturall objects we should not introduce two
circumstances the one of which is included in the other. {Such
Circumstances as necessarily Suggest one another may bee called
Synonymes}[d] The modern Sophists as Hercules Statius[e] and   [f]
Apuleius etc. are often guilty of this[10]. They will tell us that a man who
185 leant forwards | had one foot placed before another, if he leant his head
to one Side [to one Side,] they tell us he leant his body to the other.[g]
The latter of these circumstances is included in the other and would be
easily conceived from it. They were probably led to this manner of
description by seeing that those authors whose descriptions were most[h]
admired followed it. But they did not consider that those authors
described imitations of nature and not natural objects. This last species
of writing was greatly ⟨used⟩[i] in the time of Trajan and the Antonines;
and in it as we observed before the excellency ⟨is⟩ in relating every
particular, as it is in the exactness and symmetry of them that the
excellence of the workmanship consists.

186 | The Abbe du Bos[11] in his description of the Statue of the slave
who discovered the conspiracy amongst the Romans, describes every
particular attitude; But if he had been to describe the Posture of the
Slave himself, he would have told us that he stood[j] listening to what he
heard them talking of, but at the same time so as[k] to seem minding his
work tho in reality he had given it up for that time.

---

[x] *inserted by Hand B in blank left*   [y] is alto *deleted*   [z] Homer *deleted*   [a] *MS* then
[b] was *deleted*   [c] *replaces* by   [d] *Hand B*   [e] *i.e. Achilles Tatius*   [f] *blank of fourteen letters in*
MS   [g] when *deleted*   [h] *to be deleted*   [i] *supplied conjecturally*   [j] *in the deleted*   [k] not
deleted

[9] *Aeneid*, i.502, 'Latonae tacitum pertemptant gaudia pectus', based on *Odyssey*, vi.106 (γέγηθε
δέ τε φρένα Λητώ); *Iliad*, viii.559 has the same phrase with ποιμήν.

[10] Achilles Tatius (who puzzled the scribe also at i.178 above) was the second-century AD
author of the romance *Leucippe and Cleitophon*, remarkable for the minuteness of its descriptions of
things and persons. His contemporary Apuleius wrote the satiric *Golden Ass*, based on *Lucius the
Ass*, perhaps by Lucian.

[11] *Réflexions critiques sur la poésie et sur la peinture* (1719), i.sec.38. Du Bos cites Livy, ii.4; Juvenal,
viii.266. The figure is 'le *Rotateur* ou l'Aiguiseur', the Grinder. Thomas Nugent (1748 translation)
quotes Juvenal in G. Stepney's version.

7. We ought not only to avoid these circumstances that include one another which we may call synonymous circumstances but also those ⟨that⟩ are conterary to the nature of the object we would describe. Thus when a modern Poet*[l]* describes the appearance of a mountain to
87 those | who saw it at a distance from Sea, he tells us they saw it appear black, which could not be the real appearance of a mountain at a distance as it is tinged of a bluish white by the Colour of the atmosphere.—Those who think themselves bound to describe when they are very ill*[m]* qualified and know little of the object they would describe are most apt to fall into this error.

8.*[n]* It would appear needless to guard you against using*[o]* epithets that are contradictory or not applicable to the object, if we did not find that some of the Greatest English writers have fallen into it, in many places.
88 Mr Pope frequently applies adjectives to | substantives with which they can not at all agree, as when he speaks of the *brown horror of the groves*[12]

> {deepens the murmurs of the falling floods
> and shades a browner horror ore the Woods}*[p]*

Brown joined to horror conveys no idea at all.—Thomson is often guilty of this fault and Shakespeare almost continually.

---

[l] modern Poet *inserted by Hand B in blank left*   *[m]* MS all   . *[n]* MS 7   *[o]* circumsta *deleted*
[p] Hand B

---

[12] *Eloisa to Abelard*, 169–70 reads:

> Deepens the murmur of the falling floods,
> And breathes a browner horror on the woods.

The phrase is borrowed from Dryden: '. . . the lambent easy light / Gild the brown horror, and dispel the night' (*The Hind and the Panther*, 1230–1); '. . . a wood / Which thick with shades and a brown horror stood' (*Aeneid*, vii.40–1). Cf. Pope, *The First Book of Statius his Thebais* (1712), 516: 'Thro' the brown Horrors of the Night he fled'. Thomson's synaesthesia has already been criticised at i. v.68 above.

Lecture 15th ^a   *Mr Smith.*   Friday, Decr 24
                                                    1762

Having made some observations on the descriptions [on the descrip-
tion] of objects in generall and given some directions for the describing
Simple objects whether^b internall or externall, I shall proceed in the
next place to give some observations on the proper manner of
describing more complex objects. These are either the characters of
189   men or the more grand and impor|tant actions and conduct of men. I
shall begin with the first as it is Chiefly the character and disposition of
a man that gives rise to his particular conduct and behaviour, and the
manner of describing ⟨the⟩ former will be better understood when the
causes of it are first considered.

   A character,[1] then, may be described either directly or indirectly.
When we describe a character directly we relate the various parts of
which it consists, what mixture of each particular passion or turn of
mind there is in the person. To do this in any tollerable degree of
perfection requires great skill, deep penetration, an accurate observation and almost perfect knowledge of men. Accordingly we find that
very few of the ancients have attempted to describe characters in this
190   manner altogether. Sallust has described the character of | Cataline[2] in
this manner. Tacitus too tho' he seldom sets himself on purpose to give
us an account of a mans character yet generally give⟨s⟩ som⟨e⟩ strong
lines of it at first, which are illustrated afterwards by the many
reflections he afterwards make⟨s⟩ on each persons conduct, and the
pains he is at to discover and explain the motives of his conduct.

   This way is seldom sufficient, unless remarkably well executed, to
give us a just notion of the character; the general distinctions do not
serve alone to distinguish the character we describe from others
perhaps a good deal different. It is not so much the degree of Virtue or
Vice, probity or dishonesty, Courage or Timidity that form the
distinguishing part of a character, as the tinctures which these severall
191   parts have received in | forming his character.

   ^c{Turrene and Saxe[3] were both perhaps equalls in Courage, but the

---

^a *MS* 14th   ^b *MS* whather   ^{c c} *interpolation on v.189; the last sentence is in Hand B*

[1] On the Character see Introduction, p. *17.*
[2] *Bellum Catilinae* v. This sketch is compared with Cicero's in *In Catilinam* at i.194 below.
[3] Henri de la Tour d'Auvergne, Vicomte de Turenne (1611–75), described by pre-Napoleonic
Frenchmen as the greatest commander of modern times; grandson of William I Prince of Orange.
Hermann Maurice, Comte de Saxe (1696–1750). They were two of the only three pre-
Revolutionary Maréchaux de France: Turenne from 1660, Saxe from 1744. Pope includes the
'god-like' Turenne among his dead heroes (he was killed at Sassbach) in the *Essay on Man*, iv.100,
and Retz praises him in *Mémoires* (1723 edn, i.218). Cf. *TMS* VI.iii.28.

activity of the one and the caution of the other made their characters
very different. In our own Country, Cromwell and Montrose who lived
in the same period were I believe of equally military skill, but the open
boldness of the one and the suspicious designing temper of the other
sufficiently distinguished them.

Men do not differ so much in the degrees of Virtue and Wisdom as in
the Peculiar Tinges which these may Receive from the other
Ingredients of their Character}[c]

The Abbe[d] Rhetz is one of the chief writers amongst the moderns
who has followed this method, his characters a few excepted are all
drawn in this manner. His method is to set before us the different
passions and inclinations, aversions and desires of the person whose
character he would give us, and the different proportions[e] which each
of them bears to the others.

{The method followed by Cardinall du Retz was that of describing a
character as it Existed in the person, and he had perhaps in this
Excelled all others had it not been for some affectation and too much
Subtelety: for example who can have any Idea of his Strange character
of Anne of Austria,[i] that too of Madoemosselle Chevreuse is disfigured
by its Conclusion}[f]

This manner of writing as it requires very nice observation, and as it
can not give us a just Idea of the character described unless it be by
pointing out very nice and minute particularities, has frequently lead
those who followed it into too great refinements[g] in the description of
their characters. The Abbe shews frequently to have fallen into errors
of this Sort; and Tacitus too seems often to have had recourse to Causes
92 | too minute and too trivial, in order to account for the conduct of the
persons he has occasion particularly to insist on.—Many of the
characters drawn by the Abbe are altogether *unintelligible*; Some from
     [h] and others from an ill tim'd affectation. His character of the

---

[d] M. la Bruyers *written above and deleted*   [e] *replaces* degrees in   [f] *Hand B*   [g] both
deleted   [h] *blank of about twelve letters in MS*

---

[i] Jean François Paul de Gondi, Cardinal de Retz (1614–79): *Mémoirs*, 1717. Hands A and B are
reporting his descriptions of the same two ladies. Anne d'Autriche became Queen of France in
marrying Louis XIII in 1615. Hand B's note corrects Hand A's deleted guess 'Madame de
Nivers', which is difficult to account for, unless the Duchesse de Nevers (of Louis XIV's court) has
somehow become involved in the confusion. The Queen's is the first of a 'galerie de portraits',
seventeen in all; it consists of a series of twelve comparative pairs of qualities, the pattern being:
'Elle avoit plus d'aigreur que de hauteur, plus de hauteur que de grandeur, plus de maniere que
de fond . . .'. The brief characterisation of the demoiselle de Chevreuse ends with the criticised
witticism: 'La passion lui donnoit de l'esprit et même du serieux et de l'agréable, uniquement
pour ceulis qu'elle aimoit; mais elle le traitoit bien-tôt comme ses juppes, qu'elle mettoit dans son
lit, quand elles lui plaisoient, et qu'elle brûloit par une pure aversion deux heures après'. Her
mother, described at greater length just before, took her lovers much more seriously: she scorned
all scruples and 'devoirs' except that 'de plaire à son amant' (1723 edn, 214, 221, 220).

Queen of France is an instance of the first,[5] and the character of
      ⁱ of the 2.^d Who can make any thing of this character? cried I*^j* on
reading the first. The 2^d on the other hand is entirely spoiled and*^k* is
almost deprived of any meaning by the misapplyed witticism with
which it is concluded.— — — —

The indirect description of a character is when we do not enumerate
its severall component parts, but relate the effects it produces on the
193 outward behaviour and Conduct of the person.—Now | the first
⟨which⟩ strikes one in seeing a person whom they had not before
known is not the prevalency of any part of his temper but the air of the
man as we call it; this it is which first gives one an opinion of a man
whether it be ill or whether it be good. But this air is a matter of so
simple a nature that it can hardly admit of description; and
accordingly no one has attempted it.—We must therefore have
reccourse to the more particular effects of the character; and this may
be done either by relating the Generall tenor of conduct which the
person follows, which we may call the generall method, or by
descending into particulars and pointing out how he would act in such
and such instances: this we may call the particular method.

194 The General method is that in which | Mon^{sr} La Bruyer[6] has wrote
the greatest part of his characters.—This manner differs from the
direct manner as it does not relate the generall principles that govern
the conduct of men, but tells us in what manner those principle⟨s⟩
when brought into action influence the Generall conduct of the man.
{La Bruyeres character of a discontented man may be taken as an
Example of his favourite manner. Had Theophrastus[7] been to describe
it he would probably have done it thus}*^l* The difference betwixt these
two methods will be more clearly seen if we should compare the
description of the character of Cataline by Sallust, with that of the
same person drawn by Cicero. The first is in the direct way and the
latter in the Generall indirect one. We will see likewise by this
comparison that the latter is considerably more interesting and gives us
a fuller view of the character.

ⁱ Madame de Nivers *deleted, then a blank of fourteen letters in MS*   *^j* on feading (?) *deleted*
^k rendered *deleted*   *^l* Hand B

⁵ See n.4 above.
⁶ Jean de la Bruyère (1645–96): *Caractères de Théophraste traduits du grec, avec les Caractères ou les Moeurs de ce siècle*, 1688–94. Démophile, the *frondeur* or anti-establishment man, was added in the 6th edition, 1691 (section 'Du Souverain', X.11): 'Démophile se lamente, et s'écrie: Tout est perdu, c'est fait de l'État; il est du moins sur le penchant de sa ruine . . .'. Contrasted with Basilide the *anti-frondeur*.
⁷ Theophrastus (c.370–288/285 BC), pupil and successor of Aristotle. The publication of his lately discovered *Characters* by Casaubon in 1592 began the vogue of this form in western literatures. See Introduction, p. 17.

Theophrastus is one of the chief who have given us characters drawn
95 | in the particular manner. He always begins his characters with a
definition of the character he is to describe and then gives us a
description of it by telling us in what manner the person of that
character would act in such and such circumstances. This manner tho'
perhaps not always most proper is generally the most interesting and
agreable. Insomuch that tho La Bruyer has drawn his characters in
many different manners sometimes he laughs at the person he
characterizes, sometimes expostulates with him and sometimes gives
him serious advice; yet notwithstanding of this variety of methods,
there is perhaps none of them all so agreable as that of Theophrastus.
{We may observe that it would be no difficult matter to turn one of
Theop⟨hrast⟩us characters into the manner of Bruyer: the circumstances are so well chosen as readily to suggest the generall character;
But on the other hand it would be very difficult to express one of La
Bryers in the manner of Theo⟨phrastus⟩. It being a very nice matter to
pick out single instances[m] that sufficiently mark out the generall
character we would describe.}
Accordingly we find that Theophrastus is generally more read
than La Bruyer; Nay this method is so far superior with respect to the
96 pleasure it gives that the only character | La Bruyer has drawn in that
manner {viz. that of Menalcas[8] the absent man} tho perhaps worse
done than any of the others is more admired than any of them.
{Mutato nomine de te fabula narratur, said Mr Herbert of Mr
Smith.} Tho it has less variety and less spirit than perhaps any of the
rest, yet   [n] has thought it deserved to have a commedy founded
on the plan of it: none of the others have been honoured in this
manner, tho' there are few that do not deserve it as well. {or better}[o]
{This comedy was wrote by Mr   [p] a Comic Writer of Secondary
Rank an Imitator of Moliere's and no bad one} {There is a Certain
order and arrangement in the Pictures exhibited by Bruyere which the
least alteration of any member of it would destroy. But Theophrastus's
are Tumbled together without much arrangement and that
Circumstance which Concludes the whole might have stood first}

[m] *of deleted*   [n] *blank of seven letters in MS*   [o] *inserted after* well *by Hand B, who wrote the next*
two notes on v.195   [p] *blank of nine letters in MS*

[8] Ménalque, La Bruyère's best known character, was added in his 6th edition, 1691 (section 'De
l'homme', xi.7). La Bruyère noted: 'Ceci est moins un caractère particulier qu'un recueil de faits
de distraction'. It is said to be modelled on the Comte de Brancas. Smith's use of the classical form
of the name (Virgil, *Eclogues* iii,v) suggests that he may have referred his students to the English
translation of La Bruyère (1699 and reprints). 'Absent' has the common eighteenth-century
meaning 'absent-minded' (cf. La Bruyère's *distraction*); and the student Herbert—see
Introduction, p. 5—has by the tag from Horace's *Satires*, I.i.69–70 equated the character with his
professor. The comedy referred to is unidentified.

If we were to state a comparison of the excellence of these 3 methods of describing a character, we might perhaps give the preference in point of agreableness to that of Theophrastus. But in writing a history it would probably be the best method to describe the character in the same order as the different views of a character naturally present themselves to us. That is, first to give an account of the prevailing

197 temper and passions of the man, as soon | as he is brought into the scheme of the history and afterwards to give such observations on his conduct as will open up the generall principles on which he acts. {to give an account of his disposition and the generall Manner in which it lead him to act, reserving the particulars to be interwoven in the Subsequent Narration}[q] The particular manner would but ill suit the dignity of a history; A number of particular actions perhaps very trifling ones thrown all together gives a work the appearance of a commedy or a Satyre, and it is in such works only that it can be applyed with propriety. The Characters of Theophrastus[r] tho very agreable, yet have so great a Similarity both in their Plan and execution that they soon fatigue us. Bruyers again have a great deal of variety and Elegance. They of all works of this sort are most proper for those who would Study the Rhetorical art and are extremely well worth reading.

{His Book abounds with a Species of Reflexions equally distant from Trite and unentertaining ones as from the Paradoxicall ones at present so much in Vogue among authors—La Bruyeres are Sufficiently obvious at first View yet such as would not readily have occurred to one}[s]

198 | The same methods[t] that are proper to describe a Particular character are also applicable to that of a nation or body of men. La Bruyer[u] has also given us characters of severall nations and particular professions and ways of life as the Courtier etc. drawn in the same manner as those of persons. In describing the character of a nation The Government may be considered in the same view as the air of a single person; The Situation, Climate, Customs as those peculiarities which give a distinguishing tincture to the character, and form the same generall out lines into[v] very different appearances.

These authors I have mentioned are the chief who have excelled in the describing of characters. Lord Clarendon likewise in his history is at great pains to give us the characters of the severall persons as they

199 appear in it. This he does by narrating[w] the different circumstances | of

q Hand B, foot of v.195   *r replaces* Telemachus   *s Hand B, opposite* fatigue us *towards end of previous paragraph*   *t replaces* rules; *of deleted*   *u Hand B deleted* La Bruyer *and wrote* wrong *beneath*   *v* a *deleted*   *w replaces* telling us their past Life, their Education and the advances or declining State of their fortunes, and from thence indeavours to collect their character, in a manner nearly allied to the direct method. Tho he has not the penetration requisite for excelling in this way yet his being personally acquainted with the most of those whom he describes makes it almost impossibl⟨e⟩ that he should miss some circumstances that will give us at least a tollerable Idea of the persons charackter. There is always something in a character which will make an impression on those who are of ones intimate acquaintance and which they will readily express so as to make it known to others.

{An Instance of this may be seen in his character of The Earl of Arundell and Pembroke.

The Great fault we are apt to fall into in the description of characters is the making them so Generall that they Exhibit no Idea at all: who for example can form any Idea of Lord Falkland from the Character which Clarendon gives him.⁹

To avoid thisˣ there ought to be always some particular and distinguishing Circumstance annexed such as that description of Agricola¹⁰ by Tacitus. You would have | known him by his Look to be a good man, you would have rejoiced to have found him a great one. In fact when you would do honour to and perpetuate the memory of a friend you must take care not to ascribe to him those contrary Virtues which the Comprehension of the humane mind is too narrow to take in at once}.ʸ

Burnet¹¹ in the characters he gives us is so biting and sarcastical that he is not at all pleasing; he gives us a worse idea of his friends than Clarendon does of his very enemiesᶻ; this latter | whatever we may think of him as a historian certainly deserve⟨s⟩ our Love as a Man.

99

•00

ˣ *MS* the   ʸ *Hand B, on v.198 and v.199, beginning opposite* being personally acquainted *on 199*   ᶻ so that *deleted*

⁹ Edward Hyde, Earl of Clarendon (1609–74): *The History of the Rebellion and Civil wars in England*, published 1702–4. On Thomas Howard, 14th Earl of Arundel, a hostile portrait: 1702 Abridged), i.44–6; W. D. Macray ed., 69–71. On William Herbert, 3rd Earl of Pembroke, a friendly portrait: i.44–6; Macray ed., i.71–3. On Lucius Cary, 2nd Viscount Falkland, a loving portrait: ii.270–7 and also in Clarendon's *Life* (1759, written 1668) 19–23; Macray ed. *History*, iii.178–90. Clarendon once planned to work up the portrait of Falkland into a book, which would have stood to the *History* as the *Agricola* of Tacitus stands to the *Annals* and *Histories*. Pope calls Falkland 'the virtuous and the just' in *Essay on Man*, iv.99, alongside Turenne.

¹⁰ *Agricola*, xliv; cf. ii.39 n.6 below.

¹¹ Gilbert Burnet, Bishop of Salisbury (1643–1715): *History of his own Time*, 1724/1734. Examples are Charles II, Clarendon, Lauderdale, the first Earl of Shaftesbury, the second Duke of Buckingham (Villiers), Halifax. Burnet exercised his art of charactery also in his *Lives* of Rochester, Sir Matthew Hale, and the Dukes of Hamilton.

{Sir William Temple in his Essay on the Netherlands[12] has described the character of a Nation very compleatly in all the Severall three ways.

The Conclusion is an Example both of the Direct and Indirect Character of a Nation, where he says this is a place where profit is in more request than honour etc. As in the Characters of Persons the great Error we are exposed to is the making them too Generall so is it in that of Nations. The English, french and Spaniards may be equally brave yet that Valour is certainly very different in each}[a]

---

[a] *Hand B, on 200*

---

[12] Sir William Temple, *Observations upon the United Provinces of the Netherlands* (1673), ch. iv, last paragraph, 164: '*Holland* is a Countrey where the Earth is better than the Air, and Profit more in request than Honour; Where there is more Sense than Wit; More good Nature than good Humour; And more Wealth than Pleasure; Where a man would chuse rather to travel, than to live; Shall find more things to observe than desire, And more persons to esteem than to love. But the same Qualities and Dispositions do not value a private man and a State, nor make a Conversation agreeable, and a Government great: Nor is it unlikely that some very great King might make but a very ordinary private Gentleman, and some very extraordinary Gentleman might be capable of making but a very mean Prince.' Cf. i.95 n.7 above.

Lecture. 16.^{th a} Monday Decr 27 1762.

Having in the three or four foregoing Lectures considered the manner of describing Single objects as well internall as externall and given some particular Rules for the Describing the different Species of them,^b and having also given you an account of the different maners of describing a character, and the principall authors who have excelled in that art; I come now to make some observations on the proper method of describing the more complex and important actions of men.

It is only the more important objects that are ever described; others less interesting are so far from being^c thought worthy of^d description that they are not reckon'd to deserve much of our attention. As it is mankind we are chiefly connected with it must be their | actions which chiefly interest our attention; Other rationall agents we are little acquainted with and the transactions which pass amongst other animalls are never of so great importance to us as to attract our notice. 'Tis therefore the actions of men and of them such as are of the greatest importance and are most apt to draw our attention and make a deep impression on the heart, that form the ground of this species of description. The actions and perception⟨s⟩ which chiefly affect us and make the deepest impression on our minds are those that are of the misfortunate kind and give us in the perception a considerable degree of Uneasiness. These are always found to be more interesting than others of the same degree of Strength if they are of a pleasant and agreable nature.

| {Whence this superior influence of uneasy sensations proceeds} Whether^e from their being less common and so^f more distinguishd from the ordinary pitch of human happiness^g by being greatly below it, than our most agreable perceptions are by rising above it; or whether it is thus ordered by the constitution of our nature to the end that the uneasiness of such sensations as accompany what tends to our prejudice might rouse us to be active in warding it^h off, can not be easily determind: For tho pleasant Sensations from what is of advantage might perhaps[s] be dispensed with, and no great prejudice thereby acrue to our happiness, Yet it seems absolutely necessary that some considerable degree of uneasiness should attend what is hurtfull; for without this we should soon in all probability be altogether destroyed.

But whatever be the | cause of this Phenomenonⁱ it is an undoubted fact

---

^a MS 15th .... Decr 26. *Vol. ii of MS begins here*   ^b I come *deleted*   ^c *last four words replace* not   ^d being related *deleted*   ^e this proceeds *deleted*   ^f on that account *written above then deleted*   ^g than *deleted*   ^h *replaces* them   ⁱ the fact i *deleted*

that those actions affect us in the most sensible manner, and make the deepest impression, which give us a considerable degree of Pain and uneasiness. This is the case not only with regard to our own private actions, but with those of others. Not only in our own case, missfortunate^j affairs chiefly affect us; but it is with the misfortunes of others that we most commonly as well as most deeply sympathise.—A Historian who related a battle and the effects attending, if he was no way interested would naturally dwell more on the misery and lamentations of the vanquished than on the triumph and exultations^k of the Victors.

5   It is to be observed that no action^l | however affecting in itself, can be represented in such a manner as to be very interesting to those who had not been present at it, by a bare narration where it is described directly without taking notice of any of the effects it had on those who were either actors or spectators of the whole affair.—Had Livy when relating the Engagement of the Horatii and the Curiatii^1 told us that the Albans and Romans chose three brothers from each side to determine by the issue of their combat the fate of each nation; that they accordingly engaged; that the Curiatii killed two of the Romans, being at the same time wounded themselves; That the Remaining

6   Roman, betaking | himself as they imagined to flight, brough⟨t⟩ them to follow him and by that means got the victory, which he could not have expected from an enga⟨ge⟩ment with them all at once. This would have been a direct description; but very languid and uninterresting in comparison of the other Sort where the effects of the transaction as well on the actors as the Spectators are pointed^m out. The difference will appear very remarkable if we compare the above description to that which he has given us of the same^n transaction. The Account he gives of the description^o of Alba is another instance of great excellence in that method of description. Thucydides might have given us in a very few words the whole account of the sieze of Syracuse by the

7   Athenians | which has filled the best part of the 7th Book of his history, but no such account could have had [a] chance of equalling the animated and affecting description he has given of that memorable event. {There are many passages in Livy and other authors that deserve to be read on account of their excellence in this art but these I think are sufficient to confirm the Generall rule that when we mean to affect the reader deeply we must have recourse to the indirect method of des-

---

^{j} trans *deleted* ^{k} *MS* exhulations ^{l} *replaces* object ^{m} *MS* painted ^{n} *replaces* above ^{o} *for* destruction?

---

^{1} I.xxiv–xxv; I.xxix (destruction of Alba): 'one hour laid in ruins the work of four hundred years'.

cription, relating the effects the transaction produced both on the actors and Spectators.}

We observed that the emotions of Grief are those which most affect us both in reality and in description, but when these come to a very great height they are not to ⟨be⟩ expressed by the most accurate description even of their ⟨effects⟩. No words are sufficient to convey an adequate idea of their effects. The best method in such cases is not to attempt any indirect description of the grief and concern, but barely relate the circumstances the persons were in, the state of their mind before the misfortune and the causes of their passion. It is told of an eminent painter that drawing the Sacrifice of Iphigenia,[2] he expressed

8 a consi|derable degree of grief in Chalcas the augur,*p* still greater in ⟨Ulysses⟩,*q* and all that his art could reach in the countenance and behaviour of Menelaus, but when he came to Agamemnon the Father of the Victim, he could ⟨not⟩ by all his skill express a degree of grief suitable to what then filled his breast. He thought it more prudent therefore to throw a veil over his face. In the same manner when Thucydides describes the distress and confusions of the Athenians retiring from Syracuse,[3] he did not attempt to describe it by the effects it produced on them, he chose rather to relate the circumstances of

9 their Misfortunes and the causes of their distress | and left the Reader to frame an idea of the deep concern and affliction they must have been in. Dionysius Halicarn⟨assensis⟩[4] observes that Thucydides delights much more in relating the misfortunes and distresses of his countrymen than their prosperity and so far his observation is just; But the Reason he gives for it does not appear at all probable. He says that Thucydides being banished by his countrymen was so irritated by this bad usage that he was at pains to collect every thing that tended to their dishonour and was at pains to conceal all accounts of glorious and successfull conduct, that he might by this lessen their reputation*r*. For this reason he prefers Herodotus to him, who dwells more on the

---

p replaces Priest   *q supplied conjecturally for blank in MS*   *r and deleted*

---

[2] The most famous painting of Timanthes of Cythnus (late fifth century BC) is described by Cicero, *Orator*, xxii.74; Pliny the Elder, *Natural History*, XXXV.xxxvi.73; Quintilian, II.xiii.12; Valerius Maximus, viii.11; Eustathius on *Iliad*, p. 1343.60. The graduated expressions of grief and the artistic principle exemplified by the veiled face of the father greatly interested eighteenth-century writers on art: e.g. Daniel Webb, *An Inquiry into the Beauties of Painting* (1760), 158, 192, 199. Timomachos of Byzantium (first century BC) also represented the incident. S. Fazio surveys the subject in *Ifigenia nella poesia e nell'arte figurata* (1932).

[3] VII.lxxx ff. Thucydides describes the incident as the greatest of all recorded Hellenic events: for the victors the most splendid, for the vanquished the most disastrous.

[4] *Epistula ad Pompeium*, ch. iii, in *The Three Literary Letters* ed. W. Rhys Roberts (1901), 109, 104 ff. Dionysius thinks Herodotus more skilled at 'beginnings' of historical works than Thucydides: op. cit. 107–8. Cf. ii.18 n.2 below.

prosperity and Good fortune of his Countrymen: Reckoning this to be
10 a sign of a more humane and generous temper. | But if we consider the
tempers of the men as well as the nature of the thing itself we may
perhaps be of a different opinion. Their[s] tempers if we may judge from
their works were very different. Herodotus appears to have been of a
more gay disposition, was of no great experience amongst men; which
temper joind to the   [t] of Old age would make him inclined to
insist much on the Good fortune and happy incidents of the History.
Th⟨u⟩cydides again being of an age not much given to Sallies of
passion of any Sort and having seen men and things would, as it were,
be hardened against the trivial and light bursts of Joy but would not
from the innate goodness of his heart be insensible to the missfortunes
of his fellow. He perhaps considered also that these melancholy
affections were most likely to produ⟨c⟩e a good effect on the minds of
11 his readers to soften and humanize them, whereas the others would |
rather tend to make the heart insensible to tender emotions. All this
may[u] incline ⟨us⟩ to be of a different opinion from the Critic above
mentiond.

We are here also to consider, that which was before hinted, that it is
these uneasy emotions that chiefly affect us and give us a certain
pleasing anxiety. A continued Series of Prosperity would not give us
near so much pleasure in the recital as an epic poem or a tragedy which
make but one continued Series of unhappy Events. Even comedy itself
would not give us much pleasure if we[v] were not kept in suspense and
some degree of anxiety by the cross accidents which occur and either
end in or appear to threaten a misfortunate issue. For this Reason also
it is not surprising that a man of an excellent heart might incline to
dwell most on the dismal side of the Story.

---

[s] *MS* There; *this sentence interlined*   [t] *blank of nine letters in MS*   [u] *numbers written above*
change the original order This may all   [v] did *deleted*

Lecture XVII.^a

Wednesday, Jan.^{ry} 5th
1763

Having now given those observations I think necessary to the describing single objects both externall and internall, and the more important complex ones, as the characters of men and the more important and interesting actions; I might now proceed to Shew how [in] these are to be applied to the Oratoricall Composition; what objects, and what manner of describing them, and what circumstances were most Proper^b to interest us and fixing our attention on one side perswade us to be of that opinion.

But as the particular directions already laid down naturally lead us to consider how they are to be applied in the most distinct manner, and where they are all conjoin'd, I shall first consider how they are to be applied to the historicall stile. Besides the narration makes a considerable part in every^c Oration. It requires no small art to narrate 13 properly those facts which are necessary for the | Groundwork of the Oration. So that I would be necessitated to lay down rules for narration in generall, that is for the histo⟨ricall⟩ Stile, before I could thoroughly explain The Rhetoricall composition.

The End of every discourse is either to narrate some fact or prove some proposition. When the design is to set the case in the clearest light; to give every argument its due force, and by this means persuade us no farther than our unbiassed judgement^d is Convinced; this is no⟨t to⟩ make use of the Rhetoricall Stile. But when we propose to persuade at all events, and for this purpose adduce those arguments that make for the side we have espoused, and magnify these to the utmost of our power; and on the other hand make light of and extenuate all those which may be brought on the other side, then we make use of the Rhetoricall Stile.

But when we narrate transactions^e as they happened without being 14 inclined to any party, we then | write in the narrative Stile. The Didactic and the oratoricall compositions consist of two parts, the proposition which we lay down and the proof that is brought to confirm this; whether this proof be a strict one applyed to our reason and sound judgement, or one adapted to affect our passions and by that means persuade us at any rate. But in the narrative Stile there is only one Part, that is, the narration of the facts. There is no proposition laid down or proof to confirm it. When a historian brings anything to confirm the truth of a fact it is only a quotation in the margin or a parenthesis and as this makes no part of the work it can not be said to be*ʲ* a part of the didactick. But when a historian sets himself to compare the evidence that is brought for the proof of any fact and way the arguments on both Side⟨s⟩ this is assuming the Character of a Didactick writer.

15 | The facts which are most commonly narrated and will be most adapted to the taste of the generality of men will be those that are interesting and important. Now these must be the actions of men; The most interesting and important of these are such as have contributed to great revolutions and changes in States and Governments. The changes or accidents that have happend to innanimate or irrationall beings can not greatly interest us; we look upon them to be guided in a great measure by chance, and undesigning instinct; Design and Contrivance is what chiefly interests us, and the more of this we conceive to be in any transaction the more we are concerned in it. A history of earthquakes or other naturall Phenomena, tho it might Contain great variety of incidents, and be very agreable to a naturallist*¹* who had entered deeply into these matters, and by that 16 means concei|ved them to be of considerable importance, as we do of everything that we have gone so far into as to have some notion of its extent, yet it would appear very dull and uninteresting to the generallity of mankind. The*ᵍ* accidents that befall irrationall objects affect us merely by their externall appearance, their Novelty, Grandeur etc. but those which affect the human Species interest us greatly by the Sympatheticall affections they raise in us. W⟨e⟩ enter into their misfortunes, grieve when they grieve, rejoice when they rejoice, and in a word feel for them in some respect as if we ourselves were in the same condition.

The design of*ʰ* historicall writing is not merely to entertain; (this perhaps is the intention of an epic poem) besides that it has in view the 17 instruction of | the reader. It sets before us the more interesting and important events of human life, points out the causes by which these events were brought about and by this means points out to us by what manner and method we may produce similar good effects or avoid Similar bad ones.

{Should one lay down certain principles which he afterwards

ʲ said to be *replaces* called any   *ᵍ* affairs *deleted*; of naturall *deleted after* accidents   *ʰ* a *deleted*

---

¹ The common seventeenth- and eighteenth-century word for student of natural philosophy, physicist.

confirmed by examples This work would have the same end as a history but the means would be different, it would not be a narrative but a didactick writing.} — —

In this it differs from a Romance the Sole view of which is to entertain. This being the end, it is of no consequence whether the incidents narrated be true or false. A well contrived Story may be as interesting and entertaining as any real one: the causes which brought about the several incidents that are narrated may all be very ingeniously contrived and well adapted to their severall ends, but still

18 as the facts are not such as have realy existed, the end pro|posed by history will not be answered. The facts must be real,[i] otherwise they will not assist us in our future conduct, by pointing out the means to avoid or produce any event[j]. Feigned Events and the causes contrived for them, as they did not exist, can not inform us of what happend in former times, nor of consequence assist us in a plan of future conduct.

Some hints of this Sort, pointing out the view with which the author undertook his Work, whether he was induced to it by the importance of the facts or whether it was to remedy the innaccuracy or[k] partiallity of former writers, and also showing us what we may expect to find in the work, would form a much better subject for the preface or beginning of the work (where Tacitus[2] has applied them) than Commonplace-morality as that with which Sallust introduces his works. These however pretty have no connection with the matter in

19 hand, and might have been any|where else as well as where they are. This much with regard to the preface.

The next thing that comes to be considered in the course of the history is the Causes which brought about the effects that are to be narrated. And here it may be questioned whether we are to relate the remoter causes or only the more immediate ones which preceded the events. If the events are very interesting they will so far attract our attention that we can not be satisfied unless we know something of the causes which brought them about. If these causes again be very important, we for the same reason require to have some account of the causes which produced them. But these need not be so accurately

---

[i] for *deleted*   [j] This *deleted*   [k] ig *deleted*

[2] This does no justice to the skill with which both Tacitus and Sallust lead into their particular histories from an observation on the great deeds of the past, the need to preserve them from oblivion, and the disinterestedness which historians share with those they chronicle: cf. *Agricola* i and *Bellum Catilinae* I.i. But Bolingbroke thought introductions such as Sallust's or Thucydides' might introduce *any* history: see his letter to Pope, 18 Aug. 1724, *The Correspondence of Alexander Pope*, ed. G. Sherburn (1956), ii.252 (printed in Bolingbroke's *Works*, 1754, ii.501–8, as 'A plan for a general history of Europe'). He considered Machiavelli's *History of Florence*, Book i, 'a noble Original of this kind' and Paolo Sarpi's *Treatise on benefices* inimitable in this respect.

explaind as the more*[l]* immediate ones, and so on gradually diminishing
the importance of the cause till at last we satisfy the Reader.

In general the more remote any cause is the less circumstantially it
20 may be | described. Thus Sallust in his Jugurthan war, where the
immediate cause of that event was the character of that Prince and the
State of the Numidian affairs at the death of Micipsa, dwells but little
on the events that preceded that Reign. These he points out more
minutely but less so than those that happened in Jugurthas life; and in
it too those that happen'd in his infancy or when he was in the Roman
Camp are much less accurately explained than those which immediately preceded and were intimately connected with the Chief
events. Had he dwelt more on the events that happend before
Micipsa's reign, he would have been necessitated to have explained
those that preceded them and so on in infinitum. By not attending to
this method the Introduction to the   *[m]* history fills a whole folio
volume; Gordon[3] who translated Tacitus tells us that when he set
21 about writing the*[n]* Life of | Oliver Cromwell he found the Events in
that Period so connected with those before the Reformation and those
again with the former Reigns that he was obliged to go as far back as
the*[o]* Conquest, and by going on in the same way he would have
fou[u]nd himself*[p]* reduced to the necessity of tracing the whole back
even to the*[q]* fall of Adam. It is always however necessary to give some
reason for the events which more immediately preceded the Chief
cause, but this may often be done in such a manner as to prevent any
farther Curiosity. Thus Sallust when he tells us that the Cause of the
Cataline conspiracy[4] was the Temper and character of that man and
the circumstances of his life, join'd with the corrupt manners of the
people. Here we naturally demand how it came to pass that a people
once so strictly virtuous and sober should have degenerated so much,
he tells us that it was owing to the Luxury introduced by their Asiatick

---

[l] import *deleted*   *[m]* blank *of ten letters in* MS   *[n]* events in the Blac *deleted*
[o] Reformation, *deleted*   *[p]* as much *deleted*   *[q]* very *deleted*

---

[3] Thomas Gordon (1690?–1750), miscellaneous writer and pamphleteer, translated the works
of Tacitus (1728, 1731) with twenty-two extensive 'Political Discourses' on him. In the preface to
his translation of the works of Sallust (1744, p.xxi) he tells of the history of England on which he is
engaged: 'My first intention was to write the life of Cromwell only, but, as I found that, in order
to describe his times it was necessary to describe the times which preceded and introduced him,
and that I could not begin even at the Reformation without recounting many public incidents
before the Reformation, I have begun at the Conquest and gone through several Reigns, some of
these seen and approved by the ablest judges, such judges as would animate the slowest
ambitions. Half of it will probably appear a few years hence; the whole will conclude with the
"History of Cromwell".' His *History of England* (British Library Add. MS 20780) ends in mid-
sentence at 1610; but small parts were printed in his *Collection of Papers* (1748) and *Essays against
Popery, Slavery and Arbitrary Power* (1750?).

[4] *Bellum Catilinae*, I.xi.

22 conquests. This altogether | satisfies us; as those conquests and their
circumstances however interesting appear no way connected with the
matters in hand.

v.18 | '{The more lively and shocking the impression is which any
Phænomenon makes on the mind the greater curiosity does it excite to
know its Causes, tho perhaps the Phænomenon may not be intrinsically
half so grand or important as another less Striking. Thus it is that we
have have a greater Curiosity to pry into the cause of thunder and
v.19 Lightning and of the Cœlestiall Motions | than of Gravity because they
naturally make a greater impression on us. Hence it is that we have
naturally a greater curiosity to examine the Causes and Relations of
those things which pass without us than of those which pass within us,
the latter naturally making very little impression. The associations of
our Ideas, the progress and origin of our Passions, are what very few
think of enquiring into. But when one has turned his thoughts that way
and made some enquiries he begins to think these matters to be of
importance and is therefore interested in them.'

A Historian therefore is to expose the causes of every thing only in
proportion to the impression it makes. Now the Cause of the Event
makes a less impression than the Event itself and so excites less curiosity
with regard to its Cause; that cause therefore is to be touched upon
more slightly, and by being so it excites but very little Curiosity about
v.20 its Cause, which therefore | may be still more superficially mentioned.
It is thus that Salust ascribes the Conspiracy of Cataline to the
Characters and Circumstances of Certain Persons in the State; these he
traces to the Generall profligacy and Luexury then prevailing in
Rome, which at length he deduces from the Conquest of Asia, where
he leaves us fully satisfied that we know all that is necessary of the
matter and not disposed to enter into the origin of these conquests,
however convinced that the enquiry would be curious at a proper
time}'

The causes that may be assigned for any event are of two Sorts;
either the externall causes which directly produced it, or the internall
ones, that is those causes that tho' they no way affected the event yet
had an influence on the minds of the chief actors so as to alter their
conduct from what it would otherwise have been . . .' We may observe
on this head that those who have been engaged in the transactions they
relate or others of the same Sort, generally dwell on those of the first
Sort. Thus Cæsar, Polybius and Thucydides, who had all been
engaged in most of the battles they describe, account for the fate of the

---

ᵣ⁻ᵣ *Hand B's note begins on v.18 opposite* If these causes (19) *and ends opposite the appropriate point*
corrupt manners of the people (21)   ˢ *this sentence inserted by Hand A vertically in inner margin of*
v.19, keyed for insertion after into   ᵗ *so in MS*

battle by the Situation of the two armies, the nature of the Ground, the weather etc.—Those on the other hand who have little acquaintance with the particular incidents of this sort that determine events, but
23 have made enquiries into the nature of the human mind and | the severall passions, endeavour by[u] means of the circumstances that would influence them, to account for the fate of battles and other events, which they could not have done by those causes[v] that immediately determine them. Thus Tacitus who seems to have been but little versant in Military or indeed publick affairs of any sort, always account⟨s⟩ for the event of a battle by the circumstances that would influence the mind of the Combatants.

This difference in the manner of accounting for events is very plainly seen in the Description of a battle in the night; one by Thucydides and the other by Tacitus.[5] The former mentions all the causes the nature of the[w] circumstances would have on the armies; whereas the Other has entirely omitted these and mentiond solely those that would affect the minds of the Combatants with lesser courage etc. The 1st is the account of the attack of Syracuse by the Athenians and the latter of the battle betwixt Vespasian and Vitellius generall.

24 | The describing of characters is no essentiall part of a historicall narration; The temper of the person of the actors at the different times will be sufficient. Xenophon in his account of the Retreat of the 10000 Greeks describes very accurately the Characters of the 3 commanders who were betrayed by Artaxerxes.[6] {Xenophon is almost the only antient Historian who professedly draws characters}[x] In his Greek history likewise tho he does ⟨not⟩ enter on purpose on the describing of characters but[y] by the different circumstances and particular incidents he relates the characters are sufficiently plain. Herodotus and Thucydides hard[ad]ly describe any characters. Herod⟨otus⟩ indeed has[z] some exclamations on the characters of the different persons, but such generall ones as are not to be called characters, and might be equally applicable to 100 others. {as in the Exclamations on the virtues of Pericles.[7]—A man of grave or a merry, of a good nature, or morose temper, may advance to battle or scale the walls with equall intrepidity.} Tis not the degrees of virtue or vice, of courage, good nature etc. that distinguish a character, as the particular turns they have received from the temper and turn of the mind of the severall

---

[u] their *deleted*   [v] procee *deleted*   [w] Army *deleted*   [x] *Hand* B   [y] *i.e.* yet
[z] *replaces* gives

---

[5] Thucydides, VII.xliii–xlv; Tacitus, *Historiae*, III.xxii–xxiv – but the Vitellians, in the absence of Vitellius, had no 'generall'.
[6] *Anabasis*, II.vi: Clearchus, Proxenus, Menon.
[7] Not traceable in Herodotus.

25   individualls. Thucydides | gives us no account of characters at all. This
      we can not attribute to want of ability, as he was personally acquainted
      with most of the characters he would have had occasion to describe
      and has shewn his skill in this art, in the admirable Characters he has
      given of whole communities, as of the Athenians[8] after the [a]   and
      of   [a] which is still more difficult than the describing of characters
      of single persons; we must then attribute this conduct to an opinion
      that it[b] was not at all necessary.
          There is no author who has more distinctly explained the causes of
      events than Thucydides. He is in this respect far superior to Polybius,
      who is at such great pains in minutely explaining all the externall
      causes of any event that his labour appears visibly in his works and is
      not only tiresome but at the same time is less pleasant by the constraint
26   the author seems to have been in. Thucydides on the o|ther hand often
      expresses all that he labours so much in a word or two, sometimes
      placed in the middle of the narration but in such a manner as not in the
      least to confound it. Next to Thucydides come Xenophon and Tacitus;
      This last has often been censured as being too deep a Politician. The
      author of this remark was I think {Trajan Boccalini[9]}[c] an Italian, who
      has been implicit⟨l⟩y ⟨followed⟩[d] by all the petty criticks since his time.
      This remark was very naturall at that time when such subtility
      prevailed and Machiavelian politicks were in fashion; but does not
      seem at all suitable to the ingenuous temper of Tacitus, nor is it
      confirmed by his writings. In the beginning of his history of the affaires
      in the Reign of Tiberius he gives us some politicall remarks on the
      Genius and temper of that Prince,[10] but this[e] is sufficiently justified by
      the character of cunning and design given him by other authors. In
27   other parts of his work the pains he is | at to explain the causes of events
      from the[f] internall causes seems to pont out a conterary temper.
          Livy seldom endeavours to account for events in either way, by the
      external or internal causes, and those who are acquainted with
      millitary affairs affirm that he is not altogether clear in his accounts of
      battles or sieges. He supports the dignity of his narration by the
      interesting manner in which he relates the severall events; which he
      does so admirably that we enter into all the concerns of the parties and

---

[a] *a two blanks in MS of about ten letters each*   [b] *replaces* this   [c] *Hand B. correcting Hand .I's*
Bathesar Castigliond *(deleted)*   [d] *supplied conjecturally: reading doubtful*   [e] conduct *deleted*
[f] character *deleted*

---

[8] i.e. after the disaster of Syracuse (VII.lxxxvii), cf. ii.8 n.3 above. VIII.i describes the effects
on the Athenians of the news of the disaster.
[9] Traiano Boccalini: *Commentari sopra Cornelio Tacito* (1669); cf. ii.69 n.4 below.
[10] *Annales*, I.iv.

are allmost as much affected with them as if we ourselves had been concerned in them.

Events as we before observed may be described either in a direct or indirect manner. We observed also that in most cases the indirect method is much preferable, even when the objects were inanimate; 28 much more then will it be to be chosen when we describe the[g] actions | of men where the effects are so much stronger; as the actions themselves are more interesting. 'Tis[h] the proper use of this method that makes most of the ancient historians, as Thucydides, so interesting; and the neglecting it that has rendered the modern historians for the most part so dull and so lifeless. The ancients carry us as it were into the very circumstances of the actors, we feel for them as it were for ourselves. {They show us the feelings and agitation of Mind in the Actors previous to and during the Event. They Point to us also the Effects and Consequences of the Event not only in the intrinsick change it made on the Situation of the Actors but the manner of behaviour with which they supported them}[i]

One method which most modern historians and all the Romance writers take to render their narration interesting is to keep their event in Suspense. Whenever the story is beginning to point to the grand event they turn to something else and by this means get us to read thro a number of dull nonsensicall stories, our[j] curiosity prompting us to get at the important event, as {Ariosto in his Orlando Furioso.} This method the ancients never made use of, they trusted not to the readers 29 Curiosity alone, but relied on the | importance of the facts and the interesting manner in which they narrated them. Livy when he relates the affecting catastrophe of the Fabii and the[k] Battle of Cannæ does not endeavour to conceall the event but on the other hand gives us a plain intimation what will be the event of those expeditions before they are related.[11] {In cassum misse[l] Preces}[m] Yet this does not in the least diminish our concern on the relation, which by the lively manner in which he has executed it engage⟨s⟩[n] us as much as if it had been intirely unknown. This method has besides this advantage that[o] we can then with patience attend to the less important intervening accidents, which if the great event had been intirely concealed, our curiosity would make us hurry over; We would count the pages we had to read to get to

---

[g] effects *deleted*　　[h] is in *deleted*　　[i] *Hand B*　　[j] *replaces* by the; prompting us *replaces* we have　　[k] ruinous *deleted*　　[l] *or* missi (?)　　[m] *Hand B*　　[n] *replaces* interests　　[o] *replaces* which

---

[11] II.xlviii–l. The crowd cheering the Fabii on their way against the Veientes pray to the gods for their success, but 'in cassum missae preces', in vain (xlix.8). Cf. ii.43 n.9 below. The battle of Cannae, Hannibal's great victory in 216 BC, is described by Livy at XXII.xliii–xlix; cf. ii.56 n.8 below.

the event, as we generally do in a Novel. {Nay in some cases[p] this warning has a very manifest and considerable advantage. Thus after being given to know that the Generous attempt of the Fabii was to fail we read every future circumstance and the progress of their expedition with a melancholy which is extremely pleasing. Livy seems almost with design to give Warning of the Event of his battles as of Thrasymene[12] and Cannæ}[q]

30 | As newness is the only merit in a Novel and curiosity the only motive which induces us to read them, the writers are necessitated to make use of this method to keep it up. Even[r] the Antient Poets who had not reality on their side never have recourse to this method, the importance of the naration they trust will keep us interested. Virgil in the beginning of the Æneid and Homer in both his heroick poems inform us in the beginning of the chief events that are told in the whole poem.

Even in Tragedy where it is reckoned an essentiall part to keep the plot in Suspence this is not so necessary as in Romance.[s] A tragedy can bear to be read again and again, tho the incidents be not new to us they are new to the actors and by this means interest us as well as by their own importance.

{The graduall and just developement of the Catastrophe constitutes a great beauty in any Tragedy yet is it not a necessary one, otherwise we could never with any pleasure hear or see acted a play for the Second time; yet that pleasure often grows by Repetition.

Euripides often in his Prologues by means of a God or a Ghost makes us acquainted with the Events and puts us on our Guard that we may be free to attend to the Sentiments and Action of each Scene, some of which he has laboured greatly.}[t]

[p] it has *deleted* [q] *Hand B* [r] But *deleted*; Even *and* Antient *in Hand B above the line* [s] It is not the novelty alone that *deleted* [t] *Hand B, but last seven words in Hand A, last five vertically in margin*

[12] Hannibal's destruction of the army of Flaminius at Lake Trasimene in 217 BC: Livy XXII.iv–vi.

Lecture XVIII^a

Friday Jan.^{ry} 7. 1763

{The order in which I proposed to treat of historicall Composition was first to treat of the End; next of the means of accomplishing that End, of [of] the Materialls of hi⟨s⟩tory; next of the arrangement of these materials; next of the Expression; and lastly of those who have most excelled in this Subject}^b

The next thing in order that comes to be considered with regard to historicall composition is the arangement in which the severall parts of the narration are to be placed. In generall the narration is to be carried on in the same order^c as that in which the events themselves happened. The mind naturally conceives that the facts happened in the order they are related, and when they are by this means suited to our naturall conceptions the notion we form of them is by that means rendered more distinct. This rule is quite evident and accordingly few Historians have tresspassed against it.

But when severall of the events that are to be related happened in different places at the same time, the difficulty ^din this case is to determine in what order they are^d to be related:—The best method is^e to observe the connection of place, that is^f relate those that happen'd in the same place for some considerable succession of time | without interrupting the thread of the narration by introducing those that happened in a different place. 'Tis in this manner that Herodotus after having followed the course of events in one Country to some remarkable Æra passes on to those that happend during a Period nearly of the same length in another country, Resuming afterwards the former by itself where he had left it off.

But tho the connection of time and place are very strong, yet they are not to be so invariably observed as to supercede the observance of all others. There is another connection still more striking than any of the former, I mean that of cause and Effect.^g There is no connection with which we are so much interested as this of cause and effect; we are not satisfied when we have a fact told us which we are at a loss to conceive what it was that brought it about. Now there is often such a connection betwixt the facts that have happend at different^h times in different | countriesⁱ that the one can not be explaind distinct from the other. They would appear altogether unintelligible unless those which

32

33

^a MS XVII ^b Hand B ^c replaces manner ^{d-d} numbers written above change original order is to determine in what order they are, in this case deleted ^e to relate those then deleted ^f that is replaces and ^g Hand B replacing Hand A's Event ^h or at the deleted ⁱ replaces times in the catchword on 32

produced them were also understood. The Difficulty of Accommodating the explaining the causes that have produced the different events with the distinctness which is necessary to give one a clear notion of any one series of events, has lead different authors into error in[j] both the distinctness of events and the connection of causes with events. Diodorus[1] of Halicarnassus {accuses Thucidides}[k] of having adhered so much to the connection of time that the different events he relates to have happen'd in different places at the same time are so jumbled together that it is impossible to form a distinct notion of what passed in any one place. This observation[l] of the Halicarnassian is not perhaps altogether just with regard to Thucydides. The History he writes is that of a war; and the events of one campaign in each place he narrates by themselves; this period is not so short but one may form 34 a distinct enough | notion of the Events that happen'd in each place. The Criticism may however serve to shew what disadvantages would attend the writing a history with too close an attention to the connection of time. Had Thycydides chosen much shorter periods, as a month, which the compilers of the history of Europe[2] a work publishd some Years ago did, no one could form any conception of the events any more than from a chronologicall table.

Mr Rapin[3] on the other hand having adhered too much to the connection of Place has often rendered the causes of the events altogether obscure. In his account of the Saxon Heptarchy, he relates the whole affairs of each of those seperate states by themselves, in one continued account from their first establishment till their subversion by the West Saxons. The transactions that pass in any of these are so 35 connected with what passed | at the same time or a little befor⟨e⟩ in another part of England that one can not perceive by what means they were brought about unless he is before informed of what passed in the neighbouring states. So that one can not form any notions of the history of any one of these till he has read thro the whole severall times and that with no small attention. The same may be observed of his account of the disputes betwixt the people and King Charles the 1ˢᵗ which for distinctness sake as he says he relates in the same manner, and the obscurity and incoherence[m] that follows it is still greater as the affairs

---

j MS is   *k inserted by Hand B above the line*   *l replaces* criticism   *m last three words replace* and confusion

[1] For Dionysius. The comparison of Thucydides and Herodotus is in the *Epistula ad Pompeium*, ch. iii (*The Three Literary Letters*, ed. W. R. Roberts: on the order of events, pp. 111 13); cf. *On Thucydides*, 9 (*The Critical Essays*, LCL, 1974: i.480 ff.).

[2] Not identified.

[3] Paul de Rapin Thoyras (1661-1725): *Histoire d'Angleterre*, i (1724), 147 275, 475 525 (Bk 3, the Heptarchy; and 'Dissertation sur le Gouvernement . . . des Anglo-Saxons'); viii (1725), 1 724 (Bks 20-21, from 1640 to 1649).

are still more nearly connected. {For distinctness sake says he I will relate separately the affair of the Bishops, of the Militia and of the Earl of Stafford. These are unluckily so Interwoven that to understand what is done in one of them we must know what is doing in the others}*[n]*

The best method therefore is to adhere to the succession of time as long as it does not introduce an inconvenience from the want of connection; and that when there are a number of simultaneous events to be related we should relate by themselves those that happen'd in 36 each place, recapitulating under each those concerning the others so | far as is necessary to keep up the connection betwixt the Cause and the event, and place the former always in order before the latter.

I shall only observe two things farther with regard to the arangement of the narration; the 1*[st]* Is, That there is an other way of keeping up the connection besides the two abovementioned; That is, the Poeticall method, which connects the different facts*[o]* by some slight circumstances which often had nothing in the bringing about the series of the events, or by some relation that appears betwixt them.*[p]* This is the method which Livy generally has made use of, and to such good purpose that he has never been condemned for want of connection. {Thucydides*[q]* on the other hand never observes any sort of connection in the circumstances he brings in. Those mentioned in his description of the battle in the night[4] would do equally well in whatever order they were placed*[r]*. Tacitus[5] describing the distress an army was in says; They were without tents and in want of bandages.— — —}

The 2*[d]* is that, We should never leave any chasm*[s]* or Gap in the thread of the narration even tho there are no remarkable events to fill up that space. The very notion of a gap makes us uneasy for what 37 should have happened in that time. Taci|tus is often guilty of this fault. He tells us that the army of Germanicus*[t]* being attacked in their camp gained a great victory over the enemy; this is in the middle of Germany and in the next sentence we find them across the Rhine, supported by the assiduity and Care of Agrippina when they were in the utmost hazard.— — —

I shall now proceed to make some observations on the Manner in which the narration is to be expressed and the difference betwixt the didactick*[u]*, oratoricall and the Historicall Stile.

---

[n] *Hand B*   *[o]* different facts *replaces* events   *[p]* *last eight words added vertically in margin* *[q]* *Hand B replacing Hand A's* Tacitus (*deleted*)   *[r]* In an other place he says describing *deleted* *[s]* in *added to* chas *in different ink*   *[t]* *inserted by Hand B in blank left*   *[u]* *inserted by Hand B above the line*

---

[4] See ii.23 n.5 above.
[5] *Annales*, I.lxv: 'non tentoria manipulis, non fomenta sauciis'. The army of Germanicus: I.lxviii–lxix.

An historian as well as an orator may excite our love or esteem for the persons he treats of[v], but then the methods they take are very different. The Rhetorician will not barely set forth the character of a person as it realy existed but will magnify every particular that may tend to excite the Strongest emotions in us. He will also seem to be
38 deeply affected with | that affection which he would have us feel towards any object. He will exclaim, for example, on the amiable Character, the sweet temper and behaviour of the man towards whom he would have us to feel those affections. The Historian on the conterary can only excite our affection by the narration of the facts and setting them in as interesting a view as he possibly can. But all exclamations in his own person would not suit with the impartiality he is to maintain and the design he is to have in view of narrating facts as they are without magnifying them or diminishing them.—An historian in the same way may excite grief or compassion but only by narrating facts which excite those feelings; whereas the orator heightens every incident and pretends at least to be deeply affected by them himself, often exclaiming on the wretched condition of those he talks of etc.—{I could almost say damn it}[w]

39 | [x]Few historians accordingly have run in this error. Tacitus indeed has a[y] passionate exclamation in the latter part of his character of Agricola.[6] The Elder Pliny too has severall times been guilty of this foolish affectation as it certainly is in him who in other respects is a very grave author, and the more so on the subject he writes on, which is naturall history, a subject which tho' it may be very amusing does not appear[z] to be very animating.[a] Besides these there is no historian who has used them unless it be Valerius maximus,[7] and Florus (if he deserves the name of a historian) who is full of them from the beginning to the end.

As[b] the historian is not to make use of the Oratoricall Stile so neither has he any occ[c]asion for the didactick. It is not his business to bring proofs for propositions but to narrate facts. The only thing he can be
40 under any | necessity of proving is the events he relates. The best way in this case is not to set a labourd and formall demonstration but barely mentioning the authorities on both sides, to shew for what reason[c] he

---

[v] but we *deleted*   [w] *Hand B(?) at foot of 38*   [x] An historian again never enters into *deleted*   [y] *MS* an, n *deleted*; passionate *added above the line*   [z] to me *deleted*   [a] *Hand B replacing Hand A's* interesting (*deleted*)   [b] *replaces* In   [c] this *deleted*

---

[6] 'Bonum virum facile crederes, magnum libenter' (*Agricola*, xliv, quoted at i.199 above); or 'consulari ac triumphalibus ornamentis praedito quid aliud adstruere fortuna poterat?'

[7] Valerius Maximus wrote (*c.* AD 31) a handbook of moral and philosophical examples drawn from history for the use of rhetoricians. Lucius Annaeus Florus compiled an *Epitome* of Roman history up to Augustus, derived mainly from Livy; cf. i.83 n.4 above.

had chosen to be of the one opinion rather than of the other. Long demonstrations as they are no part of the historians province are seldom made use of by the ancients. The modern authors have often brought them in. Historicall truths are now in much greater request than they ever were in the ancient times. One thing that has contributed to the increase of this curiosity is that there are now severall sects in Religion and politicall disputes which are greatly dependent on the truth of certain facts. This it is that has induced almost all historians for some time past to be at great pains in the proof of those facts on which the claims of the parties they favoured depended. These proofs however besides that they are inconsistent
41 with the historicall stile, are likewise of bad con|sequence as they interrupt the thread of the narration, and that most commonly in the*d* parts that are most interesting. They withdraw our attention from the main facts, and before we can get thro them they have so far weaken⟨ed⟩ our concern for the issue of the affair that was broke off that we are never again so much interested in them.
v.39 | {The Dissertations which are everywhere interwoven into Modern Histories contribute among other things and that not a little to render them less interesting than those wrote by the Antients. To avoid a dissertation about the Truth of a Fact a Historian might first Relate the Event according to the most likely opinion and when he had done so give the others by saying that such or such a Circumstance had occasiond such or such a mistake or that such a*e* misrepresentation had been propagated by such a person for such Ends. This would be making a fact of it. The Truth and Evidence of Historicall facts is now in much more request and more critically Examined than among the
v.40 Antients because of all the Numerous Sects among us whether Civil or | Religious, there is hardly one the reasonableness of whose Tenets does not depend on some historicall fact}*f*
      Besides no fact that is called in question interests us so much or makes so lasting impression, as those of whose truth*g* we are altogether satisfied. Now all proofs of this sort show that the matter is somewhat dubious; so that on the whole it would be more proper to narrate these facts without mentioning the doubt, than to bring in any long proof.
      The same objections that have been mentioned against Long Demonstrations hold equally against Reflexions and observations that exceed the length of too or three sentences. If one was to point out to us some interesting spectacle, it would surely be very disagreable in the most engaging part to interupt us and turn our attention from it by
42 desiring us to attend | to the fine contrivance of the parts of the object or the admirable exactness with which the whole was carried on. We

d MS these, se *deleted*   *e* mistake h *deleted*   *f Hand B, v.39 (top)–v.40*   *g* of whose truth *replaces* that

would be uneasy by being thus withdrawn from what we were so much concerned in. The historian who brings in long reflections acts precisely in the same manner, he withdraws us from the most interesting part of the narration; and in such interruptions we [we] always imagine that we lose some part of the transaction; Tho' the narration is broken off we cannot conceive that the action is interrupted. The short Reflexions and observations made use of by The Cardinal de Rhetz and by Tacitus are not liable to the same objections. Of these Two[h] Tacitus has evidently the superiority; his observations do not stand out from the narration but often appear to make a part of it, whereas those of the Cardinall, tho not too long are intirely separate from the narration.

{I saw, says the Cardinall,[8] the whole extent of my danger and I saw nothing but what was terrible. There is in great dangers a Certain charm etc. etc.}[i]

43   Speeches interspersed in the narration do not appea⟨r⟩ | so faulty (tho they may be of considerable length) as long observations or Rhoricall declamations. The Stile inde⟨e⟩d is altogether different from that of the Historian as they are oraticall compositions; But then they are not in the authors own person, and therefore do not contradict the impartiality he is to maintain. Neither do they interrupt the thread of the narration as they are not considered as the authors, but make a part of the facts related. They give also an opportunity of introducing those observations and reflections which we observed are not so properly made in the person of the writer. Livy often makes this use of them; Thus he introduces his reflection on the hazard, the importance and generosity of the undertaking of the Fabii[n] not in his own person but by making their design the subject of[j] Debate in the Senate, which also adds to the sentiments he would inspire us with.

    The only objection then that can be made against the using speeches in this manner is, That tho they be represented as facts, they are not
44 genuine ones. But[k] neither does ⟨he⟩ desire you to consider | them as such, but only as being brought in to illustrate the narration. — — —

{Not a word more can I remember}[l]

---

[h] those *deleted*   [i] *Hand B*   [j] the *deleted*   [k] then *deleted*   [l] *Hand A in small writing in next line*

---

[n] 'Je voyois le peril dans toute son étendue, et je n'y voyois rien qui ne me parut affreux. Les plus grands dangers ont leurs charmes, pour peu que l'on aperçoive de gloire dans la perspective des mauvais succès; les mediocres dangers n'ont que des horreurs, quand le perte de la réputation est attachée à la mauvaise fortune': Retz, *Mémoires* (1723), 152, under Sept. 1648— italicized as an 'observation' separate from the narration. Quoted in a loose translation in TMS I.iii.2.11.

[n] II.xlvii–xlviii; cf. ii.29 n.11 above.

Lecture. XIX.^{th a}

Having in the preceding lectures given ye an account of the principall things necessary to be observed in the writing of history, I proceed to^b *the History of Historians.*

The Poets were the first Historians of any. They recorded those accounts that were most apt to suprise and strike the imagination such as the mythological history and^c adventures of their Deities. We find accordingly all the most ancient^d writings were ballads or Hymns in honour of their Gods recording the most amazing parts of their conduct. As their Subject was the marvellous so they naturally expressed themselves in the Language of wonder, that is in Poetry, for 45 in that Stile amazement and | surprise naturally break forth.

Of the actions of men, again, military exploits [as they] would be the first subject of the Poets as they are most fraught with adventures that are fit to amaze and gratify the desire men have especially in the early periods for what is marvellous. Homer accordingly has recorded the most remarkable^e war that his countrymen had been engaged in before those days. All the other poets he mentions, for he mentions no writers but what were poets, had also followed the same plan; they related the most surprising adventures and warlike exploits of the great men in or before their time. In all Countries we find poetry has been the first Species of writing, as the marvellous is that which first draws the attention of unimproved men. The oldest originall Writings in Latin, Italian, French, English and Scots, are all poets. There are indeed 46 other | writings perhaps as old as any of these Poems, that are wrote in Prose; but these are only Monkish Legends or others of that sort; which as they are wrote in a foreign Language, and in a different way from that naturally to the country, are evidently copied from the works of authors of an other Country. {and are not to be numbred with the Productions of that Country}^f

The next Species of Historians were Poets in every respect except the form of the Language. Their language was prose but their Subject altogether Poeticall—Furies, Harpys, Animalls half^g men and half Bird, or snake, Centaurs, and others half fish and half man that were bread in Tartarus and swam about in the Sea; The intercourse of Gods with Women, and Goddesses with men, and the Heroes that Sprung from them, and their exploits, were the subject of their Works

---

^a MS XVIIIth   ^b give you some account of *deleted*   ^c genea *deleted*   ^d Poets *deleted*   ^e *replaces illegible word* rer . . . . ped   ^f *Hand B*   ^g MS have

according to Dionys⟨ius⟩ of Halic⟨arnassus⟩.[1] When one reads his
account it will immediately put him in mind of the Geoffry of
47 Monmouth[2] and the other earlier | writers, their Elves and Fairies,
Dragons, Griffins and other monsters with the accounts of which the
greatest part of their Books were filled, The Creatures of an
imagination engendered by the terror and Superstitious fear which is
allways found in the ruder state of Mankind. These writers that
followed this method amongst the ancients confined their accounts to
the memorable Stories of some one country or province; and in the
same manner the monkish legends are confin'd to one town or perhaps
to one monastery.

The first author who formed the Design of extending the plan
of history was Herodotus. He chose for this reason a period of 240
Years before his time, and comprehends the history not only of all the
Grecian States but also of all the Barbarous nations. These he has
connected together in such an easy and naturall manner, as to leave no
48 gap nor | chasm in his narration. The stile is gracefull and easy; his
narration Crowded with memorable facts and those the most
extraordinary that happened in each country. He does not however
confine himself to those that produced any memorable change or
alteration in each country but chooses out whatever is most agreable.
He has[h] not near so many of those fabulous and marvellous accounts as
we are told the authors who preceded him had but then he has still a
good number scattered in his work. His design inde⟨e⟩d seems to have
been rather to amuse than to instruct. This is confirmed by the long
period he has chosen and the wide tract of Country which he has[i]
made the Subjects of his history; by this means his[j] facts could be
more easily rendered amusing and he has accordingly picked from the
history of each country those which are most intertaining whether they
be of importance or not. We can[k] learn from him rather[l] the Customs of
49 the different nations and the | series of events, than any account of the

---

[h] much fewer, greatly, *deleted*   [i] chosen *deleted*   [j] choice of *deleted*   [k] *replaces* may
[l] *replaces* chiefly

[1] *On Thucydides*, 6 (*The Critical Essays*, LCL, i.476 ff.). He quotes the historian's own defence of
his avoidance of legend however attractive, in favour of attested fact (I.xxii.4). In his *Roman
Antiquities* he attacks Greek myths as opposed to Roman piety and religion, and finds legends
misleading for ordinary people, as to the intervention of the gods in human affairs (II.lxviii ff.;
II.xx; V.liv).
[2] Geoffrey of Monmouth's early twelfth-century *History* was first published in Paris in 1508 as
Britannie utriusque regum et principum origo et gesta insignia. No edition appeared in Britain till J. A.
Giles's *Historia Britonum* in 1844, but Smith's contemporaries knew it in A. Thompson's
translation *The British History* (1718) 'from the Latin of Jeffrey of Monmouth'. It is generally now
referred to as the *Historia Regum Britanniae*, as in J. Hammer's 1951 edition.

internall government or the causes that brought about the events he relates; but in this way too we may learn a great deal.

History continued in the same state as Herodotus left it till Thucydides undertook a history of the Peloponesian war. His design was different from that of former historians, and was that^m which is the proper design of^n historicall writing. He tells us that he undertook that work that by recording in the truest manner the various incidents of that war and the causes that produced ⟨it⟩, posterity may learn how to produce the like events or shun others, and know what is to be expected from such and such circumstances. In this design he has succeeded better perhaps than any preceding or suc⟨c⟩eeding writer. His Stile is Strong and Nervous, his narration crouded with the most important events. The Subject of his work is the history of a war which he relates in the distinctest manner, giving the history of each
50 campaign by itself so as that we have a compleat notion | of the progress of the war in each place. He never introduces any circumstances that do not some way contribute to the producing some remarkable change in the affairs of the two contending states; This is a fault most other historians are often guilty of. Tacitus and many others introduce all those circumstances which give them an opportunity of displaying their Eloquence. Thus Tacitus in one place stops short to describe a Temple Titus happen'd to visit, and in another the particular circumstances of the disorder in Verres army.^{3} The only place where Thucydides is guilty of it is in describing the concern of the Soldiers at the recall of a favourite generall, and for this too he makes an apology acknowledging that such matters are not the subject of a history. His Events are all chosen so as to be of consequence to the narration, and in his account of them he abundantly satisfies his
51 design, accounting for every | event by the externall causes that produced ⟨it⟩, pointing out what circumstances of time, place, etc. in the side of either party determin'd the success of the enterprize they were engaged in. {He renders his narration at the same time interesting by the internall effects the events producd as in that before mention'd of the Battle in the night, and also by the great number of speeches he introduces into his works, and by which he opens up the different circumstances of the affairs at each time.} His narration is by this means very crouded and tho perhaps it is not so amusing as that of

^{m} of writing *deleted* ^{n} design of ⟨wri *deleted*⟩ *replaces* ly called a

^{3} While in Cyprus Titus visits the famous temple of Paphian Venus and consults the oracle; an account of the history of the cult and the treasures of the temple follows: *Historiae*, II.ii–iv. *Annales*, I.lxi is a flashback to the defeat and death of Varus (not Verres) when Germanicus visits the spot six years later. The Thucydides passage is unidentified.

Herodotus, yet (as he[o] himself says)[4] one who de[r]sires to know the truth and the causes of the different success of the war will be pleased with it. He gives a good deal more of the Politicall and Civill History of the two States engaged in the war than Herodotus, but neither does he seem to have had it much in his view.

{Thucydides is the first who pays any attention at all to Civill History, all who preceded him had attached themselves merely to the military}[p]

The next author we come to is Xenophon. His Stile is easy and agreable[q], not so strong as that of Thucydides but perhaps more pleasant; Nor is ⟨his⟩ narration so crouded as he often condescends to intermix circumstances that do not tend much to the chief events in the
52 history. His retreat of the Ten thousand Grecians[5] is com|monly Compared to Cæsar's Commentaries as they are the accounts of the[r] conduct of two generalls wrote by themselves without the least ostentation. In this point indeed they bear a great resemblance, but in other matters they differ very widely. The Plainness of Xenophon is [is] very different from that of Cæsar, and displays an ingenuity and openness of heart that does not appear in the writings of the other. Cæsars Stile is constantly crouded, he hurrys from one fact of importance to another without touching on anything that is not of importance betwixt them. It is not easy to convey a notion of Xenophons beauties, there are no passages which taken by themselves could shew his manner, and his peculiar excellencies {as he uses but a few circumstances in comparison of Thucidides in his description} {The precedent is always so much connected with every passage that we cannot enter into the beauties of any passage unless we are acquainted with what precedes}[s] He must be read through to perceive his beauties and enter into his manner. In his Expedition Of Cyrus he
53 is at pains in all the circumstances of the narration which would | otherwise often have been of little consequence, ⟨that⟩ tended to conciliate the affections of the Soldiers to their commander, and by this means he engages us so much in his favour that we are no less affected by the description he gives of the fate of the battle, tho' it be very plain and void of ornament, than we would have been by one of the most interesting of those drawn by Thucydides, with all the circumstances he brings in of the effect the ev⟨e⟩nts had on the actors both in the

[o] *numbers written above change original order* says himself [p] *Hand B* [q] *replaces* pleasant
[r] expedi *deleted* [s] *this sentence added later than* as he uses . . . description

[4] Thucydides (I.xxii.4) defines his aim as appealing, through an investigation of the facts, to readers who wish to have a clear view of what happened and may in human probability happen again, in the same or a similar way. He is not composing a prize essay to be heard once only.

[5] *Anabasis*, II.vi; cf. ii.24 n.6 above.

action and afterwards. By thus drawing us gradually on he becomes
one of the most engaging tho not one of the most passionate and
interesting of authors. {To Speak in the Painters Stile; tho neither the
Lines nor the Colouring or expression be very strong yet the
ordonnance of the piece is such that it is on the whole very engaging
and attractive.} He does not raise those violent emotions that
Thucydides does but he pleases and engages fully as much. It is evident
from this that no one passage can make us acquainted with his
beauties. On the other hand there are many passages in Cæsar which
54 will give us a compleat notion of his | manner and his beauties. As all
the events he describes are important, he is often induced to describe
them in a striking and interesting manner. Xenophon too has*t* given us
severall descriptions of characters in his works, not indeed of set
purpose but by the circumstances he mentions of the persons that occur
in the Course of his history. This he does particularly in his treatise of
the Grecian*u* affairs,[6] in which he takes up the history where
Thucydides left it off, and by this means he gives us more insight into
Politicall affairs of Gree[e]ce than the fore-mentioned historians do.

   The first writer however who enters into the Civill history of the
Nations he treats of is Polybius. This author tho inferior to Herodotus
in Grace, and to Thucydides in Strength and Xenophon in Sweetness;
and tho his manner be not very interesting; Yet by the distinctness and
55 ac|curacy with which he has related a series of events, which would by
their importance have been interesting tho handled by a less able
author; as well as by the views he has given us of the Civill constitution
of the Romans, is rendered not only instructing but agreable.

   Dio*v* [7]

56 | Of all the Latin historians Livy is without doubt the best; and if to
be agreable were the chief view of an author he would merit the chief
Rank amongst the whole number. He does not indeed enter deeply
into the causes of things, in the same manner as the Greek historians
do; but*w* on the other hand he renders his descriptions extremely
interesting by the great number of affecting circumstances he has
thrown together, and that not without any connection, as is the
method of Thucydides, but in an order naturall to the times in which
they happend and the circumstances themselves. The circumstances
mentiond in the night battle are narated in such a manner as if they

---

t oft *deleted*   *u* *replaces* military   *v* *The scribe has anticipated the name Dionysius of Halicarnassus
and failed to cancel Dio. After Dio the rest of 55 is blank*   *w* at the *deleted*

---

[6] *Hellenica*, the history of his own times, 411–362, starting where Thucydides left off.
[7] Cf. ii.57 below.

had all happened at the same time; but those Livy relates in the Confusion at Rome after the battle[8] of   [x] are all related in the order they must have succeded.

{But that which is the peculiar excellency of Livy's Stile is the Grandeur and majesty which he maintains thro' the whole of his works and in which he excells all other historians tho' perhaps he is inferiour in many other respects. Tis probably to keep up this gravity, that he pays so much attention to the ceremonies of Religion and the omens and Portents, which he never omitts.[9] For it is not to be supposed that he had any belief in them himself in an age when the vulgar Religion was altogether[y] dissregarded except as a Politicall Institution by the wiser Sort. And of this he gives a hint in}[z]

57   Livy is generally accused of | being very inaccurate in his accounts of military affairs, but I imagine he is not so faulty in this respect as[a] common fame reports. He gives us too a very good account of the Roman constitution not indeed so particular as that of the Halicarnassian; but there is enough thro the work to make us tollerably acquainted with it. It is to be co[r]nsidered too that Livy wrote to Romanes to whom it would have been impertinent to give[b] a minute account of their own Customs; Whereas Dion⟨ysius⟩ of Halicarn⟨assus⟩ wrote for Greeks unacquainted with those matters.

        Livy is[c] compared by Quintilian[10] with Herodotus and Sallust with Thucydides. But Livy without question far excells Herodotus and Sallust on the other hand falls no less short ⟨of⟩ Thycidides. He resembles him indeed in the conciseness of his manner and the suddeness of his transitions but then he has neither his strength nor his accuracy. Nor is narration so crouded in the Cataline conspiracy
58 (induced perhaps by the subject which | furnished him with no very wide field), he has thrown ⟨in⟩ severall digressions of considerable length very little connected with his subject. In both the works that are now remaining he is very defective in his descriptions, his circumstances are often so far from being adapted to the matter in hand that they are what we may call common place and such as would do equally well in any account of the same nature tho the State of the affairs were

---

x blank of six letters in MS; Cannae is intended. Livy XXII.liv.   y unrelated catchword con- *at foot of* v.55   *z interpolation on v.55–v.56 breaks off here; gap of four letters in MS after* in   *a the deleted b MS* gave   *c* Generally *deleted*

---

[8] Cf. ii.29 n.11 above.

[9] Livy dwells on the political and social motives behind the arrangements of the Roman cults: I.xx–xxi (Numa), IV.xxx.9–11 and XXV.i.12 (only Roman gods to be worshipped and in the traditional way).

[10] X.i.101.

considerably different.—His Description of the battle with Jugurtha[11] would in allmost all the circumstances suit equally to any other battle; it signifies indeed nothing more than that there was a great confusion. Thucydides[d] in his description of the night battle, tho he represents nothing more than the confusion, yet it is such a confusion as in no other place, nor in no other conditions could possibly have [have] happened. That described by Sallust is such as happen in every battle.

59 In the same way the circumstances by which | he represents[12] the Luzury of the Romans and their depraved moralls are such as attend[e] Luxury in every country. But those by which Thucyd⟨ides⟩ points[f] out the effe⟨c⟩ts of the S⟨edition⟩[g] in Greece are such as no other sort of sedition, no other state of a country could have occasioned. Besides this, his conciseness which it is plain he copied from Thucy⟨dides⟩ is rather apparent than real. For tho his sentences are always very short, Yet the one signifies nothing more than was implied[h] by the former and in the following one. In the Description of the battle abovementioned the first Sentence implies all the following ones. He supports (however) his[i] narration by the aptness of his expression in which perhaps he surpasses all the other historians, and by the variety of his Spee[e]ches which as well as those of Thucydides shall be considered when we come

60 to Deliber⟨erative⟩ Eloquence. | But from his descriptions, one would imagine that he had enquired rather into the events, than into the different Circumstances, with any accuracy. And as, by this means, he was necessitated to contrive Incidents, he would naturally fall upon Common-place ones such as would occur in every affair of the same Sort . . . [j]

---

[d] again *deleted*   [e] the *deleted*   [f] *MS* paints   [g] *rest of word supplied conjecturally; blank in MS of seven letters*   [h] *replaces* said   [i] *MS* this, t *deleted*   [j] *So in MS*

---

[11] *Bellum Iugurthinum*, xcvii–xcix. The reference below, in the description of the battle in which the troops of Marius were surprised by Jugurtha and Bocchus, must be to the sentence whose remarkable syntactic pattern re-enacts the confusion in which the Roman soldiers, 'trepidi improviso metu', fought: 'pars equos ascendere, obviam ire hostibus, pugna latrocinio magis quam proelio similis fieri, sine signis, sine ordinibus equites peditesque permixti cedere alii, alii obtruncari, multi contra advorsos acerrume pugnantes ab tergo circumveniri; neque virtus neque arma satis tegere . . .' (xcvii.5).

[12] *Bellum Catilinae*, i–xiii (cf. ii.21 n.4 above); Thucydides, III. lxxxii–lxxxiii, on the social disintegration following war.

Lecture. XX.^{th a}

Wednesday. Jan. 12

The first Historians as well as the first Poets chose the marvellous for their Subject as that which was most likely to please a Rude and Ignorant People. Wonder is the passion^b which in such a people will be most easily excited. Their Ignorance renders them Credulous and easily imposed on, and this Credulity makes them delighted with Fables that would not be relished by a [more]^c people of more knowledge.—When therefore Knowledg⟨e⟩ was improved and men 61 were so far | enlightined as to give little credit to those Fabulous relations which had been the entertainment of their Forefathers, the^d Writers would find themselves obliged to take^e some other Subject. For what has nothing to recommend it but its wonderfullness can no longer please than it is believ'd. In the same way as we now see that the Stories of withches and Fairies are swallowed greedily by the ignorant vulgar, which are^f despised by the more knowing. As the marvellous could no longer please authors had recourse to that which they imagind would please and interest most; that is, to represent such actions and passions as, being affecting in themselves, or displaying the delicate feelings of the Human heart, were likely to be most interesting. Thus it was that tragedy succeded the Fabulous accounts of Heroes and centaurs and different monsters, the subject of the first Romances; 62 and thus also, Novells which unfold | the tender emotions or more violent passions in the characters they bring before us succeded the Wild and extravagant Romances which were the first performances of our ancestors in Europe.

The Historians again made it their aim not only to amuse but by^g narrating the more important facts and those which were most concerned in the bringing about great revolutions, and unfolding their causes, to instruct their readers in what manner such events might be brought about or avoided. In this state it was that Tacitus found Historicall writing; He departed altogether from the plan of the former Historians and formed one of a very different sort for his own writings. He had observed that those passages of the historians were most interesting which unfolded the effects the events related produced on the minds of the actors or spectators of those; He imagined therefore 63 that if one could write a history consisting entirely of | such events as were capable of interesting^h the minds of the Readersⁱ by accounts of

^a *MS* XIXth   ^b *to deleted*   ^c *added above the line*   ^d Historians *deleted*   ^e the pr *deleted*   ^f *replaces* would be   ^g the *deleted*   ^h *replaces* Producing these effects on the   ⁱ to the *deleted*

the effects they produced or were of themselves capable of producing this effect on the reader.[j] If we consider the State of the Romans[k] at the time Tacitus wrote and the dispositions of the People which it must necessarily occasion we will find this plan of Tacitus to be a very naturall one. The Roman ⟨Empire⟩[l] was in the Reign of Trajan arrived to its greatest pitch of Glory, The people enjoyed greater internall Tranquillity and Security than they had done in any of the former reigns or indeed in the last 150 ⟨years⟩ of the Republick. Luxury, and Refinement of manners the naturall consequence of the former were then as far advanced as they could be in any state. Sentiment must bee what will chiefly interest such a people. They who live thus[m] in a great City where they have the free Liberty of disposing of their wealth in all the Luxuries and Refinement of Life; who are not

64 called to any publick | employment but what they inclined to[n] and obtained from the favour and Indulgence of the prince; Such a people, I say, having nothing to engage them in the hurry of life would naturally turn their attention to the motions of the human mind, and those events that were accounted for[o] by the different internall affections that influenced the persons concerned, would be what most suited their taste. The French monarchy is in much the same condition as the Romans under Trajan and we[p] find accordingly that those writers who have studied to be most agreable have made great use of Sentiment. {This is that in which the works of Marivaux and the younger Crebillon do excell}[q] Marivaux and ⟨Crebillon⟩ resemble Tacitus as much as we can well imagine in works of so conterary a nature. They are[r] Allways at great pains to account for every event by the temper and internall disposition[s] of the severall actors in disquisitions that approach near to metaphysicall ones.

65 We will find that Tacitus has exe|cuted his works in a manner most suitable to this design. We shall consider chiefly his annalls as it is in them that the character of Tacitus chiefly appears. We are told that his history was that which appeared first; perhaps he may have chosen to try first how a work would be relished in which his favourite plan was somewhat tempered with the usuall manner of writing ⟨his⟩tories before he would risk one where he kept in view intirely the notion he had conceived of the beauty of writing History.[t]

---

j last ten words deleted in MS   *k* Empire *deleted*, s *added to* Roman   *l supplied conjecturally; see pre ious note*   *m or then?*   *n* to *written above* from   *o last three words replace* lead them most into these causes that   *p* will *deleted*   *q Hand B; Hand A here left a blank with* and *in middle; another hand (not B) inserted* Marivaux *in first space, then line was drawn through all. In the following line,* Crebillon *is supplied conjecturally on the strength of Hand B's note*   *r* full of *deleted*   *s last two words replace* intellectuall (?) motion   *t added by Hand B in space at end of line after full stop*

The Period of Time that makes the subjects of both these works contains no remarkable revolutions; the only two of any consequences that happend in that time viz. the assassination of ^{u}{Caligula} and the expulsion of {Nero}^{u} have not come down to our time nor were these of a duration sufficient to fill above a book or two. None almost of the
66 events he relates tended to produce any great chang⟨e⟩s in the state of | publick affairs. He conjectured^v however and I believe justly that the incidents of private life tho' not so important would affect us more deeply and interest us more than those of a Publick nature. The Murther of Agrippina or the death of Germanicus Sons will perhaps affect us more than the Description of the battle in the night by Thucydides.[1] In Private calamities our passions are fixt on one, as it were concentrated and so become greatly Stronger than when seperated and distracted by the affecting circumstances that befell the severall persons involved in a common calamity. He describes all events rather by the internall effects and accounts for them in the same manner, and where he has an opportunity of displaying his talents in these respects and affecting our passions he is not greatly concerned whether the events^w be important or not. Thus he gives us a full description of the Storm that attackd ^{x} fleet, the Sedition of the
67 German Legions and the Buriall of Varrus soldiers[2] by Ger|manicus, altho in the first there ⟨was⟩ but a ship or two lost, the 2.^{d} was no more but a mob and the third was [of] still less important^y than either of the former; Yet the method he describes these is so interesting, he leads us so far into the sentiments and mind of the actors that they are some of the most striking and interesting passages to be met with in any history. In describing the more important actions he does not give us an account of their externall causes, but only of the internall ones, and tho this perhaps will not tend so much to instruct us in the knowledge of the causes of events; yet it will be more interesting and lead us into a science no less usefull, to wit, the knowledge of the motives by which men act; a science too that could not be learned from^z
The events he relates as they are of a private nature, as the intrigues
68 of ministers, the deaths or advancement of particular men, so they | are not connected together by any strong tie such as is necessary in the Series of a history of the common sort where the connection of one

---

$^{u\ u}$ *Hand B in two blanks left* ^{v} *MS* conjactured ^{w} *MS* evints ^{x} *blank of ten letters in MS* ^{y} *replaces* interesting ^{z} *blank of five letters in MS, followed by blank of two and a half lines; then, in inner margin, a pattern of dots apparently a caricature of a face in profile, to which Hand B added* this is a picture of uncertainty

---

[1] *Annales*, XIV.i–xiii; VI.xxiii–xxiv. For Thucydides cf. ii.23 n.5 above.
[2] The fleet of Germanicus, *Annales*, II.xxiii–xxiv; German legions, I.xxxi–xlix; soldiers of Varus, I.lxi–lxii (cf. ii.50 n.3 above).

event with another must be clearly pointed out. But here they are
thrown together without any connection unless perhaps that they
happened at the same time.

The Reflections he makes on the different events are such as we
might call observations on the conduct of the men ⟨rather⟩ than any
generall maxims deduced from particular instances such as those of
      a In his history he gives us indeed some more insight into the
causes of events, and keeps up a continued series of events; But even
here he so far neglects connection as to pass over intirely those
connecting circumstances that tend to no other purpose. Of this we saw
an instance already in the retreat of the Army of Cecina*b* after they had
69 defeated the Germans.[3] The circumstances [of] | which intervened
betwixt that defeat and the Crossing of the Rhine were probably such
as would have afforded no room for those descriptions or affecting
narrations in which he thought the chief beauty of writing consisted.*c*

{Such is the true Character of Tacitus which has been mis-
represented by all his commentators from Boccalini*d* down to
Gordon[4]} — — —

Machiavell and Guichardin*e* are·the two most famous modern
Italian historians.[5] The former*f* seems to have had*g* chiefly in his view
to prove certain maxims which he had laid down, as the impolitickness
of keeping up a standing army,*h* and others of the same sort, generally
Contradictory to the received politicks of the times. The different
70 courts of Italy*i* at that time piqued themselves greatly on a refined and |
subtle politicks; nothing could then be a greater reproach to a man of
genius than that he was of an open and undesigning character. But
these politicks he seems to have altogether despised and has therefore
given little attention to them or represented them as of no great
moment. He is to be commended above most modern writers on one
account, as he does not seem to favour any one party more than*j*

---

a blank of ten letters in MS   *b Hand B's correction of Hand A's* Socina *(deleted)*   *c blank
of three and a half lines*   *d replaces (in Hand B?)* Machiavell   *e Hand B in blank left*
f first half deleted   *g* it *deleted*   *h blank line*   *i* seem'd *deleted*   *j* the *deleted*;
and . . . relation *is squeezed in between this line and next, and overflows to v.69*

[3] Cf. ii.36 n.5 above.
[4] See ii.26 n.9 and 20 n.3 above. Gordon discusses 'the foolish censure of Boccalini and others
upon Tacitus' in *The Works of Tacitus*, i (1728), Political Discourse 2, sec. xi.
[5] Niccolò Machiavelli (1469–1527); principal historical work, *Historie fiorentine*, 1525 (cf. ii.18
n.2 above). Most of the works of Francesco Guicciardini (1483–1540) were published
posthumously. The most notable are the political and social maxims based on his historical
studies, *Ricordi politici e civili* (written 1528–30, published 1576) and *Storia d'Italia* (written 1536,
published 1561). In *Considerazioni sui Discorsi del Machiavelli* (written 1529) he disagreed with
Machiavelli's interpretations of Roman history as basis for political thought.

another and therefore is generally very candid in his relation {which is the scheme of Lord Clarendon and Bishop Burnet.}

{Machiavel is of all Modern Historians the only one who has contented himself with that which is the chief purpose of History, to relate Events and connect them with their causes without becoming a party on[k] either side}

Guichardin[l] on the other hand seems as much to have esteemd the Politicks then in fashion as Machiavel[l] dispised them and is therefor at great pains to explain[s] the schemes that brought about the severall events of importance. {His whole History is a criticall dissertation on the Schemes, the little and often crooked artifices of the times.}[m] In his account of his own country Florence he often dwells on particulars of very little moment, which makes Boccalini in his advices from Parnassus[6] cause Apollo condemn ⟨one⟩ to Read his accoun⟨t⟩ of the
71 disputes betwixt Florence and Pisa | which he receives as a very hard task.[n]

Clarendon and Burnet are the two English authors who have signalized themselves chiefly in writing history.

As the thing he[7] had in view was to represe⟨n⟩t the bad disposition of the one party[o] and justify the conduct of the other, so it is not those events which were of the greatest importance and tended most to produce a memorable change on which he insists but such as tend most to unfold the dispositions of the different parties. In this manner it is that he discusses in two or three sentences all the actions of Montrose in Scotland tho' of the Greatest importance, and on the other hand relates at length the whole proceeding of one of the Keepers of the great Seal[p] Lord Littletons flight to the King[q] tho' it producd nothing but a new Seal and a new keeper, and two protest which he is at the Pains to tell us at full length.

---

[k] *MS* or. *This interpolation,* Machiavel . . . side, *is in Hand B, above Hand A's addition* which . . . Burnet   [l-l] *Hand B in two blanks left*   [m] *Hand B, keyed in after* of importance
[n] *one blank line*   [o] *last seven words replace* in as Black a light as possible the one party *(last three words not deleted)*   [p] been *deleted*   [q] *last six words inserted by Hand B in blank left*

[6] *De' Ragguagli di Parnaso* (adjudications or notifications from Parnassus, by Apollo) appeared in two 'centuries' in 1612 and 1613. The sentence passed on a Laconic for using three words instead of two is in Century i, no 6. The work was immensely popular and influential in the seventeenth century; under various titles ('Newes', 'The New-Found Politicke', 'Advertisements', 'Advices') it appeared in six different English translations between 1622 and 1727, *Advices from Parnassus* in 1706. Among its progeny were 'Sessions of the Poets', or imaginary trials of writers for their misdeeds, before assessors and jurors. *The Great Assises Holden in Parnassus by Apollo and his Assessors* (1645; Luttrell Soc. Reprint 6, 1948) arraigns newspapers and their editors. For Boccalini see ii.26 n.9 above.
[7] i.e. Clarendon: references to his *History of the Rebellion,* Books viii–ix and v respectively.

72   For[r] | the same reason it is that he is ⟨at⟩ such pains in describing characters; not to explain the transactions but to display the characters of the parties, by shewing that of individualls; and for this reason[s] there is hardly a footman brings a message but what he gives us an account of his character. By crouding in so many trifling circumstances he has swelled the history of 18 years at most to the size of 3 folio volumes.[t]

Burnet again delivers his narration not as a Compleat history of the times but only as an account of those facts that had come to his knowledge. His business plain⟨l⟩y appears to have been to set the one party in as black a light as he could and justify the other, so that he is to be con⟨si⟩dered rather as party writer[8] than as a candid historian. His manner is lively and spirited[u], his Stile very plain, but his language and expression is low and such as we would expect from an old nurse rather

73   than from a gentleman. It has been the fate of | all modern histories[v] to be wrote in a party spirit for reasons already mentioned. Rapin[9] seems to be the most candid[w] of all those who have wrote on the affairs of England. Yet he has entered too much into the private affairs of the monarchs and the parties amongst the severall great men concern'd, so that his history as many others is rather an account of the Lives of the princes than of the affairs of the body of the people.

---

[r] *scribe started 72 with* Burnet, *by anticipation*   [s] it is that *deleted*   [t] *one blank line*   [u] but *deleted*   [v] *replaces* governments   [w] *note in inner margin*: so (*or 10?*) years ago. a better now

[8] Burnet's views on political and ecclesiastical affairs were broad church, and often too liberal for his own good. See i.v.199 n.11 above.

[9] See ii.34 n.3 above. The marginal note no doubt refers to the *History of Great Britain* [later *England*] by Smith's friend David Hume, which appeared in six volumes in 1754, 1757, 1759, 1762.

Lecture XXI.^{st a}

Friday. Jan.^{ry} 14
1763

N.B. This Lecture was delivered intirely without Book

I have now finished what I have to say with regard to the 1st Species of Writing viz. the narrative, where the business is to relate facts, and come in the next place to treat of that where the design is to prove some proposition or series of propositions. The Rules we have already given 74 with regard to the narrative composition will with | a few alterations be easily accomodated to this Species also.

We may observe also that the same rules will also be equally applicable to Poeticall compositions. For what is it which constitutes the essential difference betwixt a historicall poem and a history? It is no more than this that the one is in prose and the other in verse. Now what is that induces one to write in verse^b rather than in prose? what is his design?^c It is certainly far more difficulte, but at the same time it is much superior in beauty and strength. It is evident therefore that the authors design in writing is to amuse us[e]. {There are many other authors besides the poets who have made it their chief design to please but they are the only writers who by the very manner in which they write fairly tell us that this is their design:} The way in which he writes is of all others best calculated to answer this end. The best prose composition, the best oratoricall^d discourse⟨e⟩ does not affect us half so much. An orator will^e often tell us the same thing in many shape[r]s. 75 If we should examine | the best orations we will find that the 2^d, 3^d and 4th Sentences often contain nothing more^f than is contained in the 1st only turnd into other words. Whereas none but the lower class have such repetitions. It is even necessary for an orator to do this, if he expects that the argument shall have its full force. Some repetition is often absolutely necessary to make us affected in^g the manner the orator desires. But on the other hand repetition is so far from being necessary that anyone who is the least acquainted with Poetry either by writing or reading knows there is nothing more dissagreable than to have the next line or the next couplet express in other words the same thing that has been already expressed in the one before us. Mr Pope tells us that the Reason which induced him to write his *Essay on man* in

---

^a *MS* XXth *deleted; see end of 79*   ^b *replaces* prose   ^c Why should the Taking of Troy, the fo, *on v.73,* ^d *MS* ortaroicall   ^e *MS* wall, *replaces* of   ^f *replaces* but ^g *replaces* with

verse rather than in Prose was that he saw he could do it in a much shorter and concise manner.[1] I much doubt indeed whether this was
76 his real motive; but it shews he | was very sensible of the great superiority of Poetry over prose in this[h] respect. I mentioned this particular of the great conciseness of poetry, not that it is one of the chief of its beauties, but as it may prove the great advantage of Poetical measures, and the great effect harmony and regular movement has on us when it commands our attention so much that we are never[i] necessitated to Repeat the same thing over a second time. {It is needless to prove the superiority of Poetry over prose, every ones experience and the common consent of mankind sufficiently confirm this.} One expression in this manner has more effect on us than when the orator turns it in 3 or four different shapes.

The manner however as it is so vastly more difficult than prose writing shows sufficiently that amusement and intertainment was the chief design of the poet. It is from[j] our being satisfied that this is the design of Poetry that what we call Poeticall licence has taken its
77 ori|gin.

There are some men who distinguish themselves chiefly in conversation by a certain knack of telling a Story. They plainly shew by their manner, and the way in which they tell it that it is not their design to be believed; they do not care in the least whether they are or not; all they seem to have in view is to divert us by some ridiculous Story. As we perceive that this is their design, we are not very anxious whether the Story be just as they tell it or not. We give them a liberty to add to, or take from the Story what they think proper, to cut and carve as they please. For there is no story so compleatly of one sort that every circumstance tends to produce the same effect. There is no story, no adventure so intirely ridiculous that there is not som⟨e⟩ part of it ⟨of⟩ a grave nature, there is none so melancholy but what there is some part
78 of it[k] prosperous, nor any so | prosperous that is not somewhat tinctured with adversity. Now as we are sensible of this we are not offended tho the teller of Ridiculous Stories, a talent which[l] tho it be no very

---

[h] poetry *deleted*   [i] desirous *deleted*   [j] this *deleted*   [k] effect is very tell *deleted*   [l] a talent which *replaces* a character

---

[1] In 'To the Reader', prefixed to Epistle i of *Essay on Man* in 1733, Pope explained his choice of '*the Epistolary Way of Writing*' then in vogue; his subject, though high and of dignity, is '*mixt with* Argument, *which of its Nature approacheth to Prose*'. In 'The Design', prefixed to the whole poem in 1734, he defends his choice of verse and even rhyme: these are more striking and more memorable, and he found he could express maxims or precepts 'more *shortly* this way than in prose.' Conciseness is a source of much of the '*force* as well as *grace* of arguments. . . . I was unable to treat this part of my subject more in detail, without becoming dry and tedious; or more *poetically*, without sacrificing perspicuity to ornament, without wandring from the precision, or breaking the chain of reasoning'.

eminent one is generally well received, should throw[m] out those circumstances which would tend to diminish the Ridicule of the Rest; or add others which would heighten it; nay we can even allow him to make up a story alltogether; but this seldom takes so well. {Now if we would make the Story perfectly and compleatly ridiculous or melancholy or merry we must leave out those Jarring and dissimilar Circumstances}[n] There are also tellers of wonderfull stories, and tellers of mournfull Lamentable ones; these as well as the others are often obliged to add or take away from their Story; as they can seldom get one that will prove so very wonderfull or so very lamentable that there is nothing in it that appears little or at least of an ordinary nature. Now these are altogether dissagreable; we know that their[o] stories are forged and yet they tell them with a grave face and appear evidently to desire we should believe them. There are even some who take pains to tell illnatured Stories, and turn a thing of a very harmless nature into a
79 very Black and Shocking one, these deserve no quarter tho | they are often too well received. The wonder teller and [and] the teller of lamentable Stories are always despised. It is only the teller of Ridiculous Stories that can be at all tollerable in conversation, as we know his design is harmless[p] so we are readily inclined to grant him some licence.

    The Poet is exactly in the same condition; his design is to intertain[q] and he does not pretend that what he tells us is true; for which reason we are not offended if he make some additions to the Story he relates. But not [not] onely are ridiculous stories allowable in Poetry, but also the wonderfull and the Lamentable. The teller of Wonderfull or lamentable Stories is disagreable because he endeavours to paun them upon us for true ones. But as this is not the case of the poet, we can receive not only the Ridiculous ones but the others also. The Subjects are generally so distant we are not offended at the Poet if he imbellishes his Story with the addition of some circumstances. The Taking of
80 Troy, the foundation of the Roman Empire, or the | Life of Henry the 4th of France[2] are not so much connected with us as to make us[r] much concernd in what way they are represented. For we do not read Homer to be instructed in the Events of the Trojan war, nor Virgil to know {the origin of the Romans}[s]; Nor Milton to be informed in the Scripturall account of the Fall of Man[t]; tho inde⟨e⟩d most of the particulars be brought into it, yet no one reads it to increase his faith.

---

[m] *MS* through   [n] *Hand B*   [o] *MS* there   [p] *replaces* good   [q] *replaces* amuse   [r] *as to make us replaces* that we can   [s] *v.74 note (in Hand B) replaces* the particulars of the Vouyage of Æneas, *deleted on 80*   [t] *changed from* Adam

[2] Voltaire's epic *La Henriade* (1723).

But[u] as it is intertainment we look for from the Poet as well as the storyteller, so we make them the same concessions. As we know that no Story is so compleatly ridiculous as to tell well without some cobling, so we know that no series of adventures are so entirely of a piece, either so wonderfull and extraord⟨in⟩ary, so lamentable or so absurd that they could compleatly answer the design of a Poet without some improvement. We therefore allow the tragic writer whose Subject is the lamentabl⟨e⟩, the Comic writer who has pitched on the ridiculous 81 and absurd for his | subject, and the Epic Poet who endeavours to interest us by a series of grand and extraordinary events, each to modell[v] his Story (or even sometimes to invent one), so as to make it all suitable to his end. {Dramatick and epick Poetry differ only in the connexion of the Scenes of Action they exhibit: in the former the persons come in themselves, in the latter the connexions are made in the person of the Poiet; he says such a person came in and said so and so or did so and so, and then came another and said and did so and so}[w]

(From hence we may see that) There is one requisite absolutely necessary both to Epic and Dramatick writing, that is, Unity of Interest.[x] The greatest Critics have laboured greatly to shew in what it is that this Requisite consists, but if we attend to it we will find that it is very easily comprehended and what we meet with in every common Story.—It is no more than this; that every part of the Story should tend to some one end, whatever that be. This we find in every nurses tale; every story of a king and a Queen, of the fairies, ghosts and suchlike, have a regular beginning, a middle and an end. There is one point which all the rest tend to bring about and in which they are wound up and the Story entirely concluded. This we find in them all whether they be of a gay or grave, of a happy and joyous or a miserable nature; it may indeed be easier in them because they are shorter, but is 82 certainly attainable in all.—In the | same manner as a Storyteller would appear to have failed in his design of raising our laughter, or at least he could not answer it so well, if he should bring in any of a grave and serious nature; So it is necessary that the poet should accommodate all his circumstances so as that they tend to bring about the main event either directly or indirectly.—A comic writer should make all the parts tend to excite our sense of Ridicule and at last conclud⟨e⟩ the work with the highest piece of Ridicule which all the Rest pointed at or tended some way to bring about. The tragic[y] writer must in the same manner make all the parts of the action of a lamentable natur⟨e⟩ or some way tend to bring about the great catastrophe; and so of the Epic writer.—But it is to be observed that in Comic writings the

---

[u] as wh *deleted*   [v] *replaces* form   [w] *Hand B*   [x] *written large in MS*   [y] and Epic *added above line, then deleted*

Ridicule must consist in the Characters represented: Ridicule that is founded only on the Ridiculousness of the circumstances into which the Persons are brought without regarding themselves is the lowest
83   Species of Wit and such as is hardly tollerable in a common Story. | On the other hand in tragedy or Epic Poetry the chief art does not consist in displaying the characters; but in shewing in what manner the Chief Persons in whom we are chiefly concerned⁝ acted in Lamentable or difficult circumstances, and how at last they were either in the 1ˢᵗ altogether oppressed by their misfortunes or extricated themselves from them. The unity in Comedy consists in the Characters, whereas in tragedy or Epic poetry it consists chiefly in managing the Circumstances.

But in no part should any thing appear to have a conterary tendency to that of the whole piece. For this reason the Scene *ᵃ* in   *ᵃ* and the Scene of the Gravediggers in Hamlet tho very good s⟨c⟩enes in their Sort had better been away as the⟨y⟩ have no share in bringing about the main design of the piece and are somewhat conterary to the temper of the Rest of the Scenes.

We may see from this that tragi-comedy tho the different parts be
84   very well executed and may be very interesting, is yet a monstrous | production. Thus in the Spanish Friars³ the Tragicall part is very good and the comic part is admirable; so that the whole is no bad piece; but the parts had been much better taken seperate; the effect of the one would not have contradicted that of the other.

There is another Species of Unity viz. the Unity of Time⁴ which the more severe Criticks, tho it is not necessary in the Epic Poetry, account indispensably requisite in Dramatic Writing, both tragedy and Comedy. Now let us consider in what the difference betwixt Tragedy and Epic writings consists. It is no more than that in the one case the Persons come on the stage and speak their parts, and in the other the Poet tells us that after one had spoke so and so another spoke after him. Home⟨r⟩ tells us that a Captain spoke to such a company in one way, left them and spoke to another and did such or such action. Sophocles would on the other hand put these speeches in the mouths of the
85   person⟨s⟩ themselves and represent the actions as | then passing before us. But from this difference it must necessarily follow that the one must be vastly shorter than the other. As the one is carried on by Dialogue the connection betwixt two parts can only be kept up by the changing

---

⁝ and who must *added above line, then deleted*   *ᵃ⁻ᵃ two long blanks in MS (the omissions probably refer to the Porter scene in Macbeth, II.iii)*

---

³ Dryden's comedy *The Spanish fryar; or the double discovery*, produced Nov. 1680, published 1681.
⁴ On the Unities see Introduction, p. *21*.

of the persons, Whereas in the other the poet can in a few words, in his own person, keep up the connection. The actions of a year would take up a year to Represent them; but a poet can dispatch them in two or three words.

Shakespeare and some other English writers have been[b] chiefly guilty of omitting this; the French are generally very little; Racin⟨e⟩ never supposes more time to have been taken up in the actions than in the Representations. Shakespeare on the other hand supposes often that three or four years[5] have elapsed betwixt one scen[c]e and another. The reason generally given for the bad effect of such blanks where no action⟨s⟩ connecting them are represented is that it prevents our deception, we can not suppose that when we have been but $\frac{1}{4}$ of an hour in the play-house that two or three Years has past. But in reality

86 we are never thus deceived. | We know that we are in the play-house, that the persons before us are actors, and that the thing represented either happened before or perhaps never happend at all. The pleasure we have in a dramaticall performance no more arises from deception than that which ⟨we⟩ have in looking at Picture; No one ever imagined that he saw the Sacrifice of Iphigenia; no more did any one imagine that ⟨he⟩ saw king Richard the Third; Ever⟨y⟩one knows that at the one time he saw a picture and at the other Mr Garrick or some other actor. Tis not then from the interruption of the deception[c] that the bad effect of such transgressions of the unity of time proceed; It is rather from the uneasiness we feel in being kept in the dark with regard to what happened in so long a time. When in the scene before us there is supposed to have passed three or four years since the last was before us; We immediately become uneasy to know what has happened during that time. Many important events must have passed in that time

87 which we know nothing ⟨of⟩. We make a jump | from one time to another without knowing what connected them. The same jump is often made in Epic Poets, but they take care to smooth it over, by telling us in a few words what happened in that time. Was this small[d] connection omitted the Jump would be as uneasy in the Epic poem as the Dramaticall performance. Le Brun[e] has represented the different actions[6] of Mary of Medicis, [f]   the of   [f] and other painters

---

[b] most *deleted*   [c] *MS* deeption *replaces* action   [d] *written over* smoothe   [e] *inserted by Hand*
B *in blank left*   [f]–[f] *two blanks in MS of six and ten letters each*

---

[5] Frequently in his history plays; and in *The Winter's Tale* sixteen years explicitly elapse between Acts III and IV.
[6] Charles Le Brun (1619–90), from 1664 first Court painter in France and responsible for the decoration of the :oyal palaces, Vaux, Versailles, etc. His master was Poussin. The portrait of Marie de Medicis is not noted in Henry Jouin, *Charles Le Brun* (1889), or the catalogue of the 1963 Versailles Exhibition of Le Brun.

have represented the different transactions of an Heroick Poem. This is surely a very pretty fancy and may have a very good effect; but nothing equall to what the Poem itself would have. The Painting can only represent one moment or Point of time and the situation*g* things were in at that time; Betwixt one moment and another there must have been a very considerable time, a great number of moments must have passed; The actions of all these are unknown and can only be conjectured. {Severall Painters have emulated the Poets in giving a Suit of Actions but these labour under a defect for want of Connection; when we turn from one Picture to look at another we do not know the Persons which act there till we have studied the piece nor do we know what hath happened intermediate and preparatory to this action}*h* We
88 are uneasy here just from | the same cause as we are at an interruption of time in a drammatick performance. That it is not the*i* preventing our deception which occasions it may appear from this that we are not very uneasy at a small interruption, we can easily conceive what may have passed during the hour or two for which the action is suspended. We see also that these pieces tho' they have not all the effect they would have were it not for this defect, have yet a very considerable one, which would not be the case if the whole pleasure we take in dramaticall works proceeded from the deception.

The same things may be said with regard to the Unity of Place which some criticks reckon indispensably necessary to the Dramaticall works. In an Epic poem the connection of place is easily maintaind by the poets having it in his power to connect the different actions by a
89 few intervening words. In the dramatick works, the | Unity of place can not be altogether maintaind unless the action be such as that it be all supposed to be transacted in the same place, as well as acted.*j* Shakespeare in some of his plays breaks thro this Rule altogether; he makes one Scene be in France, and the following one in England, one at London and another at York etc. In this case the distance is so great that we are anxious to know what has happend in the intervall betwixt them. The best way, surely is to fix the action to one place if possible, as Racin⟨e⟩ and Sophocles have done, and if that is not possible we should make the distance as little as possible confining the action to the same house or thereabouts. But when this rule is not observed we find the effect of the Piece may still be very considerable, which as we said before shows that it is not deception which gives us the pleasure we find in these works and in fact we nev⟨e⟩r are deceived for one moment.
90 | There is one thing however that must be always observed, otherwise the piece can never produce any great effect; it is the

---

g MS sutuation   *h Hand B ; this note begins opposite* Le Brun has . . . *i.e. the 4th sentence of ii.87*
i unde *deleted*   *j* Time *follows in tiny writing; supply* at the same?

Propriety of character. As comedy and Tragedy are designed to produce very different effects, so the characters they place as the principal ones must be such as are suited to produce these Conterary effects.

Kings and Nobles are what make the best characters in a Tragedy. {The misfortunes of the great as the⟨y⟩ happen less frequently affect us more. There is in humane Nature a Servility which inclines us to adore our Superiors and an inhumanity which disposes us to contempt and trample under foot our inferiors}*k* We are too much*l* accustomed to the misfortunes of people below or equall with ourselves to be greatly affected by them. But the misfortunes of the great both as they seem connected with the wellfare of a multitude and as [they seem] we*m* are apt to pay great respect and attention to our superiors however unworthy are what chiefly affect us. Nay such is the temper of men, that we are rather disposed to laugh at the misfortunes of our inferiors than take part in them.

'Tis for this same principle that*n* persons of high rank make very bad actors in a comedy. Dukes and Princes and men of high rank, tho they be never so ridiculous in themselves, never appear the subject of 91 Laughter*o*, | the same prejudice which makes us be so highly interested in their misfortunes, makes us also imagine there is something respectable even in their follies. Persons in low life either equall or inferior to ourselves are the best characters for comedy. We can laugh heartily at the absurdity of a shoemaker or a burgess tho we can hardly prevail on ourselves to weep at his misfortunes. Farces where the characters are the lowest of any make us laugh more than the finest comedy, and on the other ⟨hand⟩ we can hardly enter into the humour of a comedy of the higher sort where dukes and nobles*p* are the objects of our laughter: {We can laugh at Sancho Panca in his Island[7] because we know that he was no real but only a mock governor.} We even carry this so far that we are rather apt to make sport of the misfortunes of our inferiors than sympathise with them. The Italian comedy, by applying the misfortunes of the great personages of tragedy*q* to persons in Low life and putting their speeches in their mouths, is so far from appearing lamentable, that ⟨it⟩ is the most ridiculous of any, tho no doubt persons in low life are as deeply affected with the passions of grief or sorrow [and] or joy as those of greater fortunes.

v.91 | {As it ⟨is⟩ the misfortunes or recovery of the chief persons in a

k Hand B   *l* replaces well   *m* changed from to be   *n* the deleted   *o* 90 and 91 are on a biofolium stuck in after the first leaf of quire 74 (i.e. p. 89) ; at lower outer edge of v.90 is a half-erased note written vertically in Hand A: My Dear Dory   *p* replaces princes   *q* MS traegedy

[7] Barataria, of which he was made governor briefly by the Duke: *Don Quixote*, ii.ch.36–45.

tragedy that we are to be chiefly interested in, A Villain can never be a fit person for the hero of such a piece. For this reason tho Iago makes a tollerably good actor in Othello as the latter has evidently the superiority to him in our opinion: Yet Alonzo*r* in the Revenge[8] which is nothing more than Othello Spoiled is a very unfit character, as the hero Alonso has such an inferiority of parts to Zanga*s* that we should rather take him to be the principle character.}*t*

92 | We observed before that the Ridicule*u* of Commedy consists in the Ridiculousness*v* of the characters and not of the circumstances. It will be necessary therefore that the characters should be changed. We can not always be laughing at misers, or fops, we must have a variety of characters, to make the pieces agreable. But we will find that there is no such necessity in tragedy or Epic Poetry. The Characters here are not the principall thing; The adventures or circumstances*w* and the behaviour of the different persons in these circumstances is what chiefly interests us. We are uneasy when those worthy persons are in difficult or unhappy circumstances and rejoice if they are extricated and our grief is at its height when they are altogether overwhelmed. These circumstances may be varied a thousand ways; so the Grief or concer⟨n⟩ excited by the Orphan and that by Venice preserved[9] are very different.

93   Mr   *x* however reckons this one | of the essentiall beauties of a heroick poem.[10] But when we consider that neither in Virgill nor Racine there is the variety of characters, there is no Variety in the Aeneid at all; Racine's men are all of one sort and his women also have all the same character. When we consider too, that Virgill is in the Opinion of many the 1st of Epic Poets, but by the unive⟨r⟩sall consent he is the 2^d; that Racin⟨e⟩ Is universally acknowledged to be the 2^d Tragic writer, the French perhaps preferring Corneille and the English Sophocles; When we consider, I say, that the 2^d perhaps the First of

---

r Hand B's correction of Hand A's Zara (*deleted*)   *s Hand B's correction of Hand A's* him (*deleted*)
t the v.91 notes end with the catchwords We observed Sc *and are continued on 92*   *u MS* riducule
v MS Rudiculousness   *w* may be are that which chiefly engage us, togeth *deleted*   *x blank of six letters in MS*

---

[8] Edward Young's tragedy of jealousy *The Revenge* was produced and published in 1721. Zanga is Don Alonzo's Moorish captive, taking revenge on his conqueror for his humiliation.

[9] Thomas Otway's tragedies: *The Orphan; or the unhappy marriage* (1680), *Venice Preserv'd: or a plot discover'd* (1682). On *The Orphan*: TMS I.ii.2.3, II.iii.3.5.

[10] '*Homer* has excelled all the heroic Poets that ever wrote, in the Multitude and Variety of his Characters'; '. . . but also in the Novelty of his Characters' (*Spectator*, 273, 12 Jan. 1712). Addison goes on to praise Milton for introducing all the variety of characterization his poem was capable of. His two human persons represent in fact 'four distinct Characters'; and *Spectator* 309 (23 Feb. 1712) illustrates the points made by examining the characters of the fallen angels in *Paradise Lost* in all their diversity. Addison claims to be elaborating an Aristotelian principle, but Aristotle had in mind 'manners' or *mores* rather than personalities.

Epic poets; and the 2^d perhaps the first of Tragic Poets have not^y the smallest share of this Beauty, we will be apt to think that it is not so very essentiall. Perhaps the great attention which these authors have paid to the Propriety, Decorum, and ^{z} of their works has hindered them from bringing in a variety of characters, thro all which it is almost impossible to keep up the decorum and propriety of the pieces. In this point they are indeed greatly inferior to two other Poets,

94 Homer and Shakespear. The first of these | has a vast Variety of characters and the latter still greater. But then this vast variety has often lead them into Breaches of Decency, Propriety and Uniformity of Interest.^{a} As Racine seems to have studied these last mentiond perfections still more than Virgill, so he has a still less variety of characters. And in the same manner Shakespear, as the^b incon⟨c⟩eivable variety of characters he has introduc'd far ex⟨c⟩eeds that of Homer's, so he has paid still less regard to De⟨c⟩ency and Propriety. These Different Beauties^c of Decorum and Variety seem incompatible when in their greatest perfection, and we are not to condemn one who excells in the one for not^d being equally excellent in the other.

This decorum we see is very easily maintaind in the lighter pieces of Poetry such as Odes, Elegy, and Pastorall where the length of the Piece does not admit of any great variety of incidents. {Ode, Elegy and all the other smaller compositions are the exhibitions only of a Single event or action or of one Simple disposition in a person; they have not time nor connexion Sufficient to awaken great emotions}^{e}—In all these Pieces the affection^f or temper of mind they would excite should not be

95 very violent. Great Passions as they are long of being | raised in the Persons themselves so are they not to be raised in us but by a work of a considerable Length. A temper of mind that differs very little from the common tranquillity of mind is what we can best enter into, by the perusall of a piece of a small length. A painting can only present us with the action at one point of time. For this reason it is that we are more pleased with those that represent a state not far different from that we are generally in when we view the Picture; When one takes a view of the Chartoons of Raphael, it is not Paul Preaching at Athens or Elias Struck with Blindness that first attract our attention but Peter receiving the Keys, Peter feed my Sheep. This piece represents a state of mind in all the figures not much different from that we are in. {Poussin^{11} used to say that the tranquill pieces were what he liked

^{y} obe *deleted* ^{z} *blank of six letters* (*probably* Uniformity *as in the same phrase a few lines on*)
^{a} *last three words inserted by Hand B in blank left* ^{b} has *deleted;* the *changed from* he ^{c} *replaces* Perfections ^{d} *inserted in margin in another hand* ^{e} *Hand B* ^{f} *replaces* passion

---

^{11} Nicolas Poussin: *Lettres et propos sur l'art,* ed. Anthony Blunt (1964).

best.} Whereas the emotions in the others are so violent that it takes a considerable time before we can work ourselves up so far as to enter into the Spirit of the pieces.

96 | In the same manner an Ode or Elegy {in which there is no odds but in the measure} which differ little from the common state of mind are what most please us. Such is that on the Church yard, or Eton College by Mr Grey.[12] The best of Horaces (tho inferior to Mr Greys) are all of this sort. Pastoralls too are subject to the same rule for it matters not whether the Sentiments represented to us be in the person of the poet or in a dialogue. The Pastorall poem[13] of Mr Shenstone[g] if he had put the account he gives of the effects love had on himself into the mouth of a person in the dialogue would have been precisely similar to the 3[d] pastorall of Virgil. The only difference betwixt an ode and the ordinary sort of Pastoralls is that in the one the temper of the poets mind and in the other of an other person are related.

g inserted by Hand B in blank left

---

[12] Smith often expressed his admiration of Gray: see TMS III.2.19 ('the first poet in the English language' if only he had 'written a little more'), III.3.15; EPS 225 n.20, and ii.121 n.10 below. In his life of Gray (final paragraph) Johnson, who disliked Gray's Odes, pays to the *Elegy in a Country Churchyard* a tribute similar to Smith's here: 'The *Church-yard* abounds with images which find a mirrour in every mind, and with sentiments to which every bosom returns an echo'. Smith uses the word *elegy* in the special sense it had acquired since the publication in 1743 of James Hammond's *Love elegies, written in the year 1732*. Hammond's 'measure', four-line stanzas of alternately rhyming iambic pentameters, was widely imitated (especially in the circle of Shenstone and Richard Jago) in reflective or 'moral' elegies, the genre to which Gray's (written ?1746, published 1751 with immediate success) belongs.

[13] *A Pastoral Ballad* by William Shenstone, earlier entitled *Recollection, or the Shepherd's Garland*, first appeared anonymously as an eight-stanza imitation of Nicholas Rowe's 'Colin's Complaint, or the Despairing Shepherd' (written to the tune of 'Grim King of the Ghosts'), in the *London Magazine*, Dec. 1751, 565. Written in 1743 and much revised, with a fourth section varying in successive versions from hopeful to despondent, it appeared in Dodsley's *Collection of Poems* iv.348 (1755), where Smith would read it. Shenstone was attracted by Rowe's stanza-form: anapaestic trimeters rhyming ababcdcd; that poem was said to be about Addison and the Countess of Warwick. See *The Letters of William Shenstone*, ed. M. Williams (1939), 74, 79, 87, 300, 421–2, 444, 633.

97   # Lecture XXII[d][a]

Monday Jan.ʸ 17. 1763

Having now said all I think necessary concerning the two most simple methods of Writing, the Descriptive and Historicall, I might now proceed to the 3 Method viz. the Didactick,[1] but as the Rules concerning it are very obvious, I shall here pass it over and proceed immediately to consider the Oratoricall Stile.

Eloquence as I mention'd before was divided by the ancient⟨s⟩ into three Sorts, 1ˢᵗ The Demonstrative, 2ᵈˡʸ The Deliberative, 3ᵈˡʸ The Judiciall.—I shall begin with the Demonstrative as being most Simple and as the rules which[b] regard it are almost all applicable to the other two species of Eloquenc⟨e⟩ and also because those rules which are to be given concerning it have least dependance on what I shall advance hereafter with regard to Didactic Etc.[c]

This Sort of Eloquence generally was directed to the Commendation
98 of some Great man, which was given out to be the design of | the Orator, tho' as the name of Demonstrative or Paren   [d] shows the Real design of the orator was to shew his own Eloquence. To maintain the Glory of the Person he commended was what he gave out to be his sole design in undertaking the work: But to raise his own glory was plainly the motive of his undertaking, as the Glory of the Person could not be very interesting either to the Orator or his hearers, as they were generally persons who had lived some ages before. {And this also will lead him   [e]}

In treating of this Subject the following order shall be observed. In the 1ˢᵗ Place I shall consider, I. The End Proposed in these orations. IIᵈˡʸ The means by which this may be brought about. IIIᵈˡʸ The order in which those means are to be arranged. IVˡʸ The manner in which these are to be expressed: and Vᵗʰˡʸ Lastly what authors have most excelled in this Species of writing.

1ˢᵗ As to the End proposd it will not be difficult to determine what
99 this is | to be. The nature of the Work plainly shews, that it is to Raise the Glory and Reputation of the Person commended. For tho' the increase of his own fame may be the design of the Orator, and

---

[a] MS XXIᵗ   [b] *replaces* with   [c] In treating of this subject I shall observe the following method. I *deleted*   [d] *blank of nine letters in MS* (*probably* 'Panegyrick')   [e] *blank of five letters in MS*

---

[1] See i.151 above.

ge⟨ne⟩rally is so, Yet this is to be considered only as a secondary end. The Glory of the Person praised is the thing the orator is to have in view; and the other secondary*ʲ* end is to be brought about only by acquitting himself handsomely in the principall design.

II^dly Of the means by which this end may be accomplished.—It is evident that there are but two ways in which a man*ᵍ* may be commended*ʰ*, either 1st by describing*ⁱ* his actions, or 2dly By praising his character. The manner in which actions and characters are to be described have already been explained at some length and need not be here repeated. What we are here to aim at is to point out the actions and particular parts of a character that are most proper to be described 100 | in a discourse of this Sort. We may observe then that when a mans designs*ʲ* have for the most part proved unfortunate, when he has been baffled in his chief and favourite Schemes, his actions are to be either passed over or but slightly touched, and the character or disposition of the man is chiefly to be insisted on. On the other hand if he has experienced a great flow of prosperity his actions are what we are chiefly to insist on. For as bad fortune is apt to give us a low and contemptible notion of a man tho' he be of a very different cast; so good fortune has a great tendencey to attract our admiration and applause. But there is nothing which is more apt to raise our admiration and gain our applause, than the hardships one has undergone with firmness and constancy, especially if they have at last been surmounted. We are told by Shakespeare that Othello gained the 101 Love of Desde|mona more by the difficulties he had encountered than by all his assiduities²·—We admire Ulysses*ᵏ* more for the great ha⟨r⟩dships he had to struggle with than if he had not been brought into such hazard. Uninterrupted prosperity does not*ˡ* convey such a high Idea of the person who has experienced it, as if it had been intermixed with some Strokes of adversity. The 1st seems more owing to chance, whereas the other demands all the attention and best endeavours of the Sufferer. {And as a tract*ᵐ* of adversity which ends well strikes us more than uninterrupted prosperity with admiration and respect, so a long course of Prosperity is weakend in our esteem by an unlucky or illguided conclusion. Thus Pompeys*ⁿ* Glory seems to be

---

ʲ aim *deleted by enclosing brackets*   *ᵍ replaces* a character   *ʰ* ord: *inserted above; for*
ordinarily.?   *ⁱ replaces* praising   *ʲ replaces* actions   *ᵏ* the *deleted*   *ˡ* does 'not
replaces appears   *ᵐ replaces* course   *ⁿ* character *deleted*

² *Othello*, I.iii.167–8:
   She lov'd me for the dangers I had pass'd;
   And I lov'd her that she did pity them.

Tarnished by the Battle of Pharsalia[3] and that of Massinissa and Robert the Bruce}[o].

{It is the stedfastness with which they have encountered dangers and opposed themselves to hazard which has gained men the character of heroes. The Heroes of Romance are all carried thro a series of disastrous adventures before they are brought to the happiness to which they are destined.— — — — —} Thus much with regard to the actions[p].

As to the character that is most proper to be given of a man we would extoll it is evident at first sight that it must be a virtuous one. Virtue adds to every thing that is of itself commendable wheras Vice distracts from what would otherwise be praise worthy. But all virtues are not equally proper to give us a high and exalted Idea of him who is possessed of them, nor are all vices equally | adapted to excite our contempt and dislike of the man who is guilty of them. Nay, the different virtues do not[q] claim our admiration in the proportion they bear to one another in the Scale of Virtue nor do all vices degrade in our opinion the person guilty of them[r] in the precise proportion we[s] should expect from the degree in which they are generally placed.

There are some virtues which excite or attract our respect and admiration and others which we love and esteem. {It would appear that as in externall objects the mind is pleased with two kinds, the great and the Beautifull, so also in these internall objects she discovers two species's which affect her with delight, the Grand[t] and the amiable} There are in the same way some vices which we contemn and despise and others which we abominate and detest; and (as we said) these opinions do not always keep pace with one another. Fortitude is generally more admired and respected than humanity altho this latter[u] virtue is perhaps more loved and esteemed. And on the ⟨other⟩[v]

102 (margin, left of "possessed")

---

o this interpolation by Hand A begins opposite brought into such hazard, (*above*) *and ends* Massinissa's by, *which Hand B deleted and squeezed* that of Massinissa and Robert the Bruce *into space above Hand A's second interpolation* It is . . . are destined (*below*); *there is a space of five letters after* Bruce
p sentence added later in space left in the line   *q all deleted*   *r numbers written above change original order* the person . . . opinion   *s* proportion we *replaces* degree they   *t replaces* great; *the sentence is in Hand B*   *u MS* letter   *v on the should be followed by* other ; *the scribe thought he had written* othe, *added* r, *and omitted* other

---

[3] The war between Pompey and Caesar with Pompey's defeat at Pharsalus in 48 BC was a familiar subject in the 18th century, thanks largely to the popularity of Nicholas Rowe's translation of Lucan's epic the *Bellum Civile* (often mistakenly called the *Pharsalia*), published in 1718 and reaching a fifth edition by 1753.—On Bruce, cf. i.150 n.2 above; it is difficult to fill, for him, the blank, since the disasters of Dundalk (1318) and Edward II's 1322 raids will hardly suffice. The same is true of Masinissa (c.240–148 BC) the Numidian who, by deserting the Carthaginians for alliance with Rome, aggrandised his kingdom and became its greatest monarch (Polybius xxxvi–xxxix).

hand, Cowardice and want of Resolution are[w] more contemned and
103 despised than | cruelty and Inhumanity[x], tho cruelty and Inhumanity
are more detested and abhorred. Men generally are more desirous of
being thought great than good, and are more afraid of being thought
despicable than of being thought wicked. Divines have commonly
ascribed this Inclination which prevails so much amongst men to the
depravity of human nature; and Philosophers who have taken up the
cause of our nature and endeavoured to clear her from this charge of
depravity have for the most part denied this to be the case. But it would
be easy to show were this a proper place, that there is no part of our
nature which more evidently appears to be contrivd wisely and kindly
to, or tends more to promote our happiness.

The Respectable Virtues are those which are most suited to a
commendatory discourse where we would excite the admiration and
wonder of the audience. For besides that (as we said) they are of
themselves more commonly admired than the amiable ones. For those
104 latter are often | found connected with the contemptible vices. Thus
good nature and humanity are frequently joined with timidity and
want of resolution. And on the other hand those vices which most
demean and d⟨e⟩grade one in the eyes of men are the contemptible
ones; for those which we would[y] detest are as often found connected
with the respectable virtues.

The Language of Admiration and wonder is that in which we
naturally speak of the Respectable virtues. Amplicatives and
Superlatives are the terms we commonly make use of to express our
admiration and[z] respect. But this is not the Genuine and natural
language of Love. There is none of the human passions which when it
speaks as nature dictates is less apt to address its object in amplicative
and magnifying expressions. The Romance writers of the middle age
and others on Love subjects have indeed introduc'd those terms into
their Love Language; but nature never expresses itself in that manner.
105 | Diminutives and such-like are the terms in which we speak of
objects we love. We are most ⟨apt⟩ to fondle Women and children and
others whom we esteem of less capacity and worth than ourselves; and
to these we never express ourselves in the superlative degree. 'Tis the
Respectable virtues which[a] we find most generally[b] made use of in
Panegyricks. In the Panegyricks of the Saints and Martyrs (a Species of
writing very common in France) the patience, fortitude and magna-
nimity with which they endured the torments and cruel treatment
inflicted on them is what they insist chiefly upon. The martyrs were
those who in their own time drew most the attention of the people.

---

[w] generally *deleted*   [x] and *apparently deleted*   [y] otherwise *deleted*   [z] este *deleted*
[a] *replaces* that   [b] *MS* generelly

Their virtues of patience, fortitude etc. made them be^c more admird than the Saints themselves were for their humility and Resignation and Piety. And it is their praises which we see are most extolld, and discovered in the terms of the highest admiration. Such expressions do 106 not at all | suit with the other more amiable but not so respectable virtues. Flechier^d has indeed made use of them in his panegerycks[4] on those Saints and their virtues of humility and Resignation; but they suit as ill to them and appear as Ridiculous as when Don Quixote applies them to his Lady Dulcinea del Toboso.

Thus much of the means whether actions or character by which a man may be praised^e. We may observe that in generall the same Rules are applicable to those discourses which are intended to praise or extoll a nation as are applicable to those which are wrote in Praise of a single person, and this holds both of those already deliverd and those that are to follow.

We come now in the III^d Place to consider in what order those means are to be arranged in the discourse which we have here pointed out.—The character of a man is never very^f striking nor makes any deep impression: It is a dull and lifeless thing taken merely by 107 itself. It then only appears in | perfection when it is called out into action. We are not then generally to begin our panegerick with a character of the man whose Reputation we are to raise; but are rather to begin with an account of his mere actions commencing from his birth and tracing them on in the order in which they happen'd. With^g these as we go along we may intermix some of the more minute and Private actions of^h the Person. The smallest circumstances, the most minute transactions of a great man are sought after with eagerness. Every thing that is created with Grandeur seems to be important. We watch the Sayings and catch the apothegms of the great ones with which we are infinitely pleased and are fond of every opportunity of using them altho we every day hear better from those of our intimate acquaintance which we let slip unheeded. Having thus as it were conjoind the Manners of describing a character made use of by^i Theophrastus and La Bruyer,[5] we recapitulate (or tell over a 2^d time) 108 the character of the person, in the | manner of the Abbe Rhetz. This is

---

^{c} made them be *replaces* were ^{d} *inserted by Hand B in blank left* ^{e} *this sentence written small in one and a half lines which had been left blank* ^{f} *replaces* so ^{g} *replaces* from ^{h} our *deleted* ^{i} the Abbe *deleted*

---

[4] Valentin-Esprit Fléchier (1632–1710), Bishop of Nimes from 1687: famous, like Bossuet, for his funeral orations, especially one for Turenne (see i.191 n.3 above).
[5] On the Character see Introduction, p. *17*, and j 191 above.

precisely the method which Xenophon has followed in his Panegyrick on Agesilaus.[6] He begins from his birth and gives us an account of the more memorable events of his life.[j] He gives us also many particulars of his private life which tend to illustrate his character. And Concludes the whole by drawing a character of him in the Direct manner.

This may answer very well in most cases, but is not to be so strictly adhered to as not to be deserted when circumstances require it. If it should so happen that the most actions of a mans life had ended unhappily it would be very improper to introduce our panegyric with an account of them which would in effect be an account of his failings. We should rather in these circumstances give an account of his character illustrating the severall virtues with any facts that will admit of being introduced in that manner, concealing or at most slightly touching on those of a disastrous nature.

There are other circumstances also which may make it expedient to 109 alter this method. Thus Cicero | in the Manilian Oration,[7] where his design was to Recommend Pompey for the Commander in the Mithridatick war, does not give an account of his actions in the order they happen'd. But after having enumerated the requisites in a general who should command in that expedition, Shows that Pompey[k] possessed all those necessary qualifications; which ⟨he⟩ confirms by suitab⟨l⟩e actions taken from the different stages of his life without regard to the order of time.[l] This may suffice concerning the arangement.

It may be observed that there are some other circumstances which may afford matter to a panegyric besides those above enumerated: Thus if the Person be of a good family, noble ancestors etc. {or virtuous children and good}[m] these may be recorded, as well as his own qualifications; for everything that is connected with rank, nobility or Grandeur[n] receives a tincture from them and is looked on in that light by the generality of People.

IV Of the manner in which these are to be expressed. The 110 Panegyrist will | not as the Historian content himself with barely relating any fact[o] or affirming a proposition but will embellish the one

---

j the *deleted*   *k MS* Pompess   *l illegible word in minute writing* (co Ciceros?) *follows this sentence which is squeezed into a line left blank*   *m added by Hand B above the line*   *n* com *deleted* *o replaces* thing

---

[6] In *Scripta minora*, LCL vii.60–133. The equivocal dealings of Agesilaus with his foe Tissaphernes, satrap of Lydia, touched on at the end of this lecture, are recorded at i.10–17, 29 and 35 in Xenophon.

[7] *Pro lege Manilia*, for the step taken by Gaius Manilius in putting Pompey in command of the campaign against Mithridates and Tigranes in 66BC.

with ornamentall declamations and go about to Prove the other by different methods. Thus Xenophon in the forementiond work not only affirms that Agesilaus conduct to Tissaphernes was the beginning and foundation of all his good actions, but also proves it by different methods.

Lecture XXIII[d][a]

In the Last Lecture I gave ye some account of the Design of Demonstrative orations, the means by which this end may be attained and the arrangement of those means.

I shall make some observations on those authors who have chiefly excelled in this manner of writing. There have been but very few who have turned their thoughts this way.—It is very late before this Species
11 of writing is at all cultivated, | the Subject is not one which would naturally interest very much either the Speaker or his audience. Deliberative and Judiciall Eloquence would arise much more early: Men would much sooner consider what was to be done, or consider the merit of those actions that have been done, than they would think either of commending men and actions, or of discommending them; and consequently would sooner apply themselves to the cultivation of the Deliberative and Judicial Eloquence than of the Demonstrative. Their subjects are such as would be interesting both to speaker and hearers, whereas that of the latter[b] could interest neither for tho the Speaker gave out that his design was to commend some Person or nation, yet the motive was the advancement of his own glory.

This species of Eloquence took its rise from the Old Hymns in honour of the gods and Heroes in the same manner as History arose from the ancient Ballads and Heroical Poems. The Stile of these two is
12 very different: | The one raising our opinion of the Persons whom they celebrate only by recording their actions, whereas the others celebrate the persons they extoll which are gods or Heroes in the most[c] high and exalted epithets. Thus Virgil who proposes to Celebrate the actions of Aeneas does this only by recording them and never exclaims on the danger or difficulty of the adventures with which he had to encounter. But when he comes to ⟨the⟩ Reception of Hercules by Evander, the speech he puts in the mouth of the former in praise of that Heroe is in a very different Strain.[1]

The Poeticall panegyricks were very long in use before the Prose ones. It is always late before prose[r] and its beauties come to be cultivated; Poetry is always precedent and is generally arrived to some

---

[a] *MS* XXIId   [b] has not its *deleted*   [c] extra *deleted*

---

[1] *Aeneid*, viii.293–302: young and old 'carmine laudes / Herculeas et facta ferunt', the celebratory hymn which precedes Evander's narration to Aeneas of the early history of Latium and their tour of places later to become known in Roman history. Smith has conflated Evander with the 'chorus'.

tollerable perfection. It will no doubt seem at first sight very surprising
that a species of writin⟨g⟩ so vastly more difficult*ᵈ* should be in all
113 countries prior to that in which men | naturally express themselves.
Thus in Greece Poetry was arrived to its greatest Perfection before the
beauties of Prose were at all studied. At Rome there had lived severall
poets of considerable merit before Eloquen⟨ce⟩ was cultivated in any
tollerable degree. There were English poets of very great reputation
before [before] any tollerable prose had made its appearance. We have
also sevarall poeticall works in the old Scots Language, as Hardyknute,
Cherry and the Slae, Tweedside, Lochaber, and Wallace Wight in the
originall Scotts but not one bit of tollerable prose.[2] The Erse poetry[3] as
appears from the translations lately published have very great merit
but we never heard of any Erse prose. This indeed may appear very
unnatural that what is most difficult[y] should be that in which the
Barbarous least civilized nations most excell in; but it will not be very
difficult to account for it. The most barbarous and rude nations after
114 the labours of the day are over have | their hours of merryment and
Recreation; and enjoyment with one another;*ᵉ* dancing and
Gambolling naturally make a part of these dive⟨r⟩sions; and this

---

ᵈ MS difficuld *or* difficute   *ᵉ* music and *deleted*

---

[2] *Hardyknute*: imitation ballad by Elizabeth, Lady Wardlaw (1677–1727), published anonymously as pamphlet in 1719; reprinted by Allan Ramsay with sixteen additional stanzas in his
Ever Green (1724) and in a slightly less 'antique' version in his *Tea-Table Miscellany* ii (1726). The
poem was earlier thought to contain lines remembered from some ancient lost ballad.
  The Cherrie and the Slae, an allegorical debate by Alexander Montgomerie (1556?–1610?),
published 1597 but written considerably earlier; included in Ramsay's *Ever Green* (1724).
  Tweedside: the tune 'Twide Syde' is known at least as early as 1692 (it also occurs in the Blaikie
MS as 'Doune Tweedside'). A poem with the title and fitting the tune, by Robert Crawford
(*c.*1690–1733), is included in Ramsay's *Tea-Table Miscellany* ii (1726); and in a 1753 edition of the
collection the preface quotes 'My worthy friend Dr. Bannerman ... from America' as attesting
the popularity 'round all the globe' of, among other things, 'Tweed-side'. There is a poem in
Scots with the same title by John Hay (10th Lord Yester, 2nd Marquis of Tweeddale, 1645–
1713), in David Herd's *Ancient and Modern Scottish Songs, Heroic Ballads* etc. (1769). We cannot
determine which of many popular Border poems Smith had in mind—or even rule out the most
famous of Border ballads, *Chevy Chase* or *The Hunting of the Cheviot* (Child, see below, no 162).
  Lochaber no more: 'A Song. Tune of Lochaber no more', in Ramsay's *Tea-Table Miscellany* ii
(1726). Its relevance here is not obvious.
  Wallace Wight: perhaps one of the many ballads on Wallace's exploits. F. J. Child, *English and
Scottish Popular Ballads* (1882–89), no 157, contains nine traditional versions, some reported from
several sources, though none entitled *Wallace Wight*: see iii.265–74, v.242–3. In this context a
reference to Blind Harry's late 15th century poem *The lyfe and actis of William Wallace* (printed
1570 etc.) is less likely. This was the ballad-collecting age. (But in 1722 William Hamilton of
Gilbertfield (1665?–1751) published his epic *Life and heroick actions of Sir William Wallace*, in
English).
[3] See James Macpherson (1736–96), *Fragments of ancient poetry collected in the highlands of Scotland*
(1760), *Fingal: an ancient epic poem* (1762), *Temora: an ancient epic poem* (1763). The controversy on
the authenticity of these supposed translations from 'the Galic language' began with Hugh Blair's
A critical dissertation on the poems of Ossian (1763). See Derick S. Thomson, *The Gaelic sources of Ossian*
(1952).

dancing must be attended with music.[4] The Savage nations on the coast of Africa, after they have sheltered themselves thro the whole day in*ᶠ* caves and grottos from the scorching heat of the Sun come out in the evening and dance and sing together. Poetry is a necessary attendant on musick, especially on vocall musick the most naturall and simple of any. They naturally express some thoughts along with their musick and these must of consequence be formed into verse to suit with the music. Thus it is that Poetry is cultivated in the most Rude and Barbarous nations, often to a considerable perfection, whereas they make no attempts towards the improvement of Prose. Tis the Introduction of Commerce or at least of*ᵍ* opulence which is commonly

15 the attendent of Commerce which | first brings on the improvement of Prose.[5]—Opulence and Commerce commonly precede the improvement of*ʰ* arts, and refinement of every Sort. I do not mean that the improvement of arts and refinement of manners are the necessary consequence of Commerce, the Dutch and the Venetians bear testimony against me, but only that ⟨it⟩ is a necessary requisite. Wherever the Inhabitants of a city are rich and opulent, where they enjoy the necessaries and conveniencies of life in ease and Security, there the arts will be cultivated and refinement of manners a neverfailing attendant. For in all such States it must necessarily happen that there are many who are not obliged to Labour for their livelyhood and have nothing to do, but employ*ⁱ* themselves in what most suits their taste, and seek out for pleasure in all its shapes. In this State it is that Prose begins to be cultivated.—Prose is naturally the Language of Business;*ʲ* as Poetry is of pleasure and amusement.*ᵏ* Prose is the Stile in which all the common affairs of Life all Business and

16 Agreements are made. No one | ever made a Bargain in verse; pleasure is not what he there aims at. Poetry on the other hand is only adapted for pleasure and entertainment; the very nature of Poetry, the numbers it is composed in (for there can be no poetry without numbers) declare the intention is to entertain. In the first ages of Society, when men have their necessities on their hands, they keep their business and their pleasure altogether distinct; they neither mix pleasure with their business, nor business with their pleasure; Prose is not ornamented nor is verse applied to subjects of Business. It is only

---

ᶠ changed from froin   *ᵍ* the *deleted*   *ʰ* all *deleted*   *ⁱ changed from* display   *ʲ* that *deleted*; o *written above* i *of* Business   *ᵏ* In *deleted*

---

[4] Cf. the discussion of poetry and other arts in primitive societies by John Brown, *A Dissertation on the Rise, Union, and Power, the Progressions, Separations, and Corruptions, of Poetry and Music* (1763), and Cartaud de la Villate, *Essais historiques et philosophiques sur le goût* (1734): also 'Of the Imitative Arts' II.3 ff. in EPS.

[5] See Introduction, p. *18*.

when pleasure is the only thing*[l]* sought after that Prose comes to be studied. People who are rich and at their ease cannot give themselves the trouble of anything where they do not expect some pleasure. The common transactions of life, as Deliberation and Consultation on what they are to do, are of themselves too dry and unpleasant for them, without the ornaments of language and elegance of expression. Tis then Deliberative and Judiciall eloquence are studied and every ornamen⟨t⟩ is sought*[m]* out for them.

117 | Till the Persian expedition[6] arts were unknown in the greater part of Greece. The military art was the employment of the People and as the education must be suited to the Business it was to this*[n]* that the youth was trained. But least this education should give their manners a Rudeness and Ferocity which it had a great tendency to produce, music was added to correct the bad effects of the*[o]* former part ⟨of⟩ education. These two made the whole of the education of the youth even in Athens *the most civilized of any*[p] : Philosophy and the arts were intirely neglected. In the Colonies indeed Philosophy etc. were come to some perfection before they were heard of in the mother Country. Thales[7] had taught at Miletus, Pythagoras in Italy and Empedocles in Sicily, before the time of the Persian Expeditions from which time commerce that had been cultivated in the Colonies, flourished in the continent and brought wealth, arts and Refinement along with it. Gorgias of Mitylene was the first who introduced Eloquence into
119 Greece; he is said to have astonished them with the*[q]* | elegance and force of the Oration he delivered on his embassy from his country. From that time Eloquence began to be cultivated, and was soon encouraged by the addition of wealth and opulence to the Grecian States—{which was made after the Persian expedition. This Expedition likewise added to the improvement of Eloquence as the Athenian State ordered by a public decree that anuall orations or Panegyrick⟨s⟩ should be read on the persons who had signalized themselves in the defence of their country and died in*[r]* Battle.}

As Arms and Music made the chief part, indeed the whole of the

---

[l] the only thing *replaces* so much   *[m]* is sought *written above* sought   *[n]* alone *deleted*
[o] MS their, ir *deleted*   *[p]* underlined *with double row of dots*   *[q]* 118 is blank   *[r]* the *deleted*

[6] The wars with Persia which started at the beginning of the 5th century BC. By *c.*450 State funerals had become elaborate festivals: held in October.

[7] Thales (*c.*636–*c.*546 BC) of Miletus in Ionia, one of the 'Seven Sages'; cf. Astronomy, III.5, in EPS. Pythagoras (6th century BC) emigrated from Samos to Croton in the toe of Italy *c.*531 BC. Empedocles (*c.*493–433 BC) was originally of Acragas in Sicily; master of Gorgias of Leontini in Sicily (*c.*483–376 BC), rhetorician and one of the principal sophists. The scribe oddly substitutes Mitylene (or Mytilene), chief town of Lesbos, for Leontini. The embassy of Gorgias from Leontini to Athens, epoch-making in the history of rhetoric, was in 427.

education of youth at that time, so to encour[g]age those who excelled in those arts Games were instituted[8] at which prizes were adjudged to the victors in the different exercises as running, wrestling, chariot Races etc. and to those who excelled in the other branch, Music. The Competition for the prize in Music naturally introduced a compet⟨it⟩ion amongst the Poets as their art was nearly connected with that Science. The orators seeing the success of the Poets and the great encouragement which they met with, were tempted to try their art also. There was no prize indeed assigned for those who excelled in this Science; but that could be no great discouragement for the prizes that were assigned to the victors in the others were of no value in themselves
20   and only served as a mark of Honour, which could be very well attained without that Badge. The Praises of the conquerors in these games also furnished them with an opportunity of displaying their Talents. At these games Herodotus read his History, and Isocrates his orations (at least had them read by another for his voice was so bad that he never read himself).

   The Orators at this time as they rivalled the poets so they imitated them. The Hymns and Praises of the Gods was that sort which best suited these Sort of Orators. As they imitated the' Poets in their design so they did in the Subject; The Praises of Divinitys and' Heroes who were so much obscured by antiquity as that they might pass for deities were the subj⟨e⟩ct of these Hymns. The first of these orations were" also on the same subj⟨e⟩ct. Those of Gorgias[9] as we are told and others of his time were generally in Praise of Theseus, Hercules, Achilles, Meleager or other such personages.—As they imitated the
21   subject so did they the | manner of the Hym⟨n⟩s. Those writings were all in a very desultatory and inconnected manner. They mind Connection no more than it suits them and bring in whatever they think can please the Reader not' regarding the subject. All passions especially admiration express themselves in a very loose and broken manner, catching at whatever seems connected with the Subject of the Passion, which as it seems important itself so it makes every thing which is connected with it seem to be so also. The higher the Rapture

---

' *MS* them; in *deleted*, Poets *inserted above*   ' *changed from* or   " *MS* wera   ' mind in *deleted*

---

[8] The ancient Pythian Games were reorganized in 582 BC; to the main competitions in music, drama, and recitation in verse and prose, were added athletic events in the Olympic style. Similar festivals were the Panathenaea at Athens and the Carnea at Sparta. See ii.51 n.4 above for the distinction Thucydides implies between himself and those whose work is read publicly for applause.
[9] Add the extant *Encomium of Helen* and *Defence of Palamedes*.

the more broken is the^w expression. {Thrasymachus}[10] All the Lyric Poets are in this way desultatory, and Pindar the most raptorous of all is the most unconnected or at least appears to be so.

Isocrates is the first of these writers which has come down to us. His manner is said greatly to Resemble that of Gorgias. He is as well as the old Poets and Lyrick writers very inconnected, and introduces any subject that is the least connected with that in hand; thus in his oration in praise of Helen,[11] he introduces the praises of Theseus, Paris,

122 Achilles etc. etc. | and not a 6th part is concerning Helen herself. He is fond of all sort of morall sayings, and coin⟨in⟩g figuré or ornament of Language, Metaphors, Similys, Hyperboles, Antithesis etc. The beauty he chiefly studdies is that of a sounding uniform cadence and equality of Members in the Sentenc⟨e⟩. These may all be seen in the introduction of the Oration to Democles,[12] which also shews his design and temper, how he claimed a superiority over the other Sophis[s]ts and endeavourd to Rivall the poets in sweetness and number. Brutus,[13] who had the idea that all Eloquence was to be directed to discover the truth of the matter in question and lead us to a certain conclusion with regard to the Debate, heartily despised this Orator. Whereas Cicero greaty admired him, as he considered only the beautiful, the pleasing and what would intertain and please the audience without much regarding the argument. And indeed if we should read Isocrates for Instruction in order, method, argument or strength of reasoning we

123 should lose our labour; But if we expect intertainment and pleasure | from an agreable writer he will not be dissappointed.

The Victory of the Grecians over the Persians has furnished us with

^{w} *MS* the is

[10] Thrasymachus of Chalcedon (*floruit c.*430–400 BC), rhetorician famed for his elaboration of techniques for appealing to the emotions of hearers.— The 'rapturous' quality of Pindar came to be admired in the eighteenth century and partly accounted for the vogue of the 'Pindarique Ode' (of which Gray's two examples, *The Bard* and *The Progress of Poesy*, were thought by Smith to represent 'the standard of lyric excellence': see ii.96 n.12 above, and *The Bee*, 1791, iii.6). His disconnectedness, 'immethodical to a vulgar eye', was seen by Edward Young in 'On Lyric Poetry' (prefaced to *Ocean: an Ode*, 1728) as his essential virtue: 'Thus Pindar, who has as much logic at the bottom as Aristotle or Euclid, to some critics has appeared as mad, and must appear so to all who enjoy no portion of his own divine spirit. Dwarf understandings . . .' These words were to be echoed in the classic statement of the point by Coleridge at the beginning of *Biographia Literaria*: 'Poetry, even that of the . . . wildest odes, had a logic of its own, as severe as that of science; and more difficult, because more subtle . . .'. (Cf. Hume, 'Of the Standard of Taste', 15th paragraph from end, 1757).

[11] LCL iii. 60–97.

[12] An Attic orator and opponent of the statesman Demochares (*c.*360–275 BC), nephew of Demosthenes. Isocrates (436–338 BC) could therefore not have addressed a speech to him. The scribe has apparently conflated, as to names and content, the orations to Demonicus and Nicocles, LCL i.4–35, 40–71. That to Nicocles, King of Salamis in Cyprus from 374, is advice to a ruler. References to *Dem.* §§1–4; *Nic.* §§42–4, 48–9.

[13] Cicero, *Orator*, xiii: 'leniter et erudite repugnante te'.

three orations by very eminent hands on that subject of the Praise of the Athenians. One by Lysias.[14] He is said chiefly to have excelled in Judicial private causes, where he maintaind the character of a Plain man not ve⟨r⟩sed in the chicane of the[x] Bar or courts of Justice; and lost himself much when he attempted any thing florid and extraordinary such as this subject requird. In this oration he appears to have endeavoured at all the beauties of Language and ornament of expression as well as moral sayings and Reflexions. He does not Relate many of the actions of the Greeks, these being exhausted by former authors; but those which he does relate are not well adapted with circumstances, these as well as his reflections are all trite and commonplace. He exagerates everything and often[y] affirms what was far from | being true. He is very fond not only of all sorts of figures but even is full of Exclamations and Wonder.

The 2ᵈ is Platos[15] and his Stile is more correct, his Reflexions and Circumstances well chosen and not comm⟨on⟩place like those of the former. He has still fewer actions than Lysias but in the choice he excells him and where they hit on the same one his superiority is evident, as in the account of the Battles of Marathon and Salamis. His Stile is not so extravagant[z] but is at the same time too verbose, which often conceals his other beauties.

Pericles in the oration Thucydides[16] gives as his in the Introduction of the Peloponesian war, is more correct, less exuberant and extrava⟨ga⟩nt than the form⟨er⟩, strong and nervous, Precise and pointed and carrys along not only a direct commendation of the Athenians but an indirect discommendation of the Lacedemonians then their rivalls. His beauties are | so manifest that I shall not insist on them any longer.

24

25

[x] *MS* thre   [y] brings in some *deleted*   [z] extravangt

---

[14] *Epitaphios*, for those who fell for the Corinthians, ?392 BC (LCL 30–69). Cf. ii.218 n.10 below.
[15] *Menexenus* (LCL vii), funeral oration of Aspasia the Milesian as reported by Socrates and praised as equal to the Periclean oration reported by Thucydides: §§5–21.
[16] I.cxl–cxliv, speech to the Athenians.

Lecture XXIVth ^a

Mond:? Jan:ry 24
1763

sine Libro except what he Read from Livy

Having in the two foregoing Lectures made all the observations I think
necessary on the first Sort of Eloquence viz. the Demonstrative I come
now to the 2^d Sort, The ^bDeliberative. But before I enter particularly
upon it; it will be proper to make some observations on a spe⟨c⟩ies of
writing more Simple than eithe⟨r⟩ it or the Judicial. I mean the
Didactick; In which the design of the writer is to Lay Down a
proposition and prove this by the different arguments which lead to
that conclusion.

If there be but one proposition ne⟨c⟩essary to be proved, there can
be nothing more simple; the best method here undoubtedly is; 1st To
lay down the proposition, and afterwards advance the Severall
arguments that tend to prove it; which may be summed up, or brought
to conclude in the same terms as the Proposition. It is proper to begin
126 with laying down the | proposition, as the arguments advanced will by
that means make a greater impression on the mind, as it is evident at
what they point, than if they were delivered without informing us what
was to be the conclusion.—But it will often happen that in order to
prove the capitall pro⟨po⟩sition it will be necessary to prove severall
subordinate ones. In this case we are first to lay down the proposition,
and then shew in what manner the truth of it depends on that of some
other propositions, and having proved these summ up the whole as
before.

{Tis in this manner Lord Shaftesbury proceeds in his enquiry into
the Nature^c of Virtue[1] and also in that where he endeavours to prove
that virtue is our greatest happiness. Whether his Reasoning be
sufficient or not, his method is perfect; and if the subbordinate
propositions are clearly proved the principall one must necessarily be
true.}

We are to observe however that these subordinate propositions
should not be above 5 at most. When they exceed this number the

---

^a MS XXIII^d   ^b Judicial *deleted*; Deliberative *written large, so also* Didactick *(below)*
^c Nature *inserted by Hand B in blank left*

---

[1] *An Inquiry concerning Virtue or Merit*, Treatise iv in *Characteristicks of Men, Manners, Opinions, Times* (1711). This treatise had first appeared in an unauthorised edition as *An Inquiry concerning Virtue in two Discourses* (1699). Cf. i.10 n.10 above. Also Treatise vi, Miscellany iv.1; and Treatise v, *The Moralists*, Part II.

mind can not easily comprehend them at one view; and the whole
runs into confusion. Three or there about is a very proper number;
and it is observed that this number is much more easily comprehended and appears more complete than 2 or four. In the number 3
27 there is as it were a middle and two extremes; but in two or | four
there is no middle on which the attention can be so fixt as that each
part seems somewhat connected with it. The Rule is in this matter the
same as in Architecture;[2] the mind can not there comprehend a
number at sight and without counting above 9 or 10. Three is
the number of all others the most easily comprehended; we immediately perceive a middle and one on each side. {Swift proposed
a panegyrick on the number three[3] and this was one of the
articles of its commendation. There is un[n]doubtedly something
in this number that makes it more agreable than others. In Architecture, there being a middle one to which we first turn our eyes,
is a sufficient reason, tho it appears whimsicall when applied to
writing. There are more sermons and other discourses divided
into this number of heads than into any other.} In four there is
no middle and tho in numbers of Windows or Columns it may be easily
enough comprehended yet it seems[d] awkward; and in Architecture
there is one evident defect as there is no regular place for the Door; 5 is
easily comprehended, 1 in the middle and 2 on the sides or three in the
middle and one on each side. Six and seven are in the same manner not
difficult to comprehend, and in the same manner 9 as it may be
divided into 3 times 3. But tho in Architecture we can comprehend this
number with tollerable readiness, we cannot in writing reach so far.
Columns and windows are things exactly similar and are for that
28 reason more easily compre|hended as when we know one or two we
know the whole. But the Propositions which are brought as secondary
to the primary one are often noways connected but as they all tend to
the same point; and we have not only the number but also the nature of
each proposition to remember.—It may often happen that it will be

---

[d] to be *deleted*

---

[2] This passage rests on the ancient mnemonic system recommended to orators, by which they
associated parts of their speech with places and images, especially with parts of a building, e.g. a
temple. See *Rhetorica ad Herennium* (LCL), III.xxiii–xxiv; Cicero, *De Oratore*, I.xxxiv.157,
II.lxxxvii–lxxxviii; Quintilian, XI.ii.17–26. Frances A. Yates brings the history of the idea up to
the se . enteenth century in *The Art of Memory* (1966), especially chapters VI–VII, XV–XVI.
[3] In *A Tale of a Tub*, Section I, The Introduction, §4, Swift mocks the mysticism of numbers:
'... Philosophers and great Clerks, whose chief Art in Division has been to grow fond of some
proper mystical Number, which their Imaginations have rendered Sacred. ... The profound
Number *THREE* is that which hath most employ'd my sublimest Speculations, nor ever without
wonderful Delight'. He has in the press 'a Panegyrical Essay of mine upon this Number', rescuing
certain things from its 'two great Rivals *SEVEN* and *NINE*'.

necessary to prove 14 or 15 subordinate propositions in order to confirm the principall one. In this case it is much better to form three or 5 propositions[e] on which the truth of the principal one evidently depends; and under each of these propositions to arrange 5 or 3 of those which are necessary to confirm the primary one. The mind will much more easily comprehend the 18[f] propositions in the one case or the 20 in the other, than it will 15 which immediately depend on the principall one without any intermediate steps. In the same manner in Architecture, the architect generally makes one part of the building

129 some way distinguished from the rest, either | throws the middle farther back or advances it further forwards than the sides; that is in case there be above 3 (or 5) windows or other parts. By this means one may[g] with tollerable ease remember at least 15 or 16 Propositions, whereas in the other case the mind finds a considerable difficulty in going above half that length. There are however sermons wrote about the time of the Civil wars, which have not only 15th or 16th, but 20[thly] 30[thly] or 40[thly]

In architecture we can not only comprehend a considerable number of parts by subdivisions, but by Sub-sub-divisions etc. we can go still farther. Thus if a building was to contain 81 windows or columns, let these be thrown into 3 27s distinguished remarkably from one another, the two side ones being similar; let each of these be again divided into 3 9s, and these into 3 3s, and let each subdivision be remarkably distinguished from the rest by a differen⟨t⟩ order of architecture, or

130 some other variety; and one, tho' not of very quick appre|hension will, if placed at a proper distance readily conceive the order and number of the severall parts. But in writing it is otherwise; Subsubdivisions etc. are not at all easily remembered; they always run into confusion and become too intricate for our memory to comprehend. For this reason one who was to read Aristottles Ethics or indeed any other of his works ten times over would hardly have a distinct notion of the plan; the divisions, subdivisions and subsub etc. divisions are carried so far that they produce the very effect he intended to have avoided by them Viz. Confusion.

These Divisions and Subdivisions are very usefull not only in such didactic writings as have in view the Proof of a Single proposition, but even in those where the Design is to Deliver a System of any Scien⟨c⟩e e.g. Naturall Philosophy; the divisions assist the memory in tracing the connection of the severall parts. In Judiciall Eloquen⟨c⟩e it is often

131 indispensably necessary. Facts and Points | of Law often occur which cannot be decided without the proof of severall previous propositions and in this case the Divisions and subdivisions are to be applied in the same manner as that above mention'd. But in Deliberative Eloquence

there is seldom any occasion for it. This is not to say that no order or method ⟨is⟩ to be observed, which there is without doubt, but only that the arguments to be used in this case where we would persuade others either to do or not to do something, to make peace or continue war, to fight or not to fight,[h] are either so evident and conclusive and make it so plainly appear to be honourable, attainable, and for the advantage of those we would persuade, that there is no occasion for ranging them in a set order. Or if they happen not to be entirely plain and conclusive[i] it is the business of the Orator to make them appear so. Now, a long chain of metaphysicall arguments one deduced from another do not promise to have this appearance in the opinion of such people as an
132 audience where these | orations are delivered generally consists of. And altho the arguments were really conclusive, yet the appearance of so much subtility and Laboured trains of argument would make it very much to be suspected that the arguments were not altogether solid and conclusive.

{Aristotle[4] makes no use of Division and Subdivision in any of his Deliberative Orations tho he frequently does in his Judicial ones. Cicero in those which are the best in the Deliberative makes no divisions, and very sparingly in any of that Sort.}

There are two methods in which a didacticall writing[j] containing an account of some system may be delivered; Either 1ˢᵗ we Lay down one or a very few principles by which we explain the severall Rules, or Phaenomena, connecting one with the other in a natural order, or else we beginn with telling that we are to explain such and such things and for each advance a principle either different or the same with those which went before. Virgil in his Georgics follows the latter method; His design is to give us a System of Husbandry; in the 1ˢᵗ he gives us directions for the Cultivation of corn, in the 2ᵈ of Trees, in the 3ᵈ of
133 Cattle and in the 4ᵗʰ of the Insects called the Bees. If Virgill had | begun with enquiring into the pri⟨n⟩ciple of vegetation, what was proper to augment it and e contra; In what proportions it was in different soils and what nourishment the different plants required, and putting all these together had directed us what culture and what soil was proper for every different plant, this would have been following the 1ˢᵗ method which is [k] without doubt the most philosophicall one. In the same way in Nat⟨urall⟩ Phil⟨osophy⟩ or any other Science of that Sort we may either like Aristotle go over the Different branches in the order they happen to cast up to us, giving a principle commonly a new one for every phaenomenon; or in the manner of Sir Isaac Newton we

---

h last twelve words vertically in margin   *i then deleted*   *j is delivered deleted*   *k MS in*

[4] Error for Demosthenes.

may lay[l] down certain principles known[5] or proved in the beginning, from whence we[m] account for the severall Phenomena, connecting all together by the same Chain.—This Latter which we may call the Newtonian method is undoubtedly the most Philosophical, and in every scien⟨c⟩e w⟨h⟩ether of Moralls or Nat⟨urall⟩ phi⟨losophy⟩ etc., is vastly more ingenious and for that reason more engaging than the

134 other. | It gives us a pleasure to see the phaenomena which we reckoned the most unaccountable[n] all deduced from some principle (commonly a wellknown one) and all united in one chain, far superior to what we feel from the unconnected method where everything is accounted for by itself without any referen[e]ce to the others. We need ⟨not⟩ be surprised then that the Cartesian Philosophy (for Des-Cartes was in reality the first who attempted this method) tho it does not perhaps [perhaps] contain a word of truth,[6] and to us who live in a more enlighten'd age and have more enquired into these matters it appears very Dubious, should nevertheless have been so universally received by all the Learned in Europe at that time. The Great Superiority of the method over that of Aristotle, the only one then known, and the little enquiry which was then made into those matters, made them greedily receive a work which we justly esteem one of the most entertaining Romances that has ever been wrote.

135 The Didacticall[o] method tho undoubtedly the | best in all matters of Science, is hardly ever applicable to Rhetoricall discourses. The People, to which they are ordinarily directed, have no pleasure in these abstruse deductions; their interest, and the practicability and honourableness of the thing recommended is what alone will sway with them and is seldom to be shewn in a long deduction of arguments.[p]

As there are two methods of proceeding in didacticall discourses, so there are two in Deliberative eloquence which are no less different, and are adapted to very conterary circumstances. The 1st may be called the Socratick method, as it was that which, if we may trust the dialogues of Xenophon and Plato, that Philosopher generally made use. In this method we keep as far from the main point to be proved as possible, bringing on the audience by slow and imperceptible degrees to the thing to be proved, and by gaining their consent to some things whose

136 tendency they | cant discover, we force them at last either to deny what

---

[l] MS law   [m] deduce *deleted*   [n] for *deleted*   [o] *the scribe, in error, has* Rhetoricall
[p] There are 2 metho *deleted; then new paragraph*

---

[5] This interlined word, confused with descenders and ascenders in the adjacent lines, had not been correctly read when WN (see *3*, 769 n 17) was published in this series.
[6] On Smith's views on Descartes cf. the Letter to the *Edinburgh Review* (EPS 244), TMS VII.ii.4.14, and Astronomy IV.61 ff. (EPS 92).

they had before agreed to, or to grant the Validity of the Conclusion. This is the smoothest and most engaging manner.

The other is a harsh and unmannerly one where we affirm the thing we are to prove, boldly at the Beginning, and when any point is controverted beginn by proving that very thing and so on, this we may call the Aristotelian method as we know it was that which he used.

These 2 methods are adapted to the two conterary cases in which an orator may be circumstanced with regard to his audience, they may either have a favourable or unfavourable opinion of that which he is to prove. That is they may be^q prejudiced for or they may be prejudiced against. In the 2^d Case we are to use the Socratic method, in the 1st ^{r} the Aristotelian. I do not mean by this that we are to suppose that in any case the Orator and his audience are to hold a dialogue with each
37 other, or that they | are^s to go on by granting small demand⟨s⟩ or by boldly denying what the other affirms; but only that when the audience is^t favourable we are to begin with the proposition and set it out Roundly before them as it must be most for our advantage in this case to shew at the first we are of their opinion, the arguments we advance gain strength by this precaution. On the other hand if they are prejudiced against the Opinion to be advanced; we are not to shock them by rudely affirming what we are satisfied is dissagreable, but are to conceal our design and beginning at a distance bring them slowly on to the main point and having gained the more remote ones we get the nearer ones of consequence.—The 1st is exemplified in the Oration of^u Titus Quinctius Capitolinus and the latter in that of Appius Claudius Crassus, in Livy.[7]

^{q} either *deleted* ^{r} *replaces* latter ^{s} either *deleted* ^{t} un *deleted* ^{u} Appius *deleted*

---

[7] Respectively VII.xl (speeches of Marcus Valerius Corvus and Titus Quinctius to their opposing troops, ending in reconciliation), and V.iii–vi (the 'practised orator' Appius Claudius addresses the Quirites during the Veientine campaign).

Lecture XXV.ᵃ

Wed. Jan.ʳʸ 26. 1763

Having in the foregoing Lecture given you all the observations I think necessary with regard to Deliberative Eloquence; I might now according to the method I proposed proceed to point out the proper method of choosing the arguments and the manner of arranging them as well as the Expression. But Directions of this sort can seldom be of any advantage. The arguments that are to be used before a people cannot be very intricate; the Proposition generally requires no proof at all and when it does the arguments are of themselves so evident as not to require any elaborateᵇ explanation. There must be in this case no nicety nor refinement, no metaphysicall arguments, these would both
139 be altogether superfluous in the circumstances an orator is gene|rally in and can very selldom be in any shape applicable. As the arguments are in themselves so simple, there can be no great nicety required in the arrangement. And in generall in every sort of eloquence[e] the choise of the arguments and the proper arrangement of them is the least difficult matter. Theᶜ Expression and Stile is what requires most skill and is alone capable of any particular directions. We see accordingly that Cicero, Quinctilian¹ and all the best authors who treat of Rhetoricall composition, treat of the Invention of arguments, or Topicks, and the composition or arrangement of them, as very slight matter and of no great difficulty, and never see[e]m to be in ernest unless when they give us directions concerning the ornaments of Language and Expression; and even this in the maner the⟨y⟩ have
140 handled it does not appear to be of very great | importance,ᵈ tho it might without doubt be treated of so as to be both entertaining and instructive. I shall therefore omitt these altogether and come to the last thing proposed, that is to give you some account of theᵉ authors who have excelled in this manner of writing. I shall follow the same plan too in Judicial Eloquence, for after having explain'd the Generall nature and principles of that sort of Eloquence I shall proceed to give an account of the chief orators and the manners of the different writers in

---

ᵃ MS XXIV   ᵇ proof *deleted*   ᶜ arran(?) *deleted*   ᵈ MS important   ᵉ Best *deleted*

---

¹ Invention and arrangement, says Cicero (*Orator*, xiv–xv, 44–49), are matters of *prudentia* rather than *eloquentia*, common to all activities, and he will treat them briefly. Quintilian echoes this. They are the *duties* of the orator, not *parts* of the subject-matter of rhetoric (III.iii.1); the untrained can do them (VIII.iii.2).

this manner both with respect to Greece and Rome, and the English
writers. I shall however take up some longer time on the nature of the
Judicial eloquence, as here in the proving of facts or points of Law a
good deal of nice and delicate Reasoning and argumentation may be
introduced which, as I said, the Deliberative hardly ever admit of, and
for that reason is the simplest of all the three Spe⟨c⟩ies of Eloquence.

141 | I shall in this Lecture give you some account of the Manner of
Demosthenes's Deliberative orations, and then of Ciceros.

Of 16 Deliberative orations which have come down to us under the
name of Demosthenes 2 are plainly the work of a different hand,
probably of Hegesippus;[2] they have a rusticity and coarseness of
expression with an affectation of force which is very unlike the manner
of our orator: these orations are that *ʃ*   and that   *ʃ* Of the
14 remaining ones 10 are either employed to excite the Athenians to
war with Philip of Macedon or to encourage them to prosecute it with
vigour. The other 4 are on Different Subjects but as their design is
much the same as that of the Philippics I shall say nothing concerning
them, confining my observations intirely to the Philippics, and take as
an instance of the manner of Demosthenes that of them which is called
the 3^d, and is the 2^d Olynthian oration, not that it is the most elegant or
142 the finest of his | Orations, which in my Opinion is that περι
χερσουησου, but as it will as well shew the peculiar manner of the
author.

That we may the better understand his manner and the
Observations on it, it will be necessary to consider briefly the state the
Athenian affairs were in at the time these Orations were composed.
The Government of Athens was long before that time become
altogether Democraticall; the Council of the Areopagus, which was
composed of the nobility and Chief men of the Commonwealth, was
altogether abolished and that great Check on the Fury of the People
removed. The Council[3] of   *g* and the Pritaneum which made
parts of the Aristocraticall government were then laid aside and no
barrier remaind against the unruly multitude. But still it was the
Nobility which directed the management of Publick affairs. The
Ballance of Wealth and Rank on their side gave them also the Ballance
143 of Power. The lower Rank were not conspicuous enough to have | a

---

ʃ–ʃ two blanks of about ten letters each in MS   *g blank of eight letters in MS*

---

[2] See ii.151 n.1 below.

[3] From the time of Cleisthenes at the end of the sixth century BC the Council (*boulé*) consisted of
500 members; its business was prepared by 50 of these, the *prytaneis* (the *prytaneum*, the word Smith
apparently applied to this committee).

chance for the Regulation of affairs. The Battle⁴ of Platea,ʰ where by the advice of Periclesⁱ the Soldiers first received pay from the Publick gave the first beginning to theʲ Democraticall government,ᵏ and the Commerce which followed it strengthed that change. Commerce gave the lowest of the people an opportunity of raising themselves fortunes and by that means power. They had by the government an equall chance for all magistracies with the greatest of the nobles, and by their wealth were enabled to have equall weight with the People. This it was which introduced the great change in the tempers of the people and the means of gaining their favour. Before that time one who had a mind to gain the favour of the people and have influence with them, as Riches were not to be got in the state was generally obligedˡ to make his

144 | end by planning out new expeditions and new wars, by which the people might be enriched. Those who executed these schemes best were those who had most of their favour. There was therefore no one ever at the head of affairs who had not distinguished himself by military exploits. {But afterwards we find this was little attended for at the beginning of the Peloponesian war we find Cleonᵐ at the head of the State, and in the end Theramenes⁵ and   ⁿ neither of whom had ever been any way distinguished by military glory; and of the 10 Orators who in their turn directed the affairs of Athens none unless Demosthenes had ever seen a battle.} The Athenians were on this account the most enterprising and active people in all Gree⟨c⟩e; Insomuch that the Chief Leaders and directors had as great difficulty in restraining them as afterward in rousing them to war.ᵒ Commerce and Luxury intirely altered the state of affairs; They gave the Lowest an opportunity of raising themselves to an equality with the nobles; and the nobles an easy way of reducing themselves to the state of the meanest citizen. In this state forreign wars was not the way most likely to give wealth to the People; those therefore who desired to ingratiate

---

ʰ Platea *circled in MS; then* and the B *deleted*   ⁱ *inserted by Hand B in blank left*   ʲ true Democraticall government great change *deleted*   ᵏ by the pay which was at that time appointed to the People *deleted*   ˡ to have recourse *deleted*   ᵐ *inserted by Hand B in two blanks left; in the first Hand A had written only* C   ⁿ *blank of six letters in MS*   ᵒ them to war *changed from* their Courage

---

⁴ Battle of Plataea (479ʙᴄ) at which Mardonius and the Persian forces were defeated by the Greeks under Pausanias.—The account given in this lecture of judicial and administrative procedures in Greece (and, later, in Rome) may be compared with passages in the parallel course Smith was in the habit of giving on jurisprudence: see index to LJ, s.v. Greece, democracy, judges, judicial power, Athens, Lacedaemon, etc., and under the ancient authors there cited.

⁵ On Cleon cf. ii.176 n.1 and 179 below.—Theramenes and Critias were two of the Thirty Tyrants who seized power in 404 ʙᴄ; in the reign of terror which followed, the extremist Critias had Theramenes the moderate executed, but he was himself killed in Jan. 403; after which a governing Board of Ten was appointed. Aristotle (*Politics* 1305ᵇ 26) names Charicles rather than Critias as the leader of the extremists.

45   themselves did not | take that method; they found it easier to give them
     riches which they had no title to from the Plunder of their fellow
     citizens than from the Spoils of their enemies.
        The first thing they did was to procure them a pay in war; which tho
     it might appear of no great consequence yet had a great effect on the
     nature of the government. Commerce, as it introduced trade or
     manufacture into all the*p* members of the State made them unwilling
     to attend the courts. There were three courts each of 500 men where
     private causes were tried and these 3 were joined in all public or
     criminall debates. These being*q* chosen by lot from the poorest as well
     as the richest would be very unwilling to leave their work for an
     employment which brought them no profit. Pericles therefore to gain
     the favour of the Public brought it about that every judge who at-
46   tended the court should get two Oboli about 3^d per Diem.— | Nay so
     far did this method go that one Eubulus[6] or Eubulides made a law that
     every citizen should receive the same summ from the Community in
     order to enable him to attend the Theatre, that is in our language to
     pay for his ticket to the Play. This was the foundation of all their
     dissorders. Demosthenes opposed it but without effect, and a Law was
     afterwards made which made it capitall in any one to propose to
     Repeal it. From this time the People became altogether idle and
     unnactive; they re⟨c⟩eived the same pay for sitting at home and doing
     nothing but attending the publick Diversions as they did for serving
     their country abroad, and the*r* former was without question the easiest
     duty.—Military Glory had then no weight; the orators ruled the
     People coaxing them with new schemes of additional wealth and often
     overruled the most experienced commanders, turning them, continu-
47   ing them or changing them | as they thought fit. Levies were then
     seldom voted and where they were, as seldom made. The Athenians
     from being the most enterprising people in Greece were now become
     the most idle and innactive. They who had such a spirit for enterprize
     that they had frequently in their wars with Lacedemon, Syracuse and
     other States, risqued their whole strength to the fortune of a battle,
     which sometimes ruined the state at least for a time.
        In this state were the Athenians when Philip of Macedon arose. This
     prince soon made himself formidable to them by his enterprizing and
     Politicall conduct; The States of Greece were all sensible of their

---

p State *deleted*   *q* cle *deleted*   *r* latter are *deleted*

---

[6] Eubulus (*c*.405–*c*.335) as a member of the Theoric Commission came to control the finances
of Athens and to stop state extravagance. In 348 he had a measure passed which made it difficult
for state revenue to be used for inessential military projects. The system of payments referred to
above originated long before his time; it was ended in 338 BC.

danger and wanted nothing to⁵ cause them declare war but a proper
leader. The Lacedemonians were ruined by the Battle of Leuctra.⁷ The
Thebans were powerfull but universally hated. The Athenians alone
148 remained fit for this post. They accordingly were pitched | upon for the
Leaders of the War And immediately declared war. But tho they
declared war they did not go to action. Levies where decreed were
never made. Fleets and treasure were to be sent out but never sailed,
and nothing was done with any spirit or activity. They saw their
danger, but as warᵗ did not promise them any advancement of their
fortunes they could hardly be prevaild toᵘ engage in it. Demosthenes
took upon him to stir up the Athenians to a more vigorous Conduct,
and this is the Subject of his Philippick orations.⁸ His manner is that of
one who spoke to a favourable audience; for tho the Athenians were
sluggish and Dilatory in undertaking the war they saw well enough
that it was for the good of the State but as it promised them no private
advantage they would not be very eager to engage in it. For this
reasonᵛ he never insists much on the reasonableness of the war; nor on
149 the practicability of succeeding | in it, for it was universally allowd that
they were a match for their enemies. He dwells more on the growing
Power of Philip and the Danger Delay would expose them to and
prompts them to exert themselves and Repeal the Law of Eubulus. His
expression and manner is such as becomes one of Sense and dignity,
with a sort of Innate pride, and contempt for those who opposed him.
This makes him frequently rather expostulate with themʷ on the folly
of their conduct than shew them the practicability or advantage of
more vigorous measures. In this strain he often condescends to
downright Scolding and gives them very opprobrious and Scurrilous
language, but never in a manner improper for a man of Dignity and
authority. He does it in a manner natural to one who reproves those
whom he is sorry to see acting amiss tho they know the right; and
hence he is always remarkably strong and passionate. {He however
never lays the blame on the peoples want of courage or spirit but on the
false arguments and seductive counsel of the Orators who, bribed as he
said by Philip and from other private motives, dissuaded the People
from what they well knew was their real interest. It is to be observed
that in no former war, tho they were often carri'd on with more
wealthy nations than Macedon, yet this accusation was never so much
v.149 as mentioned. The reason is not because the oratorsˣ were | thenʸ less

---

ˢ end *deleted*   ᵗ *replaces* it   ᵘ follo *deleted*   ᵛ they *deleted*   ʷ *MS* him
ˣ *replaces* people   ʸ much more *deleted*

---

⁷ 371 BC, victory of Epaminondas and the Thebans over Cleombrotus and the Spartans.
⁸ See ii.141 above: four *Philippic* orations, 351–41 BC; three *Olynthiacs*, 349 BC.

liable to take such gratuities, but because what was conterary to the interest of the country could not then be of any weight, nor would be at all Received.}

150 In the Course | of the affairs with Philip it happened that the City of Olynthus a port of some note on the coast of Macedon was brought by Presents and sollicitations into the interest of Philip. The Athenians were very sollicitous to bring them over to their interest. This they accordingly obtain; the Olynthians declared war on Philip.[9] But when Demosthenes was using his best endeavours to prompt the Athenians to a vigorous defence of their allies, the other Orators amused them with debates concerning what Punishment they should inflict on Philip when they had got him into their Power. 'Twas on this occasion Demosthenes spoke the Olynthian oration above mentiond.—We may observe that Sallust has copied this speech[10] in that which he puts into the mouth of Cato and has even gone so far as to translate the first sentence, which could not suit that Cause.

[9] In 349 BC Demosthenes delivered his three speeches advocating Athenian support for Olynthus against Philip II of Macedon: cf. ii.141 above.
[10] *Bellum Catilinae*, lii; Marcus Porcius Cato's speech to the Senate is an echo of Demosthenes, *Olynthiac* iii.1: take precautions against plotters instead of discussing how you will punish them when you have caught them.

Lecture XXVI^{th a}

Monday Jan.ʳ 31. 1763

In the last Lecture I endeavoured to give you some notion of the Manner and Spirit of the Deliberative orations of Demosthenes. Besides them there have no Deliberative orations of any of the Greek Orators come down to our time: Unless we should reckon those two περι χαλονησον and περι των μετ' Ἀλεξανδρον συνθηκων,[1] which are commonly ascribed to Demosthenes; But more probably were composed by Hegesippus. But who ever be the author of them, they are certainly not Demosthenes's, they are altogether silly and triviall and are not of merit sufficient to deserve any consideration.

We shall therefore proceed ⟨to⟩ the Deliberative orations of Cicero which are the chief ones that remain in the Latin Language. These we shall find are of a very different Genius from those of Demosthenes. They have a certain Gravity and affectation of dignity which ⟨those⟩ of the latter want[b]. It is commonly said the Latin is a grave and Solemn Language and much more so than the Greek which is | said to be a merry and Sprightly one. It were easy to shew that all languages Greek and Latin not excepted are equally ductile and equally accommodated to all different tempers. The Stile indeed of the Latin authors has much more of Solemnity and affected dignity and ornament than that of the Greek authors. The difference betwixt Stile and Language is often not attended to, and has not been observed by severall authors, tho they be in themselves very different: And to this[c] it is owing that what is true only of the Stile of the Writers has been ascribed to the nature and temper of the Language itself.

That we may better understand the particular temper and Genius of Ciceros manner of writing and the Causes of it; It will be proper to make some observations on the State of the Roman Commonweal and the temper of the People at the time he wrote. Which tho one of the most important parts of History is generally too little insisted on by authors, and understood | by very few.

Before this time the great distinctions of the people had been in a

---

a MS XXVth   *b* They . . . want *written vertically in margin*   *c* MS thus; *changed from* And thus are

---

[1] The titles of the two non-Demosthenic speeches already referred to at ii.141 above were misheard by the scribe: περὶ Ἀλοννήσου, *On Halonnesus*, and περὶ τῶν πρὸς Ἀλέξανδρον συνθηκῶν, *On the Treaty with Alexander*. The first was generally attributed to Hegesippus, an equally vigorous opponent of Philip, though Dionysius of Halicarnassus thought Demosthenes the author: see *On the Style of Demosthenes*, 9 (*The Critical Essays*, i. LCL). Hyperides was once credited with the second; for his works see *Minor Attic Orators* ii (LCL).

great measure abolished; all magistracies were now become attainable by the whole of the multitude. Those magistracies which were formerly the peculiar province of the Patricians were laid upon to every one. The Senatoriall dignity, the office of the Praetor, Censor, Ædile etc. (which were called the Curule magistracies) were no longer confind to the old Patricians. The factions of the State were formerly those of the Patricians and Plebeians; the differences and contentions which sprung up after the expulsion of the Kings all arose from the rivalship of those two bodies. But by these continu'd contentions the magistracies and all of power and profit were by degrees open'd to the People. From these immense riches and immence power and interest 154 were often acquired by individualls, both of the | Patrician and the nobler Plebeian Families. There are many instances of immense fortunes raised by the oppression of those who were under the Power and direction of the different officers. The Proconsul Verres may serve as an instan⟨c⟩e of this; and there are many of as extraordinary and immense power obtain'd by those who instead of oppressing chose to ingratiate themselves with those whom they had under their Subjection, Ma⟨r⟩ius, Cinna etc.—The authority of the Senate was now indeed little more than nominal; they could make no Laws nor transact any business of importance without the consent and approbation of the people; Some few offices remaind at their disposall; but their approbation to the decrees of the people was in most cases no more than a mere form. There had indeed been some attempts to 155 reinstate the Patricians in their former authority and | Sylla even made laws to this effect, but the alteration made by them was so great that they were^d allowed to subsist no longer than the power of him who introduced them. By this means the old Parties of Patrician and Plebeian were at an end. It was now as much the interest of the chief men of the Plebeians to support the authority of the^e Senate and other dignified offices as it had formerly been to curb them. The power or wealth they had acquired or had a prospect of acquiring by them, were sufficient motives for them to promote the authority of those office[e]s and the depression of those who were subject to them. This joint interest formed a division amongst the Citizens somewhat similar but considerably different from the old one. On[e] the one side were all the 156 Richer and more powerfull of the Citizens, whe|ther Patrician or Plebeians; all who had either enjoyed the offices of Power and profit or those who had a prospect of reaping those advantages. That is to say the People of fashion; all who would go under the Denomination of Gentlemen. These were called Optimates, a word signifying no more than that they were, as we would say, the better sort, people of

^d they were *replaces* it was   ^e Patricians *deleted*

fashion.—The other faction was those of the Plebeians who had not power nor riches to make them considerable nor any hopes of arriving at those offices which would make it in their power to obtain them. These were the lowest most despicable people imaginable, supported chiefly by the Donations of the nobles. They were the Rabble and Mob, and a most wretched and miserable set of men imaginable.

157 These would for their | own safety oppose the Oppression and extortion of the nobles, and attach themselves to those who to gain Power and weight in the common wealth courted the favour of this order. The method ⟨of⟩ these men, who from their attachment to the Populace were called Populares, was to propose Laws for the equall division of Lands and the distributing of Corn at the Publick charge, or else by Largesses and bounties bestowed out of their own private fortune.*ʲ* Of this sort were Clodius, Marius and others.

The effects therefore of the communication of the magistracies and the laying them open to all the people were very different at Rome from what they were at Athens. Neither the territory of the commonwealth nor the authority of the magistrates was so con-

158 siderable as to put it in the power | of those who filled the offices of State to acquire any extraordinary Riches and consequently gave them less opportunity of courting the favour of the multitude with success. By this means the magistracies continued open to all those who had merit enough to deserve them and gaind the favour of their fellow citizens. The innequality of fortune was not so great as to make any distinction amongst the Citizens. 5 Talents was reckon'd a great*ᵍ* estate for an Athenian citizen; for we find Demosthenes Reproaching his Rival Æschines[2] with not having celebrated with sufficient magnificence some public Show; for says he 'You can not plead poverty in your defence as you was then worth above 5 Talents'.*ʰ* A 100 times that would have been but a very moderate fortune at Rome. And Demosthenes*ⁱ* also mentions that his Brother in Law would have been

159 one of the richest men in Athens as his Father left him 52 Tals. | The poorest Citizens might here by trade raise themselves fortunes equall to those of the most wealthy. As there was therefore no considerable distinction of Fortune, so there was properly but one rank of Citizens; the highest were Citizens and no more and the lowest had the same priviledge. In Rome on the other hand, the great power and immense wealth which were attendant on all the Chief offices of the State soon

---

ʲ MS fertune   *ᵍ* MS greet estates, s *deleted*   *ʰ* ten *deleted*   *ⁱ* a line above and below in MS

---

[2] The reproach of Demosthenes against Aeschines is in *De Corona*, 312; apart from his own resources he had inherited more than five talents from the estate of his father-in-law Philo, and had contributed nothing to the state's projects.

destroyed that equality which the communication of the magistracies meant to establish. The People was therefore divided into two Factions, that of the Optimates and that of the Populares. The first comprehended all those who had either enjoyed or had a reasonable expectation of enjoying the magistracies; that is, the few Remaining Old Patricians and all the Noble Plebeian familys and those who had power or interest to advance themselves. In the other were all the Plebeians who were not noble nor had any expectations of raising
160 themselves to offices by which they might attain Power or Riches. | These (as I said) were a most wretched and destitute set of men; they depended for their very subsistence 1st on the liberality of the Candidates in their Largesses at Elections, which were indeed often prohibited^j and could not afterwards be publickly avowed; but it was a vain attempt to hinder the people from accepting of such presents for their votes, or the Candidates from endeavouring to carry their Elections by that means; or 2dly on the Distributions of Corn or other necessarys which were made^k by the publick either for no price or at a low one. There was here no middle Rank betwixt those who had the greatest^l wealth and power and those who were in the most abject poverty and dependance. The Knights in the earlier periods were a sort of middle betwixt the Plebeians and the Patricians and somewhat restrained the extravagancies of either. They were at this time horsemen, Equites, and were distinguished from the rest of the people by the manner of their service.
161 | We may observe that knights in all countries were mere horsemen originally, but when military service was not so much used they have become of a very different Rank.^{m} A knight in this country is a very different person from a dragoon.—In the same manner the Roman Equites were at first those who composed the Cavallry. But after the Victory of Marius over the Cimbri, they were never employed in that service. They were soon[er] after allowed to be Elected into the Senate, and from that time became of the same party with the remaining Patricians and other nobles. As there was but one order at Athens so there was properly only two^n orders at Rome, the great and the populace.

Besides this the Athenians and the Romans treated their favourites^o in a very different manner. All appearance ⟨of⟩ pride or extra-o⟨r⟩dinary authority or presumption of any sort was looked ⟨on⟩ at Athens with a jealous eye. The people were offended with Alcibiades
162 their greatest favourite, for wearing a dress | somewhat more splendid than was ordinarily worn by the Citizens. But the Luxury of Lucullus

---

^{j} as by the Lex Servia (?) *deleted* ^{k} out *deleted* ^{l} power *deleted* ^{m} They *deleted*
^{n} *replaces* one ^{o} with a *deleted*

or the Splendor of Pompey, were not objects of Jealousy to the Romans. Tho the Athenians could not allow Alcibiades to go gayly dressed the Romans beheld without suspicion Pompey attended by the flower of the young nobility, a great part of the Senate and the chief men of the City.

{The people never at this time opposed the growing power of their favourites, all they did was looked on with the greatest ease. The only check they met with was from the opposition and conterary endeavours of the other nobility who in the same manner strove to get to the head of affairs.}

The Nobleman of Rome would, then, find himself greatly superior to the far greater part of [a] mankind; He would see at Rome 1000 who were his inferiors for one who was even his equalls; and anywhere else there would be none would could[p] compare with him in power or wealth. Finding himself thus superior to most about him he would contract a great opinion of his own dignity. He would have an air of superiority in all his behaviour. As he spoke generally to his inferiors he would talk in a manner becoming one in that Station. Respect and deference would be what he thought his due as one of superior dignity and his behaviour would aim at approving himself to be such. His

163 discourse | would be pompous and ⟨o⟩rnate and such as appeard to be the language of a superior sort of man.

At Athens on the other hand the Citizens were all on equall footing; the greatest and the meanest were considered as being noway distinguished, and lived and talkd together with the greatest familiarity. Difference of fortune or employment did not hinder the ease and familiarity of behaviour. It is observed that there is no Politeness or Compliments in the Dialogues of Plato; whereas those of Cicero abound with them. Particularly in his Dialogues de Oratore, the noblemen he introduces talk in the most Polite manner and pay one another the greatest respect, and commend in the most complimenting Stile. Plato again introduces persons of the most unequall Dignity or Power in the State talking with the greatest freedom And familiarity such as would appear very odd at this day amongst people of such differen⟨t⟩ stations[q]; and there is generally one person who roasts, tiezes and exposes the others without mercy, and often with a turn of humour which would not ⟨be⟩ at this day altogether polite or even decent.—In the one country the People at

164 least the Nobles would converse[r] and harangue with Dignity, | Pomp and the air of those who speak with authority. The language of the others would be that of freedom, ease and familiarity. The one is that

where the speaker is supposed to be of Superior Dignity and author⟨ity⟩ to his hearers and the other is that of one who talks to his equalls. Pomp and Splendor suit the former well enough but would appear presumption in the other.

These considerations may serve to explain many of the differences in the manners and Stile of Demosthenes and Cicero.—The latter' talks with the Dignity and authority of a superior and the former with the ease of an equall. Cicero therefore studies allways' to add what ever'' may give this appearance to his Stile even on the most trivial occasions, and the other talks with ease and familiarity even when he is the most earnest and vehement. {Demosthenes abounds with all the Common phrases and Idioms, and Proverbs; Cicero on the other hand avoids all Idiomaticall turns or other Vulgar expressions with the greatest care.} Cicero abounds with all those figures of spee⟨ch⟩ which are thought to give dignity to language; his Stile is always correct and to the highest
165 degree, | with the greatest propriety of expression and the strictest observance of grammaticall propriety. This makes it evident that the author conceives himself to be of importance, and dignity; For this exact and ornate stile shows that every word is premeditated and that he has settled before he begun the sentence in what manner he was to conclude it.

There are certain forms of Speech which are peculiar to common conversation; and plainly appear to proceed from the carelessness of the speaker, who had not resolved when he begun his sentence in what manner he was to end it. These are called ἀνακολουθα i.e. unconnected, without consequence; Where the one part of the sentence is of a different Grammaticall construction from the other. The Greek writers abound with this figure, but none more than Xenophon and Demosthenes. I shall mention an instance from each to explain the matter. Xenophon: The sentence in Latin would run thus, Hephaestus et Menon, quoniam sunt amici vestrum, remittite nobis; the gram⟨maticall⟩ const⟨ruction⟩ plainly would require here that he
166 should have Hephestum et Menona etc. In the same manner | we would say in easy conversation, Hephestus and Menon as they are your friends, send them back to us; instead of, Send back etc. Or, John or James suchathing'', I know not what is become of him; instead of, I do not know, or I know no⟨t⟩ what is become etc. The one we would use in conversation or familiar letter'' writing and the latter in a formal discourse or in writing a history. This has been much used by Demosthenes and other Greeks; but Cicero and most Latin[e] writers have entirely rejected it, as well as almost all modern authors; as it

testifies a great degree of carelessness in the speaker. The instance in Demosthenes[x] I do not remember, but there are two places in the same sentence where the forgoing [me]member by the means of some words would require the subsequent to have been altogether of an other form.

Again Demosthenes' periods are for the most part short and concise,[y] without any redundancy of expression; Whereas Cicero always runs out into a long train of connected [me]members even on the most simple subject. And even when Demosthenes is obliged by the quantity 167 of matter which crouds | in upon him to form a long period he never affects those ornaments of similarity of cadence and uniformity of length in the severall members, which is so much studied by Cicero.— This difference is very visible in their Deliberative orations but still more in their Judiciall ones.

Again, the familiar[z] ease with which Demosthenes writes makes him often use illustrations or examples as well as expressions that appear rather low and ludicrous[a]. This is remarkable in his comparisons where he often compares things of the greatest importance to others of a very conterary nature. Thus he compares the p⟨eople⟩[b] sending a fleet to [c] after it had been plundered and destroyed to a Boxer who always clapt his hand to the place where he felt the smart of the last blow, without attending to parry off the approaching ones or *lay on* any himself.[3] Cicero on the other hand compares the most triviall things, and that too when he is Rallying, with the most serious, as for instance; he says[4] that the conduct of Mithridates in leaving his treasure in 168 Pontus, which by employing the troops in plunder | gave the King himself time to escape, was like that of Medea who to retard the pursuit of her father tore her Brother in pieces and strewed his limbs on the sea, that she whil[e]st her father was employed in taking them up might have time to escape.[d]

These differences in the Stile of these orators may probably arise from the different condition of the countries in which they lived; the tempers of the men had[e] no doubt also have had their effects. The vanity and pride if you will call it so which Cicero was possessed of may perhaps have made him more ornate and pompous than the temper of

---

[x] (WFL) *deleted: i.e.* wait for laugh?　　　[y] *with* ⟨blank⟩ *and even when deleted (three-letter blank)*　　　[z] *MS* familiari, *final* i *deleted*　　[a] *replaces* mean　　[b] *rest of word supplied conjecturally for blank in MS; initial letter might be* h　　[c] *blank of five letters in MS*　　[d] mistaken criticism I think *inserted vertically in margin*　　[e] *for* may?

---

[3] In *Philippic* I.40 the Athenians are blamed for always, despite their great military and material resources, fighting the previous battle, sending expeditions which arrived too late (e.g. to Pagasae in southern Thessaly already taken by Philip).

[4] *Pro Lege Manilia* (cf. ii.109 n.7 above), 22. Cicero refers in a different context to Medea, her brother Absyrtus and her father Aeetes: *De Natura Deorum*, III.xix.48.

his audience would have required, and on the other hand the severity
and downright plainess of Demosthenes may have made him more
bare and careless than even the familiarity and equallity of his
countrymen would have required. To this too it may be owing that
Demosthenes is at no pains to Repeat or expatiate on his subject, which
Cicero as we hinted always studies.

169   This much with regard to the expression and man|ner of writing. As
to the matter and the arrangement these two great Orators seem to
have succeded with equall good fortune. The matter and the
arrangement of Demos⟨thenes⟩ as we said is almost always the same, as
his Design is the same and his audience favourable. Those of Cicero are
more various in all these respects; but his success in adapting himself to
the severall exigencies of the cause is no less conspicuous.

        Such then are the different manners of Dem⟨osthenes⟩ and Cicero,
both adapted to the state of their country, and perhaps had they been
practised in the other countries they would have been less
succ[c]essfull. Brutus*f* and   *g* we are told attempted this which
they called the Attick eloquence, and blamed Cicero for the unpolishd
and bold method of his orations. But we do not find that their success
was at all comparable to that of Cicero, or of Hortensius[5] and   *h*
the first of*i* which if we may believe Cicero was still more florid and
170   ornate | than he; and the other appears from the fragments preserved
by Quintilian[6] to have been *very pretty* and *very florid, just like Cicero.* This
study of Ornament and Pomp was common not only to all the Roman
orators but to the Historians and the poets themselves. Thus Livy and
Tacitus are much more ornate etc. than Herodotus and Thucydides;
Virgill and, Propertius than Homer and Hesiod;   *j* than
Theognis[7] etc.; and Lucretius the most simple of all the Roman Poets is
far more ornate than Hesiod. When this Study is so generall we may be
well assured that it proceeded not from any pecularity or humour of

---

f squeezed into blank left before and   *g blank of five letters in MS*   *h blank of seven letters in MS*
(*The blanks referred to in this and the preceding note can be supplied from Brutus, lxxxi–lxxxii. 280–4. C.
Licinius Calvus 82–? 47 BC, leader of the 'Atticist' movement in Rome, to which he gave the name; and lxxix.
273, M. Caelius Rufus 82–48 BC, pupil and initially follower of Cicero, and successfully defended by him in
the Pro Caelio*).   *i these deleted   j blank of about ten letters in MS; short blank after etc.*

[5] In *Brutus*, xcv.325 ff. Cicero discusses types of 'Asiatic' oratory: see Introduction. p. *16.*
Quintus *Hortensius* Hortalus (114–50 BC) was the leading forensic orator in the 70s BC, and noted
for his theatrical style; cf. ii.239 below.
[6] Quintilian has comments on Caelius at IV.ii.27, 123 ff.; X.i.115; XII.x.11; XII.xi.6 (taught
by Cicero); quotations from him at I.v.61; I.vi.29, 42; VI.iii.25, 39, 41; VIII.vi.53; IX.iii.58;
XI.i.51.
[7] The scribe has confused the pairing: Theognis (*c.*544 BC) the elegiac poet clearly goes with
Propertius, and Virgil as both epic and didactic poet is paired with Homer and Hesiod. Thus no
blanks are left unfilled.

the writers but from the nature and temper of the nation. Tis this
ornate manner I would have you chiefly remark in Cicero. It appears
indeed most in his Judiciall orations. The one I shall translate is the
fourth Catalinan one.[8] I translate it not because I in the least imagine
171 there are any of you here who would not understand the originall | but
because it would be unfair to compare an originall of Cicero with a
translation of Demosthenes. The occasion was when Cato and
S⟨ilanus⟩[k] counselled the Senate to put those unworthy and abom-
inable cives[l] to Death and Caesar and   [m] counselled to spare
their lives as the Senate had not, after the Sempronian law, the power
of condemning to capitall punishment, but to confine them for life
alledging this to be a more severe and heavier punishment on
Courageous men. Cicero, then Consull, was afraid to counsell Death
least the odium should fall on him alone, but yet inclined and offered
to execute the commands of the Fathers to do it. Betwixt these he
wavers and his whole oration is one continued train of Tergiversation;
Which tho a most weak and pusillanimous temper and which
afterwards caused him to be banished for that very action which he
was afraid to avow, yet is managed in a most artfull, ornate and
172 elegant manner. And | when in this case he is ornate, we may conceive
what he must be in other cases.

---

k supplied conjecturally by JML for a blank beginning S   *l word partly illegible through blotting.*
(Cives as the term for Glasgow students might occur naturally to the scribe)   *m blank of five letters in MS*

---

[8] Cicero, *In Catilinam*, IV.7: Decimus Silanus pressed for the death sentence on the
conspirators, Caesar though arguing for the full rigour of the law opposed him. Cicero makes
oblique reference to Crassus (perhaps the blank after Caesar?), absent in order to avoid the
odium of voting in a capital case. The passage echoes Silanus' argument: 'hoc genus poenae saepe
in improbos civis in hac republica esse usurpatum', and conduct which disqualifies a man from
being worthy of *citizenship*.

Lecture XXVII*a*

Friday Feb. 4th 1763

The Deliberative orations of Demosthenes and Cicero are the only ones of that Sort that have come down to us either in the Greek or Latin languages. And as these are pretty much on the same occasions and designed to bring about the same ends it would be unfair to form a judgement of the Deliberative eloquence of those two nations from so small and confined a specimen. It may not therefore be improper to take also into our consideration those deliberative orations which the severall Greek and Latin Historians have inserted in their works. We are certain it is true that these orations are not genuine and those which were spoke on the occasions they are introduced. But at the same time they will serve to shew what notion those writers had formed 173 of De|liberative Eloquence. They will also perhaps appear to be as perfect in their kinds as*b* those either of Demosthenes or Cicero. The Writers had more leisure to correct and polish them than those two great Orators had, who often spoke them on sudden and unexpected occasions.

I shall first consider those which Thucidides has inserted in his history. I mentiond already in treating of the Historicall writers the particular end which that author had in view in composing his history; Which was to explain the causes which brought about the severall important events that happened during this period. I observed also that it was chiefly the externall causes which he calls in to this purpose. Now all his Orations are excellently adapted to this Idea of historicall writing.*c* There are three things which are principally concerned in bringing about the great events of a war (and as it is the history of a war which he writes it is in such he is principally concerned), Viz. The 174 Relative Strength of the conten|ding powers at the commencement of the war; The Strength, Fidelity and Good will of their severall allies; and the circumstances in which the*d* armies on both sides were placed, and the different incidents which influenced the success of each particular battle. The*e* whole of his orations are employed in explaining some one or other of these causes. They*f* are sometimes supposed to be deliverd before the commencement of the war and are employed either to persuade the people to enter upon the war or to dissuade them from it; or they are the orations of*g* Ambassadors either asking an Alliance, or defending the condu[e]ct of their countries, or

---

a MS XXVI; *date squeezed in as afterthought*   *b* eith *deleted*   *c* For *deleted*   *d* y were *deleted*   *e* fa *deleted*   *f* either *deleted*   *g* the *deleted*

settling the demands of the contending powers either before the war
broke out or in order to bring about an accommodation; or they are
those of Generalls at the head of their armies encouraging them to
battle.*h*

    Of about 48 Orations which there are inserted in Thucidides history,
175 there | are about *12 or 13* which are represented as the orations of those
who were recommending war to their countrymen. These evidently
tend to make us acquainted with the comparative strength, the valour,
the designs and interests of the*i* contending parties. In these and indeed
in all his other orations he has made chief use of those arguments which
in deliberative orations are alone convincing and conclusive. The
arguments as I mentioned before which may be used to persuade one
to undertake any enterprise are 3 sorts; they either shew the utility*j*
and the honourableness of it, or 2dly The Practicability, or thirdly they
are such as take in both these considerations together, and shew that
the Undertaking is both usefull and Practicable to them in their
present situation. These latter are those which are conclusive and
convincing as they alone are suited to the particular occasion on which
they are deliverd.

176   There ⟨is⟩ also a good number of Orations of Am|bassadors, asking
alliance with particular States, etc. But the far greater part of his
Orations are those of Generalls at the head of their armies. There are 6
or 7 orations besides which do not touch upon either of these Subjects,
but then they are very well adapted to bring about the generall end of
his history. The 1st is that which I formerly mentioned of Pericles
where he draws the Characters of the Athenians and Lacedemonians.
It is evident that this will tend greatly to explain the events of the war,
as nothing [nothing] gives greater light into any train of actions than
the characters of the actors. The Consultation of the Athenians
concerning the Punishment that should be inflicted by the Athenians
on the   *k* who had broke their allian⟨c⟩e and were then reduced
into subjection fournishes matter for 4 Orations, two of which
reccommend the Greatest Severity and the other two a mitigation of
their punishment. The Reduction of Mytylene also affords the Subject
of two others on the head of their*l* punishment. The first day of the
177 assembly Creon advised the putting of the whole inhabitants | to the
sword, which was accordingly agred to, and a boat dispatched with the
orders. But the next day Democritus, a man of a milder and more
humane temper, called them together and so changed the temper of
the Athenians that they took the whole people again into their

---

h one blank line follows   *i* worst o *deleted*   *j* of the *deleted*   *k* Mytilenians *supplied
conjecturally by JML for a blank of eight letters in MS beginning with part of* M   *l* head *deleted*

protection and Alliance, or more properly subjection in the same manner as they had been before.[1]

The affair of the Megareans,[2] who had been attacked by the Lacedemonians as Refusing their Commerce, has been the subject of severall of his Deliberative Orations; that which Pericles is said to have delivered on this occasion may serve as an ensample of his particular manner and Stile in the Deliberative orations. In this Oration, the point he insists most upon is the practicability of succeeding in a war against the Lacedemonians. He passes over the Utility and Reasonableness of it as he had explained that in the former Orations on this head. He does not however consider those in the abstract, but
78 has shewed the justness of the causes that influenced them | to declare war and the great necessity of doing so, and in this he sets forth the great superiority the Athenians had over the Lacedemonians. In this Oration as his design is to inform the Reader of the Situation of the Athenians at that time and the motives for undertaking the war, but chiefly of their superiority over the Lacedemonians at that time, so for the better understanding of these he thought it proper to divide his oration into these seperate parts; and tho he does ⟨not⟩ divide the discourse into a 1st, 2^{d} and 3^{d} part, yet the transition from the one subject to the other is distinctly marked. As the instruction of his Reader is what he has chiefly in view, so he has no occasion to introduce any ornamentall and what are called oratorial expressions; far less any exageratory or hyperbolicall ones. Plain downright strong arguments are what best suited with his design and are accordingly what is the matterialls of all his Orations. From this it procee[e]ds that
179 his orations are all so much alike. | The character of the Speaker has no influence; for as the instruction of the Reader in the causes of the chief events is what he aims at here as well as in the other parts of his book, the arguments which are deduced from these are what chiefly suit his design. {An old man and a young, a passionate and a calm, talk^{m} in the same way. The ^{n} and the ^{n} the Superstitious and Solemn Cleon, and the loose, merry and debauched Alcibiades harangue in the same Stile.}

---

^{m} MS take $^{n-n}$ *two blanks of about ten letters each in MS*

---

[1] The Athenian debate on how to treat the defaulting Mytilenians becomes an argument between Cleon (not Creon) son of Cleaenetus, who advocates putting them to death, and Diodotus (not Democritus) son of Eucrates, who takes a humane position (Thucydides, III.xxxvi–xlviii). It therefore resembles the Roman case referred to at ii.170 n.8 above. On Cleon cf. ii.144 n.5. He appears as a ruthless demagogue with crude but effective oratorical methods; but his treatment by Aristophanes in (e.g.) the *Knights* is still harsher: mean, ignorant and venal. 179 below is another comment on him.
[2] Thucydides, I.cxl–cxliv; cf. ii.124 n.15 above.

The whole of the Orations therefore which are introduced in debates with regard to peace or war before the commencement of it are of the same sort. There is no more variety in those where the ambassadors of one state*ᵘ* ask the alliance of another; the arguments here all tend to shew the advantage such an alliance would be of to the parties and the disadvantage of rejecting it; and in the same manner his orations for Generalls all tend to the same end; to set forth the necessity of engaging and the probability they had to conquer from the nature and circumstances of their situation. {The arguments he uses are in all cases such as would have most weight with the hearers, without considering what those were which would most naturally occurr to one of such a particular temper and would most strongly prompt him to such or such a scheme of conduct or particular action.} By this means tho his 180 Orations have properly speakin[n]g no character at all which they | display, yet they tend greatly to illustrate the particular incidents. His Orations on peace and war have none of those Generall expression⟨s⟩ which are so common in other historians, no declamations on the Glory of Conquering or falling in the defense of liberty nor other such like. Nor his Ambassadorianones any of those highflown expressions generally used on such occasions, as the Glory and Heroism of Defending the oppressed etc.—Nor those of the generalls any one generall and commonplace expression[s] on the magnanimity of expos[s]ing themselves to the haza⟨r⟩d either of conquering or of falling in the field*ᵖ* of honour etc. By this means, tho the Orations on each Subject are of the same kind, yet those regarding one debate on peace and war could not apply to any other, nor those of one allian⟨c⟩e to the circumstances of any other in the whole Book; And tho he has above 20 Orations of Generalls, yet none of them could be interchanged without being easily perceivd.

181 | The Deliberative orations of Livy have a considerable resemblance to those of Thucidides and are at the same time very different. For this reason it will perhaps tend to give us the more distinct notion of both to make a comparison betwixt their different manners. The design of Livy seems to be much the same with that of Thucidides, to wit, to explain the causes of the severall remarkable events whose history he relates. The causes too which he assigns are in generall the externall ones. But tho this be his chief plan yet he does not adhere so much by it, as not to give place to what appears to be entertaining and amusing to his Readers. Thucidides never relates any fact but what is some way connected with the principall events of the history, nor does he introduce any speeches but such as tend to illustrate the causes or circumstances of some important event or one nearly connected with

ᵘ are the deleted   ᵖ changed from bed

them. In both of these respects he is widely different from Livy. That
82 author | never omitts any event which promises to be interesting and
affecting to his Readers however little connected with the chief events
he is to relate. And as he never omitts any event of this sort, so he
commonly puts a speech into the mouth of the person chiefly affected
expressing his sentiments on that head. As an instance of this we may
observe the account he gives of the discord betwixt Demetrius and
Persius, the sons of Philip of Macedon the 2ᵈ of that Name.³ These he
tells us came to such a pitch that the one at length told his father that
his brother intended to murder⁹ him. The father then calls his sons
before him to hear the cause, and we have a speech of his on this
occasion; not after he had heard the cause as a judge summing up the
arguments and ballancing them together; but before he had heard the
cause expressing how greatly he was affected by his situation; being the
judge betwixt his sons and obliged to discover either one guilty of an
83 attempt of Patricide, or one who had falsely accused his brother etc. |
We have also the speeches of the brothers, where there is indeed some
attempt to record a proof, but the far greater part is employd in
expressing how greatly they were affected in being obliged to justify
themselves each by accusing his brother, etc. But Philip at last
concludes that he would not determine the cause by one hearing but
examine into all the actions of their lives and the generáll tenor of their
behaviour. So that Livy has here bestowed 3 speeches⁴ on an event
which tends not in the least to illustrate the principall ones, nor had
even any effect on the fate of the persons concerned.

There are two speeches, on⟨e⟩ in Thucydides and the other in Livy,
which are on very similar circumstances and in many things resemble
one another so much that Brissonius affirms that Livy has copied his
from Thucidides.⁵ The occasion of that in Thucidides was the Embassy
of the Corcyrians to Athens asking their Alliance against the
Corinthians with whom the Athenians were then at war. The
184 Reasoning here is the strongest pos|sible: They represent how that they

q changed from murther

³ Philip V of Macedon (238–179 BC).
⁴ The rivalry between Philip's sons, the jealous elder Perseus and Demetrius whom he accuses
before his father of being a traitor, is recorded in Livy XL.v–xv: the agonised speech of the father
called on to be judge (viii), Perseus' charge (ix–xi), Demetrius' answer (xii–xv).
⁵ The notes on Livy by the jurist Barnabé Brisson, President of the Parlement of Paris, were
collected from his juridical works (especially *De Formulis*) with those of Justus Lipsius and others
in the edition of Livy by the Flemish jurist François Modius (1588 and later editions). The note
on Livy VII.xxx points to borrowing from the account of a similar incident by Thucydides. The
latter (I.xxxii–xliii) professes to report the opposing speeches of the Corcyrean and Corinthian
ambassadors to the Athenians; the Corinthians are anxious that the Athenian fleet should not join
the Corcyrean. In Livy the Campanian ambassadors address to the Roman Senate a plea that
Capua may be spared.

were under a necessity of joining themselves to one or the other party.
They were then the 2^d maritime power, as Holland; Athens the 1st, as
Britain; and Corinth the 3^d, as France. They represent therefore that if
the Athenians accepted of their alliance they would without doubt
⟨be⟩ superior to their foes; but if they rejected it and obliged them to
join with the Corinthians they would then be equall if not superior to
them; and other arguments no less convincing. The Case of the
Capuans and the speech of their ambassadors is exactly similar to this.
The Samnites were to them as the Corinthians to the people of
Corcyra. The arguments in both are so similar that it is very probable
Livy borrowed those of greatest strength from Thucidides. But besides
these there are many which tend only to shew how much the
Ambassadors and the people of Capua were interested in it and how
much they themselves were affected by it, but tend little to make it
185 appear reasonable to the | Romans. The arguments used thro the
whole of his Orations are such as rather shew the great affections and
desires of the speaker than tend to convince the audience; they are very
strong to the speaker but not of great weight with the hearer. As his
speeches are those of persons deeply and passionately interested in the
cause they have consequently no set division, no transition distinctly
marked from one part of the subject to another. But altho they are not
thus regularly divided yet the^r sentences follow one another in a
naturall order, each one suggestin⟨g⟩ that which follows it. Whereas in
Thucidides there is no connection particularly observ'd in the severall
sentence[e]s altho the whole be distinctly divided. The one is the
naturall language of one deeply interested in the subject he spoke on,
the other that of a calm sedate man who valued nothing but strong
and^s solid arguments.
    The Deliberative orations of Tacitus are considerably different
either from those of Thucidides or of Livy. They are however very
186 consi|stent with that Idea of Historicall writing which Tacitus enter-
taind and which we have already explained. He is at no pains in any
of them to unfold the causes of events in his orations, they are altogether designed to interest and affect the reader. The arguments
therefore which he brings into them are such as would have been
very strong with the speaker but would have no effect with the
audien⟨c⟩e. Thus in the speech which Germanicus,^{6} makes to
the soldiers to bring them from the sedition there is not one argument
which would induce them to quit it, all that he says tends only to

---

^{r} arguments *deleted* ^{s} *illegible word deleted*

---

^{6} *Annales*, I.xlii–xliii: the moving speech of Germanicus grieving and indignant over the
treatment of his wife and young son.

shew his own desire that they should leave it, and the great effects
which it had on him. We will see that Tacitus carries this to a much
greater length than Livy if we compare this speech with one in the 2ᵈ
Book of Livy,[7] which he puts in the mouth of Valerius Corvus addressed to the soldiers who had revolted and obliged Tit⟨us⟩
187 Quinctius to take the command. In this speech | the sedi⟨tio⟩n was far
from being of such consequence as that of the Legions under
Germanicus, yet there is greatly more of argument and Reasoning
than in that which Tacitus gives Germanicus.

Livy, we may observe here, tho he uses a great many arguments in
his Deliberative orations which could be of no weight with the
audience, carefully avoids them in his Judiciall ones of which he has
severall. It would be altogether absurd to introduce one defending
himself barely by alledging how sorry he was to die etc. etc. etc. As
Livy is a sort of Medium betwixt Tacitus and Thucidides, so is
Xenophon betwixt Thucidides and Livy. In his Judiciall orations he
introduces a great deal more of strong argument than Livy and more
convincing Reasoning; But at the same time he has a great deal more
of the affecting and interesting arguments which display the character
of the speaker than is to be met with in Livy. The Oration[8] which he
188 says he delivered himself to the soldiers | when they demanded the
plunder of   ᵗ may serve to shew all these particulars. It will also
serve as an instance of thatᵘ Simplicity and innocence of manners
which is so conspicuous in all his works.ᵛ

ᵗ *blank of seven letters in MS*   ᵘ plai *deleted*   ᵛ *rest of 188 blank*

---

[7] VII.xl–xli. The scribe has misheard 'seventh book' as 'second'.

[8] *Anabasis*, VII.i.25–31: the Athenians have entered on this war with the Lacedaemonians
possessed of great military and material resources, and many cities, including 'this very city of
Byzantium' and its plunder (27).

Lecture XXVIII^{th a}

Monday Feb.^{ry} 7.
1763.

Having now said all I think necessary to observe concerning Demonstrative and Deliberative Eloquence, I come to the 3^d and last Species of Eloquence viz. the Judicial; which is employed either in the Defense of some particular person, or the Support of some particular right or claim as vested in some certain person, or in the contrary of these. That is, it is either Judicial or Civil. In treating of this I shall consider, 1st What matters may be the Subject of a Judicial oration; 2dly What arguments may be used in these discourses; 3dly In what order they are to be placed; 4^{thly} How they are to be expressed; and 5^{thly} What writers have chiefly excelled in this manner of Writing with some observations on the distinguishing marks and characteristicks of each.

Ist We are to consider what may be the Subject of a Judicial Oration. This may be either a matter of fact which is affirmed by the one party 190 and denied by the other, | or the Question may respect a certain point of law. This latter again divides into two. For the question may be either whether such a point be law or not; or whether the circumstances of the fact are such as that they bring it within the Verge of that Law. So that all Judiciall questions may be comprehended under some or other of these three heads: either 1st The question may be concerning the reality of a fact which is alledged by one party and denied by the other; or 2dly concerning the Existence of a certain Point of Law; or 3dly concerning the Extent of that law, that is, Whether the circumstances of the fact are such as that they bring it within the Verge of the Law. These 3 heads we will find exactly corresponding to the division given by the ancient writers on this Subject. They said all questions were either De Re, which corresponds to the 1st of our division; or concerning the circumstances and particularities of the 191 fact, which they said was De Re finita; or after the affair was fixed^b | it might be disputed whether or not it was agreable to law or not.

Thus much concerning the Subject of Judicial orations; we come now to the 2^d thing proposed viz.^c what arguments may be used on these heads, in a judicial oration. We shall consider this 1st with regard to the case where the question is concerning a matter of fact.

Now arguments may be drawn to prove a matter of fact^d in two

---

^a MS XXVIIth   ^b some . . . deleted   ^c by deleted   ^d numbers written above change original order a matter . . . be proved

ways, either 1st from its causes, or 2dly from its effects.—Now as it is the actions of men which^e commonly are to be examined into, the causes that must be advanced for the proof of any events of this sort are those which generally tend to bring about human actions. Now the proof of any event from the causes that are imagined to have produced it is generally not very satisfactory as there seldom can be causes shewn which infallibly will produce such or such an event. But in no case is the proof of facts from the causes more uncertain than in that of

192 Human actions. The causes | of Human actions are motives; And so far is Certain that no one ever acts without a motive. But then it is no Sufficient proof that one committed any action, that he had a motive to do so. There are many things which may occasion the conterary. If the action be not suitable to the character of the person the motive will not influence him to commit the action it prompts him to. Besides tho one had a motive to such or such an action and tho it was altogether suitable to his character it is still requisite that he should have an opportunity, otherwise the action could not have been committed. In proving therefore^f an action to have happend by proving that its causes subsisted, we must not only prove that one had a motive to commit such an action, but also that it was one that suited his character, and that he had an opportunity also. But even when all this is done it does by no means amount to a proof of the action. The character of man is a thing so fluctuating that no proof which depends

193 on it can be altogether conclusive. | There may many circumstances interfere which will entirely alter the designs and disposition of the person for that time, and prevent the execution of an action even when there is a strong motive for it, the disposition and character of the person agreable to the action and the fairest opportunity offers. In ^{g} oration^1 to prove that   murdered ^{g} it is said Haereditatem sperabat et magnam Haereditatem etc. etc., each of which arguments taken singly have a considerable weight, but when considered in the gross, the shewing that he had a motive, and that the action was suitable to his character, may serve to shew that he^h might possibly have had an intention to have comitted the action; and where the motive, character and opportunity all coincide there is a proof that the person may [have] possibly have committed it; but can not amount

---

^{e} are *deleted* ^{f} a thing *deleted* ^{g} *three blanks in MS of seven letters each* ^{h} probabl *deleted*

^{1} Apparently a reference to the intricate and sensational story behind Cicero's *Pro Aulo Cluentio*, in which a Roman Blue-Beard named Statius Abbius Oppianicus had been condemned for murder. In this case, the victim may be Dinaea his first mother-in-law: Cluentia, aunt of Cicero's client; or one of several others. See vii–xvii (19–48) of the oration. But the Latin phrase does not occur in it, though the motive is recurrent. See ii.210–11 below.

to a proof that the fact was actually committed. But altho these can not
make out cl⟨e⟩arly an affirmative proof yet they will be very
194 suffi⟨cient⟩ | to prove that an action was not committed. The want of
opportunity alone is sufficient to prove that the action was not
committed. The want of a motive is also a very strong proof, but not so
conclusive as the other, since sometimes men act altogether un-
reasonably and without any strong motive. The actions being
conterary to the character of the person is a great proof of the
conterary, but neither is it altogether certain as there are many
occasions on which one will deviate from the ordinary tenor of his
conduct. Cicero in his defense of Roscius[2] endeavours to shew that he
had no motive to kill his father, that it was altogether unsuitable to his
character etc . . .[*i*] It is this sort of arguments which the Rhetoricians
chiefly insist upon and are at greatest pains to divide and subdivide.
Thus with regard to the motive they say we do an action either to
increase, or procure, or preserve something good, or to diminish,
divide, shun, or get free from something evill etc. They insist in the
195 same manner on the character | and consider the Age, the Sex, the
Family etc. and even the very name of the person. In the same manner
they divide the consideration of the Opportunity into that of   [*j*]
Time and place, and so ⟨on⟩. This may serve to account why the later
Orators have insisted almost solely on this sort of arguments, as they
alone are fully treated of by the Rhetoricians, on whose directions they
seem to have moddelled their orations. This may suffice concerning
those arguments which are used to prove a fact from its causes. {Even
Cicero himself insists greatly on these arguments, and seems sometimes
to strain them rather too far as in the Case of Milo, in which he would
shew that he had no reason to kill Clodius, tho this man was
continually seeking his life.}

The proof of an event from its effects is sometimes altogether
Certain. Thus if one has been seen committing the fact and the
witnesses testify it there is no other proof necessary. But there are many
cases where the effects either of the action[*k*] itself or of the intention to
do it are not altogether conclusive at first sight, tho they may be very
strong presumptions. Thus in the old cause[3] which is commonly quoted

---

[*i*] *so in MS*   [*j*] *blank of four letters in MS*   [*k*] to *deleted*

---

[2] *Pro Roscio Amerino*: young Cicero's first major case, 80вc.— Smith is specially fond of the *Pro
Milone* (cf. ii.209 ff., 215), since this virtuoso defence illustrates so many aspects of Cicero's skill at
the bar—though it was never delivered. Titus Annius Milo was a political gangster and
opportunist, and the killing of Clodius by his associates on the Via Appia called for a display of
special pleading, and all the barrister's techniques of suggestion, with a masterly manipulation of
'proof, paradox, pathos'. Quintilian drew some sixty-four of his illustrations from this speech.
[3] Not identified.

196 the man who had been seen some days before | the murder of a certain
person walking about very pensive and melancholy as if he was
meditating some horrid or dreadfull action, and was amissing all that
night that the murder was committed and could give no account of
himself, might very probably be presumed from these effects of the
intention of killing one to have had some hand in it but could not be
absolutely concluded to have been guilty of it. But when these effects of
the intention are joined with those of the action itself the proof is still
stronger, as in the case where one who bore an other an ill will was
found near his dead body, with his hands bloody, and a great
appearance of terror*l*, he would appear to be very probably the
murderer; Especially if the arguments from the cause of the action are
joind with them. But tho these arguments give a great probability of
the commission of the action by the person in whom they are found, yet
197 the want of them does by no means prove the Innocence of the person. |
If one should be found whose hands were altogether clean of blood and
no appearance of concern after the murther nor anxiety before it, we
could not conclude from this that he was innocent. For there are some
people such consummate Dissemblers that the⟨y⟩ can go about the
most horrid actions without the least emotion or anxiety either before
or after the perpetration.

The Rhetoricians divide all these topicks into many orders and
Classes (these will be found in Quinctilian[4] by those who incline to
read them; for my part Ill be at no farther trouble about them at
present.)*m*

{It is in the proper ordering and disposal of this sort of arguments
that the great art of an orator often consists. These when placed
seperately have often no great impression, but if they be placed in a
naturall order on⟨e⟩ leading to the other their effect is greatly
increased. The best method to answer this is to throw them into a sort
of a narration, filling up in the manner most suitable to the design of
the Speaker what intervalls there may otherwise be. By this means tho
he can bring proof but of very few particulars, yet the connection there
is makes them easily comprehended and consequently agreable, so
that when the adversary tries to contradict any of these particulars it is
pulling down a fabric with which we are greatly pleased and are very
unwilling to give up — —}

l changed from horror   *m of* I.W. *inserted at end of parenthesis. One blank line follows with* x *as key
for the interpolation opposite*

---

[4] At V.x.55 Quintilian describes 'definition', *finitio*, in terms of *genus, species, differens,* and
proprium; cf. ii.204 below. Quintilian devotes V.x.73 and V.xi to proof by *similia* of various
orders; see also on these topics V.x.25 ff., VII.i.1 and 23 ff.; VIII.xxx ff.; IX.ii.105. He refers to
Cicero, *De Inventione,* I.xxx ff. On Smith's indifference cf. ii.205 below.

We shall now make some observations concerning the topicks or foundations of argument̄s that may be brought to prove anything to be Law or not.—Now when the Law is plainly expressed in the statute there can be no question on this head". The only two methods in which
198 any thing can be shewn to be law, are either to shew how | it follows from some Statute {by abstract Reasoning} or how it has been supported as Law by former practise and similar adjudged causes or precedents. This last which is so much in use amongst modern Lawyers was not at all used by the antients either Greeks or Romans. The Rhetoricians amongst all their topicks make not the least mention of Precedents. They have inde⟨e⟩d one order of Topicks which they title de similibus {et dissimilibus}° In this they mention all the different sorts of Similitude except that of precedents. They are such as the persons having done the like actions before, or other persons in similar circumstances etc., which are evidently altogether different from praecedents (or praec̄edents). As therefore there is such a remarkable difference betwixt the modern and the ancient practise in this respect it may not be improper to make a digression in order to explain it.

   In the early periods the same persons generally exercise the duties of
199 Judge, | Generall and Legislator, at least the two former are very commonly conjoined. The first thing which makes men submit themselves to the authority of others[5] is the difficulty they feel in accomodating their matters either by their own judgement or by that of their opponents, and find*p* it most adviseable to submit it to some impartiall person. By this means some persons of eminent worth came to be settled as judges and Umpires. When men especially in a Barbarous State are accustomed to submit themselves in some points they naturally do it in others. The same persons therefore who judged them in peace lead them also to battle. In this twofold capacity of Judge and Generall the 1st Kings and Consulse of Rome and other magistrates would reckon the Judiciall part of their office a Burthen rather than that by which they were to obtain honour and Glory, that was only to be got by military exploits. They therefore were very bold in passing sentence. They would pay very little regard to the conduct
200 of their predecessors as this was the least | important part of their office. This part was therefore for their ease seperated from the other and given to another set of magistrates. These as the Judicial was their only office would be at much greater pains to gain honour and Reputation

---

n Those that are either not justly *deleted*   *o* Hand B   *p* ing *deleted*

---

[5] Cf. the tenor of this passage with Rousseau, *Discours de l'inégalité*, which much occupied Smith's mind at this period; see EPS 250 ff. and Languages, §2, n.3 below; and LJ on judges and judicial power.

by it. {Having less power they would be more timid}^{q} They would be at pains even to strengthen their conduct by the authority of their predecessors^r. When therefore there were a few Judges appointed these would be at great pains to vindicate and support their conduct by all possible means. Whatever therefore had been practised by other judges would obtain authority with them and be received in time as Law. This is the case in England. The Sentences of former Cases are^s greatly regarded and form what is called the common law, which is found to be much more equitable than that which is founded on Statute only, for the same reason as what is founded on practise and experience must be better adapted to particular cases than that which is derived from theory only.

01　　These judges when few in number will be much more | anxious to proceed according to equity than where there is a great number; the blame there is not so easily laid upon any particular person, they are in very little fear of censure and are out of danger of suffering much by wrong procee[e]dings; {besides that a great number of Judges naturally confirm each others prejudices and enflame each others Passions}^{t} We see accordingly that the Sentences of the Judges in England are greatly more equitable than those of the Parliament of Paris or other Courts which are secured from censure by their number. The House of Commons when they acted in a Judicial Capacity have not always proceeded with the greatest wisdom; altho their proceedings are kept upon record as well as those of the other Courts, and without doubt in imitation of them. {In censuring any of their own members or in any other such case they have not distinguished themselves by their Justice.}^{u} The House of Lords have indeed proceeded in a very equitable manner but this is not to be attributed to their number but rather to—.　　　　　^{v}

　　The case was the same with regard to the Areopagus and the
202　Councill^6 of the 500 | at Athens; there number was too great to restrict them from arbitrary and summary proceedings. They would here pay as little regard to the proceedings of former Judges as those did who at the same time possessd the Office of Generall allong with that of Judge. The Praetor at Rome indeed often borrowed from the de⟨c⟩rees, but then Nothing could be quoted as Law to him but what was found in his edict, which was put up at the beginning of each year and in which he declared in what manner he was to regulate his conduct. (This was the

---

^{q} *Hand B*　　^{r} By *deleted*　　^{s} abo *deleted*　　^{t} *Hand B*　　^{u} *Hand B*　　^{v} *one and a half blank lines follow*

---

^{6} See ii.142 n.3 above.

custom till the time of the Edictum perpetuum.)⁷ He would have taken
it as a great affront to his judgement to have been told that such an one
before had done so or so. And no part of the former edicts could be
quoted but what was transcribd into his, and in his name it was always
to be quoted. There was therefore no room for præcedents in any
203 Judiciall pleadings amongst | the Greeks or Romans; tho no⟨t⟩hing can
be more common than it is now. And it may be looked on as one of the
most*ʷ* happy parts of the British Constitution tho introduced merely by
chance and to ease the men in power that this Office of Judging causes
is committed into the hands of a few persons whose sole employment it
is to determine them.

{This Separation of the province of distributing Justice between
man and man from that of conducting publick affairs and leading
Armies is the great advantage which modern times have over antient,
and the foundation of that greater Security which we now enjoy both
with regard to Liberty, property and Life. It was introduced only by
chance and to ease the Supreme Magistrate of this the most Laborious
and least Glorious part of his Power, and has never taken place untill
the increase of Refinement and the Growth of Society have multiplied*ˣ*
business immensely}*ʸ*

It is evident that in quoting præcedents the more dire⟨c⟩tly they
agree with the case in hand in all its circumstances it will be so much
the better. For where it differs in many or in any [ony] important parts
it will require a good deal of abstract Reasoning to shew the Similitude
and bring them to the same case.

The other way to prove any thing to be Law is to shew that it follows
from some statute Law by abstract Reasoning. The other is always to
204 be preferred to this where it can be made use of, as the abstract |
reasoning renders it less easily comprehended*ᶻ*. To shew that any thing
is or is not comprehended within any point of Law there are 2 methods.
We may either shew, first, that the Law could not have its desired effect
unless it was extended thus far, or 2*ᵈˡʸ* that the Law by the manner in
which it is expressed must comprehend it.—The 1*ˢᵗ* method is but very
seldom applicable and in most cases not conclusive as the precise
intention of the Law is not always evident[s], and besides it requires a
great deal of abstract Reasoning. In the other manner we must (to
shew the meaning of the Law) give a Definition of the meaning of the

---

ʷ replaces Great   *ˣ era deleted*   *ʸ Hand B*   *ᶻ* This however when necessary may be
done in *deleted*

---

⁷ The consolidation *c.* AD 130 of the praetorian *edicta* into a permanent corpus of law by P.
Salvius Julianus Aemilianus (L. Octavius Cornelius), 100–*c.*169, on the order of Hadrian. Salvius
Julianus was the most creative of Roman jurists, and his work was freely incorporated in
Justinian's *Digesta* (AD 533).

severall parts and shew the extent of each. (We all know how the[a]
Rhetores made their definitions by Genus, Species and differentia.)
205 This is very difficult in all things of a | very generall nature and can not
be applied on many occasions. The best way of defining generally is[b] to
enumerate the severall qualities of the thing to be defined. But in this
case it is most adviseable not to go about to define ever⟨y⟩ part of the
law and shew the whole extent of it but to shew by some part of it
which we are to explain clearly that the thing in question is
comprehended by it; and leave the rest to others, as I do the
Rhetoricall divisions of these heads.

[a] *MS* they; y *deleted and* Rhetores *written above*   [b] *numbers written above reverse original* is
generally

Febry. 14.th   Lecture XXIX^a   Monday

In the last lecture I gave ye an account of the severall things which may be the Subject of a Judiciall oration and also of the severall topics from which arguments for the proof of those severall questions^b may be drawn. The next thing which writers on this Subject generally treat of is the method of a Judiciall oration.

They tell us that every regular oration should consist of 5 parts.[1]
206 There are it is true two chief parts, the Laying down | the proposition and the Proof. But in the Connecting these two properly together and [and] setting them out in the^c brightest light, the Oration they say naturally divides itself into 5 parts. The 1st of these is the Exordium, in which the orator [explains] briefly explains the purpose of his discourse and what he intends^d to accuse the adversary of, or to acquit his Client of. 2^d Part is, according to them, the Narration. The orator in this Relates not only those facts which he is afterwards to prove but puts the whole Story into a connected narration, supplying those parts of himself, in the manner mos⟨t⟩ suitable ⟨to his⟩ design, which he can not prove. The reason they give for this is that the severall parts being thus connected gain a considerable strength by the appearance of probability and connection so that it is difficult afterwards to wrest our belief from them. And by this means tho we can prove but a very small part of the facts yet those which we have proved give the others by the
207 close connection they have with^e them a great appearance of | truth and the whole Story has the appearance, at least, of considerable probability. In the practise of the modern courts of Judicature the Narration is never introduced; The pleader barely relates the things he is to prove, without giving us a detail of the whole transaction; and it is only where there is very little attention and great ignorance that this can have much weight. The Innatention and confusion which prevailed in the ancient courts is such as we have no conception of, and the ignorance and folly of the Judges as great as can well be imagined. By this means a well told story would have a great influence upon them. The Courts were then in very little better order than the mob in the pit of an ill regulated play house and easily turned to either side. We see in one of Demosthenes[2] orations^f viz. that upon   ^g when

---

^a MS XXVIII   ^b replaces subjects   ^c most deleted   ^d either deleted   ^e those that inserted above, then deleted   ^f last four words replace Diogenes Phillipoppicks;   ^g blank of eight letters in MS (cf. note 2)

[1] See ii.213 below.
[2] The scorn expressed by Demosthenes (De Corona 51–2) for anyone who calls him a friend of Philip shows the blank (note g above) to represent 'the Crown'.

his adversary Æschines had accused him of calling him the friend of
Philip and Alexander, he said he did no such thing, he called him,
208 indeed, the Slave of Philip who had been bribed by his gold, but | had
never given him the name of his friend. And this, he says, was the name
he undoubtedly best deserved. We shall appeal, says he, to these
Judges, What think ye my Countrymen: Is this man to be called the
friend or the Slave of Philip? The judges we find called out, The Slave,
The Slave; for he goes on, 'ye see what is their opinion.' Some
pe⟨r⟩sons which he had place[e]d among them and hired or
encouraged to that purpose, called out as he wanted them and the rest
seconded them without hesitation. The orators then managed the
courts of Judicature in the same manner as these Managers of a play
house do the Pit. They place some of their friends in different parts of
the pit and as they Clap or hiss the performers the rest join them; And
so the orators then got some persons who began the Cry which the rest
for the most part accompanied. This was the case at Athens. The
Courts at Rome were much more Regular and in better order and to
this in a great measure we may attribute the stability of their
209 Commonwealth. The | Athenian State did not continue in its Glory for
above 70 years; viz. from the Battle of Platea from which we may date
the commencement of the democracy till the Taking^h of the City and
the Settling of the Tyrants under Lysander.[3] The Roman State again
continued in its grandeur for above 500 years[4] viz. from the Expulsion
of the Tarquins till the Ruin of the Republick under Julius Caesar.

But even in these Courts the Orators made a very great use of those
narrations, and in cases where the facts they could prove were but
very few and often little tending to the main point. Thus in the Oration
for Milo[5] Cicero gives us a very particular and minute detail of the
whole transaction, how they met, fought, etc. etc. He would have us to
believe that not Milo but Clodius had lain in wait for his adversary,
tho it^i was well known at Rome at time that their meeting was
intirely accidentall. He proves indeed pretty plainly that Milo^j had not
210 lain in | wait for Clodius, as he staid in the Senate till the ordinary
time, that he went home, changed his shoes and put of his cloak etc.,
but he proves no more; the rest^k depends intirely on its connection
with these circumstances.—In the same manner in his oration for

---

^{h} *replaces* Conquest ^{i} *replaces* the conterary ^{j} *replaces* Clodius ^{k} *must* deleted

[3] 497 BC; cf. ii.143 n.4 above. The Spartan general Lysander supported the setting up of the
Thirty Tyrants after the surrender of Athens in spring 404 BC (cf. ii.144 n.5 above); i.e. seventy-
five years later.
[4] 510–44 BC (the assassination of Caesar): i.e. 466 years.
[5] Cf. ii.194 n.2 above, and 215 below.

Cluentius, which I believe is*[l]* the finest as well as it is the longest of all his orations, he endeavours to prove that it was not Cluentius but his accuser*[m]* ⟨Oppianicus⟩ who had bribed the Judges. He does not pretend to deny that they had been bribed, as there had been severall[s] banished on that account by a court in which severall[s] of the judges then sitting had been present, but he gives the bribery to a different person. Cluentius had been acquitted and ⟨Oppianicus⟩ condemned; the most probable account of the Bribery in this case was that they had been bribed by the person acquitted. But he endeavours to prove in a very pretty manner that the Bribe had been given by the other. The only fact he proves in support 211 of | this is that ⟨Oppianicus⟩ had given one ⟨Staienus⟩*[m]* 640000[6] Sesterii, perhaps for a very different cause than the Bribing of the Judges. This he says must have certainly been to bribe the Judges as it made 40000 to each of them, else what would have been the design of the odd 40000. The whole story is told in a very pleasant and entertaining manner and had such an effect on the Judges that Cluentius was acquitted, in all appearance conterary to Justice. And we[e] see that Cicero glories more on this occasion of his Address in*[n]* fooling the Judges than on any other. {We may observe also with regard to this Oration that Cicero gains the favour of his Judges in the Exordium or Preface to his Client and prejudices them against his opponent, by telling before them the great and uncontrovertible crimes he had been guilty of.}

The Regularity and order of the Procedure of the Courts, however, made the lives and property of the subjects pretty safe in most cases, whereas at Athens*[o]* the disorder (as we said) was such that it was just heads or tails whether the sentence was given for or against one*[p]*. We see from the accounts we have of the Condemnation of Socrates[7] that it was not any crime he was convicted of, for all the Judges inclined to

---

[l] one of *deleted*   *[m–m] proper names in angled brackets supplied for four blanks in MS*   *[n]* the *deleted*   *[o] replaces* in Greece   *[p]* From this it followed *deleted*

---

[6] Cf. ii.193 n.1 above. The failure of the notetaker to catch the often repeated name of the notorious villain in this extraordinary case (Oppianicus) can be explained only by his bewilderment over the familial, testamentary, and judicial complexities of the melodrama—if Smith attempted to unravel them. The forensic skill of the orator is matched only by the virtuosity he attributes to the poisoner. (For Staienus see xxiv.65 ff.). No wonder this speech was used even more often than the *Pro Milone* by Quintilian, and that so many writers quote Quintilian's report of Cicero's boast of his fooling of the judges in the cause: 'se tenebras offudisse iudicibus in causa Cluentii gloriatus est' (II.xvii.21).

[7] For the accusation of Socrates by Anytus and his two instruments Lycon (an orator) and Meletus (a poet), see the two *Apologies* by Plato (an eye-witness at the trial) and Xenophon. Plato's *Euthyphro*, *Crito* and *Phaedo* present Socrates at and after the time of his trial. Xenophon cites the evidence of Hermogenes, the intimate friend of Socrates.

212 acquit him, but his | behaving*q* somewhat haughtily and not making the acknowledgements he required, which brought him under a Capitall punishment. This Uncertainty and Variableness of the Courts at Athens*r* was so great that none allmost cared to stand their trial. When Alcibiades[8] had performed the most Gallant exploits at Syracuse and heard that he was accused at home of impiety he would not stand his trial, but fled to Lacedemon (which was in effect the cause of the Ruin of that State). When they asked why he would not trust his life in the hands of his countrymen he told them that he would trust them with any thing but that, and with it he would not trust his own mother, least she should put in the black bean instead of the white one. This however is not now in use as the Courts of Judicature are brought into a different form; So that I shall not insist on the proper manner of executing it.

213 | The other 3 parts are the Confirmation*s*, the Refutation and the Perroration. The Confirmation consists in the proving of all or certain of the facts alledged, and this is done by going thro the Arguments drawn from the severall Topicks I mention'd in the last Lecture; and the Refutation or the Confuting of the adversaries arguments is to be gone thro in the same manner. The later*t* Orators adhered most strictly to the Rules laid down by the Rhetoricians. We see that even Cicero himself was scrupulously exact in this point, so that in many indeed most of his Orations he goes thro all of these topicks. It would probably have been rekoned a defect to have ommitted any one, and not to have lead an argument from the topic de Causa, Effectu, Tempore etc. This may serve to shew us the low state of philosophy at that time. Whatever branch of Philosophy had been most Cultivated and has

214 made the greatest progress will necessarily be most agreable | in the prosecution. This therefore will be the fashionable science and a knowledge in it will give a man the Character of a Deep philosopher and a man of great knowled⟨ge⟩. If Naturall Phil⟨osophy⟩ or Ethicks or Rhetor⟨ick⟩ be the most perfect Science at that time then it will be the fashionable one. Rhetorick and Logic or Dialectick were those undoubtedly which had made the greatest progress amongst the Ancients, and indeed if we except a little of moralls were the only ones which had been tollerably cultivated. These therefore were the fashionable sciences and every fashionable man would be desirous of being thought well skilled in them. Cicero therefore attempted and has succeeded in the attempt to display in all his writings a compleat knowledge of these Sciences. He adheres however so strictly to these

q with *deleted*   *r* made *deleted*   *s* and *deleted*   *t* Rhet *deleted*

[8] Plutarch, *Apophthegmata of Kings and Commanders*, in *Moralia*, 186E 6.

Rules that had it not been*ᵘ* looked on as mark of ignorance not to be acquainted with every particular, nothing else could have induced him
215 to it. In his Oration in defence of Milo | he has arguments drawn from all the 3 topicks with regard to the Cause: That is that he had no motive to kill Clodius, that it was unsuitable to his character, and that he had no opportunity. These one would have thought could not take place in this case, and yet he goes thro them all. He endeavours to shew that he had no motive, tho they had been squabling and fighting every day and ⟨he⟩ had even declared his intention to kill him; That it was unsuitable to his character altho he had killed 20 men before; and that he had no opportunity altho we know he did kill him.

Altho however a science that is come to a considerable perfection be generally the fashionable one yet it takes some time to establish it in that character. Antiquity is necessary to give any thing a very high reputation as a matter of Deep knowledge. One who reads a number of modern books altho they be very excellent will not get thereby the Character of a Learned man; The acquaintance of the ancients will alone procure him that name. We see accordingly that tho Cicero
216 when Dialectick | and Rhetorick were come to be sciences of considerable standing is at great pains to display his knowledge in all their Rules, Demosthenes, who lived at a time when they had no long standing in Greece, has no such affectation but proceeds in the way which seemed most suitable to his subject.

The Perroration contains a short summary*ᵛ* of the whole arguments advanced in the preceding part of the discourse, placed in such a way as naturally to lead to the conclusion proposed. To this the Roman Orators generally add some arguments which might move the Judge to decide in one way rather than in another; By either shewing the enormity of the crime if the person accused be his opponen[en]t, and setting it out in the most shocking manner; or if he is a defendant by mitigating the action and shewing the severity of the punishment etc. This latter the Greeks never admitted of; the other is the naturall conclusion of every discourse.

We have a great number of Greek orations still remaining. We have
217 severall[s] of | Lysias,⁹ a good number of Isaeus, some of Antiphon, one

---

ᵘ the fashion nothing could have e *? deleted* ᵛ *replaces* state

---

⁹ Of the ten Attic orators recognised as the 'canon' some time before Dionysius of Halicarnassus (including Lycurgus, whom he names in *On Imitation*, IX.v.3), Isocrates has already been dealt with at ii.121–2 above. This leaves Hyperides, Dinarchus and Andocides unaccounted for. Since Dionysius wrote a short treatise on Dinarchus (though he considered Hyperides a much better orator) he may have been in Smith's mind here; but Quintilian omits him from his roll-call of orators at XII.x.12–26.—It is useful to distinguish a first generation (5th to early fourth century ʙᴄ), Antiphon, Andocides, Lysias, Isaeus, Isocrates; and a second (latter fourth century).

of^w Lycurgus, of ^{x} and also severall[s] of Æschines, besides about 45 of Demosthenes. We need not take examples of the peculiar manner of each of these, as they are now but obscurely understood, at least the more ancient ones.

The Judiciall orations of the Greeks may be considered as of two sorts: 1st those which they called Publick, and 2dly the private ones. In the causes which regarded only the private affairs of an individuall it was not allowed for any one to plead the cause but the party concerned. The Patrons and Clients of Rome were never established in Greece in any shape. The only cases wherein any one but the person concerned was allowed to plead was where the party could not thro sickness or other incapacity appear at the Judgement of the Cause and when he who undertook it was a near relation of the | persons whose cause he plead; bothe these circumstances were necessary. The orator in this case therefore did not pronounce the oration himself, but composed one to be delivered by the party concern'd and adapted to his character and station. In the Publick ones in which the community was someway concerned the Orator spoke in his own person. I shall give you examples of both of these manners from Isaeus ^{y} and Demosthenes, betwixt whom and Cicero I shall make a comparison.[10]

Lysias is the most ancient of all the Orators whose works have come to our hands. He wrote^z private Orations to be delivered by the persons concerned; and in these he studied to adapt them to the Character of a simple good natured man not at all versed in the Subtility and Chicane of the Law. Isaeus ⟨was⟩ the Disciple of Lysias and the master of Demosthenes. He seems to have had neither the Fire of the latter nor the Simplicity of the former^a. The character he studied in his orations which were on private | causes as well as those of Lysias, was that of a plain sensible honest man,[11] and to this his orations are very well adapted. He is said however to have resembled Lysias so much that many could not distinguish betwixt the stile of the one and the other.

218

219

^{w} MS of one ^{x} *blank of about nine letters in MS* ^{y} De *deleted, then a blank of five letters in MS* (*the following paragraph supplies Lysias to fill the surprising gap. See note 10 below*) ^{z} as *deleted* ^{a} MS latter (*see below, ii. 219–221*)

Aeschines, Demosthenes, Lycurgus, Hyperides, Dinarchus 'the last of the ten'; with the minor orator Demades.

Of the sixty-one extant speeches once attributed to Demosthenes, the eighteenth-century critics accepted forty-five as genuine; later scholarship has reduced the number to under thirty.

[10] Four days before this lecture Smith referred (LJ iii.64, 10 Feb. 1763) to the oration of Lysias *Against Diogeiton*, 'which I will perhaps read in the other lecture'. There is no sign here that he did so; the notetaker's initial failure to catch the orator's name makes it seem unlikely. At LJ iv.78 (28 Feb. 1763) he praises the way in which in his *Funeral Oration* Lysias uses the Athenians' conduct at the time of the victory at Megara as an example to his hearers.

[11] See i.85 n.5 above, and ii.235–6 below.

Dionysius of Halicarnassus has however shewn us severall differences,[12] and by what we can now judge of their Stile and Language it seems to have been still greater than he makes it. The Exordium of their orations is much the same. They in it barely give us an account of the thing they are to prove, without any incentive arguments to either side; But their narrations are very different. There is so far alike in both that they do not wrest or torture any matter of fact to make it suit their purpose but deliver it as it realy happened. But as Lysias studied the Character of a Simple man, so his narration is altogether suitable to that Character. He introduces it barely by telling the Judges that they would understand it better on hearing the whole story. In the course of the narration he observes no order but delivers | the severall facts in the same order as they occurred and seems to tell the story as much to refresh his own memory as to inform his Judges; And for the same reason he relates not only those which are necessary to the cause but those which are noway connected with it. And as they are delivered in this dissorderly method, so it would be unnaturall for him to Recapitulate them, and therefore in the Conclusion he only draws an inference from the whole. Isaeus on the other hand in the Character of a plain and sensible man, appears to have considered and weighed maturely his subject before he ventures to speak on it, and for this reason they are all classed in proper order and are excellently adapted to the Subject he has in hand. He introduces his narration not only by telling[b] that[c] they will understand the cause the better if they hea⟨r⟩d the story, but specifies the particular points he intends it should illustrate, and introduces such facts only as tend to this end. And as they are deliverd in this orderly manner, so he summs them up exactly[d] and in order at the end. We may take as an example of his method his oration concerning the succession of Appollodorus.[13] N.B. Regard to Dead and keeping up house. Pub. Off.[e]

220

---

b in *deleted*   *c* he *deleted*   *d* exactly, *deleted, then rewritten above*   *e last sentence squeezed minutely into remaining space at end of quire 105*

[12] The treatises by Dionysius of Halicarnassus on Isaeus and Lysias as well as the short prologue on *The Ancient Orators* are in his *Critical Essays* i (LCL) and in his *Opuscules rhétoriques* i (ed. G. Aujac, Budé series, 1978).

[13] *On the Estate of Apollodorus* (no 7 in LCL edn): on the unjust treatment of a nephew's inheritance by his sole surviving uncle, Eupolis, and the claim now made for the estate of the deceased nephew by Thrasyllus (his half-sister's son) whom he was in the process of adopting at the time of his death. 'Pub. Off.' refers to Thrasyllus having been inscribed in the public official register as the adopted son of Apollodorus. Of the twelve surviving speeches of Isaeus all but one concern inheritances.

221 # Lecture. XXX[a]

Friday Febry. 18th 1763

In the last Lecture I mentioned to you that all the orations of the Greeks may be considered as of two sorts, viz. either the publick or the private ones; The first[b] tho composed by orators who made that their profession were nevertheless spoke by the persons themselves and of consequence were adapted to the character of those persons. They[c] are therefore generally adapted to the Character of a Plain or Simple country man who was not in the least acquainted with the[d] niceties of the law. Of this sort I gave you an example from Isaeus. The character he endeavours to maintain is that of a plain sensible man. Lysias again endeavours to appear in the character of a man of the greatest simplicity such as we might expect in a countryman not acquainted with the more refined manners. The Private orations of Demosthenes very much resemble those of Isaeus, as to the character kept up in them. He has not however the orderly arrangement of Isaeus, in the severall parts of his oration, but has in that point more of the manner of
222 Lysias. And if you can conceive the Plainness and Sense[e] | joined with the Simplicity and Elegance of Isaeus you will have a compleat notion of the private Judic[c]iall[f] orations of Demosthenes.

Of Public Orations we have no such great number. There is one of Lycurgus, and 3 of Æschines[g] and of all those of Demosthenes[1] that remain there are but three or four which appear to have been spoken by himself; if we except the Philippicks which are more properly Deliberative orations. Of these orations there are two in which Demosthenes and Æschines[h] accuse each other, as well as those wherein they make their defense.[2] Those are περι στεφανου and περι

[a] *MS* XXIX [b] *for* second*?* [c] *changed from* and [d] Proceedings usuall *deleted*
[e] *supply* of Lysias*?* [f] *numbers written above reverse the original* Judicciall private
[g] *MS* Æschyles, *with note in margin in Hand B*(*?*) Lege Eschines semper, *corrected to* Æschines
[h] *MS* Æschylus *for* Æschines; *so repeatedly up to 230*

[1] Lycurgus, *Against Leocrates*; Aeschines, see n.2 below; Demosthenes, speeches 18–24, but *Against Meidias* (see LJ ii.138, and Longinus xx.1) was never delivered. Demosthenes therefore delivered six.

[2] To summarize the altercations: Demosthenes and Aeschines went on embassage to Macedon in 346BC; the prosecution of Aeschines for misconducting it by Demosthenes and Timarchus was delayed by Aeschines charging Timarchus with vices incompatible with public office—*Against Timarchus*, 345BC; Demosthenes alone in 343BC prosecuted Aeschines, who successfully defended himself—the two speeches περὶ τῆς παραπρεσβείας (usually called *De falsa legatione*, since Cicero in *Orator*, xxxi.111, spoke of the first as 'contra Aeschinem falsae legationis') in 366 BC Ctesiphon carried a motion to award Demosthenes a golden crown for services to the state, but Aeschines prosecuted him in 330 BC for unconsitutional action—*Against Ctesiphon*—with Demosthenes defending successfully in the speech usually called περὶ τοῦ στεφάνου or *De Corona* (but of course both speeches are 'on the Crown'). Aeschines left Athens in mortification (not banished).

παραπρεσβειας, which are two of the most perfect and noblest of any of the Greek orations. That particularly of Demosthenes is the most instructive and most elegant of any wrote by him. In it he accuses Æschines by name of great misconduct in the Embassy he had been sent upon. In that περι στεφανου Æschines directs his accusation against one Ctespihon[i] who had proposed that a Crown should be

223 decreed to Demosthenes; but as the design of it is to prove that | Demosthenes was unworthy of it, the greatest part of the Oration is taken up with him. Neither of these orations produced what they were intended for. But that of Æschines was still less successfull than that of Demosthenes. It was a maxim at Athens that if one had not the 5th part of his judges on his side, who were very ignorant and generally easily influenced, he was to be accounted guilty of Calumny and suffer the Punishment the person accused would if he had been found guilty. Demosthenes tho he seems to have accused Æschines unjustly had nevertheless $\frac{1}{5}$ of the Judges, which Æschines had not and was accordingly banished.

The manner of these two orators is considerably different. Æschines has a certain gaiety and livelyness thro all his works which we do not find in the other; who tho' he has a great deal more of Splendor than the former orators has not near so much as Æschines and still less than Cicero. That disposition for mirth often takes away from the force of his orations in other points, and indeed is not at all fitted for raising any of those passions which are chiefly to be excited by oratory, viz.

224 Compassion | and indignation. This we see[j] is the case in many passages which were proper to have been described in the serious manner, in which he frequently introduces touches of humour which entirely prevent all that effect and prevent either indignation or compassion from being excited as nothing can be more conterary to those passions: But though[k] they do not at all suit with grave parts, are admirably adapted to a genteel and easy railing which appears to have been his peculiar excellence. His humour is always agreable and polite and such as we can attend to with great pleasure; Whereas Demosthenes whenever[l] he attemp⟨t⟩s to Rally runs into downright Scurrility and abuse, and abuse such as we could never attend to with patience, as nothing can be more dissagreable than this Coarse sort of Railery, were it not that the earnestness and sincerety of the orator is hereby displayed. As Gaiety and Levity appear in Æschines works so does a certain austere Severity and Rigidity in those of Demosthenes;

225 as it is very well adapted to feel and excite the more violent passions, | so it indisposes him to humour and Ridicule, and we see accordingly

---

[i] *i.e.* Ctesiphon   [j] often *deleted*   [k] ugh *inserted later below line*   [l] MS when every, y *deleted*

that where the best opportunities offered of Rallying his adversary he*m* hardly ever makes advantage of them; tho Æschines never fails to turn them to the best account.*n* This last mentioned orator is so agreable in this gay and entertaining temper that even those parts which are in most cases the driest and dullest of any, as the division of the Subject of his Oration, are made as entertaining as we can well conceive anything of that sort will admit of. Thus in the division of that part of his Oration where he intends to shew the misconduct of Demosthenes in his generall conduct,*o* he tells the Judges that Demosthenes said his life might be divided into four periods from one time to another and so on;[3] And that when he came to this part of his Oration Demosthenes was to ask him in which of these he was to accuse him of bad conduct, and that if he did not answer him he was to drag him to the forum and compell to determine which it was or else to give up his accusation.

226 When he does this, says he, I will tell him that it is | not against any of these particularly that my accusation is directed, but that I accuse him in them all together and in them all equally. This manner tho rather somewhat pert, is at the same time very entertaining and would probably fix the division he was to follow in the minds of the Judges.

But tho Demosthenes may be inferior perhaps to his Rivall in some of these more triviall points he has greatly the advantage over him in the more important and weighty parts of his orations. The severe and passionate temper which appears in his works is admirably adapted to the graver and serious parts which alone are capable of raising the passions of Compassion and Indignation, of which the latter particularly all his Orations tend*p* greatly to excite. His Judiciall Orations in most points indeed resemble his Deliberative ones, excepting that we find in the [the] latter more eloquence and passion than*q* is the case which all other authors. For as the Subject of Deliberative orations is politicks or something nearly allied to it, the object of this must be the concerns of a whole people; at a debate

227 concerning | peace or war etc. which tho very important will never affect the passions so highly as the distress of a single person or Indignation against the Crimes of an individuall. When Æschines*r*

---

m often *deleted*   *n* But tho Demosthenes may be inferior to his Rivall in the *deleted (anticipation of next paragraph)*   *o* general conduct *replaces* oratory (?)   *p replaces* are des   *q MS* which   *r This time changed from* Æschylus

---

[3] References as follows: *Against Ctesiphon*, 54–6—the four periods of Demosthenes' political activity equated with four periods in the city's history (Aeschines misuses this); ibid. 149–50—Demosthenes' frantic behaviour in jumping up in the assembly and swearing an oath by Athena, as if Pheidias had made her statue expressly for Demosthenes to perjure himself by—all out of pique at not sharing the bribe-money; ibid. 157 ff.—Aeschines on capture of Thebes, contrasted with Demosthenes on news of the capture of Elateia by Philip (*De Corona*, 169); cf. i.74 n.2 above.

enters upon these subjects he often misses the effect by the interruption of some stroke of Raillery, as that where he represents Demosthenes hopping into the market place thro grief that he had receivd none of the money which was distributed amongst the Thebans. And when he sets himself purposely to affect the passions in a high degree he generally runs into bombast. As we see in the Exclamation ˢ etc. {and severall other passages.} Those actors who enter least into their parts are observed to use more grimace and Gesticulation than those who are greatly affected by what they act; for whatever is affected is found always to be overdone. This is the case with Æschines, his temper was not adapted to gravity, or to be any ways greatly affected by those things which would stir up the [the] passions of more earnest men, so that whenever he attempts any thing of this sort he always outdoes. In all such more interesting events, Æschines has generally little more than Commonplace remarks, and such incidents as happen

228 on every | such like occasion. Thus in the Description he gives of the taking of Thebes, on⟨e⟩ of the most important events that happened about that time, he dwells greatly on the carrying the old men into Captivity, the Rape of the Virgins and matrons, and other such like which happen on the taking of every City; whereas Demosthenes in describing the taking of Elatea and the confusion this occasiond all Athens, tho the event was of much less moment and the danger which threatend Athens was still at a distance; yet I say he points out the severall circumstances of the confusion, theˡ croud which gathered at the Forum, how everyone looked on the others in expectation that they had discovered some expedient which had escaped him etc. etc. in such an interesting manner and with circumstances so peculiar to the event that it is highly interesting and striking etc.

However as no one is altogether perfect, it is greatly to be suspected that Demosthenes has not dividedᵘ his Orations in the most happy order; a talent which Æschinesᵛ and Cicero have possessed in a very high degree. There is in all his orations a confusion in the order of the

229 Arguments and the different parts it consists of, which will appear | to anyone on the slightest attention. Dionysius of Halicarnassus, a Critick of great penetration but whose observations appear sometimes to be rather nice and refind than solid, would persuade us that this confusion is merely apparent and that the order he has chosen is the most happy he could possibly have hit upon. But as far as I can see there is not only an apparent but a realʷ confusion. Thus in the orationˣ περι

ˢ *blank of about ten letters in MS*   ˡ con *deleted*   ᵘ *replaces* arranged   ᵛ *changed from* Æschylus *in a different hand*   ʷ *numbers written above change original order* a real but an apparent ˣ *of deleted*

παραπρεσβειας he begins his oration[4] with telling the people that there were 5 things which a people may[y] [to] expect from an ambassador and these he repeats in order. One should expect from this that he was to begin with the 1st and having discussed it proceed to the 2[d], from that to the 3[d] and so on; but of this we find nothing thro the whole; he begins at the first to give us a narration of the whole story as it happened, and tho we might perhaps reduce all that he has thrown together in that Oration[z] to one or other of these, yet they are not at all classed in that order but told in the very order they happened; and from the whole it appears most probable that this division was added

230   after the oration was wrote, and that when ⟨he⟩ | begun it he had no thought of dividing it, but finding before he got to the conclusion that it would be difficult to observe at what the several parts pointed, he has afterwards prefixed[a] the division, to point out what the hearers were chiefly to consider in the Oration. Æschines on the other hand is very happy in his divisions and, as I said before, attains in them a perfection very seldom met with, as he renders them even entertaining, and to these divisions he adheres very strictly. The best apology we can make for Demosthenes in this defect is that his eagerness, vehemence and passion have hurried him on both in speaking and writing to deliver the severall parts of his oration in the manner they affected him most, without considering in what manner they would give the hearer[b] or reader the clearest notion of what he delivers. {And we see this accordingly is most remarkably the case in those orations which he himself delivered and in which he was most interested}

The characters of these two Orators were we are informed very agreable to that which we would be apt to form from the consideration of their writings. Æschines who was bred a player,[5] an employment as creditable at that time as it is discreditable now, had all the mirth,

231   gaiety and levity which we | find in most of his profession. This temper made his company be greatly sought after by all the young people of his time, as he himself tells us and Demosthenes throws up to him as being noway to his honour. He seems also to have had a goo[o]d deal of

---

y changed from had   *z for* narration   *a replaces, in inner margin,* added   *b MS* hearre

[4] *De falsa legatione*, 4: an ambassador's responsibilities embrace his reports, the advice he offers, observance of his instructions, use of times and opportunities, and integrity.—For Dionysius of Halicarnassus and his praise of the methods of Demosthenes see his *Critical Essays* i (LCL).

[5] Aeschines as a small-part actor with two 'Growlers' ('Ετριταγωνίστεις), see *De Corona*, 262–6; and Demosthenes' mocking question at 180, 'What part do you wish me to assign you . . . in the drama of that great day?'; also *De falsa leg.* 246. For the equivocal response of Aeschines to taunts about his licentious and unsavoury private life: *Against Timarchus*, 135; *Against Ctesiphon*, 216. Demosthenes addresses Aeschines as a 'disreputable quill-driver', a 'third-rate tragedian', at *De Corona* 209.

the mimick about him; and there are some passages in the oration abovementioned which are evidently intend⟨ed⟩ to mimick Demosthenes and must have been delivered with his tone and Gesture. This talent of mimickry recommended him to the favour and patronage of Philip, who we are told was extremely delighted with all sorts of mimicks and Buffoons.

Demosthenes on the other hand was of an austere and rigid disposition, which made him not be affected with anything which was not of importance, but at the same time his vehemence made him enter into every thing which was of any moment with the greatest warmth; and prosecute those who seemed to deserve his indignation. This temper made ⟨him⟩ not much entertained with common conversation as there are but few things of importance generally canvassed in it, and at the same time made him not be much desired as a companion, as men
232 of this character | can neither be much intertained by other⟨s⟩ or be very entertaining. He therefore lived for the most part shut up in his own house seeing and seen by very few. He spent much of his time in the study of the Stoick and Platonick Philosophy, to the latter of which he seems to have been most addicted. He has in most of his passionate and animated passages many of the sentiments of those philosophers, particularly in that where he introduces the famous Oath mentioned by Longinus.[6] And there ⟨are⟩ many pass[s]ages which resemble Plato so much even in the expression that I have been often tempted to believe that he had Copied them from him. I should have given you a translation of these two orations[7] were it not that they are both of them very long and could not be abriged without loosing greatly in their merit. I would however reckommend them greatly to your perusall as they are not only excellent in their way, but also as they give us a very good Abrigement of the History of Greece for a period of considerable length.

There are severall other Greek orators whose works are still remaining but as they are but little read and are generally in private
233 causes | which are commonly not*ᶜ* [not] the most entertaining I shall pass them over altogether and proceed to make some observations on Cicero and the Differences betwixt his manner and that of Demos⟨thenes⟩.

ᶜ *numbers written above reverse the original order* not commonly; *then a superfluous* not

---

[6] *On the Sublime* cites the two most famous passages in *De Corona*: at x.7 the news of Elateia (see i.74 n.2, ii.228 above); at xvi.2, Demosthenes' impassioned oath (*De Cor.* 208) by those who fought at Marathon, Plataea, Salamis, by all brave men who rest in public sepulchres—much admired by Quintilian (IX.ii.62, XI.iii.168, XII.x.24) and other rhetoricians.
[7] *De Corona* and *De falsa legatione*: apparently the speeches of Demosthenes, though as at ii.222 above the context is ambiguous.

I have already*d* pointed out some of the Differences betwixt those
two great Orators,[8] which appear to me to proceed chiefly from the
different conditions and Genius of their two nations. I shall now
observe more particularly those which proceed from the differences of
character and circumstances of the men themselves.

There is no character in antiquity with which we are better
acquainted than with that of Cicero, which is evidently displayed in all
his works and in particular must receive great light from his Epistles.—
But we may perhaps discover more of the real*e* spirit and turn of his
writings by considering his naturall temper, his Education, and the
Genius of the times he lived in, than from the Observations of his
Criticks. But altho these men have a very extraordinary knack at
mistaking his meaning, yet they have not been able to err so grosely
with respect to his character, so clearly does it shine out, as the sun now

234 does*f* | thro all his writings. He seems to have*g* by nature [nature] had
along with a great degree of Sensibility and Natural parts a
considerable share of Vanity and Ostentation. Sensibility is without
doubt a most amiable character, and one which is of all others most
engaging; We may therefore with justice make some allowance if it be
joind with some failings. Now there are no two tempers of mind which
are so often combind as Levity in a certain proportion and a great
degree of Sensibility. The same temper which disposes one to partake
in the joys or misfortunes of others, or to be much affected with ones
own, is naturally connected with a disposition that makes one both
easily buoyed up by the smallest circumstances of the pleasant kind
and depressed with those which are in the least distressing, and at the
same time prompts them to communicate their feelings with others no
less at the one time than at the other. One who is of a Joyous temper
turns every thing that*h* happens to him into an object of pleasure, and
dwells on the most minute circumstances; and is no less inclined to
communicate it to others. If it happens that he has nothing which

235 immediately calls for any exertion of this happy temper | his happy
condition becomes an object of his joy, he looks on himself and his
condition with a certain complacense and his joy becomes the object of
his Joy; the same disposition which makes him communicate his joy at
other times and expatiate on the agreableness of certain things around,
makes him now dwell upon himself and be continually talking of the
happiness of his circumstances and the joy of his own mind. A morose
or melancholy man on the other hand takes everything in the worst

d shewn *deleted*   *e* geni *deleted*   *f* last five words added (scribe's remark?) at foot of page
g been *deleted*   *h* can *deleted*

[8] Cf. ii.151 ff. above.

light and finds something in it which distresses[i] him, and when nothing
occurrs which can give him any real distress his own unhappiness
becomes his vexation. He continually dwells on the misery of his own
disposition which thus turns every thing to his misery.—He talks of
himself no less than the Joyous man, and as the one dwells on the
happiness of his condition so he insists on the misery of his. A man of
great Sensibility, in the same manner, who enters[j] much into the
happiness or distress either of himself or others is no less inclind to
236 display these sensations to others, and | in this way will frequently talk[k]
of himself and frequently with a good deal of vanity and ostentation.
We see that the women, who are generally thought to have a good deal
more of Levity and vanity in their temper, are at the same time
acknowledged to have more sensibility and compassion in their
tempers than the men. The French nation who are thought[l] ⟨to have⟩
more levity and Vanity than most others are reckoned to be the most
humane and charitable of any.

  Cicero seems in the same way to have been possessed of a very high
degree of Sensibility and to have been very easily depressed or elated
by the missfortunes or prosperity of his friends {as his letters to them
evidently shew, where he enters intirely into their misfortunes[m]} or of
himself; which levity of temper tho it might indispose him for Publick
business and render him somewhat unsettled in his behaviour would
nevertheless be of no small advantage to him as a speaker. {Men of the
greatest Calmeness and Prudence are not generally[n] the most sensible
and Compassionate} It would also make him a very agreable and
237 pleasant companion and dispose him frequently to mirth and |
Jovialty. We are told accordingly that his apothegms[9] or sayings were
no less esteemed than his orations; Volumes of them were handed
about in his life time and his servant Tyro published 7 volumes of them
after his death. We may reasonably suppose that one of this temper
would be very susceptible of all the different passions but of none more
than of pity and compassion, which accordingly appears to have been
that which chiefly affected him.

  Cicero lived at a time when learning had been introduced into
Rome and was indeed but just then introduced. It was in very high
reputation and as Novelty generally inhances the value of a thing it
was perhaps more highly esteemed than it deserved, and than it was

---

[i] *changed from* depresses   [j] *changed from* partakes   [k] ing *deleted*   [l] thought *deleted*,
wrongly?   [m] and *deleted*   [n] best *deleted*

---

  [9] Quintilian (VI.iii.5) wishes Tiro had shown more judgment in selecting the *three* volumes of
Cicero's jests or obiter dicta than zeal in collecting them. Cicero (*Ad Familiares*, IX.xvi.4) reports
that Caesar, who was making a collection of apophthegms, had instructed his friends to bring him
any *mots* they picked up in Cicero's company.

afterwards when they became better acquainted with it. Rhetorick and Dialectick were the Sciences which had then arrived to the greatest perfection and were the most fashionable study amongst all
238 the polite men of Rome. Their | Dialectick was pretty much the same with that of Aristotle though somewhat altered and improved by the Stoicks, who cultivated it more than the Peripatiticks. Their Rhetorick was that of Henagoras[o] which I have already touched upon. To these studies Cicero applied himself with great assiduity till the age of 25. He tells that he disputed under the inspection of some of the most Renowned masters severall hours every day. After this having appeared in two or three causes, one of which was that of Roscius[10] of Almeira,[p] and gain'd no little reputation as a speaker, he went over into Gree⟨c⟩e where he staid [a] about two years. This time he employed in attending the Harangues and Discourses of the most Celebrated Orators and Philosophers of the time, under whose direction he wrote and delivered harangues and orations of all sorts. The Eloquence then in fashion in Greece had deviated a good deal from the Simplicity and easiness of Demosthenes but still retained a
239 great deall of familiarity | and Homelyness, which was unknown in[q] the Pleadings at Rome for the reasons I have already pointed out. When he returned from his travells he found a more florid and Splendid Stile to be fashionable at Rome than what he had met with at Athens or the other parts of Greece; and Hortensius,[11] the most Celebrated orator of his time, was more florid and aimd more at the Splendor and Grandeur then esteemd than any other. We would naturally expect of a man of this temper, this Education and in these circumstances the very conduct that Cicero had followd in his works. We should expect that he would aim at that Splendor and dignity of expression which was then fashionable tho conterary to the familiar method which was esteemed in Greece. We may expect that he will be at considerable pains to display his knowledge in those Sciences which were then in highest repute; That we will find in ⟨his⟩ Orations the whole of those parts which were reckoned proper to the form of a regular oration; a Regular exordium, narration where ever the Subject will admit of it, a
240 Proof, a confu|tation, and perroration, all regularly marked out [all regularly marked out]. We might expect also that he would even

---

[o] *i.e.* Hermagoras; *line above and below in MS*   [p] *i.e.* Ameria   [q] Greece *deleted*

[10] Cf. ii.213 ff. above, 242 below. Hermagoras (*c.* 150 BC), a very influential teacher of rhetoric, whom Cicero (*Brutus*, lxxvi.263 ff., lxxviii.271) found unhelpful for embellishment of style but a purveyor of useful precepts and guidelines of general applicability in argument: 'ad inveniendum expedita Hermagorae disciplina'. Hence frequent references to him in Cicero's early *De Inventione*. On *Pro Roscio Amerino* cf. ii.194 n.2 above.

[11] Q. Hortensius Hortalus (114–50 BC). See ii.169 n.5 above.

sometimes adhere to the Rhetoricall divisions and topicks where they appeared to be very unsuitable to the cause in hand, as we saw in his Oration for Milo. We may expect also that one of his cast as his temper naturally leads him to compassion will be more inclind to undertake a defense than to accuse; whic⟨h⟩ we see was the case, and when he has been necessitated to accuse he will insist rather on the missfortunes of the injurd than on the guilt of the Offender; As we see he does in his orations in Verrem,¹² where he dwells chiefly on the misfortunes of some of the oppressed Syracusans etc., touching but little on the crimes' of the Praetor. We may expect too that he would have some part of his oration where he would purposely endeavour to move the Compassion of the Judges towards the Injurd persons. This he generally places' immediately before the perroration; Which is much

241 preferable | to one placed nearer the beginning; for compassion even when strongest is but a short lived passion. So that the whole influence' of it would be lost if it was placd near the beginning before the time came where it was to produce its effect. ᵘ observes that Cicero generally draws the attention of the Reader from the cause to himself and tho we admire the Orator we do not reap great instruction with regard to the Cause.¹³ This observation so far as it is just proceeds from the Digressions which Cicero introduces in many parts of his Orations to raise the passions of his audience, tho sometimes they do not tend to explain the cause.

Demosthenes was very different from this both in naturall temper and the Genius of the Country. He was of an austere temper which was not easily moved but by things of a very important nature, and in all cases his indignation rose much higher than his compassion. His earnestness makes him hurry on from one thing to another without

242 attending to any particular order. Logice or Dialectick was not then | nor was it or Rhetorick ever in such high reputation as they were afterwards at Rome, and accordingly we find no traces of their divisions in his Orations. He frequently has no exordium, at least none distinc⟨t⟩ly marked from the narration, and the other parts are in like manner blended together. The Florid and Splendid does not appear in his works, a more easy and familiar one was more esteemd in his time. The passion which animates him in all his orations is Indignation, and

---

ʲ *inserted later in short blank left*   ˢ *scribe wrote* im *of* immediately, *then repeated* places
ᵗ *replaces* effect   ᵘ *blank of five letters in MS*

---

¹² For Gaius Verres, pro-praetor of Sicily 73–71 BC, cf. ii.154 above; prosecuted by Cicero for the people of Sicily in 70 BC.—*Verrine orations*, (LCL).
¹³ Cicero's critic here is almost certainly Quintilian; cf. his report of Cicero's famous boast over the Cluentius case, II.xvii.21 (ii.211 n.6 above).

this as it is a more lasting passion than Compassion he often begins with and continues in thro a whole oration. The free and easy manner of the Greeks would not admit of any such perroration designed to move the passions as those we meet with in Cicero; and it is not accordingly to be met with in any of the Greek orators. Upon the whole Cicero is more apt to draw our Pity and love and Demosthenes to raise our Indignation. The one is strong and commanding, 243 the other persuasive | and moving. The character Quinctilian gives of Cicero intirely corresponds with this.——

Of all the immense number of Orators who are enumerated[v] by Quinctilian,[14] none have come down to us excepting Cicero. With regard to those who preceded him and were his contemporaries we surely may[w] regreat the loss; but as to those who came after him, they are perhaps as well buried in oblivion as if they remained to perplex us.—— We see that even Cicero introduces in his Orations severall digressions which tended merely to amuse the Judge without in the least explaining the cause. This became the universall and ordinary practise after his time, insomuch that there were fixt pla[e]ces where these digressions were introduced. There was one betwixt the narration and the proof, of which I can see no design unless it was make the judge forget what they were to prove. There was another betwixt the proof and the confutation and another betwixt that and the perroration, for 244 which I can see no purpose but the same as the former. The whole | of their orations was also filled with figures as they called them, no less usefull than these digressions. We may see how far this was come so soon after Cicero's time as that of Tiberius, by the Story of one[x] ⟨Albucius⟩. He when pleading against one ⟨Arruntius⟩[y] offered to referr it to his oath, which he accepted;[15] But says he, you must swear by the ashes of your father which are unburied etc.; and so on, laying all sort of crimes to his charge. The man accepted the condition but ⟨Albucius⟩[z] refused to allow him to swear saying that it was only a figure. And when the man insisted on his standing to his word he told them if that was the case there would be an end of all figures. ⟨Arruntius⟩[a] told him he believd men could live without them, and still

---

[v] *MS* neumerated   [w] *replaces* are with   [x] *, He wh deleted; then blank, for which JML supplies* Albucius   [y] *blank in MS: JML supplies* Arruntius   [z] *blank in MS: supply* Albucius
[a] *blank in MS: supply* Arruntius

[14] XII.x.12–26, following a list of ancient painters (3–6) and sculptors (7–9).
[15] The advocate Albucius is infuriated when his challenge to his opponent Arruntius, 'Will you swear by the ashes of your father?', is taken literally and accepted, since he insists it was a *figure* (the Omotic). 'Nota enim fabula est' (Quintilian, IX.ii.95). See Seneca the Elder, *Controversiae*, VII. praefatio 6–7 (Albucius incidentally is breathless with admiration for Hermagoras, 5). LCL edn. cites also Suetonius, *De grammaticis et rhetoribus*, XXX.3.

insisted on the oaths being put to him, which the judges agreed to. But
⟨Albucius⟩*b* was so enraged at his figures being thus laid hold on that he
swore he should never appear at the bar for the future. He kept his
word and we are told he used to brag that he had more hearers at his
house listening to his declamations on feigned Causes than others had
245 at their pleading on real ones. | In a short time their Orations came to
be nothing but a String of Digressions and figures of this sort one after
another, so that we need not wonder at what Quinctilian informs us of,
that there were many orations delivered for which the pleader was
highly commended when at the same time no one could tell on which
side of the cause he was.[16] We need not therefore regret much the loss of
these later orations.

I shall now give ye some account of the state of the Judicial
eloquence of England, which is very different from that either of
Gree⟨c⟩e or of Rome. This difference is generally ascribed to the small
progress which has been made in the cultivation of language and Stile
in this country compared with that which it had arrived to in the Old
World. But ⟨tho⟩ this may be true in some degree, yet I imagine there
are other causes which must make them essentially different. The
eloquence which is now in greatest esteem is a plain, distinct, and
perspicuous Stile without any of the Floridity or other ornamentall
parts of the Old Eloquence. This and other differences must necessarily
246 arise from the nature of the | courts and the particular turn of the
people. The Courts were then*c* much in the same manner as the Jury is
now; they were men unskilld in the Law, whose office continued but
for a very short time and were often in a great part chosen for the trial
of that particular cause, and not from any particular set of men, but
often by ballot or rotation from the whole body of the people; and of
them there was always no inconsiderable number. The Judges in
England on the other hand are single men, who have been bred to the
law and have generally or at least are supposed to have a thorough
knowledge of the law and are much versed in all the different
circumstances of cases, of*d* which they have attended many before*e*
either as Judges or pleaders, and are supposed to be acquainted with
all the different arguments that may be advanced on it. This therefore
cutts them out from a great part of the substance of the old orations.

---

b required, but no blank in MS   *c composed deleted*   *d changed from and*   *e the deleted*

[16] The remark is not in Quintilian; but its spirit informs the little portrait in Persius, *Satire* i.85–
8, of the advocate Pedius (the name is from Horace, *Satires* I.x.28) to whom the fate of his client is
indifferent as long as the beauty of his speech ('rasis/librat in antithetis, doctas posuisse figuras') is
admired; and Quintilian's own question (XI.i.49–50) on what we should think of a man pleading
his imperilled case and hunting only for fine words ('verba aucupantem et anxium de fama
ingenii'), with leisure to show off his eloquence ('diserto').

47 There can here be no room for a narration, | the only design of which
is*ʲ* by interweaving those facts for which*ᵍ* proof can be brought with
others for which no proof can be brought, that these latter may gain
credit by their connection with the others. But as nothing is now of any
weight for which direct proof is not brought this sort of narration
should serve no end. The pleader therefore can do no more than tell
over what facts*ʰ* he is to prove, which may often be very unconnected.
The only case indeed where he can give a compleat narration of the
whole transaction is when he has ⟨a⟩ witness who has been present thro
the whole, which can happen but very rarely. {And if he should assert
any thing as a fact, as the old orators frequently did, for which he can
bring no proof he would be severely reprimanded.} The pleader has
here no opportunity of smoothing over any argument which would
make against him, as the Judge will perceive it and pay no regard to
what he advances in this manner. Nor can he conceal any weak side by
placing it betwixt two on which he depends for the proof of it, as this

48 would be | soon perceived. All these*ⁱ* were particularly directed by the
antient Rhetoricians; the innatention and ignorance of the Judges was
the sole foundation of it; as [as] this is not now to be expected they can
be of no service. The Pleader must be much more Close than those of
ancient R⟨ome⟩ or G⟨reece⟩, and we find that those Pleaders are most
esteemed who point out the Subject in the clearest and distinctest
manner and endeavour to give the Judge a fair idea of the Cause.*ʲ*

A great popular assembly is a great object which strikes the Speaker
at first with awe and dread, but as they begin to be moved by the cause
and the Speaker himself to be interested in it they then animate him
and embolden him. The confusion which he will perceive amongst
them will give him courage and rouse his passions. A Single Judge is
but a single man and he, attended with a pityfull Jury, can neither
strike such awe nor animate the passions. Florid speakers are not at all
in esteem. One who was to Storm and Thunder before 5 or 6 persons

49 would be taken for a fool or a madman; Tho the same | behaviour
before a Great assembly of the People would appear very proper and
suitable to the occasion. It might perhaps seem that the House of Lords
which consist of a considerable number might give an opportunity of
being more animated and passionate. But in most private causes there
are not above 30%*ᵏ* of them together. In State trials indeed they are all
met, but then the great order and decorum which is kept up there gives
no opportunity for expatiating. In all the State trialls which have been
published those speeches were most commended which proceeded in
the most naturall and plain order; and if ever one brings in any thing

---

ʲ that *deleted*   *ᵍ* there *deleted; numbers written above change original order* can proof   *ʰ* MS
parts   *ⁱ* replaces* which   *ʲ* The *deleted*   *ᵏ* reading doubtful

that may appear designed to move the passions it must be only by the
by, a hint and no more. The order and Decorum of Behaviour which is
now in fashion will not admit of any the least extravagancies. The
behaviour which is reckoned polite in England is a calm, composed,
250 unpassionate serenity¹ | noways ruffled by passion. Foreigners observe
that there is no nation in the world which use so little gesticulation in
their conversation as the English. A Frenchman in telling a story that
was not of the least consequence to him or any one else will use 1000
gestures and contortions of his face, whereas a well bread Englishman
will tell you one wherein his life and fortune are concerned without
altering a muscle in his face.—Montain in some of his essays¹⁷ tells us
that he had seen the same Opera acted before both an English and an
Italian audience; the difference of their behaviour he says was very
remarkable; At the time where the one would be dying away in
extasies of pleasure the others would not appear to be the least moved.
This is attributed by that Judicious Frenchman to their want of
Sensibility and ignorance of Music: But in this he seems to be
mistaken; For if there is any art thoroughly understood in England it is
Musick. The lower[s] sort often*ᵐ* evidence a great accuracy of
251 Judgement in it, and the better sort often | display a thorough and most
masterly knowledge of it. The real cause is the different idea of
Politeness.

The Spaniards notion of Politeness is a Majestick Proud and
overbearing philosophic Gravity. A Frenchman again places it in an
easy gaiety, affableness and Sensibility. Politeness again in England
consists in Composure, calm and u⟨n⟩ruffled behaviour. The most
Polite persons are those only who go to the Operas and any emotion
would there be reckoned altogether indecent. And we see that when
the same persons go out of frolick to a Beargarden or such like
ungentlemanny entertainment they preserve the same composure as
before at the Opera, while the Rabble about express all the various
passions by their gesture and behaviour.

We are not then to expect that any thing passionate or exagerated

---

¹ *MS* serenay   ᵐ *scribe started to write* display, *by anticipation*

---

¹⁷ The word 'essays' betrays that the scribe is thinking of Montaigne, in error for Montesquieu:
De l'esprit des lois (1748), XIV.ii (entitled 'Combien les hommes sont différens dans les divers
climats'), §8: 'Comme on distingue les climats par les degrés de latitude, on pourroit les
distinguer, pour ainsi dire, par les degrés de sensibilité. J'ai vû les Opéra d'Angleterre et d'Italie;
ce sont les mêmes pieces et les mêmes Acteurs; mais la même Musique produit des effets si
différens sur les deux Nations, l'une est si calme, et l'autre si transportée, que cela paroît
inconcevable'. The 18th century saw much controversy over the relative musical capacities of
different peoples and their languages; Rousseau was involved in one over French and Italian.

will be admitted in the house of Lords.[n] Nothing will be receivd there
which is not or at least appears not to be a plain, just and exact
account. The pleadings[o] for this reason of the most Celebrated
252 Speakers | appear to us to be little more than the heads of a discourse as
we are here accustomed with a more loose way of pleading. If however
under this appearance of plainess and candidness the pleader can
artfully interweave something which favours his side the effect may
often be very great.[p]

The Lords in their speeches to one another always observe the same
rules of Decorum and if any thing of passion be hinted at it must be a
hint only. We see that those who have made great figures as speakers in
the house of Commons, where a very loose manner and often a great
deal of Ribaldry and abuse is admitted of, lost their character when
transferred into the upper house. For tho they were sensible that the
manner they had been acc[o]ustomed to[q] was not at all proper there
yet it was not in their power to lay it aside all at once. Many of the
253 speeches of the | State trials must have had a great deal of their effect
from the delivery and Emphasis with which the different heads, for
little more can here be admitted of, were delivered: That of
Atterbury[18] which is spoken of with Rapture by all who heard it,
appears to us confused and unnanimated, tho it certainly produce⟨d⟩ a
wonderfull effect on the hearers.[r]—Floridity and Splendor has
allway⟨s⟩ been disliked. Sir Robert Walpoles speech on [s] was for
its being somewhat of this sort called by way of derision an Oration.

[n] *replaces* commons [o] that *deleted* [p] *barely decipherable sentence deleted*: This the the delivery mentioned is that which all the speakers of Repute have practised: Many of the Ora [q] the *deleted* [r] *MS* Hearres [s] *blank of five letters in MS*

[18] The speech which Henry Sacheverell delivered on 7 March 1710 at his impeachment before the House of Lords differed so much in tone and style—quiet and modest, with balanced phrasing and an edge of paradox—from the two offending sermons he had preached at Derby Assizes and at St Paul's in August and November 1709, that everyone believed it to be by Francis Atterbury (1662–1732), later Bishop of Rochester. It was printed in *A compleat history of the whole proceedings of the Parliament of Great Britain against Dr. Henry Sacheverell: with his Tryal before the House of Peers, for High Crimes and Misdemeanors*, 1710: 2.66–84; reprinted as 'universally ascribed to Dr. Atterbury when originally published', in *The Epistolary Correspondence, Visitation Charges, Speeches and Miscellanies* of Atterbury, iii (1784), 456–502.

Any identification of the 'oration' of Sir Robert Walpole referred to would be guesswork. He eschewed flights of oratory, but his speeches were often praised. Burke, in *An Appeal from the New to the Old Whigs*, thought Walpole's speech on the Sacheverell trial a clear exposition of constitutional principle. In his refutation of Pulteney's vote of censure in January 1742 'he exceeded himself . . . He actually dissected Mr Pulteney', according to Sir Robert Wilmot. But the reference above may be to his only speech, as Earl of Orford, in the House of Lords, speaking on 24 February 1744 on an apprehended French invasion in support of Prince Charles Edward: 'a long and fine speech', said his son Horace, a connoisseur in such matters. See W. Coxe, *Memoirs of . . . Sir R.W.*, 1798; and J. H. Plumb, *Sir Robert Walpole*, 1956–61.

I shall only observe farther on this head that the idea of English Eloquence hinted at here is very probably a just one, as the two most admired orators, Lord Mansefield and Sir Wm. Pym, spoke exactly in the same manner tho very distant in their time.[19] The former however[f] is to us more agreable on account of the langu[e]age and is without doubt greatly more perspicuous and orderly.

[f] *MS* howvear

---

[19] William Murray (1705–93), judge and parliamentarian, was created Baron Mansfield of Mansfield in 1756; first Earl, 1776. 'In all debates of consequence [he] had greatly the advantage over Pitt in point of argument' (Waldegrave, 1755); Horace Walpole, an opponent, 'never heard so much argument, so much sense, so much oratory united' (*Memoirs of the reign of George II*, iii.120), as in a 1758 speech of Mansfield's. The lucidity and sharpness of his forensic oratory are even more highly praised by contemporaries.

Pym is the parliamentarian John Pym (1583–1643), a leading speaker in the Commons from 1621 onwards; bibliographical details in S. R. Brett, *John Pym 1583–1643: the statesman of the Puritan Revolution*, 1940. The scribe confuses him no doubt with William Prynne (see i.10 n.9 above), much better known as a pamphleteer than as a parliamentary orator.

CONSIDERATIONS
CONCERNING THE FIRST
FORMATION of LANGUAGES,
AND THE
Different Genius of original and compounded
LANGUAGES.

Considerations
Concerning the First
Formation of Languages,
&c. &c.[1]

1 THE assignation of particular names, to denote particular objects, that is, the institution of nouns substantive, would probably, be one of the first steps towards the formation of language. Two savages,[2] who had never been taught to speak, but had been bred up remote from the societies of men, would naturally begin to form that language by which they would endeavour to make their mutual wants intelligible to each other, by uttering certain sounds, whenever they meant to denote certain objects. Those objects only which were most familiar to them, and which they had most frequent occasion to mention, would have particular names assigned to them. The particular cave whose covering sheltered them from the weather, the particular tree whose fruit relieved their hunger, the particular fountain whose water allayed their thirst, would first be denominated by the words *cave, tree, fountain,* or by whatever other appellations they might think proper, in that primitive jargon, to mark them. Afterwards, when the more enlarged experience of these savages had led them to observe, and their necessary occasions obliged them to make mention of other caves, and other trees, and other fountains, they would naturally bestow, upon each of those new objects, the same name, by which they had been accustomed to express the similar object they were first acquainted with. The new objects had none of them any name of its own, but each

---

[1] For full title (set out in capitals in *3–5*) see Note on the Text; only *6* abbreviates it thus. Smith seems to show some indifference to what his essay is called.

[2] This fanciful account could have been suggested by the passage in the Abbé Étienne Bonnet de Condillac's *Essai sur l'origine des connoissances humaines* (1746) referred to in Rousseau's *Discours* (see below). Adam and Eve had the gift of speech as part of their God-given perfection; 'mais je suppose que, quelque temps après le déluge, deux enfans, de l'un et de l'autre sexe, aient été égarés dans des déserts, avant qu'ils connussent l'usage d'aucun signe.' Eventually their child develops the use of lingual signs: II.sec.1 préambule, to sec.7. Condillac cites the *Essai sur les Hiéroglyphes des Égyptiens* (1744, 48) by 'M. Warburthon', i.e. the translation by M. A. Leonard des Malpeines of Warburton's *The Divine Legation of Moses Demonstrated* (1741, Bk IV sec.iv). Warburton himself refers to Diodorus Siculus ii and Vitruvius ii.1, on the beginnings of articulate human sounds in mutual association; also to Gregory of Nyssa, *Adversus Eunomium* xii; the seventeenth century Hebraist Richard Simon, *Histoire critique du Vieux Testament* i.14–15, iii.21; and J. F. Lafitau, *Moeurs des sauvages amériquains, comparées aux moeurs des premiers temps* (1724), i.482; cf. LJ(A), ii.96. Smith had copies of both Condillac's *Essai* (1746) and of his *Traité des sensations* (1754), part of the background of the essay 'Of the External Senses' in EPS.

of them exactly resembled another object, which had such an appellation. It was impossible that those savages could behold the new objects, without recollecting the old ones; and the name of the old ones, to which the new bore so close a resemblance. When they had occasion, therefore, to mention, or to point out to each other, any of the new objects, they would naturally utter the name of the correspondent old one, of which the idea could not fail, at that instant, to present itself to their memory in the strongest and liveliest manner. And thus, those words, which were originally the proper names of individuals, would each of them insensibly become the common name of a multitude. A child that is just learning to speak, calls every person who comes to the house its papa or its mama; and thus bestows upon the whole species those names which it had been taught to apply to two individuals. I have known a clown, who did not know the proper name of the river which ran by his own door. It was *the river*, he said, and he never heard any other name for it. His experience, it seems, had not led him to observe any other river. The general word *river*, therefore, was, it is evident, in his acceptance of it, a proper name, signifying an individual object. If this person had been carried to another river, would he not readily have called it a river? Could we suppose any person living on the banks of the Thames so ignorant, as not to know the general word *river*, but to be acquainted only with the particular word *Thames*, if he was brought to any other river, would he not readily call it a *Thames?* This, in reality, is no more than what they, who are well acquainted with the general word, are very apt to do. An Englishman, describing any great river which he may have seen in some foreign country, naturally says, that it is another Thames. The Spaniards, when they first arrived upon the coast of Mexico, and observed the wealth, populousness, and habitations of that fine country, so much superior to the savage nations which they had been visiting for some time before, cried out, that it was another Spain. Hence it was called New Spain; and this name has stuck to that unfortunate country ever since. We say, in the same manner, of a hero, that he is an Alexander; of an orator, that he is a Cicero; of a philosopher, that he is a Newton. This way of speaking, which the grammarians call an Antonomasia, and which is still extremely common, though now not at all necessary, demonstrates how much mankind are naturally disposed to give to one object the name of any other, which nearly resembles it, and thus to denominate a multitude, by what originally was intended to express an individual.

2   It is this application of the name* of an individual to a great

---

multitude of objects, whose resemblance naturally recalls the idea of that individual, and of the name which expresses it, that seems originally to have given occasion to the formation of those classes and assortments, which, in the schools, are called genera and species, and of which the ingenious and eloquent M. Rousseau of Geneva* finds himself so much at a loss to account for the origin. What constitutes a species is merely a number of objects, bearing a certain degree of resemblance to one another, and on that account denominated by a single appellation, which may be applied to express any one of them.

3   When the greater part of objects had thus been arranged under their proper classes and assortments, distinguished by such general names, it was impossible that the greater part of that almost infinite number of individuals, comprehended under each particular assortment or species, could have any peculiar or proper names of their own, distinct from the general name of the species. When there was occasion, therefore, to mention any particular object, it often became necessary to distinguish it from the other objects comprehended under the same general name, either, first, by its peculiar qualities; or, secondly, by the peculiar relation which it stood in to some other things. Hence the necessary origin of two other sets of words, of which the one should express quality; the other, relation.

4   Nouns adjective⁴ are the words which express quality considered as qualifying, or, as the schoolmen say, in concrete with, some particular subject. Thus the word *green* expresses a certain quality considered as qualifying, or as in concrete with, the particular subject to which it may be applied. Words of this kind, it is evident, may serve to distinguish particular objects from others comprehended under the same general appellation. The words *green tree*, for example, might serve to distinguish a particular tree from others that were withered or blasted.

5   Prepositions are the words which express relation considered, in the

* Origine de l'Inegalité.³ Partie Premiere, p. 376, 377. Edition d'Amsterdam des Oeuvres diverses de J. J. Rousseau.

³ (inegalité *PM 3*; premiere *PM 3–5*). The reference is to *Discours sur l'origine et les fondemens de l'inégalité parmi les hommes* Par Jean Jaques Rousseau citoyen de Genève (1755), I.§§23–31. The dilemma there posed is that generalization is possible only if we possess words but that words are made possible only by the power to generalize; and so 'on jugera combien il eût falu de milliers de Siécles, pour développer successivement dans l'Esprit humain les Opérations, dont il étoit capable.' A few months after the appearance of the *Discours* on 24 April 1755 Smith had quoted extensively from it in his Letter to the *Edinburgh Review* No 2 (see EPS 250–4).

⁴ The grammatical terms *noun adjective* and *noun substantive*, taken from late Latin *nomen adiectivum* and *nomen substantivum*, were normal usage from the late fourteenth century, but were rivalled from *c.*1500 by the simple *adjective* and *substantive* (the latter eventually almost wholly replaced by *noun*). The first probably sounded a little archaic, and ambiguous, in 1761. 'What is an Adjective? I dare not call it Noun Adjective' (Horne Tooke, *Diversions of Purley*, 1786, II.vi).

same manner, in concrete with the co-relative object. Thus the prepositions *of, to, for, with, by, above, below,* &c.*ᵈ* denote some relation subsisting between the objects expressed by the words between which the prepositions are placed; and they denote that this relation is considered in concrete with the co-relative object. Words of this kind serve to distinguish particular objects from others of the same species, when those particular objects cannot be so properly marked out by any peculiar qualities of their own. When we say, *the green tree of the meadow,* for example, we distinguish a particular tree, not only by the quality which belongs to it, but by the relation which it stands in to another object.

6   As neither quality nor relation can exist in abstract, it is natural to suppose that the words which denote them considered in concrete, the way in which we always see them subsist, would be of much earlier invention than those which express them considered in abstract, the way in which we never see them subsist. The words *green* and *blue* would, in all probability, be sooner invented than the words *greenness* and *blueness*; the words *above* and *below,* than the words *superiority* and *inferiority.* To invent words of the latter kind requires a much greater effort of abstraction than to invent those of the former. It is probable, therefore, that such abstract terms would be of much later institution. Accordingly, their etymologies generally shewᵉ that they are so, they being generally derived from others that are concrete.

7   But though the invention of nouns adjective be much more natural than that of the abstract nouns substantive derived from them, it would still, however, require a considerable degree of abstraction and generalization. Those, for example, who first invented the words *green, blue, red,* and the other names of colours, must have observed and compared together a great number of objects, must have remarked their resemblances and dissimilitudes in respect of the quality of colour, and must have arranged them, in their own minds, into different classes and assortments, according to those resemblances and dissimilitudes. An adjective is by nature a general, and in some measure an abstract word, and necessarily presupposes the idea of a certain species or assortment of things, to all of which it is equally applicable. The word *green* could not, as we were supposing might be the case of the word *cave,* have been originally the name of an individual, and afterwards have become, by whatᶠ grammarians call an Antonomasia, the name of a species. The word *green* denoting, not the name of a substance, but the peculiar quality of a substance, must from the very first have been a general word, and considered as equally

---

ᵈ *&c PM 3–5*   ᵉ show *PM 3–5*   ᶠ *PM has* the *before* Grammarians

applicable to any other substance possessed of the same quality. The man who first distinguished a particular object by the epithet of *green*, must have observed other objects that were not *green*, from which he meant to separate it by this appellation. The institution of this name, therefore, supposes comparison. It likewise supposes some degree of abstraction. The person who first invented this appellation must have distinguished the quality from the object to which it belonged, and must have conceived the object as capable of subsisting without the quality. The invention, therefore, even of the simplest nouns adjective, must have required more metaphysics than we are apt to be aware of. The different mental operations, of arrangement or classing, of comparison, and of abstraction, must all have been employed, before even the names of the different colours, the least metaphysical of all nouns adjective, could be instituted. From all which I infer, that when languages were beginning to be formed, nouns adjective would by no means be the words of the earliest invention.

8   There is another expedient for denoting the different qualities of different substances, which as it requires no abstraction, nor any conceived separation of the quality from the subject, seems more natural than the invention of nouns adjective, and which, upon this account, could hardly fail, in the first formation of language, to be thought of before them. This expedient is to make some variation upon the noun substantive itself, according to the different qualities which it is endowed with. Thus, in many languages, the qualities both of sex and of the want of sex, are expressed by different terminations in the nouns substantive, which denote objects so qualified. In Latin, for example, *lupus, lupa; equus, equa; juvencus, juvenca; Julius, Julia; Lucretius, Lucretia*, &c. denote the qualities of male and female in the animals and persons to whom such appellations belong, without needing the addition of any adjective for this purpose. On the other hand, the words *forum, pratum, plaustrum*, denote by their peculiar termination the total absence of sex in the different substances which they stand for. Both sex, and the want of all sex, being naturally considered as qualities modifying and inseparable from the particular substances to which they belong, it was natural to express them rather by a modification in the noun substantive, than by any general and abstract word expressive of this particular species of quality. The expression bears, it is evident, in this way, a much more exact analogy to the idea or object which it denotes, than in the other. The quality appears, in nature, as a modification of the substance, and as^g it is thus expressed, in language, by a modification of the noun substantive,

g PM omits as

which denotes that substance, the*[h]* quality and the subject are, in this case, blended together, if I may say so, in the expression, in the same manner as they appear to be in the object and in the idea. Hence the origin of the masculine, feminine, and neutral genders, in all the ancient languages. By means of these, the most important of all distinctions, that of substances into animated and inanimated, and that of animals into male and female, seem*[i]* to have been sufficiently marked without the assistance of adjectives, or of any general names denoting this most extensive species of qualifications.

9   There are no more than these three genders in any of the languages with which I am acquainted; that is to say, the formation of nouns substantive can, by itself, and without the accompaniment of adjectives, express no other qualities but those three above mentioned*[j]*, the qualities of male, of female, of neither male nor female. I should not, however, be surprised, if, in other languages with which I am unacquainted, the different formations*[k]* of nouns substantive*[l]* should be capable of expressing many other different qualities. The different diminutives of the Italian, and of some other languages, do, in reality, sometimes, express a great variety of different modifications in the substances denoted by those nouns which undergo such variations.

10   It was impossible, however, that nouns substantive could, without losing altogether their original form, undergo so great a number of variations, as would be sufficient to express that almost infinite variety of qualities, by which it might, upon different occasions, be necessary to specify and distinguish them. Though the different formation of nouns substantive, therefore, might, for some time, forestall the necessity of inventing nouns adjective, it was impossible that this necessity could be forestalled altogether. When nouns adjective came to be invented, it was natural that they should be formed with some similarity to the substantives, to which they were to serve as epithets or qualifications. Men would naturally give them the same terminations with the substantives to which they were first applied, and from that love of similarity of sound, from that delight in the returns of the same syllables, which is the foundation of analogy in all languages, they would be apt to vary the termination of the same adjective, according as they had occasion to apply it to a masculine, to a feminine, or to a neutral substantive. They would say, *magnus lupus, magna lupa, magnum pratum*, when they meant to express a great *he wolf*, a great *she wolf*, a great *meadow*.

11   This variation, in the termination of the noun adjective, according

---

[h] substance. The *PM*   *[i]* seems *PM 3*   *[j]* above-mentioned *PM 3*   *[k]* formation *PM*   *[l]* Substantives *PM 3*

to the gender of the substantive, which takes place in all the ancient languages, seems to have been introduced chiefly for the sake of a certain similarity of sound, of a certain species of rhyme, which is naturally so very agreeable to the human ear. Gender, it is to be observed, cannot properly belong to a noun adjective, the signification of which is always precisely the same, to whatever species of substantives it is applied. When we say, *a great ᵐman, a great woman*ᵐ, the word *great* has precisely the same meaning in both cases, and the difference of theⁿ sex in the subjects to which it may be applied, makes no sort of difference in its signification. *Magnus, magna, magnum,* in the same manner, are words which express precisely the same quality, and the change of the termination is accompanied with no sort of variation in the meaning. Sex and gender are qualities which belong to substances, but cannot belong to the qualities of substances. In general, no quality, when considered in concrete, or as qualifying some particular subject, can itself be conceived as the subject of any other quality; though when considered in abstract it may. No adjective therefore can qualify any other adjective. A *great good man,* means a man who is both *great* and *good.* Both the adjectives qualify the substantive; they do not qualify one another. On the other hand, when we say, the *great goodness* of the man, the word *goodness* denoting a quality considered in abstract, which may itself be the subject of other qualities, is upon that account capable of being qualified by the word *great.*

12   If the original invention of nouns adjective would be attended with so much difficulty, that of prepositions would be accompanied with yet more. Every preposition, as I have already observed, denotes some relation considered in concrete with the co-relative object. The preposition *above,* for example, denotes the relation of superiority, not in abstract, as it is expressed by the word *superiority,* but in concrete with some co-relative object. In this phrase, for example, *the tree above the cave,* the word *above* expresses a certain relation between the *tree* and the *cave,* and it expresses this relation in concrete with the co-relative object, *the cave.* A preposition always requires, in order to complete the sense, some other word to come after it; as may be observed in this particular instance. Now, I say, the original invention of such words would require a yet greater effort of abstraction and generalization, than that of nouns adjective. First of all, a relation is, in itself, a more metaphysical object than a quality. Nobody can be at a loss to explain what is meant by a quality; but few people will find themselves able to express, very distinctly, what is understood by a relation. Qualities are

ᵐ⁻ᵐ *Man, . . . Woman, PM 3*   ⁿ *PM 3 omits* the

almost always the objects of our external senses; relations never are. No wonder, therefore, that the one set of objects should be so much more comprehensible than the other. Secondly, though prepositions always express the relation which they stand for, in concrete with the co-relative object, they could not have originally been formed without a considerable effort of abstraction. A preposition denotes a relation, and nothing but a relation. But before men could institute a word, which signified a relation, and nothing but a relation, they must have been able, in some measure, to consider this relation abstractedly from the related objects; since the idea of those objects does not, in any respect, enter into the signification of the preposition. The invention of such a word, therefore, must have required a considerable degree of abstraction. Thirdly, a preposition is from its nature a general word, which, from its very first institution, must have been considered as equally applicable to denote any other similar relation. The man who first invented the word *above*, must not only have distinguished, in some measure, the relation of *superiority* from the objects which were so related, but he must also have distinguished this relation from other relations, such as, from the relation of *inferiority* denoted by the word *below*, from the relation of *juxtaposition*, expressed by the word *beside*, and the like. He must have conceived this word, therefore, as expressive of a particular sort or species of relation distinct from every other, which could not be done without a considerable effort of comparison and generalization.

13 Whatever were the difficulties, therefore, which embarrassed the first invention of nouns adjective, the same, and many more, must have embarrassed that of prepositions. If mankind, therefore, in the first formation of languages, seem to have, for some time, evaded the necessity of nouns adjective, by varying the termination of the names of substances, according as these varied in some of their most important qualities, they would much more find themselves under the necessity of evading, by some similar contrivance, the yet more difficult invention of prepositions. The different cases in the ancient languages is a contrivance of precisely the same kind. The genitive and dative cases, in Greek and Latin, evidently supply the place of the*[o]* prepositions; and by a variation in the noun substantive, which stands for the co-relative term, express the relation which subsists between what is denoted by that noun substantive, and what is expressed by some other word in the sentence. In these expressions, for example, *fructus arboris, the fruit of the tree; sacer Herculi, sacred to Hercules;* the variations made in the co-relative words, *arbor* and *Hercules*, express the

---

[o] PM 3 omits the

same relations which are expressed in English by the prepositions *of* and *to*.

14   To express a relation in this manner, did not require any effort of abstraction. It was not here expressed by a peculiar word denoting relation and nothing but relation, but by a variation upon the co-relative term. It was expressed here, as it appears in nature, not as something separated and detached, but as thoroughly mixed and blended with the co-relative object.

15   To express relation in this manner, did not require any effort of generalization. The words *arboris* and *Herculi*, while they involve in their signification the same relation expressed by the English prepositions *of* and *to*, are not, like those prepositions, general words, which can be applied to express the same relation between whatever other objects it might be observed to subsist.

16   To express relation in this manner did not require any effort of comparison. The words *arboris* and *Herculi* are not general words intended to denote a particular species of relations which the inventors of those expressions meant, in consequence of some sort of comparison, to separate and distinguish from every other sort of relation.*p* The example, indeed, of this contrivance would soon probably*q* be followed, and whoever had occasion to express a similar relation between any other objects would be very apt to do it by making a similar variation on the name of the co-relative object. This, I say, would probably, or rather certainly happen; but it would happen without any intention or foresight in those who first set the example, and who never meant to establish any general rule. The general rule would establish itself insensibly, and by slow degrees, in consequence of that love of analogy and similarity of sound, which is the foundation of by far the greater part of the rules of grammar.

17   To express relation, therefore, by a variation in the name of the co-relative object, requiring neither abstraction, nor generalization, nor comparison of any kind, would, at first, be much more natural and easy, than to express it by those general words called prepositions, of which the first invention must have demanded some degree of all those operations.

18   The number of cases is different in different languages. There are five in the Greek, six in the Latin, and there are said to be ten in the Armenian[5] language. It must have naturally happened that there

---

p relation; the *PM 3*   *q* would probably soon *PM*

---

[5] The ancient Greeks were acquainted through their colonies in Asia Minor with the Armenian language, which they associated with Phrygian; but I have found no source for this statement on its cases. Primitive Indo-European had, besides the six cases of Latin, a locative and an

should be a greater or a smaller number of cases, according as in the terminations of nouns substantive the first formers of any language happened to have established a greater or a smaller number of variations, in order to express the different relations they had occasion to take notice of, before the invention of those more general and abstract prepositions which could supply their place.

19   It is, perhaps, worth while to observe that those prepositions, which in modern languages hold the place of the ancient cases, are, of all others, the most general, and abstract, and metaphysical; and of consequence, would probably be the last invented. Ask any man of common acuteness, What relation is expressed by the preposition *above?* He will readily answer, that of *superiority*. By the preposition *below?* He will as quickly reply, that of *inferiority*. But ask him, what relation is expressed by the preposition *of*, and, if he has not beforehand employed his thoughts a good deal upon these subjects, you may safely allow him a week to consider of his answer. The prepositions *above* and *below* do not denote any of the relations expressed by the cases in the ancient languages. But the preposition *of*, denotes the same relation, which is in them expressed by the genitive case; and which, it is easy to observe, is of a very metaphysical nature. The preposition *of*, denotes relation in general, considered in concrete with the co-relative object. It marks that the noun substantive which goes before it, is somehow or other related to that which comes after it, but without in any respect ascertaining, as is done by the preposition *above*, what is the peculiar nature of that relation. We often apply it, therefore, to express the most opposite relations; because, the most opposite relations agree so far that each of them comprehends in it the general idea or nature of a relation. We say, *the father of the son*, and *the son of the father; the fir-trees of the forest,'* and the *forest of the fir-trees.* The relation in which the father stands to the son, is, it is evident, a quite opposite relation to that in which the son stands to the father; that in which the parts stand to the whole, is quite opposite to that in which the whole stands to the parts. The word *of*, however, serves very well to

ʳ forest; *3*

---

instrumental, and Old Armenian had an additional objective case formed by the prefix z-. The plural in -k may be confusing the issue; but, if authentic, the statement may partly involve the large non-Indo-European element absorbed by the Armenians into their vocabulary when *c.*1200 BC they overran the speakers of Urartian and Hurrian. In Smith's time the Armenian of the classical period, AD 400–460, had been artificially revived as a literary language; but in that period the cases had fallen together into only four forms. In 1710 Leibniz described Armenian in a paper to the Berlin Academy as a mixed language and as in need of more study. Modern treatments include A. Meillet, *Esquisse d'une grammaire comparée de l'arménien classique* (ed. 2, 1936) and H. Jensen, *Altarmenische Grammatik* (1959); on the history of the study, H. Zeller in *Geschichte der indogermanischen Sprachwissenschaft,* iv (1927).

denote all those relations, because in itself it denotes no particular relation, but only relation in general; and so far as any particular relation is collected from such expressions, it is inferred by the mind, not from the preposition itself, but from the nature and arrangement of the substantives, between which the preposition is placed.

20   What I have said concerning the preposition *of*, may in some measure be applied to the prepositions *to, for, with, by*, and to whatever other prepositions are made use of in modern languages, to supply the place of the ancient cases. They all of them express very abstract and metaphysical relations, which any man, who takes the trouble to try it, will find it extremely difficult to express by nouns substantive, in the same manner as we may express the relation denoted by the preposition *above*, by the noun substantive *superiority*. They all of them, however, express some specific relation, and are, consequently, none of them so abstract as the preposition *of*, which may be regarded as by far the most metaphysical of all prepositions. The prepositions, therefore, which are capable of supplying the place of the ancient cases, being more abstract than the other prepositions, would naturally be of more difficult invention. The relations at the same time which those prepositions express, are, of all others, those which we have most frequent occasion to mention. The prepositions *above, below, near, within, without, against*, &c. are much more rarely made use of, in modern languages, than the prepositions *of, to, for, with, from, by*. A preposition of the former kind will not occur twice in a page; we can scarce compose a single sentence without the assistance of one or two of the latter. If these latter prepositions, therefore, which supply the place of the cases, would be of such difficult invention on account of their abstractedness, some expedient, to supply their place, must have been of indispensable necessity, on account of the frequent occasion which men have to take notice of the relations which they denote. But there is no expedient so obvious, as that of varying the termination of one of the principal words.

21   It is, perhaps, unnecessary to observe, that there are some of the cases in the ancient languages, which, for particular reasons, cannot be represented by any prepositions. These are the nominative, accusative, and vocative cases. In those modern languages, which do not admit of any such variety in the terminations of their nouns substantive, the correspondent relations are expressed by the place of the words, and by the order and construction of the sentence.

22   As men have frequently occasion to make mention of multitudes as well as of single objects, it became necessary that they should have some method of expressing number[6]. Number may be expressed either

[6] On number cf. Rousseau's *Discours* as above; note 11 (pp. 250–2, 1755 ed.).

by a particular word, expressing number in general, such as the words *many, more,* &c. or by some variation upon the words which express the things numbered. It is this last expedient which mankind would probably have recourse to, in the infancy of language. Number, considered in general, without relation to any particular set of objects numbered, is one of the most abstract and metaphysical ideas, which the mind of man is capable of forming; and, consequently, is not an idea, which would readily occur to rude mortals, who were just beginning to form a language. They would naturally, therefore, distinguish when they talked of a single, and when they talked of a multitude of objects, not by any metaphysical adjectives, such as the English *a, an, many,* but by a variation upon the termination of the word which signified the objects numbered. Hence the origin of the singular and plural numbers, in all the ancient languages; and the same distinction has likewise been retained in all the modern languages, at least, in the greater part of words.

23   All primitive and uncompounded languages seem to have a dual, as well as a plural number. This is the case of the Greek, and I am told of the Hebrew, of the Gothic, and of many other languages[7]. In the rude beginnings of society, *one, two,* and *more,* might possibly be all the numeral distinctions which mankind would have any occasion to take notice of. These they would find it more natural to express, by a variation upon every particular noun substantive, than by such general and abstract words as *one, two, three, four,* &c. These words, though custom has rendered them familiar to us, express, perhaps, the most subtile and refined abstractions, which the mind of man is capable of forming. Let any one consider within himself, for example, what he means by the word *three,* which signifies neither three shillings, nor three pence, nor three men, nor three horses, but three in general; and he will easily satisfy himself that a word, which denotes so very metaphysical an abstraction, could not be either a very obvious or a very early invention. I have read of some savage nations, whose language was capable of expressing no more than the three first numeral distinctions. But whether it expressed those distinctions by three general words, or by variations upon the nouns substantive, denoting the things numbered, I do not remember to have met with any thing which could determine.

24   As all the same relations which subsist between single, may likewise subsist between numerous objects, it is evident there would be occasion for the same number of cases in the dual and in the plural, as in the singular number. Hence the intricacy and complexness of the

[7] Examples nearer home would be the Old Irish noun and the 1st and 2nd personal pronouns in Old English.

declensions in all the ancient languages. In the Greek there are five cases in each of the three numbers, consequently fifteen in all.

25   As nouns adjective, in the ancient languages, varied their terminations according to the gender of the substantive to which they were applied, so did they likewise, according to the case and the number. Every noun adjective in the Greek language, therefore, having three genders, and three numbers, and five cases in each number, may be considered as having five and forty different variations. The first formers of language seem to have varied the termination of the adjective, according to the case and the number of the substantive, for the same reason which made them vary it according to the gender;[s] the love of analogy, and of a certain regularity of sound. In the signification of adjectives there is neither case nor number, and the meaning of such words is always precisely the same, notwithstanding all the variety of termination under which they appear. *Magnus vir, magni viri, magnorum virorum; a great man, of a great man, of great men;* in all these expressions the words *magnus, magni, magnorum,* as well as the word *great,* have precisely one and the same signification, though[t] the substantives to which they are applied have not. The difference of termination in the noun adjective is accompanied with no sort of difference in the meaning. An adjective denotes the qualification of a noun substantive. But the different relations in which that noun substantive may occasionally stand, can make no sort of difference upon its qualification.

26   If the declensions of the ancient languages are so very complex, their conjugations are infinitely more so. And the complexness of the one is founded upon the same principle with that of the other, the difficulty of forming, in the beginnings of language, abstract and general terms.

27   Verbs must necessarily have been coëval[u] with the very first attempts towards the formation of language. No affirmation can be expressed without the assistance of some verb. We never speak but in order to express our opinion that something either is or is not. But the word denoting this event, or this matter of fact, which is the subject of our affirmation, must always be a verb.

28   Impersonal verbs, which express in one word a complete event, which preserve in the expression that perfect simplicity and unity, which there always is in the object and in the idea, and which suppose no abstraction, or metaphysical division of the event into its several constituent members of subject and attribute, would, in all probability, be the species of verbs first invented. The verbs *pluit, it rains; ningit[v], it snows; tonat, it thunders; lucet, it is day; turbatur, there is a*

---

[s] Gender, *PM 3*   [t] tho *PM 3–5*   [u] coeval *PM 3–5*   [v] nigit, *PM*

confusion, &c. each of them express a complete affirmation, the whole of
an event, with that perfect simplicity and unity with which the mind
conceives it in nature. On the contrary, the phrases, *Alexander ambulat,
Alexander walks; Petrus sedet, Peter sits,* divide the event, as it were, into
two parts, the person or subject, and the attribute, or matter of fact,
affirmed of that subject. But in nature, the idea or conception of
Alexander walking, is as perfectly and completely one simple
conception, as that of Alexander not walking. The division of this
event, therefore, into two parts, is altogether artificial, and is the effect
of the imperfection of language, which, upon this, as upon many other
occasions, supplies, by a number of words, the want of one, which
could express at once the whole matter of fact that was meant to be
affirmed. Every body must observe how much more simplicity there is
in the natural expression, *pluit,* than in the more artifical expressions,
imber decidit, the rain falls; or *tempestas est pluvia, the weather is rainy.* In
these two last expressions, the simple event, or matter of fact, is
artificially split and divided in the one, into two; in the other, into
three parts. In each of them it is expressed by a sort of grammatical
circumlocution, of which the significancy is founded upon a certain
metaphysical analysis of the component parts of the idea expressed by
the word *pluit.* The first verbs, therefore, perhaps even the first words,
made use of in the beginnings of language, would in all probability be
such impersonal verbs. It is observed accordingly, I am told, by the
Hebrew grammarians, that the radical words of their language, from
which all the others are derived, are all of them verbs, and impersonal
verbs.

29   It is easy to conceive how, in the progress of language, those
impersonal verbs should become personal. Let us suppose, for example,
that the word *venit, it comes,* was originally an impersonal verb, and that
it denoted, not the coming of something in general, as at present, but
the coming of a particular object, such as *the Lion.*[w] The first savage
inventors of language, we shall suppose, when they observed the
approach of this terrible animal, were accustomed to cry out to one
another, *venit,* that is, *the lion comes;* and that this word thus expressed a
complete event, without the assistance of any other. Afterwards, when,
on the further progress of language, they had begun to give names to
particular substances, whenever they observed the approach of any
other terrible object, they would naturally join the name of that object
to the word *venit,* and cry out, *venit ursus, venit lupus.* By degrees the word
venit would thus come to signify the coming of any terrible object, and
not merely the coming of the lion. It would now, therefore, express, not

---

[w] the Lion *PM 3*

the coming of a particular object, but the coming of an object of a particular kind. Having become more general in its signification, it could no longer represent any particular distinct event by itself, and without the assistance of a noun substantive, which might serve to ascertain and determine its signification. It would now, therefore, have become a personal, instead of an impersonal verb. We may easily conceive how, in the further progress of society, it might still grow more general in its signification, and come to signify, as at present, the approach of any thing whatever, whether good, bad, or indifferent.

30   It is probably in some such manner as this, that almost all verbs have become personal, and that mankind have learned by degrees to split and divide almost every event into a great number of metaphysical parts, expressed by the different parts of speech, variously combined in the different members of every phrase and sentence*. The same sort of progress seems to have been made in the art of speaking as in the art of writing. When mankind first began to attempt to express their ideas by writing, every character represented a whole word. But the number of words being almost infinite, the memory found itself quite loaded and oppressed by the multitude of characters which it was obliged to retain. Necessity taught them, therefore, to divide words into their elements, and to invent characters which should represent, not the words themselves, but the elements of which they were composed. In consequence of this invention, every particular word came to be represented, not by one character, but by a multitude of characters; and the expression of it in writing became much more intricate and complex than before. But though particular words were thus represented by a greater number of characters, the whole language was expressed by a much smaller, and about four and twenty letters were

---

* As the far greater part of verbs' express, at present, not an event, but the attribute of an event, and, consequently, require a subject, or nominative case, to complete their signification, some grammarians, not having attended to this progress of nature, and being desirous to make their common rules quite universal, and without any exception, have insisted that all verbs required a nominative, either expressed or understood; and have, accordingly, put themselves to the torture to find some awkward nominatives to those few verbs, which still expressing a complete event, plainly admit of none. *Pluit*, for example, according to *Sanctius*, means *pluvia pluit*, in English, *the rain rains*. See Sanctii Minerva, l. 3. c. 1.[8]

ˣ Verbs *PM 3 4*

---

[8] *Minerva, seu de causis Linguae Latinae Commentarius* by Franciscus Sanctius (i.e. Francisco Sanchez of Salamanca), first published 1587. (Smith owned the 5th ed. 1733). Lib. III.cap.i (194–6 in ed. 3, 1704), 'De Constructione verborum. Exploduntur Impersonalia Grammaticorum', refutes the absurd *impersonalia* falsely called *naturae* by the grammarians. There is nothing to prevent *pluit* etc. occurring in the 1st person 'si modo loquatur Deus. Integra ergo est oratio, *pluit pluvia, fulget fulgur, lucescit lux*: licebit tamen pro proprio recto suppresso, aliud exprimere; Ut. *Deus pluit*, et *pluunt lapides*'. Examples follow from Plautus, Martial, Tibullus, etc.

found capable of supplying the place of that immense multitude of characters, which were requisite before. In the same manner, in the beginnings of language, men seem to have attempted to express every particular event, which they had occasion to take notice of, by a particular word, which expressed at once the whole of that event. But as the number of words must, in this case, have become really infinite, in consequence of the really infinite variety of events, men found themselves partly compelled by necessity, and partly conducted by nature, to divide every event into what may be called its metaphysical elements, and to institute words, which should denote not so much the events, as the elements of which they were composed. The expression of every particular event, became in this manner more intricate and complex, but the whole system of the language became more coherent, more connected, more easily retained and comprehended.

31   When verbs, from being originally impersonal, had thus, by the division of the event into its metaphysical elements, become personal, it is natural to suppose that they would first be made use of in the third person singular. No verb is ever used impersonally in our language, nor, so far as I know, in any other modern tongue. But in the ancient languages, whenever any verb is used impersonally, it is always in the third person singular. The termination of those verbs, which are still always impersonal, is constantly the same with that of the third person singular of personal verbs. The consideration of these circumstances, joined to the naturalness of the thing itself, may serve to convince us that verbs first became personal in what is now called the third person singular.

32   But as the event, or matter of fact, which is expressed by a verb, may be affirmed either of the person who speaks, or of the person who is spoken to, as well as of some third person or object, it became necessary to fall upon some method of expressing these two peculiar relations of the event. In the English language this is commonly done, by prefixing, what are called the personal pronouns, to the general word which expresses the event affirmed. *I came, you came, he* or *it came*[y]; in these phrases the event of having come is, in the first, affirmed of the speaker; in the second, of the person spoken to; in the third, of some other person, or object. The first formers of language, it may be imagined, might have done the same thing, and prefixing in the same manner the two first personal pronouns, to the same termination of the verb, which expressed the third person singular, might have said *ego venit, tu venit,* as well as *ille* or *illud venit.* And I make no doubt but they would have done so, if at the time when they had first occasion to

---

[y] came, *PM*

express these relations of the verb, there had been any such words as either *ego* or *tu* in their language. But in this early period of the[z] language, which we are now endeavouring to describe, it is extremely improbable that any such words would be known. Though custom has now rendered them familiar to us, they, both of them, express ideas extremely metaphysical and abstract. The word *I*, for example, is a word of a very particular species. Whatever speaks may denote itself by this personal pronoun. The word *I*, therefore, is a general word, capable of being predicated, as the logicians say, of an infinite variety of objects. It differs, however, from all other general words in this respect; that the objects of which it may be predicated, do not form any particular species of objects distinguished from all others. The word *I*, does not, like the word *man*, denote a particular class of objects, separated from all others by peculiar qualities of their own. It is far from being the name of a species, but, on the contrary, whenever it is made use of, it always denotes a precise individual, the particular person who then speaks. It may be said to be, at once, both what the logicians call, a singular, and what they call, a common term; and to join in its signification the seemingly opposite qualities of the most precise individuality, and the most extensive generalization. This word, therefore, expressing so very abstract and metaphysical an idea, would not easily or readily occur to the first formers of language. What are called the personal pronouns, it may be observed, are among the last words of[a] which children learn to make use. A child, speaking of itself, says, *Billy walks, Billy sits*, insteads of *I walk, I sit*. As in the beginnings of language, therefore, mankind seem to have evaded the invention of at least the more abstract prepositions, and to have expressed the same relations which these *now* stand for, by varying the termination of the co-relative term, so they likewise would naturally attempt to evade the necessity of inventing those more abstract pronouns by varying the termination of the verb, according as the event which it expressed was intended to be affirmed of the first, second, or third person. This seems, accordingly, to be the universal practice of all the ancient languages. In Latin, *veni, venisti, venit*, sufficiently denote, without any other addition, the different events expressed by the English phrases, *I came, you came, he* or *it came*. The verb would, for the same reason, vary its termination, according as the event was intended to be affirmed of the first, second, or third persons plural; and what is expressed by the English phrases, *we came, ye came, they came*, would be denoted by the Latin words, *venimus, venistis, venerunt*. Those primitive languages, too, which, upon account of the difficulty of inventing numeral names, had introduced a dual, as well as a plural number, into the declension of their nouns substantive, would probably, from analogy, do the same thing in the conjugations of their verbs. And thus in all those original languages, we might expect to find, at least six, if not eight or nine variations, in the termination of every verb, according as the event which it denoted was meant to be affirmed of the first, second, or third persons singular, dual, or plural. These variations again being repeated, along with others, *b*through all its different tenses, through all its different modes, and through*b* all its different voices, must necessarily have rendered their conjugations still more intricate and complex than their declensions.

33   Language would probably have continued upon this footing in all countries, nor would ever have grown more simple in its declensions and conjugations, had it not become more complex in its composition, in consequence of the mixture of several languages with one another, occasioned by the mixture of different nations. As long as any language was spoke by those only who learned it in their infancy, the intricacy of its declensions and conjugations could occasion no great embarrassment. The far greater part of those who had occasion to speak it, had acquired it at so very early a period of their lives, so insensibly and by such slow degrees, that they were scarce ever sensible of the difficulty. But when two nations came to be mixed with one another, either by conquest or migration, the case would be very different. Each nation, in order to make itself intelligible to those with whom it was under the necessity of conversing, would be obliged to learn the language of the other. The greater part of individuals too, learning the new language, not by art, or by remounting to its rudiments and first principles, but by rote, and by what they commonly heard in conversation, would be extremely perplexed by the intricacy of its declensions and conjugations. They would endeavour, therefore, to supply their ignorance of these, by whatever shift the language could afford them. Their ignorance of the declensions they would naturally supply by the use of prepositions; and a Lombard, who was attempting to speak Latin, and wanted to express that such a person was a citizen of Rome, or a benefactor to Rome, if he happened not to be acquainted with the genitive and dative cases of the word *Roma*, would naturally express himself by prefixing the prepositions *ad* and *de* to the nominative; and, instead of *Roma*, would say, *ad Roma*, and *de Roma*. *Al Roma* and *di Roma*, accordingly, is the manner in which the present Italians, the descendants of the ancient Lombards and Romans, express this and all other similar relations.

b b thro' *in all three cases 3 5*

And in this manner prepositions seem to have been introduced, in the room of the ancient declensions. The same alteration has, I am informed, been produced upon the Greek language, since the taking of Constantinople by the Turks. The words are, in a great measure, the same as before; but the grammar is entirely lost, prepositions having come in the place of the old declensions. This change is undoubtedly a simplification of the language, in point of rudiments and principle. It introduces, instead of a great variety of declensions, one universal declension, which is the same in every word, of whatever gender, number, or termination.

34   A similar expedient enables men, in the situation above mentioned, to get rid of almost the whole intricacy of their conjugations. There is in every language a verb, known by the name of the substantive verb; in Latin, *sum*; in English, *I am*. This verb denotes not the existence of any particular event, but existence in general. It is, upon this account, the most abstract and metaphysical of all verbs; and, consequently, could by no means be a word of early invention. When it came to be invented, however, as it had all the tenses and modes of any other verb, by being joined with the passive participle, it was capable of supplying the place of the whole passive voice, and of rendering this part of their conjugations as simple and uniform, as the use of prepositions had rendered their declensions. A Lombard, who wanted to say, *I am loved*, but could not recollect the word *amor*, naturally endeavoured to supply his ignorance, by saying, *ego sum amatus. Io sono amato*, is at this day the Italian expression, which corresponds to the English phrase above mentioned.

35   There is another verb, which, in the same manner, runs through all languages, and which is distinguished by the name of the possessive verb; in Latin, *habeo*; in English, *I have*. This verb, likewise, denotes an event of an extremely abstract and metaphysical nature, and, consequently, cannot be supposed to have been a word of the earliest invention. When it came to be invented, however, by being applied to the passive participle, it was capable of supplying a great part of the active voice, as the substantive verb had supplied the whole of the passive. A Lombard, who wanted to say, *I had loved*, but could not recollect the word *amaveram*, would endeavour to supply the place of it, by saying either *ego habebam amatum*, or *ego habui amatum. Io avevá amato*, or *Io ebbi amato*, are the correspondent Italian expressions at this day. And thus upon the intermixture of different nations with one another, the conjugations, by means of different auxiliary verbs, were made to approach towards the simplicity and uniformity of the declensions.

36   In general it may be laid down for a maxim, that the more simple any language is in its composition, the more complex it must be in its

declensions and conjugations; and, on the contrary, the more simple it is in its declensions and conjugations, the more complex it must be in its composition.

37   The Greek seems to be, in a great measure, a simple, uncompounded language, formed from the primitive jargon of those wandering savages, the ancient Hellenians and Pelasgians, from whom the Greek nation is said to have been descended. All the words in the Greek language are derived from about three hundred primitives, a plain evidence that the Greeks formed their language almost entirely among themselves, and that when they had occasion for a new word, they were not accustomed, as we are, to borrow it from some foreign language, but to form it, either by composition, or derivation from some other word or words, in their own. The declensions and conjugations, therefore, of the Greek are much more complex than those of any other European language with which I am acquainted.

38   The Latin is a composition of the Greek and of the ancient Tuscan languages. Its declensions and conjugations accordingly are much less complex than those of the Greek; it has dropt the dual number in both. Its verbs have no optative mood distinguished by any peculiar termination. They have but one future. They have no aorist distinct from the preterit-perfect; they have no middle voice; and even many of their tenses in the passive voice are eked out, in the same manner as in the modern languages, by the help of the substantive verb joined to the passive participle. In both the voices, the number of infinitives and participles is much smaller in the Latin than in the Greek.

39   The French and Italian languages are each of them compounded, the one of the Latin, and the language of the ancient Franks, the other of the same Latin, and the language of the ancient Lombards. As they are both of them, therefore, more complex in their composition than the Latin, so are they likewise more simple in their declensions and conjugations. With regard to their declensions, they have both of them lost their cases altogether; and with regard to their conjugations, they have both of them lost the whole of the passive, and some part of the active voices of their verbs. The want of the passive voice they supply entirely by the substantive verb joined to the passive participle; and they make out part of the active, in the same manner, by the help of the possessive verb and the same passive participle.

40   The English is compounded of the French and the ancient Saxon languages. The French was introduced into Britain by the Norman conquest, and continued, till the time of Edward III. to be the sole language of the law as well as the principal language of the court.[9] The

9 Parliament was first opened in English, by Edward III, in 1362, and in the same decade English began to be used in the law courts.

English, which came to be ʿspoken afterwards, and which continues to be spokenʿ now, is a mixture of the ancient Saxon and this Norman French. As the English language, therefore, is more complex in its composition than either the French or the Italian, so is it likewise more simple in its declensions and conjugations. Those two languages retain, at least, a part of the distinction of genders, and their adjectives vary their termination according as they are applied to a masculine or to a feminine substantive. But there is no such distinction in the English language, whose adjectives admit of no variety of termination. The French and Italian languages have, both of them, the remains of a conjugation;[d] and all those tenses of the active voice, which cannot be expressed by the possessive verb joined to the passive participle, as well as many of those which can, are, in those languages, marked by varying the termination of the principal verb. But almost all those other tenses are in the English eked out by other auxiliary verbs, so that there is in this language scarce even the remains of a conjugation. *I love, I loved, loving*, are all the varieties of termination which the greater part of English verbs admit of. All the different modifications of meaning, which cannot be expressed by any of those three terminations, must be made out by different auxiliary verbs joined to some one or other of them. Two auxiliary verbs supply all the deficiencies of the French and Italian conjugations; it requires more than half a dozen to supply those of the English, which, besides the substantive and possessive verbs, makes use of *do, did.; will, would; shall, should; can, could; may, might.*

41   It is in this manner that language becomes more simple in its rudiments and principles, just in proportion as it grows more complex in its composition, and the same thing has happened in it, which commonly happens with regard to mechanical engines. All machines are generally, when first invented, extremely complex in their principles, and there is often a particular principle of motion for every particular movement which it is intended they should perform. Succeeding improvers observe, that one principle may be so applied as to produce several of those movements;[e] and thus the machine becomes gradually more and more simple, and produces its effects with fewer wheels, and fewer principles of motion. In language, in the same manner, every case of every noun, and every tense of every verb, was originally expressed by a particular distinct word, which served for this purpose and for no other. But succeeding observation discovered, that one set of words was capable of supplying the place of all that infinite number, and that four or five prepositions, and half a dozen

---

ᶜ⁻ᶜ spoke *in both cases* P.M   ᵈ conjugation, *P.M 3–5*   ᵉ movements. *P.M 3–5*

auxiliary verbs, were capable of answering the end of all the declensions, and of all the conjugations in the ancient languages.

42   But this simplification of languages, though it arises, perhaps, from similar causes, has by no means similar effects with the correspondent simplification of machines. The simplification of machines renders them more and more perfect, but this simplification of the rudiments of languages renders them more and more imperfect, and less proper for many of the purposes of language:*ꟳ* and this for the following reasons.

43   First of all, languages are by this simplification rendered more prolix, several words having become necessary to express what could have been expressed by a single word before. Thus the words, *Dei* and *Deo*, in the Latin, sufficiently show, without any addition, what relation the object signified is understood to stand in to the objects expressed by the other words in the sentence. But to express the same relation in English, and in all other modern languages, we must make use of, at least, two words, and say, *of God, to God*. So far as the declensions are concerned, therefore, the modern languages are much more prolix than the ancient. The difference is still greater with regard to the conjugations. What a Roman expressed by the single word, *amavissem*, an Englishman is obliged to express by four different words, *I should have loved*. It is unnecessary to take any pains to show how much this prolixness must enervate the eloquence of all modern languages. How much the beauty of any expression depends upon its conciseness, is well known to those who have any experience in composition.

44   Secondly, this simplification of the principles of languages renders them less agreeable to the ear. The variety of termination in the Greek and Latin, occasioned by their declensions and conjugations, gives*ᵍ* a sweetness to their language altogether unknown to ours, and a variety unknown to any other modern language. In point of sweetness, the Italian, perhaps, may surpass the Latin, and almost equal the Greek; but in point of variety, it is greatly inferior to both.

45   Thirdly, this simplification, not only renders the sounds of our language less agreeable to the ear, but it also restrains us from disposing such sounds as we have, in the manner that might be most agreeable. It ties down many words to a particular situation, though they might often be placed in another with much more beauty. In the Greek and Latin, though the adjective and substantive were separated from one another, the correspondence of their terminations still

---

ꟳ Language: *PM*   *ᵍ* give *PM 3-5*

showed their mutual reference, and the separation did not necessarily occasion any sort of confusion. Thus in the first line of Virgil,[h]

> Tityre tu patulæ recubans sub tegmine fagi;

we easily see that *tu* refers to *recubans*, and *patulæ* to *fagi*; though the related words are separated from one another by the intervention of several others; because the terminations, showing the correspondence of their cases, determine their mutual reference. But if we were to translate this line literally into English, and say, *Tityrus,[i] thou of spreading reclining under the shade beech.* OEdipus himself could not make sense of it; because there is here no difference of termination, to determine which substantive each adjective belongs to. It is the same case with regard to verbs. In Latin the verb may often be placed, without any inconveniency or ambiguity, in any part of the sentence. But in English its place is almost always precisely determined. It must follow the subjective and precede the objective member of the phrase in almost all cases. Thus in Latin whether you say, *Joannem verberavit Robertus*, or *Robertus verberavit Joannem*, the meaning is precisely the same, and the termination fixes John to be the sufferer in both cases. But in English *John beat Robert*, and *Robert beat John*, have by no means the same signification. The place therefore of the three principal members of the phrase is in the English, and for the same reason in the French and Italian languages, almost always precisely determined; whereas in the ancient languages a greater latitude is allowed, and the place of those members is often, in a great measure, indifferent. We must have recourse to Horace, in order to interpret some parts of Milton's literal translation;[j]

> Who now enjoys thee credulous all gold,
> Who always vacant, always amiable
> Hopes thee; of flattering gales
> Unmindful—[10]

are verses which it is impossible to interpret by any rules of our language. There are no rules in our language,[k] by which any man could discover, that, in the first line, *credulous* referred to *who*, and not to *thee*; or that *all gold* referred to any thing; or, that in the fourth line,

---

[h] Virgil: *then line Ecl. I.1 in italic, full stop, then* We . . . *PM* 3–5   [i] *Tyterus, PM* 3   [j] *Milton's lines in italic PM* 3–5; *then full stop and* Are *PM* 3 (are 4). *or semicolon and* are 5   [k] *PM* 3–5: 6 *has* lahguage

[10] Milton's unrhymed translation of the Pyrrha ode of Horace (I.v) was metrically influential in the 1740s. The brothers Thomas and Joseph Warton imitated its stanza, and probably led to their friend William Collins choosing it for his 'Ode to Evening' (in *Odes on Several Descriptive and Allegoric Subjects*, Dec. 1746, dated 1747; often reprinted).

unmindful, referred to *who*, in the second, and not to *thee* in the third; or, on the contrary, that, in the second line, *always vacant, always amiable*, referred to *thee* in the third, and not to *who* in the same line with it. In the Latin, indeed, all this is abundantly plain.

> ᵐQui nunc te fruitur credulus aurea,
> Qui semper vacuam, semper amabilem
> Sperat te; nescius auræ fallacis.¹¹

Because the terminations in the Latin determine the reference of each adjective to its proper substantive, which it is impossible for any thing in the English to do:ⁿ How much this power of transposing the order of their words must have facilitated the composition of the ancients, both in verse and prose, can hardly be imagined.¹² That it must greatly have facilitated their versification it is needless to observe; and in prose, whatever beauty depends upon the arrangement and construction of the several members of the period, must to them have been acquirable with much more ease, and to much greater perfection, than it can be to those whose expression is constantly confined by the prolixness, constraint, and monotony of modern languages.

FINIS.

ˡ thee *PM*   ᵐ Horace's lines in italic *PM 3–5*; aurea *PM 3 5*, aureâ 4 6   ⁿ do. *PM 3–5*

¹¹ *PM* and *3* print *Fallacis* as a fourth line; the practice of running the third and fourth lines of Latin lyric stanzas together (as *4–6* here do) was not uncommon. More curious is the presence in all editions of the 'Considerations' of the redundant *te* in line 3: curious that the metrically sensitive Adam Smith should have misremembered the Pherecratean third line of the Fourth Asclepiad, to which this ode belongs.

¹² On this familiar truth cf. Du Bos, *Réflexions critiques sur la poésie et sur la peinture* (1719), ch. xxxv: 'Avantage des Poëtes qui ont composé en latin sur ceux qui composent en François'. It accounts for the prominence given to word-order (the resources of rhythm, significant juxtaposition, emphasis etc.) by the ancient rhetoricians, e.g. Dionysius of Halicarnassus, *De compositione verborum*; Longinus, *On the Sublime*, xxix–xxxii; Quintilian, IX.iv; Demetrius, *De elocutione*, II.38–74, IV.199 ff.

Appendix 1
(see p. *32*)

(see p. *32*)

THE BEE,

OR

LITERARY WEEKLY INTELLIGENCER,

FOR

WEDNESDAY, MAY 11, 1791.

Anecdotes tending to throw light on the character and opinions of the late Adam Smith, L L D,—author of the wealth of nations, and several other well-known performances.

It has been often observed, that the history of a literary person consists chiefly of his works. The works of Dr. Adam Smith are so generally known, as to stand in need neither of enumeration nor encomium in this place;—nor could a dry detail of the dates when he entered to such a school or college, or when he obtained such or such a step of advancement in rank or fortune, prove interesting. It is enough, if our readers be informed, that Mr. Smith having discharged for some years, with great applause, the important duties of professor of moral philosophy in Glasgow, was made choice of as a proper person to superintend the education of the Duke of Buccleugh, and to accompany him in his tour to Europe. In the discharge of this duty, he gave so much satisfaction to all the parties concerned, as to be able, by their interest, to obtain the place of commissioner of customs and salt duties in Scotland; with the emoluments arising from which office, and his other acquirements, he was enabled to spend the latter part of his life in a state of independent tranquillity. Before his death, he burnt all his manuscripts, except one, which, we hear, contains a history of Astronomy, which will probably be laid before the public by his executors in due time.

Instead of a formal drawn character of this great man, which often tends to prejudice rather than to inform, the Editor believes his readers will be much better pleased to see some features of his mind fairly delineated by himself, as in the following pages, which were transmitted to him under the strongest assurances of authenticity;—concerning which, indeed, he entertained no doubt after their perusal, from the coincidence of certain opinions here mentioned, with what he himself had heard maintained by that gentleman.

SIR,

In the year 1780, I had frequent occasion to be in company with the late well-known Dr. Adam Smith. When business ended, our conversation took a literary turn; I was then young, inquisitive, and full of respect for his abilities as an author. On his part, he was extremely communicative, and delivered himself, on every subject, with a freedom, and even boldness, quite opposite to the apparent reserve of his appearance. I took down notes of his conversation, and have here sent you an abstract of them. I have neither added, altered, nor diminished, but merely put them into such a shape as may fit them for the eye of your readers.

Of the late Dr. Samuel Johnson, Dr. Smith had a very contemptuous opinion. 'I have seen that creature,' said he, 'bolt up in the midst of a mixed company; and, without any previous notice, fall upon his knees behind a chair, repeat the Lord's Prayer, and then resume his seat at table.—He has played this freak over and over, perhaps five or six times in the course of an evening. It is not hypocrisy, but madness. Though an honest sort of man himself, he is always patronising scoundrels. *Savage*, for instance, whom he so loudly praises, was but a worthless fellow; his pension of fifty pounds never lasted him longer than a few days. As a sample of his economy, you may take a circumstance, that Johnson himself once told me. It was, at that period, fashionable to wear scarlet cloaks trimmed with gold lace; and the Doctor met him one day, just after he had got his pension, with one of these cloaks upon his back, while, at the same time, his naked toes were sticking through his shoes.'

He was no admirer of the Rambler or the Idler, and hinted, that he had never been able to read them.—He was averse to the contest with America, yet he spoke highly of Johnson's political pamphlets: But, above all, he was charmed with that respecting Falkland's Islands, as it displayed, in such forcible language, the madness of modern wars.

I inquired his opinion of the late Dr. Campbell, author of the Political Survey of Great Britain. He told me, that he never had been above once in his company; that the Doctor was a voluminous writer, and one of those authors who write from one end of the week to the other, without interruption. A gentleman, who happened to dine with Dr. Campbell in the house of a common acquaintance, remarked, that he would be glad to possess a complete set of the Doctor's works. The hint was not lost; for next morning he was surprised at the appearance of a cart before his door. The cart was loaded with the books he had asked for;—the driver's bill amounted to *seventy pounds*! As Dr. Campbell composed a part of the universal history, and of the Biographia Britannica, we may suppose, that these two ponderous articles formed a great part of the cargo. The Doctor was in use to get a number of copies of his publications from the printer, and keep them in his house for such an opportunity. A gentleman who came in one day, exclaimed; with surprise, 'Have you ever read all these books'.—'Nay', replied Doctor Campbell, laughing, 'I have written them'.

Of Swift, Dr. Smith made frequent and honourable mention. He denied, that the Dean could ever have written the Pindarics printed under his name. He affirmed, that he wanted nothing but inclination to have become one of the greatest of all poets. 'But in place of this, he is only a gossiper, writing merely for the entertainment of a private circle'. He regarded Swift, both in stile and sentiment, as a pattern of correctness. He read to me some of the short poetical addresses to Stella, and was particularly pleased with one Couplet.—'Say, Stella, feel you no content, reflecting on a life well-spent'.— Though the Dean's verses are remarkable for ease and simplicity, yet the composition required an effort. To express this difficulty, Swift used to say, *that a verse came from him like a guinea*. Dr. Smith considered the lines on his own death, as the Dean's poetical master-piece. He thought that upon the whole, his poetry was correct, after he settled in Ireland, when he was, as he himself said, surrounded 'only by humble friends'.

The Doctor had some singular opinions. I was surprised at hearing him prefer Livy to all other historians, ancient and modern. He knew of no other who had even a pretence to rival him, if David Hume could not claim that honour. He regretted, in particular, the loss of his account of the civil wars in the age of Julius Caesar; and when I attempted to comfort him by the library at Fez, he cut me short. I would have expected Polybius to stand much higher in his esteem than Livy, as having a much nearer resemblance to Dr. Smith's own manner of writing. Besides his miracles, Livy contains an immense number of the most obvious and gross falsehoods.

He was no sanguine admirer of Shakespeare. 'Voltaire, you know,' says he, 'calls Hamlet the dream of a drunken savage'.—'He has good scenes, but not one good play'. The Doctor, however, would not have permitted any body else to pass this verdict with impunity: For when I once afterwards, in order to sound him, hinted a disrespect for Hamlet, he gave a smile, as if he thought I would detect him in a contradiction and replied, 'Yes! but still Hamlet is full of fine passages'.

He had an invincible contempt and aversion for blank verse, Milton's always excepted. 'They do well, said he, to call it *blank*, for blank it is; I myself, even I, who never could find a single rhime in my life, could make blank verse as fast as I could speak; nothing but laziness hinders our tragic poets from writing, like the French, in rhime. Dryden, had he possessed but a tenth part of Shakespeare's dramatic genius, would have brought rhyming tragedies into fashion here as well as they are in France, and then the mob would have admired them just as much as they now pretend to despise them'.

Beatie's minstrel he would not allow to be called a poem; for it had, he said, no plan, no beginning, middle, or end. He thought it only a *series of verses*, but a few of them very happy. As for the translation of the Iliad, 'They do well,' he said, 'to call it *Pope's* Homer; for it is not Homer's Homer. It has no resemblance to the majesty and simplicity of the Greek'. He read over to me l'Allegro, and Il' Penseroso, and explained the respective beauties of each, but added, that all the rest of Milton's short poems were trash. He could not imagine what had made Johnson praise the poem on the death of Mrs. Killigrew, and compare it with Alexander's Feast. The criticism had induced him to read it over, and with attention, twice, and he could not discover even a spark of merit. At the same time, he mentioned Gray's odes, which Johnson has damned so completely; and in my humble opinion with so much justice, as the standard of lyric excellence. He did not much admire the Gentle Shepherd. He preferred the *Pastor Fido*, of which he spoke with rapture, and the Eclogues of Virgil. I pled as well as I could for Allan Ramsay, because I regard him as the single unaffected poet whom we have had since Buchanan.

Proximus huic longo, sed proximus intervallo.

He answered: 'It is the duty of a poet to write like a gentleman. I dislike that homely stile which some think fit to call the language of nature and simplicity, and so forth. In Percy's reliques too, a few tolerable pieces are buried under a heap of rubbish. You have read perhaps Adam Bell Clym, of the Cleugh, and William of Cloudeslie'. I answered yes. 'Well then', said he, 'do you think that was worth printing'. He reflected with some harshness on Dr. Goldsmith; and repeated a variety of anecdotes to support his censure.

They amounted to prove that Goldsmith loved a wench and a bottle; and that a lie, when to serve a special end, was not excluded from his system of morality. To commit these stories to print, would be very much in the modern taste; but such proceedings appear to me as an absolute disgrace to typography.

He never spoke but with ridicule and detestation of the *reviews*. He said that it was not easy to conceive in what contempt they were held in London. I mentioned a story I had read of Mr. Burke having seduced and dishonoured a young lady, under promise of marriage. 'I imagine', said he, 'that you have got that fine story out of some of the magazines. If any thing can be lower than the Reviews, they are so. They once had the impudence to publish a story of a gentleman's having debauched his own sister; and upon inquiry, it came out that the gentleman never had a sister. As to Mr. Burke, he is a worthy honest man. He married an accomplished girl, without a shilling of fortune'. I wanted to get the Gentleman's Magazine excepted from his general censure; but he would not hear me. He never, he said, looked at a Review, nor even knew the names of the publishers.

He was fond of Pope, and had by heart many favourite passages; but he disliked the private character of the man. He was, he said, all affectation, and mentioned his letter to Arbuthnot, when the latter was dying, as a consummate specimen of canting; which to be sure it is. He had also a very high opinion of Dryden, and loudly extolled his fables. I mentioned Mr. Hume's objections; he replied, 'You will learn more as to poetry by reading one good poem, than by a thousand volumes of criticism'. He quoted some passages in Defoe, which breathed, as he thought, the true spirit of English verse.

He disliked Meikle's translation of the Lusiad, and esteemed the French version of that work as far superior. Meikle, in his preface, has contradicted with great frankness, some of the positions advanced in the Doctor's inquiry, which may perhaps have disgusted him; but in truth, Meikle is only an indifferent rhymer.

You have lately quoted largely from Lord Gardenstoun's Remarks on

English Plays; and I observe, that this lively and venerable critic, damns by far the greater part of them. In this sentiment, Dr. Smith, agreed most heartily with his Lordship; he regarded the French theatre as the standard of dramatic excellence.*

He said, that at the beginning of the present reign, the dissenting ministers had been in use to receive two thousand pounds a year from government, that the Earl of Bute had, as he thought, most improperly deprived them of this allowance, and that he supposed this to be the real motive of their virulent opposition to government.

If you think these notes worthy a place in your miscellany, they are at your service. I have avoided many personal remarks which the Doctor threw out, as they might give pain to individuals, and I commit nothing to your care, which I believe, that I could have much offended the Doctor by transmitting to the press.

I am, Sir, Yours &c,
AMICUS.

Glasgow
April 9th 1791.

---

* It is entertaining to observe men of abilities contradict each other on topics apparently simple. Dr. Smith admired as the very climax of dramatic excellence, Voltaire's Mahomet; on the other hand, Lord Gardenstoun pronounces, that every line in the play betrays a total want of genius, and even of taste for tragic composition. It is not my business to balance accounts between his Lordship and the Doctor.

Appendix 2

ii.88	119	ii.128	137–8
ii.89	119	ii.129	138
ii.90	120	ii.130	138
ii.91	120–1	ii.131	138–9
ii.v.91	121	ii.132	139
ii.92	121	ii.133	139–40
ii.93	121–2	ii.134	140
ii.94	122	ii.135	140
ii.95	122–3	ii.136	140–1
ii.96	123	ii.137	141

Lecture XXII		*Lecture XXV*	
ii.97	124	ii.138	142
ii.98	124–5	ii.139	142
ii.99	125	ii.140	142–3
ii.100	125	ii.141	143
ii.101	125–6	ii.142	143–4
ii.102	126	ii.143	144
ii.103	126–7	ii.144	144
ii.104	127	ii.145	144–5
ii.105	127	ii.146	145
ii.106	127–8	ii.147	145–6
ii.107	128	ii.148	146
ii.108	128–9	ii.149	146–7
ii.109	129	ii.v.149	147
ii.110	129–30	ii.150	147

Lecture XXIII		*Lecture XXVI*	
ii.110	130	ii.151	148
ii.111	130	ii.152	148
ii.112	130–1	ii.153	148–9
ii.113	131	ii.154	149
ii.114	131	ii.155	149
ii.115	131–2	ii.156	149–50
ii.116	132	ii.157	150
ii.117	132–3	ii.158	150–1
ii.119	133	ii.159	151
ii.120	133–4	ii.160	151
ii.121	134	ii.161	151–2
ii.122	134–5	ii.162	152
ii.123	135	ii.163	152–3
ii.124	135	ii.164	153
		ii.165	153–4
Lecture XXIV		ii.166	154
ii.125	136	ii.167	154–5
ii.126	136–7	ii.168	155
ii.127	137	ii.169	155

General Index to Text, Appendices and Notes

DATE DUE

1/13/12			